Wissenschaftliche Untersuchungen
zum Neuen Testament

Herausgeber/Editor

Jörg Frey (Zürich)

Mitherausgeber/Associate Editors

Markus Bockmuehl (Oxford) · James A. Kelhoffer (Uppsala)
Tobias Nicklas (Regensburg) · Janet Spittler (Charlottesville, VA)
J. Ross Wagner (Durham, NC)

488

Ephesos as a Religious Center under the Principate

Edited by

Allen Black, Christine M. Thomas,
and Trevor W. Thompson

Mohr Siebeck

ALLEN BLACK, since 1983 Dean and Professor of New Testament at Harding School of Theology.

CHRISTINE M. THOMAS, since 1996 Associate Professor at the University of California, Santa Barbara.

TREVOR W. THOMPSON, currently PhD (Candidate), University of Chicago.

ISBN 978-3-16-152515-5 / eISBN 978-3-16-156861-9
DOI 10.1628/978-3-16-156861-9

ISSN 0512-1604 / eISSN 2568-7476
(Wissenschaftliche Untersuchungen zum Neuen Testament)

The Deutsche Nationalbibliothek lists this publication in the Deutsche Nationalbibliographie; detailed bibliographic data are available at *http://dnb.dnb.de*.

© 2022 Mohr Siebeck Tübingen, Germany. www.mohrsiebeck.com

The book was typeset by epline in Böblingen using Minion typeface, printed on non-aging paper by Gulde Druck in Tübingen, and bound by Buchbinderei Spinner in Ottersweier.

Printed in Germany.

Table of Contents

II. Ephesos in Christian Memory

Abbreviations

AA	*Archäologischer Anzeiger*
AAWW	*Anzeiger der Österreichischen Akademie der Wissenschaften in Wien, Philos.-Hist. Klasse*
ABD	*Anchor Bible Dictionary*
AE	*Archaiologike Ephemeris*
AF	Archäologische Forschungen
AJA	*American Journal of Archaeology*
AnBib	Analecta Biblica
ANRW	*Aufstieg und Niedergang der römischen Welt*
ASCSA	American School of Classical Studies at Athens
ATLA	American Theological Library Association
AvP	Altertümer von Pergamon
AYB	Anchor Yale Bible
AYBRL	Anchor Yale Bible Reference Library
BECNT	Baker Exegetical Commentary on the New Testament
BEFAR	Bibliothèque des Écoles Françaises d'Athènes et de Rome
BerMat	Berichte und Materialien
BGU	*Aegyptische Urkunden aus den königlichen Museen zu Berlin*
BK	*Bibel und Kirche*
BNTC	Black's New Testament Commentaries
BSNA	Biblical Scholarship in North America
BTS	Biblical Tools and Study
BZNW	Beihefte zur Zeitschrift für die neutestamentliche Wissenschaft
CGTSC	Cambridge Greek Testamnet for Schools and Colleges
CHANE	Culture and History of the Ancient Near East
CIJ	*Corpus Inscriptionum Judaicarum*
CIL	*Corpus Inscriptionum Latinarum*
CRAI	Comptes rendus des séances de l'Académie des inscriptions et belles-lettres
EA	Epigraphica Anatolica
EC	*Early Christianity*
ECC	Eerdmans Critical Commentary
EEC	*Encyclopedia of Early Christianity*
EDB	*Eerdmans Dictionary of the Bible*
EPRO	Études préliminaires aux religions orientales dans l'Empire romain
ExpTim	*Expository Times*
FCNTECW	Feminist Companion to the New Testament and Early Christian Writings
FiE	Forschungen in Ephesos
FWF	Fonds zur Förderung der Wissenschaftlichen Forschung
HThKNT	Herders Theologischer Kommentar zum Neuen Testament

HTR	*Harvard Theological Review*
HTS	Harvard Theological Studies
IByz	*Die Inschriften von Byzantion*
ICC	International Critical Commentary
IGSK	*Inschriften Griechischer Städte aus Kleinasien*
IGUR	*Inscriptiones Christianae Urbis Romae*
ILS	*Inscriptiones Latinae Selectae*
Int	*Interpretation*
IvE	*Die Inschriften von Ephesos*
JAC	*Jahrbuch für Antike und Christentum*
JBL	*Journal of Biblical Literature*
JDAI	*Jahrbuch des Deutschen Archäologischen Instituts*
JHS	*Journal of Hellenic Studies*
JÖAI	*Jahreshefte des Österreichischen Archäologischen Institute*
JRA	Journal of Roman Archaeology
JRS	*The Journal of Roman Studies*
JSNT	*Journal for the Study of the New Testament*
JSNTSup	Journal for the Study of the New Testament Supplement
JTS	*Journal of Theological Studies*
KlPauly	*Der kleine Pauly*
LCL	Loeb Classical Library
LIMC	*Lexicon Iconographicum Mythologiae Classicae*
MDAI (I)	*Mitteilungen des Deutschen Archäologischen Instituts (Abt. Istambul)*
MDAI (R)	*Mitteilungen des Deutschen Archäologischen Instituts (Röm. Abt.)*
MTSR	*Method and Theory in the Study of Religion*
Neot	*Neotestamentica*
NewDocs	*New Documents Illustrating Early Christianity*
NIB	*The New Interpreter's Bible*
NTD	Das Neue Testament Deutsch
NICNT	The New International Commentary on the New Testament
NTG	New Testament Guides
NTL	New Testament Library
NTS	*New Testament Studies*
NovT	*Novum Testamentum*
NovTSup	Supplements to Novum Testamentum
ÖAI	Österreichisches Archäologisches Institut
ÖAW	Österreichische Akademie der Wissenschaften
OGIS	*Orientis Graeci Inscriptiones Selectae*
RAC	*Reallexikon für Antike und Christentum*
RAr	*Revue archéologique*
RE	*Die Realenzyklopädie für protestantische Theologie und Kirche*
RGZ	Römisch-Germanisches Zentralmuseum Mainz
RHM	*Römische Historische Mitteilungen*
RQ	*Restoration Quarterly*
SBL	Society of Biblical Litearture
SBLStBL	Society of Biblical Literature Studies in Biblical Literature
SEG	Supplementum Epigraphicum Graecum
SIG	*Sylloge Inscriptionum Graecarum*

SNTSMS	Society for New Testament Studies Monograph Series
SP	Sacra Pagina
SPCK	Society for Promoting Christian Knowledge
SPhiloA	*Studia Philonica Annual*
STAC	Studien und Texte zu Antike und Christentum
TAD	*Türk Arkeoloji Dergisi*
TDNT	*Theological Dictionary of the New Testament*
TS	Texts and Studies
ThesCRA	*Thesaurus Cultus et Rituum Antiquorum*
WBC	Word Biblical Commentary
WTJ	*Westminster Theological Journal*
WUNT	Wissenschaftliche Untersuchungen zum Neuen Testament
ZNW	*Zeitschrift für Neutestamentliche Wissenschaft*
ZPE	*Zeitschrift für Papyrologie und Epigraphik*

List of Figures and Illustrations

Preface

Allen Black

> *The editors and contributors dedicate this book to Richard E. Oster, scholar, teacher and friend.*

I met Richard E. Oster in the late 1970s. He began teaching at Harding School of Theology (HST) in 1978 and, although I had finished most of my classwork there in 1977, he was a reader for my thesis. Rick provided advice and encouragement as I pursued my PhD, especially as I wrote my dissertation. I began teaching at HST in 1983 and from that time forward he has in many ways remained a mentor to me. More importantly, in the ensuing decades he has been a great colleague and a faithful friend.

As a New Testament professor at HST, Rick has maintained a strong tradition first established in the 1950s by Jack Lewis, who holds a Ph.D. from Harvard in New Testament and another from Hebrew Union College in the Hebrew Bible. Jack established a tradition of high standards that Rick has continued. Rick's classes have primarily focused on New Testament backgrounds, the Pauline letters, Acts of the Apostles, the Book of Revelation, the theology of the New Testament, and Greek. His course on the New Testament World has had a long-standing reputation as the most difficult course in the curriculum. He augments it by teaching one-hour specialty courses in subjects like ancient inscriptions, iconography, the Septuagint, and the Dead Sea Scrolls. Throughout his work as a researcher and teacher Rick has emphasized the historical setting of the Graeco-Roman world, with special attention to material culture.

Rick's educational background is unusual for a New Testament scholar trained in the United States. His undergraduate program at Texas Technical University was in classical Greek and Latin. For his thesis at Rice University he wrote an introduction, translation, and commentary on Julius Firmicus Maternus's *De errore profanarum religionum (On the Error of Profane Religions)*. His dissertation at Princeton Theological Seminary then set the course for a career of study. The title was "A Historical Commentary on the Missionary Success Stories in Acts 19:11–40." In the methodological section at the beginning of his dissertation,[1]

---

[1] "A Historical Commentary on the Missionary Success Stories in Acts 19:11–40." PhD diss., Princeton Theological Seminary, 1974, 5.

Rick observes that Robert M. Grant in a 1968 essay for the *Journal of Biblical Literature* "aggressively attacked New Testament scholars in America for neglecting 'the concrete actuality of the ancient historians, of papyri, inscriptions, coins, and other archeological remains' and attempting instead 'to advance learning in their field by reading one another's books.'"[2] Grant's argument became the mantra for Rick's career, which has focused on helping to fill this lacuna in the field. He has sought to do this both through his own research and through training students to use ancient primary sources, especially the often-neglected non-literary material remains.

In 1974–1975, the year following the completion of his dissertation, Rick received a grant that allowed him to spend the academic year in Europe doing independent research. He chose to work at the Franz J. Dölger-Institut at Bonn University, a major German research institute for the study of Christianity and its Graeco-Roman environment, and the publisher of the *Reallexikon für Antike und Christentum* and its supplementary annual *Jahrbuch für Antike und Christentum*. During that year he worked on his first academic publication: "The Ephesian Artemis as an Opponent of Early Christianity," published in the *JAC*.[3] His studies there focused heavily on material backgrounds relevant to the New Testament, and included weekend visits to numerous European museums with major Graeco-Roman antiquities collections.

Throughout his career, Rick has sought to understand the documents that comprise the New Testament in the light of the prevailing features of their ancient cultural matrices, with a special emphasis on material cultural remains such as inscriptions, coins, and various forms of iconography. He has published several materials related to Ephesos. While on sabbatical in 1985 he pursued independent study at the Österreichisches Archäologisches Institut in Vienna (the primary excavators at Ephesos since 1895). Part of the outcome of that research was his *A Bibliography of Ancient Ephesus: With Introduction and Index*, published in the ATLA Bibliography Series in 1987.[4] That book, and his article "Ephesus as a Religious Center Under the Principate Paganism Before Constantine," published in *Aufstieg und Niedergang der römischen Welt* (1990),[5] are perhaps his most well-known contributions to studies of Ephesos. However, beginning with his first publication (mentioned above) he has published five journal or *Festschrift* articles[6] directly related to Ephesos as well as entries on "Ephesus" and re-

---

[2] Citing ROBERT M. GRANT, "American New Testament Study, 1926–1956," *JBL* 87 (1968): 48.

[3] "The Ephesian Artemis as an Opponent of Early Christianity," *JAC* 19 (1976): 24–44.

[4] *A Bibliography of Ancient Ephesus: With Introduction and Index,* ATLA Bibliography Series (Metuchen, NJ: Scarecrow, 1987).

[5] "Ephesus as a Religious Center Under the Principate Paganism Before Constantine," *ANRW* 2.18.3 (1990) 1661–728.

[6] "Ephesian Artemis as an Opponent"; "Christianity and Emperor Veneration in Ephesus: Iconography of a Conflict," *RQ* 25 (1982): 143–49; "Notes on Acts 19:23–41 and an Ephesian

lated items in the following dictionaries or encyclopedias: *Encyclopedia of Early Christianity,*[7] *Anchor Bible Dictionary,*[8] and *The Oxford Companion to the Bible.*[9] In addition Rick has published on numismatics,[10] inscriptions,[11] and various iconographical representations.[12]

Rick has been a member of the Society of Biblical Literature throughout his career. He co-chaired the SBL Archaeology of the New Testament group in the 1980s. His presentations at annual national meetings of the SBL further illustrate his academic interests: "Numismatic Windows into the Social World of Early Christianity: A Methodological Inquiry" (1979), "Research and Reference Tools for New Testament Archaeology" (1987), "Use, Misuse and Neglect of Archaeological Information in Recent Works on 1 Corinthians" (1989), "Religion and Philosophy in Ephesian Epigraphy" (1994), "Thoughts on Archaeological Resources for New Testament Studies in the Classroom" (1996), "Greek Inscriptions from Roman Oinoanda and the World of Early Christianity" (2001), "Ephesian Epigraphy and New Testament Studies" (2003), and "Archaeology and Ephesus" (2013). He was voted into the Society for New Testament Studies in 1989 and made presentations at annual SNTS meetings in 1986, 1994, and 1995.

Rick has spent his career at an institution that emphasizes teaching over research. His teaching loads have been heavy. A significant part of his contribution to scholarship concerning the New Testament and the Graeco-Roman world has been through his students. He has been devoted to students, making himself accessible in numerous ways. As part of his service he has offered tutoring in Greek and other subjects to students who are struggling in his classes. In addition, Rick works with students with special interests in the ancient world both for ministerial enrichment and for scholarly pursuits. His students who have contributed to this volume (Greg Stevenson, Jerry Sumney, and Trevor Thompson) are illustrative of those who have gone on to pursue PhDs and who continue to contribute academically to the intersection of the New Testament and the Graeco-Roman world. This volume, a collection of articles written by archaeologists and

---

Inscription," *HTR* 77 (1984): 233–37; "Holy Days in Honor of Artemis," in *NewDocs* 4 (1979): 74–82; "The Ephesian Artemis 'Whom All Asia and the World Worship' (Acts 19:27): Representative Epigraphical Testimony to Ἄρτεμις Ἐφεσία outside Ephesos," in *Transmission and Reception: New Testament Text-Critical and Exegetical Studies,* Texts and Studies 4 (Piscataway, NJ: Gorgias Press, 2006), 212–31.

[7] "Ephesians, Ephesus."

[8] "Ephesus," "Demetrius the Silversmith," "Christianity in Asia Minor."

[9] "Ephesus," "Artemis of Ephesus."

[10] "Numismatic Windows into the Social World of Early Christianity: A Methodological Inquiry," *JBL* 101 (1982): 195–223; "'Show Me a Denarius': Symbolism of Roman Coinage and Christian Beliefs," *RQ* 28 (1985–1986): 107–15; and the article on "Numismatics" in the *EEC.*

[11] "Greek Inscriptions," in the *EDB.*

[12] This interest is especially seen throughout his most recent book: *Seven Congregations in a Roman Crucible: A Commentary on Revelation Chapters 1–3* (Eugene, OR: Wipf & Stock, 2013).

by New Testament scholars with a deep interest in the intersection of archaeology and New Testament study, is a fitting tribute to his academic interests.

The editors thank Kevin Burr and Ryan Replogle for their editorial assistance in bringing this volume to completion.

Introduction

Christine M. Thomas

Richard E. Oster has contributed in a sustained and rigorous fashion to our understanding of how archaeology can elucidate the world of the New Testament. He was in the vanguard of a constellation of scholars who turned back to this issue in the 1980s, after more than two generations in which archaeological resources had been mostly overlooked within New Testament studies. Before this period of new work, so-called Biblical Archaeology meant above all excavations in and around Israel. For scholars of the Hebrew Bible, the geographic and chronological range of these materials was extensive and highly relevant, and the pursuit of archaeology revolutionized that field. For scholars of the New Testament, however, projects usually concentrated on Jerusalem and the Galilee, and were largely restricted to the lifetime of Jesus and his immediate disciples. This research concerned, above all, the gospels. When Oster and his colleagues began to turn to archaeology as a context for the letters of Paul in the 1980s, they were explicitly and consciously shifting the focus to the Aegean basin, to sites in Greece and Turkey.

Ephesos figures prominently among these sites. It is home to some of the most spectacular Roman imperial ruins outside Rome itself. Because of decades of diligent work by the Austrian Archaeological Institute, Ephesos has been extensively excavated, restored, and published over the course of the twentieth century. One can walk once again up and down its ancient streets, and view reconstructions of temples and public buildings that vividly recall how the ancient inhabitants themselves had seen them. Under Hermann Vetters, the Terrace Houses[1] became an important focus of excavation and publication, furnishing precious information about the everyday life of inhabitants of this highly relevant city of the Roman world, and providing materials that helped explore the domestic spaces that were the earliest meeting places of the Christians.

Accessing these publications, however, was challenging for novice students of archaeology. The assiduous discipline of prompt publication by members of the

---

[1] Published in a series extending back to the 1970s by the Austrian Archaeological Institute. The two latest volumes are HILKE THÜR and ELISABETH RATHMAYR, ed., *Das Hanghaus 2 in Ephesos: Die Wohneinheit 6: Baubefund, Ausstattung, Funde*, FiE 8.9 (Vienna: ÖAW, 2014); and ELISABETH RATHMAYR, *Das Hanghaus 2 in Ephesos: Die Wohneinheit 7: Baubefund, Ausstattung, Funde*, FiE 8.10 (Vienna: ÖAW, 2016).

Ephesos excavation team meant, for the researcher, a protracted period of paging through long series of extensive annual excavation reports, sometimes topping fifty pages of technical German for each individual year. The reports were not user-friendly: they usually lacked headings to set off the passages treating the individual structures. One would spend hours fruitlessly skimming every annual report for the two relevant paragraphs out of hundreds. A plethora of articles also presented detailed studies of particular items, but these were scattered among a variety of journals and series, like the billowing dust of the excavations. Or else the articles were interred in that sacred graveyard of scholarly publication, the *Festschrift*. Even the flagship journal, the redoubtable *Jahreshefte des Österreichischen Archäologischen Instituts (JÖAI)* was something of a bibliographic challenge. Each individual volume had two sets of identical page numbers, one for the main volume, and the other for the *Beiheft* (supplementary volume).

This is, in part, a long account of how I myself met Oster, who became the guardian angel of my graduate studies, even before I met him personally. I had worked at the Austrian excavations in Ephesos for a number of years in the 1990s, during my graduate student days, the beneficiary of the tireless efforts of my advisor, Helmut Koester, to develop professional contacts with field archaeologists for the benefit of his New Testament students; and I returned in every subsequent year through 2010 to pursue excavations and museum publications at Ephesos and in Turkey generally. Oster's *Bibliography on Ancient Ephesus*[2] was one of the first scholarly books I bought and placed on the tiny shelf in my graduate dorm, opting to own it rather than depend on the dilapidated copy at the Andover-Harvard Theological Library. It was the one absolutely indispensable book in those days for anyone working with the material culture of Ephesos as a context for early Christianity. In this age of online databases, of digital library catalogues with live links to PDFs of the actual articles, and – gasp! – of searchable PDFs, it is important to remember what it meant to do research in the decades before these advances, and to recall that the research of a generation of scholars was built upon the foundation of Oster's wonderful *vademecum*.

But this signature service to scholarship was only part of the fundamental work that Oster did in what was a new and emerging area of research. The article in the *Aufstieg und Niedergang der römischen Welt (ANRW)* after which this volume is named[3] was the first work of its kind on Ephesos, or any city central to Paul's mission. It provided a scholarly and up-to-date overview of the entire religious landscape of a single city, with attention to various forms of religious activity, and to all the relevant archaeological evidence. It reflected intensive engagement with the sources, and also a sustained dialogue with the excavators

---

[2] *A Bibliography on Ancient Ephesus: With Introduction and Index*, ATLA Bibliography Series19 (Metuchen, NJ: Scarecrow Press, 1987).

[3] "Ephesus as a Religious Center Under the Principate I: Paganism Before Constantine," *ANRW* 2.18.3 (1990): 1661–728.

themselves. As we learn from Allen Black's preface, the *Bibliography on Ancient Ephesus* was merely a side product and a preliminary study for this magisterial treatment of religion at Ephesos in the Roman imperial period.

Oster was also far ahead of his colleagues in the sophistication of his approach to material culture. He penned a number of articles that are concise gems of theoretical reflection. In his article, "Use, Misuse and Neglect of Archaeological Evidence in Some Modern Works on 1 Corinthians," he pushes his peers to consider questions of method more seriously:[4]

Since archaeological data are not self-interpreting, issues of methodology are essential to the responsible and productive use of these materials in the study and interpretation of the New Testament.

His work throughout also shows a sensitivity not only to material culture as evidence for the social, spatial, and religious context of the New Testament, but also an awareness of the value of the non-discursive forms of communication that material culture presupposes:[5]

In a culture and civilization not undergirded by the dissemination of the printed page, visual language was part of the lingua franca in a way foreign to our present experience ... To dismiss or neglect these visual testimonies from antiquity, to expel them to the field of artistic trivia, is to confine the historian of the Empire and the early church to a Braille-like encounter with ancient civilization.

The present volume attempts to honor Oster's contribution in two ways. First, it reflects the intense and dialogical engagement with the material culture of Ephesos that characterizes his work by presenting, side by side, studies by both field archaeologists at Ephesos and by New Testament scholars working with the Pauline correspondence. In a sort of interdisciplinary turnabout, we present some articles by archaeologists at Ephesos treating the topic of religion, and some articles by scholars of religion treating the topic of Ephesos. This reversal of roles is only possible because of decades-long engagement of New Testament scholars with the archaeological evidence, in which Oster himself was a forerunner, and which he also facilitated.

The second important emphasis are the clear advances in method that these articles represent. Instead of using archaeology simply as illustrative materials, the contributions in this volume reflect a deeper engagement with the archaeological materials in terms of their visual and spatial import, their "textual" aspect as communicative objects, and their position in a landscape of religious attitudes and activities. In this way, they also follow in the path that Oster cleared for us.

---

[4] "Use, Misuse and Neglect of Archaeological Evidence in Some Modern Works on 1 Corinthians," *ZNW* 83 (1992): 52–73, esp. 53.

[5] "Numismatic Windows into the Social World of Early Christianity: A Methodological Inquiry," *JBL* 101.2 (1982): 195–223, esp. 200.

The first brace of articles explicitly treats the ruins of Ephesos and their use as sources for the religious life of the ancient city. Elisabeth Rathmayr presents evidence from the ongoing investigations of the Terrace Houses located southeast of the famous Library of Celsus. Terrace House 2 is famous for the beautifully preserved busts of Tiberius and his mother Livia on display in the Efes Müzesi in Selçuk. The latest research confirms that the busts were components of an important construction in the first century CE, including an altar and an offering table, that purposefully created a space within the house for the worship of the emperors. She proposes a motive and a date, and provides a family tree of the owners of the dwelling who set up this area of worship.

Hilke Thür explores the Dionysiac scenes in Unit 6 of Terrace House 2, and concludes that, since the apartment lacks any of the rooms typically devoted to private habitation, it existed primarily for public meetings. Because of the pervasive Dionysiac imagery, complemented with Aphrodite and her entourage, she proposes that the space might have been used as a Dionysiac clubhouse for meetings, and provides valuable comparanda of similar structures in the Roman Empire. Because of the restricted access to some of the rooms, there is a good possibility that the worship of Dionysus here included the performance of mystery initiations.

Ulrike Muss documents a little-explored aspect of one of the seven wonders of the ancient world, the appearance of the Temple of Artemis during the Roman imperial period. She investigates in detail the buildings particular to that period, which include a late first-century CE odeon, part of the second-century Damianus Stoa, and two late first-century CE structures built on top of an earlier structure. She uses the most recent archaeological and epigraphic discoveries to propose that these last three structures belong to a precinct within the Temple of Artemis devoted to the imperial cult, that is, the sanctuary of Augustus and Roma known from literary and epigraphic sources.

Guy MacLean Rogers collects and analyzes all the epigraphically attested *prytaneis* of Ephesos, a central office in the civic government similar to a mayor or city councillor, held by prominent citizens of Ephesos who also served in other civic offices. He notes important trends in participation, particularly the increase in women holding the office in the high imperial period, and the steady proliferation of Roman citizens in the office.

Steven J. Friesen analyzes the famous customs-house inscription from Ephesos. The inscription contains a list of donors for the construction of a building to facilitate the taxation of the Ephesian fishing industry. Friesen observes that the list has been used inaccurately as an example of an association similar to the Pauline communities, and as a map of a socio-economic profile similar to that found in the Pauline communities. Neither is compellingly supported by evidence. Instead, Friesen uses discourse analysis to highlight misrecognitions in the portrayal of economic exchanges, and to emphasize the role of divine beings in these exchanges: they appear where surpluses are generated, and at points where severe gaps exist between ideology and practice.

Daniel Schowalter assesses the impact of the construction of the various monuments crowding the space known as the Domitiansplatz: the Memmius Monument, the Chalcidicum, the Pollio Monument, the Domitian Fountain, and the façade on the north terrace of the Flavian temple, along with the three roads entering and exiting the plaza. Each of the three routes into the *Domitiansplatz*, which correspond to three different religious processions attested epigraphically, offers a unique view of this monumental space where the Roman identity of the city intersects with the older traditions of Ephesian history and benefaction.

The second part of the volume engages directly with the text of the New Testament. Paul Trebilco explores the recent proposal of John Muddiman that Ephesians was a document written to Pauline and Johannine Christians in Ephesos. Trebilco establishes the likelihood that the Gospel of John and the epistles of John were penned in Ephesos and argues for the influence of Johannine language and imagery upon the letter to the Ephesians, if not from the text itself, then from the oral traditions that preceded the composition of the gospel. He identifies the presence of four prominent Johannine themes in Ephesians: realized eschatology, unity, the church, and the language of darkness and light, and concludes that the author of Ephesians was employing Johannine language and concerns to address more effectively the community of Christians at Ephesos, who depended upon both Pauline and Johannine traditions.

Greg Stevenson investigates the Temple of Artemis at Ephesos as a site of asylum for suppliants. His analysis emphasizes the uptick in asylum claims during times of political conflict and war, the investment of the Roman government in regulating asylum, and the extension of asylum from temples to the cities that surrounded them. The practice and ideology of Greek asylum afford a rich conceptual background for reading the passages in the book of Revelation in which God protects the righteous as suppliants, usually in the context of a war between the powers of good and the powers of evil. The safe places for innocent suppliants in Revelation are first the altar before the throne of God, then the temple in the heavens, and then the entire city of the New Jerusalem.

Jerry Sumney explores the language of sonship and inheritance in Ephesians in light of the varying practices of adoption and inheritance among Jews, Greeks, and Romans in the early imperial period, attested in epigraphic and archaeological materials. In particular, he demonstrates how the pervasive filial language in Ephesians serves as a basis for unity among Jews and Gentiles, for the establishment of community boundaries, and for the provision of a legal basis for salvation.

We the authors and editors present this volume to Richard E. Oster in gratitude for his generosity and with congratulations for a scholarly life well spent.

I. Ephesos the City

New Evidence for Imperial Cult in Dwelling Unit 7 in Terrace House 2 in Ephesos

Elisabeth Rathmayr

The results presented in this article are based on the contextual analysis of Dwelling Unit 7 undertaken by the author in the context of a three-year project, which was financed by the Austrian Research Fund (FWF).[1] Before discussing the archaeological evidence of imperial cult in Dwelling Unit 7, I will briefly describe Terrace House 2 and specifically Dwelling Unit 7 during its construction periods.

A. Terrace House 2

Terrace House 2 is situated in the city center of the Hellenistic-Roman town of Ephesos (fig. 1). It is an *insula* with seven peristyle houses (Dwelling Units) with varying dimensions. The so-called Kouretes Street, one of the main thoroughfares of the town and an important processional way, borders Terrace House 2 to the north; in the south the so-called Hanghausstrasse ("Terrace House Street") is located, and on the east and west sides the dwelling units are flanked by steep alleys, the so called Stiegengassen ("uphill alleys," STG). Although in the early 60s of the last century, a test pit was undertaken in the area of Dwelling Unit 4, the actual excavation of Terrace House 2 started in 1967 and lasted until around 1985. Dwelling Unit 7, the focus of this contribution, was excavated by Hermann Vetters between 1975 and 1982.[2]

The Dwelling Units 1 to 7 of Terrace House 2 were newly built after the abandonment of the Hellenistic structures on this area in the second quarter of the

---

[1] FWF-Project P 22102-G19 entitled "Dwelling Unit 7 of Terrace House 2 in Ephesos: Analysis of the Building and the Finds in Their Context." The project, which started in 2010, has been published in the series Forschungen in Ephesos (FiE): Elisabeth Rathmayr, *Das Hanghaus 2 in Ephesos: Die Wohneinheit 7: Baubefund, Ausstattung, Funde*, FiE 8.10 (Vienna: ÖAW, 2016). The project was carried out at the Institute for the Study of Ancient Culture at the Austrian Academy of Sciences in Vienna.

[2] Hermann Vetters, "Ephesos: Vorläufiger Grabungsbericht 1980," *AAWW* 118 (1981): 148–51; Hermann Vetters, "Ephesos: Vorläufiger Grabungsbericht 1981," *AAWW* 119 (1982): 72–76; Hermann Vetters, "Ephesos: Vorläufiger Grabungsbericht 1982," *AAWW* 120 (1983): 111–22.

first century CE.[3] Building period 2 is a major rebuilding phase that can be observed in all the Dwelling Units in the late Trajanic – early Hadrianic era. The
following building period 3, in the middle of the second century CE, is mainly
defined by the erection of the Apsidal Hall 8 in the neighboring Dwelling Unit 6,
while building period 4, around 220–230 CE, can again be observed in all the
Dwelling Units. The Units were finally destroyed by a series of earthquakes in
the third quarter of the third century CE and not rebuilt afterwards. Only some
parts of Terrace House 2 were used after the destruction,[4] but for functions other
than habitation.

B. Dwelling Unit 7

Dwelling Unit 7 was built as a peristyle house on two terraces (fig. 2).[5] With the
exception of the western parts, the ground floor is well preserved. The central
peristyle 38b.1 from the upper terrace is destroyed, and there, only the southern
rooms still remain. Each floor was probably entered from STG 3. One entrance
might have led from the alley directly into the peristyle 38b on the ground floor,
and another into room 37 on the upper floor. From the second entrance, the
service area in the southern part would have been accessible. The ground floor
and the upper floor were connected by the interior staircase 39.

---

[3] Although in the previously published volumes of Dwelling Units 1, 2 and 4, building period 1 was considered to have a late Augustan to early Tiberian date, on grounds of the stratigraphic analysis of Dwelling Units 6 and 7 it is clear that the Hellenistic structures in the area of
Terrace House 2 were destroyed in the first quarter of the first century CE; immediately after-
ward, the Dwelling Units 1 to 7 were built; for the latest results see HILKE THÜR, "Zur Datierung
der Bauphasen: Anmerkungen zur Methodik," and ELISABETH RATHMAYR, ALFRED GALIK,
MARTINA SCHÄTZSCHOCK, HILKE THÜR, BARBARA TOBER, and ALICE WALDNER, "Hellenistische Strukturen und Funde: Ergebnisse und Interpretationen," in *Das Hanghaus 2 in Ephesos:
Die Wohneinheit 6: Baubefund, Ausstattung, Funde,* ed. HILKE THÜR and ELISABETH RATH-
MAYR, FiE 8.9 (Vienna: ÖAW, 2014), 13–15 and 833–36. For the chronology of Terrace House 2
see SABINE LADSTÄTTER, "Die Chronologie des Hanghauses 2," in *Das Hanghaus 2 von Ephesos:
Studien zu Baugeschichte und Chronologie,* ed. FRIEDRICH KRINZINGER, AF 7 (Vienna: ÖAW,
2002), 9–39; HILKE THÜR, *Das Hanghaus 2 in Ephesos: Die Wohneinheit 4: Befund, Ausstattung,
Funde,* FiE 8.6 (Vienna: ÖAW, 2005), 9–40; SABINE LADSTÄTTER and ELISABETH RATHMAYR,
"Rekonstruktion der Bauphasen," in *Hanghaus 2 in Ephesos: Die Wohneinheiten 1 und 2: Baubefund, Ausstattung und Funde,* ed. FRIEDRICH KRINZINGER, FiE 8.8 (Vienna: ÖAW, 2010), 81–
104 and 426–42.

[4] Mills and a stone saw were installed in the western parts of Terrace House 2; see
FRITZ MANGARTZ, *Die byzantinische Steinsäge von Ephesos: Baubefund, Rekonstruktion, Architekturteile,* Monographien RGZ 86 (Mainz: RGZ, 2010); STEFANIE WEFERS, *Die Mühlenkaska-
de von Ephesos: technikgeschichtliche Studien zur Versorgung einer spätantiken bis frühbyzanti-
nischen Stadt,* Monographien RGZ 118 (Mainz: RGZM, 2015).

[5] The building periods of Dwelling Unit 7 are described in detail by ELISABETH RATH-
MAYR, "Rekonstruktion der Bauphasen," in RATHMAYR, *Wohneinheit 7,* 103–46.

The layout of the ground floor shows a large open court surrounded by three halls in the north, west and east. The main rooms are arranged around these halls; only room 38 in the south opens with a large door directly onto the court. The floor and wall decoration of this phase is not preserved. In building period 2, several conversions took place, affecting the placement of the columns in peristyle 38b, adaptations of rooms, and the installation of a fountain on the north stylobate of peristyle 38b as well as a bath in the northern part of the house, made possible by the connection of Dwelling Unit 7 to a water line. The bath included at least the rooms 38e with a water basin for cold baths, and the heated room 38h with a *praefurnium* in room 38 f.[6] In this phase room 38d was enlarged to the east, and room 38c was rebuilt and equipped with a vaulted ceiling. On the upper floor, besides the service rooms and a latrine (rooms 33, 34, 35 and 37), an Ionic peristyle 38b. 1[7] and a second smaller court in the south-eastern area of the house (32c, 32d, 32e. 1, 38a. 1) can be inferred from the surviving architectural members.[8] Furthermore, this building period includes the mosaic floors in the rooms 38c, 32e, 32c and in the halls of peristyle 38b, as well as portions of the wall paintings in rooms 38c, 32e, 38d, 32c and in the halls of peristyle 38b;[9] marble, the most precious furnishing element, was used for the floors of the court and room 38, and also for the central niche of the south wall of this room.[10] In the last building phase, period 4, only a few renovations took place: whereas the changes on the ground floor were insignificant, the rooms 36c. 1, 36d. 1 and 36e. 1 on the upper floor lost their door connections to the small court; they were now affiliated to the peristyle 31a. 1 in the upper floor of Dwelling Unit 6.[11] The changes in this period concerned mainly new decorations of floors and walls.[12] Most of the floorplan and decor of Dwelling Unit 7 dating to building periods 2 and 4 continued in use until the destruction of the house in the third quarter of the third century CE. Therefore all the finds from the levels of destruction can be associ-

---

[6] Since the western part of Dwelling Unit 7 has been overbuilt with Byzantine structures, the bath may have extended to the west and included more than the two preserved rooms; see RATHMAYR, "Rekonstruktion der Bauphasen."; ELISABETH RATHMAYR, "Ergebnisse", in RATHMAYR, *Wohneinheit 7*, 664–68.

[7] For the architecture of peristyles 38b and 38b. 1 see GEORG A. PLATTNER, "Architekturausstattung," in RATHMAYR, *Wohneinheit 7*, 147–69.

[8] The Ionic capitals of the larger peristyle are dated by PLATTNER, "Architekturausstattung," to the first half of the second century CE.

[9] For these decorations see NORBERT ZIMMERMANN, "Wandmalerei," and VERONIKA SCHEIBELREITER-GAIL, "Mosaiken," in RATHMAYR, *Wohneinheit 7*, 175–231 and 273–83.

[10] KARIN KOLLER, "Marmor," in RATHMAYR, *Wohneinheit 7*, 259–71.

[11] HILKE THÜR, "Rekonstruktion der Bauphasen: Erstes Obergeschoss," in THÜR and RATHMAYR, *Wohneinheit 6*, 136–37; RATHMAYR, "Rekonstruktion der Bauphasen," 131–36.

[12] While room 38d was entirely furnished with a new mosaic floor and new wall paintings, rooms 38, 38c, 32e and the peristyle 38b received only a new wall decor; see ZIMMERMANN, "Wandmalerei"; KOLLER, "Marmor"; and SCHEIBELREITER-GAIL, "Mosaiken."

ated with the latest period of habitation between 220/230 and the third quarter of the third century CE.

C. Evidence for Religious Activity in Dwelling Unit 7

A large cylindrical stone altar and a large marble table were found in the center of the open court of peristyle 38b[13] (fig. 3). The altar was undamaged and is still standing *in situ;* the table was broken into fragments, but its position to the south of the altar, where it is standing now, was indicated by imprints on the floor. Both objects prove that sacrifices took place in Dwelling Unit 7. As an ensemble they are unique in Terrace House 2; only one other cylindrical monument, this one undecorated, was probably used as an altar as well.[14] Though, the combination of an altar and a table is nothing new. It occurs, for example, in a Hellenistic dwelling house in Eretria[15] and on Hellenistic votive reliefs.[16] While the use of altars is obvious, tables could be employed as surfaces for sacrificial implements and for sacrifices as well.[17] Yet, because of the domestic setting, instead of animal sac-

---

[13] In detail see URSULA QUATEMBER, "Marmorinventar," in RATHMAYR, *Wohneinheit 7,* 536 no. MI 1 and MI 2 pl. 250–53; ELISABETH RATHMAYR, "Ergebnisse," in RATHMAYR, *Wohneinheit 7,* 650–51.

[14] It was found *in situ* on the western stylobate in the peristyle SR 22/23 of Dwelling Unit 2 and is aligned to a Heros Equitans bas-relief placed in a niche in the south wall; for this interpretation and the religious function of these objects see ELISABETH RATHMAYR, "Auswertung," in Krinzinger, *Wohneinheiten 1 und 2,* 693 pl. 180.22; the cylindrical base in the north hall of the peristyle of Dwelling Unit 7 was very probably not used as an altar as Vetters had assumed, but as a statue-base or something similar (VETTERS, "Ephesos: Vorläufiger Grabungsbericht 1981," 74–75, fig. 20 pl. 12); see for this new interpretation RATHMAYR, "Rekonstruktion der Bauphasen," 131–36.

[15] KARL REBER, "Die Architekturelemente" in *La Quartier de la Maison aux mosaïques, Eretria: Fouilles et recherches VIII,* ed. PIERRE DUCREY, INGRID R. METZGER, and KARL REBER (Lausanne: Payot, 1993), 55–74.

[16] GÜNTHER SCHÖRNER, *Votive im römischen Griechenland* (Stuttgart: Steiner, 2003), 566 R 58 pl. 2.

[17] INGRID KRAUSKOPF, et al., "Cult instruments," *ThesCRA* 5:230; ANNE VIOLA SIEBERT, *Instrumenta sacra: Untersuchungen zu römischen Opfer-, Kult- und Priestergeräten* (Berlin: Dd Gruyter, 1999), 98–102, 253–55; for marble tables and their use during offerings see CHRISTOPHER F. MOSS, "Roman Marble Tables" (PhD Diss., Princeton, 1988), 260–68; in this regard compare an inscription from Gytheion on the Peloponnese, that informs us that in the theater of this town paintings of Augustus, Iulia Augusta und Tiberius should be set up, and that municipal officials should sacrifice on a table placed before these images; although this request was rejected by Tiberius, it is important for us, because the text deals with details concerning the imperial cult; for the inscription see *SEG* (1929): 99–100, 922–923; for the interpretation see KAJA HARTER-UIBOPUU, "Kaiserkult und Kaiserverehrung in den Koina des griechischen Mutterlandes," in *Die Praxis der Herrscherverehrung in Rom und seinen Provinzen,* ed. HUBERT CANCIK and KONRAD HITZL (Tübingen: Mohr Siebeck, 2003), 218–21; JAMES HENRY OLIVER, *Greek Constitutions of Early Roman Emperors from Inscriptions and Papyri* (Philadelphia: American Philosophical Society, 1989), 58–65.

rifices, *ture ac vino*, incense offerings and libations are more likely.[18] Additionally, it cannot be a coincidence that only *libations* are depicted on the wall paintings of Terrace House 2, of which two are still *in situ*: one – discussed later on – is
on the south wall of room 38d in Dwelling Unit 7 (fig. 4), the other in a niche
used for religious purposes on the western wall of room 45b, which is situated
north of Dwelling Unit 7 on the lowest terrace of Terrace House 2.[19] They seem
to hint at the most common forms of sacrifice that took place in this house.

Next to the altar and the offering table, two *putealia* in the room 38 and in the
peristyle 38b (fig. 5), which represent a type of wellhead familiar from houses in
Rome and Italy,[20] seem to have had a ritual function too. Their main feature was
to protect the water from contamination, and people from falling into the wells.
Moreover, as their cylindrical form is similar to altars, they seem to have been
intentionally used for creating a sacred atmosphere.[21] Considering this, and that
putealia have not been found in the other dwelling units of Terrace House 2, a
connection with the sacrifices that took place in the peristyle court 38b is obvious. They were very likely installed to add to an atmosphere of religious devotion during the sacrifices; and the water used during the religious activities[22]
might have been taken from the wells they were protecting.

In the large room 38 which is adjacent to the court of peristyle 38b, imperial
busts of Tiberius and Livia, a statuette of Athena, and a large bronze snake were

---

[18] Francesca Prescendi, "Sacrifices," *ThesCRA* 1:199, considers also small animals like
chickens or eggs as sacrifices in the private sphere; Theodor Fröhlich mentions wine, incense, flowers, and pigs, as offerings for household deities (*Lararien- und Fassadenbilder in den
Vesuvstädten: Untersuchungen zur 'volkstümlichen' pompeianischen Malerei*, MDAI [R], Supp. 32
[Mainz: Zabern, 1991]: 58). They are named in literary sources and also appear on wall paintings
in the *lararia*.

[19] For the painting see Norbert Zimmermann and Sabine Ladstätter, *Wandmalerei
in Ephesos* (Vienna: Phoibos, 2010), 126 fig. 224; for the interpretation of the painting – Artemis
with a deer offering at an altar – and of the niche as a place of worship, see Ursula Quatember,
"Das Hanghaus 2 in Ephesos im Spiegel seiner Hausheiligtümer" (Masters Thesis, University of
Vienna, 2000), 129–33; Elisabeth Rathmayr, "Anhang," in Rathmayr, *Wohneinheit 7*, 769–
70 pl. 489; 503 fig. 18.

[20] Thomas Matthias Golda, *Puteale und verwandte Monumente: eine Studie zum römischen Ausstattungsluxus* (Mainz: von Zabern, 1997).

[21] Golda states: "Daß die Existenz der Denkmälergruppe nicht schon während der augus-
teischen Zeit endete, ist dem Umstand zu verdanken, dass Putealia sigillata in ihrem Ambiente
wohl immer auch die Funktion der Altarattrappe hatten" (*Puteale*, 19). This religious function is
also demonstrated by the fact that these objects also occur as consecrations in sanctuaries. For
example, one *puteal* from Ostia names the benefactress, one Terentia, who had set up the *puteal*
in the second half of the first century BCE in the sanctuary of Bona Dea; for the latter see also
Anna-Kathrina Rieger, *Heiligtümer in Ostia: Architektur, Ausstattung und Stellung öffentlicher Heiligtümer in einer römischen Stadt*, Studien zur antiken Stadt 8 (Munich: Pfeil, 2004),
239, fig. 204.

[22] Water was used for purifications before the sacrifices proper, because sacred purity was
required for sacred activities, see Ingrid Krauskopf, "Cult Instruments (Greek)," *ThesCRA*
5:165–66: and Tonio Hölscher and Günther Schörner, "Cult Instruments (Roman)," *Thes-
CRA* 5:183.

found (fig. 6).[23] Pictures of these finds, which were taken during the excavation in 1980, clearly show that the portraits together with the statuette were found standing in the central niche of the southern wall, whereas the snake was discovered standing on the debris in front of the niche. Despite this, the snake was placed inside the niche soon afterwards, and consequently this assemblage, newly created by the excavators, was transferred to its presentation in the museum (fig. 7). The former excavator Hermann Vetters, who immediately realized the importance of these findings, and Luis Robert, who discussed the finds directly after their publication by Vetters, assumed that the snake and the portraits stood together in the niche of room 38.[24] But whereas Vetters interpreted the snake as Glykon,[25] Robert rejected this reading because of the iconographic differences between the snake found in Dwelling Unit 7 and Glykon.[26] According to Robert, the snake was set up together with the portrait busts because of the apotropaic power ascribed to snakes in antiquity.[27] This assumed apotropaic power of snakes could explain the large number of snake representations in Terrace House 2, where we find them not only as sculptures, but also on wall paintings.[28] In the case of the

---

[23] Tiberius: Selçuk, Efes Müzesi, inv. no. 81.59.80; Livia: Selçuk, Efes Müzesi, inv. no. 80.59.80; snake: Selçuk, Efes Müzesi, inv. no. 83.59.80; statuette of Athena: Selçuk, Efes Müzesi, inv. no. 82.59.80. The statuette of Athena was found facing the southeast corner. Therefore it is not clear if the figure stood in the niche before the catastrophe or if it was found in the debris and put inside the niche afterwards.

[24] HERMANN VETTERS, "Der Schlangengott," in *Studien zu Religion und Kultur Kleinasiens: Festschrift für Friedrich Karl Dörner zum 65. Geburtstag*, ed. FRIEDRICH KARL DÖRNER, SENCER ŞAHIN, ELMAR SCHWERTHEIM, and JÖRG WAGNER, EPRO 66.2 (Leiden: Brill, 1978), 967–79; HERMANN VETTERS, "Ein weiterer Schlangengott in Ephesos," in *Echo: Beiträge zur Archäologie des mediterranen und alpinen Raumes: Johannes Trentini zum 80. Geburtstag*, ed. BRINNA OTTO and FRIEDRICH EHRL (Innsbruck: University of Innsbruck, 1990), 315–20; LOUIS ROBERT, "Dans une maison d'Éphèse un serpent et une chiffre," *CRAI* (1982): 126–32.

[25] Already on the day of its discovery (04.09.1980) the snake was interpreted as Glykon by VETTERS in the excavation diary; he kept up this view in all of his publications; see VETTERS, "Ephesos: Vorläufiger Grabungsbericht 1980," 149–50, pl. 23–28; VETTERS responds to criticism by Robert: "Es mag sein, daß uns bisher nur ein Typus des Glykon bekannt ist. Wer kann aber beweisen, daß es nicht auch andere Darstellungen des Gottes gab?" ("Ein weiterer Schlangengott," 320).

[26] ROBERT, "Serpent," 129; for the iconography of Glykon see G. B. BATTAGLIA, "Glykon" *LIMC* 4 (1988), where the snake from Dwelling Unit 7 is listed under no. 21 as "documenti incerti."

[27] ROBERT, "Serpent," 129–30; for snakes in household religion, see HARTMANN, "Schlange," *RE* 2 (1923): 508–13; W. RICHTER, "Schlange," *KlPauly* 16; FRÖHLICH, *Lararien- und Fassadenbilder*, 167–68.

[28] In Terrace House 2 snakes are depicted on Heros Equitans- and Totenmahl-reliefs; they also occur as attributes of Asclepius, and a single marble snake was found in Dwelling Unit 6. For the representations of snakes in Terrace House 2 and their meaning, see ELISABETH RATHMAYR, "Götter- und Kaiserkult im häuslichen Bereich anhand von Skulpturen aus dem Hanghaus 2 in Ephesos," *RHM* 48 (2006): 125 with n. 84; ELISABETH RATHMAYR, "Skulpturenfunde," in THÜR and RATHMAYR, *Wohneinheit 6*, 370–72, 412–13, no. S 79; QUATEMBER, "Hanghaus 2," 76–99, 114–28; FRÖHLICH suggests the same functions, i. e., apotropaic and protection of the

bronze snake from Dwelling Unit 7, which has a raised head, it is depicted in a fashion similar to a snake painted on a wall in Dwelling Unit 4.[29]

The portrait busts of Tiberius and Livia mentioned above stood in the central niche of room 38 (fig. 2, 5 and 6). This niche is situated opposite the door opening of room 38 onto the peristyle 38b. Through this wide entrance the niche with the busts were connected with the and visible from the altar and offering table there (fig. 5). Yet, altar and table show an axial alignment with the middle of the north, west and east stylobate, but not with the niche, which lies to the east, a bit off the middle axis (fig. 2). A possible reason for this placement might be seen in the fact that symmetry was an important design element in ancient houses,[30] which was only very seldom neglected. Beyond that, a direct spatial relation and orientation between altar and niche – that is, the sculptural display in it – was ensured in any case because of the wide door opening of room 38 onto the court. The importance of room 38, or better the objects kept there, is furthermore indicated by specific details of construction on the marble pillars flanking the entrance into the room, because they indicate that the room could be closed off by a barrier.[31] Thus the room was not easily accessible, but what was in it would always have been visible. Comparable constructions in Dwelling Unit 6 of Terrace 2 can be explained by its similar function as a meeting place for a religious association.[32] In general, similar barriers are well known from ancient religious buildings and from Christian churches.[33]

---

house (*Lararien- und Fassadenbilder*, 59), as the reason for the many representations of snakes in the Lararia of the houses in Pompeii and Herculaneum.

[29] For the wall painting in Dwelling Unit 4 see NORBERT ZIMMERMANN, "Wandmalerei," in THÜR, *Wohneinheit 4*, 105–31, esp. 114; ZIMMERMANN and LADSTÄTTER, *Wandmalerei*, 125 fig. 222; for another wall painting in Dwelling Unit 6 showing a snake being fed by a priestess see ZIMMERMANN and LADSTÄTTER, *Wandmalerei*, 127 fig. 229.

[30] One can observe this in peristyle houses as well as in atrium houses in the arrangement of rooms, but also in the positioning of niches and statues.

[31] For the reconstruction of this element see PLATTNER, "Architekturausstattung," 134.

[32] HILKE THÜR in this volume; HILKE THÜR, "Die WE 6: Vereinshaus eines dionysischen Kultvereins?" in THÜR and RATHMAYR, *Wohneinheit 6*, 849–53.

[33] Barriers are frequently found in structures with a religious function; cf. barriers in the apse of the "Kaiserkultraum" and in the hypostyle hall leading to it in the Egyptian temple in Luxor; for this JOHANNES DECKERS, "Die Wandmalereien im Kaiserkultraum von Luxor," *JDAI* 94 (1979): 607, 614, fig. 3, 17, 18; compare the *temenos*-walls marking off the sanctuaries from the surrounding land, or the choir screen in Christian churches; furthermore there were also barriers, such as curtains, made from materials which did not survive, whereby in this regard I want to note an interesting text listing a temple inventory on a papyrus from Egypt (P. Oxy. 1449). Here curtains or covers are listed which became riddled with holes and therefore could not be used any more. Since they are listed immediately after busts or statues of certain emperors, KARSTEN DAHMEN hypothesized that the covers were perhaps used closely in connection with the portraits (*Untersuchungen zu Form und Funktion kleinformatiger Porträts der römischen Kaiserzeit* [Münster: Scriptorium, 2001], 263).

D. The Chronology of the Architectural Evidence
for Religious Activity in Dwelling Unit 7

After presenting the items related to religious activity, let me expand on the chronology of their placement in Dwelling Unit 7. The altar und the table in the peristyle court 38b were covered with debris from the final destruction of Dwelling Unit 7, which can be dated to the third quarter of the third century CE. For this reason both altar and table must have been part of the display of Dwelling Unit 7 at least during the last phase of habitation in the third century CE, although, they were produced much earlier: while cylindrical altars like that in Dwelling Unit 7 are attested from the Hellenistic period onward,[34] the slim form of the altar in question and its decoration with a figural relief (fig. 5) seem to derive from Roman influence.[35] The nearly three-dimensional and realistic representation of the relief and the restrained use of drilling (fig. 3) suggest that the altar was produced not much later than the first century CE. Similar to the altar, the form of the offering table corresponds to examples from the late Hellenistic and early imperial period.[36] And the *putealia* went out of fashion after the first century CE as the dwellings underwent a direct connection to a water line[37] in the early second century CE (building period 2).[38] Therefore the instal-

---

[34] The altar in Dwelling Unit 7 belongs to the cylindrical type, attested from the late classical to the early Hellenistic period: CONSTANTINE GEORGE YAVIS, *Greek Altars: Origins and Typology: Including the Minoan-Mycenaean Offertory Apparatus: An Archaeological Study in the History of Religion* (St. Louis: St. Louis University Press, 1949), 142–43, fig. 73–75; PETER M. FRASER, *Rhodian Funerary Monuments* (Oxford: Clarendon, 1977), 25–27; the form or type seems to be adopted from statue bases, see MARGRIT JACOB-FELSCH, *Die Entwicklung griechischer Statuenbasen und die Aufstellung der Statuen* (Waldsassen: Stiftland, 1969), 77–78, 91; for examples with figural reliefs, attested since the Roman period see YAVIS, *Greek Altars*, 143; OLAF DRÄGER suggests that the themes of the decor correspond to the function of the altars (*Religionem significare: Studien zu reich verzierten römischen Altären und Basen aus Marmor*, MDAI [R] Supp. 33 [Mainz: von Zabern, 1994], 71).

[35] Cylindrical altars, which are found primarily in Greece and Asia Minor, are the commonest altar type in the east. Although figural reliefs are attested since the Classical period, they increase in popularity in Roman times; see YAVIS, *Greek Altars*, 143; WERNER HERMANN, *Römische Götteraltäre* (Kallmünz: Lassleben, 1961), 29–32.

[36] WALDEMAR DEONNA, *Le mobilier délien*, Exploration archéologique de Délos 18 (Paris: de Boccard, 1938), 24 pl. 12 fig. 92–93; 29 pl. 14 fig. 102–3; GUSTAVE MENDEL, *Catalogue des sculptures grècques, romains et byzantines 1* (Constantinople: Musée imperial, 1912), 573–80, no. 251–2; THEODOR WIEGAND and HANS SCHRADER, *Priene: Ergebnisse der Ausgrabungen und Untersuchungen in den Jahren 1895–1898* (Berlin: Reimer, 1904) 152–4 fig. 121–2 (two tables from the sanctuary of Demeter), 176, fig. 169–70 (examples from the so called sacred house); because of the find context the above mentioned tables are interpreted as offering tables. For the table type see GISELA M. A. RICHTER, *The Furniture of the Greeks, Etruscans and Romans* (London: Phaidon, 1966), 71–72 (type 5), 113 (type 5); in the dissertation of MOSS ("Roman Marble Tables") this type of table is not considered.

[37] GOLDA, *Puteale*, 19.

[38] The connection can be assumed in this period because the earliest water lines supporting toilets, fountains and baths in Terrace House 2 with fresh water can be dated by small finds (ce-

lation of the *putealia* of Dwelling Unit 7 can be dated earlier, to building period 1 or shortly thereafter.

The dating and interpretation of the busts of Tiberius and Livia, and the bronze snake (fig. 6), was much discussed. Hermann Vetters and Louis Robert, who examined the busts and the snake shortly after their discovery, had differing views about the time of their installation in the house: while Vetters postulated a date in late antiquity,[39] Robert assumed that the busts and the snake were already displayed in the niche in the early imperial period[40]. Important and helpful for answering this crucial question is the state of deposition of the objects in question. One photo, which was taken when the snake was unearthed in 1980, shows very clearly that it was found standing with its underside on a flat surface above layers of debris that extended slightly beneath the floor of the niche (fig. 6). For that reason, the snake cannot have fallen out of the niche and therefore it was not necessarily standing together with the portraits in this place at any time. The date of the deposition of the snake results from the date of the finds in the debris on which it was standing. As coins, ceramic and glass finds excavated there stem from the late Hellenistic period to the later third century CE,[41] which is the date of destruction for Dwelling Unit 7, the snake was set up on the layers of debris of this catastrophe. Since the rubble does not reach the height of the bottom of the niche, the portrait busts and the statuette were still visible after the destruction of the house. The position of the bronze snake in alignment with the middle axis of the niche suggests that it was put here purposefully and in relation to the portrait busts, which had already been standing in the niche. Due to the apotropaic power ascribed to these creatures in antiquity, the snake was probably set up to protect the busts. For whatever reason the portrait busts were kept in the niche even after the ruin of the house. Most likely, there were laws that forbade the removal of emperor portraits.[42] The portraits there were protected by the snake

---

ramic, glass) to this period; see recently HIKE THÜR, "Wasserwirtschaftliche Einrichtungen," in THÜR and RATHMAYR, *Wohneinheit 6*, 197–218; ELISABETH RATHMAYR, "Wasserwirtschaftliche Einrichtungen," in RATHMAYR, *Wohneinheit 7*, 144–46.

[39] VETTERS, "Schlangengott"; and later, VETTERS, referring to ROBERT ("Serpent," 130), notes that "... das gesamte Ensemble des Speisesaales ist erst in der Spätantike entstanden. Ich halte es für sicher, daß der Hausherr kaum wußte, daß die beiden Büsten Mutter und Sohn, Kaiser und Kaisermutter, darstellen. Man hat sie zum Schmuck des Raumes verwendet, sicher waren das nicht mehr, wie Robert glaubt, 'Loyalitätsbezeugungen' für das Kaiserhaus. Auch bin ich jetzt nicht mehr überzeugt, ob die Schlange noch unversehrt in der Nische gestanden hat, vielleicht war auch sie schon beschädigt" ("Ein weiterer Schlangengott," 320).

[40] ROBERT, "Serpent," 130.

[41] For the coins see STEFAN KARWIESE, "Ephesos 1980: Liste der Fundmünzen," *AAWW* 118 (1981): 154–68; the coins of Dwelling Unit 7 are published contextually in NIKOLAUS SCHINDEL, "Fundmünzen," in RATHMAYR, *Wohneinheit 7*, 425–28; for the chronology of the ceramic and glass objects I want to thank MARTINA SCHÄTZSCHOCK and ALICE WALDNER, who worked on these objects and provided information in advance of their publication in RATHMAYR, *Wohneinheit 7*, 311–423, 429–65.

[42] For laws concerning the treatment of Emperor portraits see THOMAS PEKÁRY, *Das rö-*

until the room was completely backfilled, which is dated by finds (ceramic and glass objects, coins) to the fourth century CE.[43] Since the date of the installation of the snake can be established in the late third century or in the first half of the fourth century CE, the placement of the imperial busts in Dwelling Unit 7 becomes clearer.

The portraits of Tiberius and Livia of Dwelling Unit 7 occur in many publications on Roman portraiture[44] in which their date and original form – bust or statue – is discussed. For stylistic, formal and iconographic reasons and also because the portraits and the bust of Tiberius seem to made of the same marble it is very likely that they were originally made as an ensemble of bust-portraits. For their dating, a date between 14 and 29 CE is obvious as in this period a number of ensembles of Tiberius and Livia can be found[45].

In room 38, the findspot of the imperial portraits, as well as other elements in Dwelling Unit 7 which can be related to religious activity will be discussed: the wall and floor decoration in building period 1 did not survive in room 38, but the door opening onto the peristyle court 38b, which is the width of the room, and the existence of narrow niches on the walls are clearly attested (fig. 5). Furthermore the position of the two niches in the central wall, which are some distance out from the middle of the wall, were probably built along with a central niche (fig. 2 and 5). A set of three niches is a common architectural element in dwellings since the Hellenistic period.[46] In building period 2 in the early second century CE when Dwelling Unit 7 was massively renovated and newly decorated,

---

mische Kaiserbildnis in Staat, Kult und Gesellschaft, dargestellt anhand der Schriftquellen, Herrscherbild 3.5 (Berlin: Mann, 1985) 35, 114–15; for Ephesos see *IvE* 25, a letter in which Marcus Aurelius und Lucius Verus commented the handling of damaged imperial portraits in the Gerousia. The close connection between imperial portraits and their places of display becomes apparent in a law of Tiberius whereupon he ordered that portraits of Augustus were to be handled like *simulacra*; they were treated like fixed parts of the houses and therefore upon resale were sold together with the buildings; for this see Tacitus, *Ann.* 1.73.3.

[43] For the coins see Karwiese, "Ephesos 1980"; for the glass and ceramic finds see Waldner, "Keramik," and Schätzschock, "Glas," in Rathmayr, *Wohneinheit 7.*

[44] Maria Aurenhammer, "Römische Porträts aus Ephesos. Neue Funde aus dem Hanghaus 2," *JÖAI* 54 (1983): 108–18; Maria Aurenhammer, "Late Hellenistic and Early Roman Imperial portraits from Ephesos," in *Roman Sculpture in Asia Minor: Proceedings of the International Conference to Celebrate the 50th Anniversary of the Italian Excavations at Hierapolis in Phrygia,* ed. Francesco D'Andria and Ilaria Romeo (Portsmouth, RI: JRA, 2011), 107; Charles B. Rose, *Dynastic Commemoration and Imperial Portraiture in the Julio-Claudian Period* (Cambridge: Cambridge University, 1997), 174, no. 113; Wolf-R. Megow, "Tiberius in Ephesos," *JÖAI* 69 (2000): 250, 295, fig. 5–9; Dietrich Boschung, Hans-Markus von Kaenel, and Hans Jucker, *Die Bildnisse des Caligula,* Das römische Herrscherbild 1.4 (Berlin: Mann, 1989), 91; Rolf Winkes, *Livia, Octavia, Iulia: Porträts und Darstellungen,* Archaeologia Transatlantica 13 (Providence, RI: Brown University, 1995), 172 no. 98; Elizabeth Bartmann, *Portraits of Livia* (Cambridge: Cambridge University, 1999), 172, no. 61.

[45] For details see Elisabeth Rathmayr, "Skulpturen," in Rathmayr, *Wohneinheit 7,* 562–63 cat.-no. S 6 and S 7 pl. 260–61.

[46] Monika Trümper, *Wohnen in Delos: Eine baugeschichtliche Untersuchung zum Wandel*

room 38 received a marble floor and stuccoed walls, and the niche was riveted with colored marble.[47] It was the most sumptuous decor in Dwelling Unit 7. In the last building period 4, around 220–230 CE, the room was again redecorated; inter alia all the narrow niches were abandoned, and in addition to the central niche, a second rather large one, also furnished with marble revetment, was installed on the east wall. Moreover not only the floor, but also the main parts of the walls were decorated with marble.

In building period 2, when Dwelling Unit 7 was connected to a water line, a fountain was built in the middle of the north stylobate of the peristyle 38b (fig. 8).[48] It consisted of a small marble pillar with a lead pipe on its backside, which is still *in situ* (fig. 5), and a rather large marble basin, now standing in the exhibit of the Selçuk museum.[49] It was set up directly north of and aligned with the altar (fig. 5), and perhaps the water used for religious activities was taken from here and no longer from the well protected by the *puteal* right behind it. Besides these items, the halls of the peristyle 38b were newly decorated with representations of gods, among them an Asclepius and a Victoria (fig. 9).[50] This new decoration presumably showed a procession of gods, heroes and personalities of various kinds,[51] a theme that would have perfectly added to the sacred ambience during the religious activities. The same is true for the new wall paintings in room 38d, a space directly connected by a wide door opening onto the eastern hall of the peristyle, flanked by windows. The paintings which have a religious content refer to religious activities in this room. While most of the paintings did not survive due to the subsequent decorations, one on the south wall showing a person with a veiled head (*Romano ritu*) while pouring a *libation* on an altar is still visible (fig. 4).[52] Here a theme was depicted which was acted out in reality in

---

der Wohnkultur in hellenistischer Zeit, Internationale Archäologie 46 (Rahden: Marie Leidorf, 1998), 68–76.

[47] According to KOLLER, the marble incrustation of the walls of the niche can be dated earlier than building period IV and can very probably be connected to phase II ("Marmor").

[48] RATHMAYR, "Wasserwirtschaftliche Einrichtungen," in RATHMAYR, *Wohneinheit 7*, 144–46, and RATHMAYR, "Rekonstruktion der Bauphasen" in RATHMAYR, *Wohneinheit 7*, 122–30.

[49] Selçuk, Efes Müzesi, inv. no. 3.2.94; its measurements: L 1.38 m x W 0.64 m x H 0.37 m.

[50] ZIMMERMANN and LADSTÄTTER, *Wandmalerei*, 126 fig. 227–28; ZIMMERMANN, "Wandmalerei."

[51] In this regard compare for Ephesos the themes of the statues listed in the Salutaris inscription. Next to Artemis and the Emperor and his wife are, among others, statues of the Senate, the Boule, the Populus Romanus, the Gerousia of Ephesos, of the *ordo equestris*, the Demos of Ephesos, Lysimachos, Athena Pammysia, Roma, and the Divus Augustus; for the inscription see *IvE* 27; JAMES HENRY OLIVER, *The Sacred Gerusia* (Athens: ASCSA, 1941), 55–85; and also the reliefs from the front hall of the Hadrian temple in Ephesos; see ROBERT FLEISCHER, "Der Fries des Hadrianstempels in Ephesos," in *Festschrift für Fritz Eichler*, ed. EGON BRAUN (Vienna: ÖAI, 1967), 23–71; ROBERT FLEISCHER, "Die Amazonen und das Asyl des Artemisions von Ephesos," *JDAI* 117 (2002): 185–216.

[52] ZIMMERMANN and LADSTÄTTER, *Wandmalerei*, 126, fig. 225; ZIMMERMANN, "Wandmalerei."

the neighboring peristyle court 38b. It was most likely supplemented by a painting with a similar theme on the opposite wall. Besides this new wall decoration, room 38d was also enlarged to the east, whereby the new back section was separated by short walls spanned over by an arch (fig. 2). In this newly emphasized area, two niches emerged; they reached to the floor and were facing one another. Probably items with a religious function were placed here.[53] These objects conceivably flanked a major religious painting on the east wall that is not preserved due to subsequent decorations painted over it.

In the last building period 4 of the late Severan period, restorations of the architecture and new decorations can be observed. Nearly all the walls were covered with new paintings or with marble revetments. Furthermore, the altar was restored in this period or in the period shortly before the ruin of the house (pl. 3).[54] And the same can also be supposed for the portrait of Livia, because her simple base – a flat block of dark stone hollowed out on the top – seems to stem not from the first display in Dwelling Unit 7, but from a restoration in one of these periods (pl. 6).[55]

E. The Recipients of the Sacrifices

Now, who were the recipients of the sacrifices that took place at altar and table in Dwelling Unit 7? A hint for identifying them is given by the bas-relief of an eagle on the altar (fig. 3). The eagle is depicted with spread wings standing on a thunderbolt in the middle of the eastern vertical surface. Since the eagle is very closely associated with Zeus/Jupiter,[56] one would think in the first instance of this god as the addressee of the sacrifices. The worship of Zeus/Jupiter has a long tradition in ancient Greek domestic religious activity: he was worshipped for example in houses in Delos as is attested by altars.[57] In the Terrace Houses in Ephe-

---

[53] Unfortunately no finds which could have belonged to the niches were found in room 38d.

[54] A piece from the lower part of the cylinder, which was broken out, had to be attached.

[55] For renovation of sculptures in Ephesos in antiquity see DIETER KNIBBE, HELMUT ENGLEMANN, and BÜLENT İPLİKÇİOĞLU, "Neue Inschriften aus Ephesos XII," *JÖAI* 62 (1993): 146–47 no. 74 (first half of first century CE); *IvE* 519 (imperial period), *IvE* 286 (imperial period).

[56] For the relation of Zeus and the eagle see for example W. RICHTER, "Adler," *KlPauly*: "Als θεῖος ὄρνις (Aristot. 619 b 6. Anth. Pal. 9.222.2) und mantischer Vogel (Hes. b.Arisot. 601b 2. Sen. Nat 2,32 u. a.) steht er in vielfachen Beziehungen zu Zeus als Siegverkünder, Bote, Helfer (…) sowie zu vielen Königen des Orients, bes. den Achämeniden (danach bei Alexander d. Gr., den Diadochen und Augustus als Münz- und Wappentier, …).'; as Zeus ἑρκεῖος he was tutelary god of the house, whereby an altar of Zeus with this epithet stood in the house of Odysseus (*Il.* 13.624–25); furthermore he was worshipped as Zeus Ktesios, Meilichios and Soter in the private realm; see DIETRICH WACHSMUTH, "Zeus," *KlPauly* (1979) 1522–23.

[57] PHILIPPE BRUNEAU, *Recherches sur les cultes de Délos à l'époque hellénistique et à l'époque impériale*, BEFAR 217 (Paris: de Boccard, 1970), 223, 641 pl. 1, 7 (one from a dwelling "vers l'an-

sos, on the contrary, he is almost not present at all.[58] Next to this god there are still other possible candidates for the worship in Dwelling Unit 7. These are Tiberius and Livia who were present in portrait-busts found in the niche of room 38. Through the wide door opening of this room onto the peristyle 38b, they were immediately connected to altar and offering table.

Generally speaking, Roman emperors were publicly worshipped in Asia Minor already since the time of Augustus.[59] For the private sphere there is evidence as well:[60] Ovid[61] informs us that he had silver statuettes of Caesar Augustus, Livia, Tiberius, Germanicus and Drusus minor in his house while in exile, which he worshipped regularly. According to Suetonius the same is true for a bronze image of Augustus, which the Emperor Hadrian worshipped in the Lararium of his house.[62] For Tiberius, we are told by Tacitus that a senator had a statue representing this Emperor in his house.[63] In Ephesos we have clear evidence for imperial cult in a private house – very likely Dwelling Unit 2 in the same Terrace House 2 – by the famous Salutaris inscription from the theater.[64] It is referring to a donation of C. Vibius Salutaris from 104 CE, in which the donor decided that silver statuettes of Trajan and his wife Plotina should be displayed in his house and worshipped by religious personnel.[65] Moreover in Dwelling Unit 6 a greater than life-sized portrait-bust of Marcus Aurelius was found, and a bust of Hadrian in a smaller format very probably also comes from Dwelling Units 6 or 7.[66] Because of its small scale it seems to have been used for religious purposes

---

gle Nord-Ouest du péribole" and the other from the "quartier de Skardhana, maison III de l'îlot des bijoux"); BIRGIT TANG, *Delos, Carthage, Ampurias: The Housing of Three Mediterranean Trading Centres*, Analecta Romana Instituti Danici, Suppl. 36 (Rome: "L'Erma" di Bretschneider, 2005), 53.

[58] For religious activity in Terrace House 2 see RATHMAYR, "Götter- und Kaiserkult"; for the worship of Zeus in Ephesos see RICHARD E. OSTER, "Ephesus as a Religious Center under the Principate," *ANRW* 2.18.3 (1990) 1691–95.

[59] For imperial cult in Asia Minor and Ephesos see BARBARA BURRELL, *Neokoroi: Greek Cities and Roman Emperors*, Cincinnati Classical Studies n. s. 9 (Leiden: Brill, 2004).

[60] For private worship of the Roman emperors see for example: MANFRED CLAUSS, *Kaiser und Gott: Herrscherkult im römischen Reich* (Munich: Sauer, 2001), 413–19; KOSTAS BURASELIS, et al., "Heroization/Apotheosis," *ThesCRA* 2:193.

[61] Ovid, *Pont.* 2.8.1–6, 8.55–6 and 4.9.105–14.

[62] Suetonius, *Aug.* 7.1; literary and epigraphic sources are collected by DAHMEN, *Porträts*, 58–60, 251–64; PEKÁRY, *Kaiserbildnis*, 53–54.

[63] Tacitus, *Ann.* 4.64.3.

[64] RATHMAYR, "Auswertung," 694.

[65] *IvE* 27, ll. 150–57: "... ἐφ' ᾧ εἰκὼν ἀργυρέα τοῦ κυρίου]/[ἡμῶν Αὐτοκράτορος Καίσαρος Νέρουα Τραϊαν]ο[ῦ Σεβαστοῦ, Γερ]-/[μανικοῦ, Δακικοῦ, ὁλκῆς λειτρῶν –',] οὐνκιῶν γ', καί εἰκὼν [ἀργυρέα]/[Πλ]ω[τείνης Σεβαστῆς, ὁλ]κῆς λειτρῶν γ', νεοκορῶνται πα[ρ' αὐτῶι]/ Σαλο[υταρίωι] τῶι κ[αθι]ερωκότι, μετὰ δὲ τὴν Σαλουταρίο[υ τελευτὴν]/ἀποδοθ[ῶ]σιν αἱ προδηλούμεναι εἰκόνες τῶι Ἐφεσίων γραμμ[ατεῖ ἐπὶ τῶι]/προγεγραμμένωι σταθμῶι ἀπὸ τῶν κληρονόμων αὐτοῦ, ὥ[στε καὶ αὐ]-/τὰς τίθε[σ]θαι ἐν ταῖς ἐκκλησίαις ἐπάνω τῆς σελίδος τῆς βουλ[ῆς μετὰ τῆς]/χρυσέας Ἀρτέμιδος καὶ τῶν ἄλλων εἰκόνων."

[66] RATHMAYR, "Götter- und Kaiserkult," 128–31, fig. 16–17.

as well.[67] In any case, both portraits show the connection of the homeowners to the emperors and testify their loyalty to the Roman Empire. In contrast to the worship of the emperors, the worship of Zeus/Jupiter in the public and in the private spheres of Ephesos was not very common. On these grounds, I would consider Tiberius and Livia to have been the objects of worship in Dwelling Unit 7. Moreover there must have been a specific reason for setting up the busts in such a prominent place and in such a close visual connection to the altar and the table. The depiction of an eagle on the altar can be explained by the common practice that Roman emperors presented themselves as earthly representatives of this highest god. The eagle as the very sign of Roman power given by Jupiter was used as an attribute of Roman generals, imperators and emperors;[68] and a depiction as Zeus/Jupiter "was generally reserved for the emperor alone."[69] Moreover, the game board cut into the offering table in the peristyle court 38b can be connected to emperor cult as well.[70]

F. Possible Reasons for Honoring the Emperors in Dwelling Unit 7

Portrait statues and busts of Emperors were regarded as the representatives of the depicted persons.[71] They were always set up for specific reasons.[72] In Ephesos, Livia was honored together with Augustus in the basilica on the Upper Agora.[73] Together with her son and the successor of Augustus, Tiberius, she was wor-

---

[67] Cf. DAHMEN, *Porträts*, 59–60; ANNEMARIE KAUFMANN-HEINIMANN, *Götter und Lararien aus Augusta Raurica: Herstellung, Fundzusammenhänge und sakrale Funktion figürlicher Bronzen in einer römischen Stadt*, Forschungen in Augst 26 (Augst: Römermuseum, 1998), 309, no. GF114 and GF115.

[68] For the identification of emperors with Zeus or Jupiter in texts and material culture see: FULVIO CANCIANI, "Zeus/Jupiter," *LIMC* 8 (1997): 401–16 and the commentary on p. 461; KOSTAS BURASELIS, et al. "Heroization/Apotheosis," *ThesCRA* 1.186–214; compare in this sense Hellenistic and Roman rulers like Seleukos I (Zeus Nikator) or Augustus (Zeus Eleutherios, Zeus Soter) who used Zeus epithets, see for example DIETRICH WACHSMUTH, "Zeus," *KlPauly*, 1523; see also the so-called "Basis Borghese," on which the sculptural decoration shows an interrelation between a god and an emperor, in this case Jupiter and Augustus; for this monument see DRÄGER, *Religionem significare*, 81–82, 212 no. 40 pl. 84–85; and a niche used for religious purposes in the Temple of Amun in Luxor with paintings of Diocletian and his co-regents, crowned by a figure of an eagle holding a *corona gemmata*; see DECKERS, "Wandmalereien," 600–52; ERIC M. MOORMANN, *Divine Interiors: Mural Paintings in Greek and Roman Sanctuaries*, Amsterdam Archaeological Studies 16 (Amsterdam: Amsterdam University Press, 2011), 146, fig. 72–73.

[69] KOSTAS BURASELIS, et al. "Heroization/Apotheosis" *ThesCRA* 1:189, 201.

[70] ULRICH SCHÄDLER, "Der Spieltisch im Peristylhof 38b," in RATHMAYR, *Wohneinheit 7*, 519–24.

[71] PEKÁRY, *Kaiserbildnis*, 118–19.

[72] PEKÁRY, *Kaiserbildnis*, 22–28.

[73] PETER SCHERRER, *Der neue Führer* (Vienna: ÖAI, 1995), 216–17 fig. 1–2; JALE İNAN and ELISABETH ALFÖLDI-ROSENBAUM, *Römische und frühbyzantinische Porträtplastik aus der Türkei: Neue Funde* (Mainz: von Zabern, 1979), 57 no. 2 pl. 2.1, 3, 4; 57–8 no. 3 pl. 2.2; 4.1; 61 no. 5 pl.

shipped in the neokorate temple in the nearby town of Smyrna.[74] Altogether three portraits of Tiberius from Ephesos survived. While all of them come from the public sphere,[75] the bust from Dwelling Unit 7 is the only one from a private context. When we think of possible reasons for the display of the portrait busts in Dwelling Unit 7, first of all the assistance from the emperor after the earthquake of 23 CE comes to mind,[76] which is also considered to be the reason for the erection of the temple in Smyrna noted above.[77] Evidence for this support of the town of Ephesos is given by a stone inscription, a decree, which was published in the Artemision[78]: the text lists donations paid into the bank of the Artemision, whereby the interest income should finance something, which should relate to a particular event. Since the text also mentions Tiberius as *grammateus* and the installation of an *archiereus* in complement to him, it is consensus in the scholarly community that the event that motivated the donation was the support of Tiberius after the earthquake of 23 CE.[79] In the particular case of Terrace House 2, certain stratigraphic layers which were recorded during the excavation of the Dwelling Units 6 and 7 led to the conclusion that the earthquake of 23 CE caused the destruction of the Hellenistic structures on the area of the later dwelling units.[80] It is likely that the support of the Emperor accelerated the subsequent

---

4.2; 5.1, 2; DIETRICH BOSCHUNG, *Die Bildnisse des Augustus*, Herrscherbild 1.2 (Berlin: Mann, 1993), 120 no. 26 pl. 24.2–4; 220.3; 186 no. 186 pl. 175; 224.3.

[74] The resolution for building a temple for the cult of Tiberius, Livia and the senate was accepted in 23 CE; see Tacitus *Ann.* 4.15, 55–56; MICHAEL DRÄGER, *Die Städte der Provinz Asia in der Flavierzeit: Studien zur kleinasiatischen Stadt- und Religionsgeschichte*, Europäische Hochschulschriften 3: Geschichte und ihre Hilfswissenschaften 576 (Frankfurt a. Main: Lang, 1993), 123; BURRELL, *Neokoroi*, 61.

[75] Besides the portrait bust in Dwelling Unit 7 only two other portraits of Tiberius were found in Ephesos; one comes from the area of the Oktogon (Selçuk, Efes Müzesi, inv. nos. 59.30.77 and 12.54.88), the other was used as a *spolium* in a byzantine wall in front of the Celsus Library (Selçuk, Efes Müzesi, inv. no. 1359); see AURENHAMMER, "Imperial Portraits," 106–7 with older literature; MEGOW, "Tiberius," 249–95, fig. 1–11.

[76] There were two big earthquakes in this region under the reign of Tiberius: one which took place in 17 CE affected twelve towns in Lydia (Tacitus, *Ann.* 2.47), the other, which happened 23 CE, caused considerable damage in Ephesos and Kibyra; see Tacitus, *Ann.* 4.13.1; in gratitude for the help of Tiberius all fourteen towns erected a huge monument on the Forum Iulium in Rome in 29 CE; see *CIL* 10.1624 (= *ILS* 1546); WERNER ECK, *Monument und Inschrift* (Berlin: de Gruyter, 2010), 64.

[77] DETLEV KREIKENBOM, *Griechische und römische Kolossalporträts bis zum späten ersten Jahrhundert nach Christus* (Berlin: de Gruyter, 1992), 76.

[78] SEG 241. In addition, eight inscriptions on statue bases that are dedicated to the health of Tiberius can possibly be evaluated as a response to his support; the texts are published in *IvE* 510, 510A, 511, 511A, 512, 513 and 514; the base carried statues not of Tiberius, but of famous sculptors, who are also named in the texts.

[79] PETER SCHERRER, "Anmerkungen zum städtischen und provinzialen Kaiserkult: Paradigma Ephesos: Entwicklungen von Augustus bis Hadrian," in *"… und verschönerte die Stadt …": Ein ephesischer Priester des Kaiserkultes in seinem Umfeld*, ed. HILKE THÜR, Sonderschriften 27 (Vienna: ÖAI, 1997), 97–98 and n 46.

[80] See above n 4.

construction of the dwellings.[81] In addition to this clear and specific motive, it is also possible that the homeowners were grateful for other benefits from Tiberius, such as appointments to offices.

G. The Owners of Dwelling Unit 7

It is certain that the furnishings discussed above, which were connected to the imperial cult, were installed by the homeowners. In general, inhabitants can be known through inscriptions, graffiti, and literary sources. Although in the case of Dwelling Unit 7, as of many other houses, no such information has come down to us, there is one building element that is pertinent to this question. This is a door connection between Dwelling Unit 7 and the neighboring Dwelling Unit 6, which already existed at their construction period: through doors in room 32b, the service area and the small peristyle of Dwelling Unit 7 in the upper storey were accessible from Dwelling Unit 6, and, conversely, through the same doors, Dwelling Unit 6 could be entered from Dwelling Unit 7 (fig. 1 and 2).[82] Since a close connection between these Units existed, it is likely that both belonged to the same owners.[83] Through inscriptions and graffiti in Dwelling Unit 6, we are in the happy position of knowing the owners of that house, who are familiar from inscriptions in the public realm of Ephesos as well.[84] They name family members and their offices, and also their connections to other families of Ephesos and beyond (chart 1). Inter alia, family members occupied the offices of *Asiarch* and *Archiereus Asias* – prominent positions within the imperial cult – since the middle of the first century CE onwards.[85] In the first half of the second cen-

---

[81] While the earthquake is attested 23 CE, the construction of the dwelling units in Terrace House 2 took place between 25 and 50 CE; see THÜR, "Datierung."

[82] There was a door between the rooms 32b and 32a, the latter the staircase of Dwelling Unit 6; HILKE THÜR, "Baubeschreibung," in THÜR and RATHMAYR, *Wohneinheit 6*, 101–2.

[83] Thür once supposed that all the dwelling units of Terrace House 2 belonged to one and the same family of owners; see HILKE THÜR, "Die Bauphasen der Wohneinheit 4 (und 6)," in *Das Hanghaus 2 von Ephesos: Studien zu Baugeschichte und Chronologie*, ed. FRIEDRICH KRIN-ZINGER, AF 7 (Vienna: ÖAW, 2002), 63; HILKE THÜR, "Die WE 4: Zusammenfassung und Ergebnisse," in THÜR, *Wohneinheit 4*, 430 n 35. Now, after the analysis of all dwelling units of Terrace House 2, it seems that only Dwelling Units 4, 6, and 7 belonged to the same family.

[84] Recently see ELISABETH RATHMAYR, "Die Besitzerfamilie," in THÜR and RATHMAYR, *Wohneinheit 6*, 846–48; ELISABETH RATHMAYR, "Das Haus des Ritters C. Flavius Furius Aptus: Beobachtungen zur Einflussnahme von Hausbesitzern an Architektur und Ausstattung in der Wohneinheit 6 des Hanghauses 2 in Ephesos," *MDAI (I)* 59 (2009): 307–36.

[85] For these offices see STEFAN CRAMME, "Die Bedeutung des Euergetismus für die Finanzierung städtischer Aufgaben in der Provinz Asia" (PhD diss., Cologne, 2001), 58, 150; 279–80; MICHAEL F. LEHNER, "Die Agonistik in Ephesos der römischen Kaiserzeit" (PhD diss., Munich, 2004) esp. 83–89, 115, 154, 166; SOFIE REMIJSEN, "The *alytarches*, an Olympic *agonothetes*," *Nikephoros* 22 (2009): 129–43.

tury CE a C. Fl. Furius Aptus is attested as the owner of Dwelling Unit 6. He held the offices of an *alytarch*, a priest of *Dionysos pro poleos* and maybe also a *neokoros*.[86] All these functions are closely related to the imperial cult. His son, T. Fl. Lollianus Aristobulus, the last known member of the family, who was active from the middle to the end of the second century CE, achieved the most honorable position of a senator.[87] The close affiliation between this family and the emperors at least since the Flavian period is not only obvious by the offices they occupied, but also by the display of a greater than life-sized portrait bust of Marcus Aurelius in Dwelling Unit 6, and the right to use precious marbles from the imperial quarries for decorating their own home.[88]

Whereas we know the owners of Dwelling Units 6 and 7 from the early second century CE onwards, we have no evidence that the houses were owned by this family at the time of their construction around the second quarter of the first century CE. In this period an ancestor of C. Fl. Furius Aptus was named Python. Through an inscription we are informed that he was *neopoios* of Artemis and therefore responsible for the temple of the goddess.[89] While Python is a name which occurs only seldom in the inscriptions from Ephesos,[90] we find it in the above mentioned donors list from the Artemision: here one Pythion, son of a Pythion, is listed among other benefactors, all of them members of the Ephesian elite in this period.[91] As the ancestral chart of the family who owned Dwell-

---

[86] For his Dionysiac priesthood and the interpretation of Dwelling Unit 6 as a club house see HILKE THÜR in this volume; for the relation of these offices to (imperial) cult see STEVEN J. FRIESEN, *Twice Neokoros: Ephesos, Asia, and the Cult of the Flavian Imperial Family* (Leiden: Brill, 1993), 50–59; for relationships between priests of Dionysos clubs and the imperial cult see FRANZ POLAND, *Geschichte des griechischen Vereinswesens* (Leipzig: Teubner, 1909), 232–36.

[87] He is attested through two inscriptions on statue bases from Ephesos, which presumably carried statues of him: *IvE* 864 was found near Dwelling Unit 6, the other, *IvE* 675, comes from the Lower Agora; for the findspots see RATHMAYR, "Haus des Ritters," 328–29.

[88] The date during the reign of Hadrian is attested by graffiti on the back side of marble slabs used in the marble hall 31 in Dwelling Unit 6; for the graffiti see HANS TAEUBER, "Graffiti und Steininschriften," in THÜR and RATHMAYR, *Wohneinheit 6*, 331–44. A small bust of this emperor was found north of the Dwelling Units 6 and 7; it presumably belonged to one of these houses; for this see RATHMAYR, "Götter- und Kaiserkult," 128–29 fig. 16.

[89] FRIESEN, *Twice Neokoros*, 23: "Individuals who served as neopoioi normally were part of a commission whose responsibility it was to administer temple finances. In some cases, groups of neopoioi functioned as a building committee for a new temple, but the normal responsibilities for such a group in the Roman period was the maintenance of buildings and oversight of a temple's income"; BURRELL, *Neokoroi*, 349: "... Such officials were in charge of the temple's fabric ...."

[90] In the database http://epigraphy.packhum.org/inscriptions/main the name Πυθίων occurs only in sixteen inscriptions (*IvE* 20, 488, 858+Add., 901, 1035, 1036, 1072, 1500, 1578A+Add., 1970, 3033, 3034, 3064, 4103, 4342; *JÖAI* 55: 139 no. 4359), and among these, six of them name T. Fl. Python, who was active in the Trajanic period (*IvE* 858+Add., 1500, 3033, 3034, 3064, 4342). For this person see the family tree in the addendum to this article.

[91] SEG 241: Λεύκιος Κοσ.....ος .ερα[-]/**Πυθίων Πυθίωνος** [-]/Ἐπαφρᾶς Φιλομούσου σὺν γ[υναικὶ -]/Ἑρμογένης Νεικάνδρου σὺν γυναι[κὶ -]/Γάιος Ἄρριος Βαργάθης [-]/Δέκμος

ing Unit 6 is not quite certain in late Hellenistic-early imperial times, it seems quite possible that this person was a member of the family in question. He might have been the son of the Pythion who was *neopoios*, and the father of T. Fl. Perigenes, the first family member who possessed Roman citizenship (chart 1). Now, if Dwelling Units 6 and 7 were already in the possession of the same family that is attested as the owner-family from the second century CE onwards, then the person who installed the imperial cult might have been one of the two named Pythion in the list; but it is also possible that a later family member established it in the memory of one of his ancestors. As all elements bearing a relationship to domestic religious activity were installed in Dwelling Unit 7 in building period 2 at the latest, this person could have been C. Fl. Furius Aptus.[92]

H. Conclusions

For Dwelling Unit 7 of Terrace House 2 in Ephesos, built in the second quarter of the first century CE, religious activity is attested through the existence of a marble altar and an offering table in the centre of the peristyle court 38b. These objects were set up in building period 2, the late Trajanic – early Hadrianic period, at the latest. The *putealia* covering two wells in the north hall of the peristyle 38b and in room 38 are to be considered as relating to them. Their cylindrical form recalled altars of this same type, and therefore they contributed perfectly to a sacred atmosphere. *Putealia*, which had their apex from the late Hellenistic period to the first century CE, went out of fashion and use in the beginning of the second century CE. When Dwelling Unit 7 was linked to a water line in building period 2, a marble fountain was installed near one of the *putealia*. It was oriented towards the altar and the table. Presumably now the water used during the offerings was drawn from there. In the same period, the floor of the court was covered with white marble slabs, the halls received a mosaic floor and the walls were decorated with figures of gods (Victoria, Asclepius). Furthermore, room 38d connected with the east hall of the peristyle 38b was also newly decorated with wall paintings: among them one should note a *libation*-scene *Romano ritu* at an altar, a theme that could recall the same ritual activities in the adjacent court. Room 38, which was equipped with a *puteal* since the erection of the house, was now furnished with marble and stucco of the highest quality on its floor and walls, whereby the central niche on the southern wall was reveted with colored marble. Here the portrait busts of Tiberius and Livia were set up in the

---

Σπέδιος Ῥοῦφος σὺν γυνα[ικὶ καὶ]/τέκνῳ δη. ι'/Λεύκιος Δειδιήνος Ἀθηνίων [-]/Μᾶρκος Κλώδιος Πρεῖμος σὺν θυ[γατρὶ -]/Χαρεῖνος Τρύφωνος [-.

[92] In this regard I want to point out that Furius Aptus erected a statue of his grandfather T. Fl. Pythion in the Lower Agora (*IvE* 3064), which probably stood next to a statue of himself and other members of his family; see RATHMAYR, "Die Besitzerfamilie."

second half of the first century CE at the earliest and in building period 2 at the latest. Through the wide door opening they were directly linked to the altar and table in the court. Furthermore this door was flanked by marble pillars, which bore apertures for barriers to fence off the room, i. e. what was kept in it.

Concerning the addressees of the sacrifices offered at altar and table, the first thought should be of the emperors, who were present in the portrait busts set up in the niche of room 38. The eagle shown in a relief on the altar in the court can be interpreted as a sign of power given to the Roman emperors by Zeus/Jupiter. In this regard Victoria and Asclepius, present in the wall paintings in the peristyle halls, had very close connections to the Roman emperors as well; we only have to think of the Victoria Augusta for instance.[93] As portraits were always set up for a certain reason, the most plausible cause for the honors of Tiberius – the inscriptions and the statues – are the benefactions that he granted to the people of Ephesos after the earthquake of 23 CE. An inscription (SEG 241) informs us that in return for his help, the emperor received a priest (*archiereus*) for his worship. Peter Scherrer identified an annex-room of the basilica on the Upper Agora as a possible location where the offerings took place.[94] Emperors were in general honored only on special occasions such as their birthdays, New Year, or dedication days of their portraits.[95]

In Dwelling Unit 7 the worship of Tiberius and Livia was supposedly established by the homeowner himself. A member of the family was presumably named in the inscription of the donor list from the Artemision honoring Tiberius for his assistance after the earthquake of 23 CE. In the house the sacrifice with the subsequent festivities might have been held on the day commemorating the imperial support.[96] In this regard Dwelling Unit 7 could have been used by certain Ephesian families as a clubhouse on particular days of the year, whereas the remaining time the house seems to have functioned as a normal dwelling.[97]

---

[93] Tonio Hölscher, *Victoria Romana: Archäologische Untersuchungen zur Geschichte und Wesensart der römischen Siegesgöttin von den Anfängen bis zum Ende des 3. Jhs. n. Chr.* (Mainz: von Zabern, 1967), 164: "Die Victoria Augusta hat sich mit dem Kaisertum wie der Name Augustus auf Tiberius vererbt." Die späteren Kaiser "übernahmen seine [des Augustus] persönliche Siegesgöttin zunächst in dynastischer Tradition, dann einfach mit der Übertragung der Kaisergewalt, mit deren rechtlicher Formulierung die Victoria des Kaisers eng zusammenhing." Concerning Asclepius, the Emperor could take on his role insofar as he, like the god, was responsible for the wellbeing of humankind; cf. a club in Ephesos whose members worshipped Asclepius and the emperor together; see *IvE* 719.

[94] Scherrer, "Anmerkungen," 97–98 n 47.

[95] For festivities concerning the Emperors see Pekáry, *Kaiserbildnis*, 110–12.

[96] At the ceremony of the *hymnodes* of Pergamon, offerings such as wreaths, cakes, incense, and lamps to celebrate the birthday of Augustus are mentioned, whereby the latter were used for illuminating his cult statue; see Poland, *Vereinswesen*, 265.

[97] The architecture and all of the finds (sculptures, terracotta figurines, ceramic and glass objects, small finds, etc.) and graffiti as well do not differ from those from the other dwelling units in Terrace House 2 and from dwellings generally; see Rathmayr, *Wohneinheit 7*.

Perigenes (*IvE* 1578A)
↓

Perigenes (*IvE* 1578A)
↓

Python: son of one Perigenes, who
himself was son of one Perigenes;
office: Neopoios of Artemis
(*IvE* 1578)
?↓?

Python[98]: son of one Python
(SEG 241)
↓

T. Fl. Perigenes[99]: son of one
Python; offices: Prytan is Asiarch
(*IvE* 1270, 3033, 3034)
↓

T. Fl. Python: Gramma- teus, Gymnasiarch of Artemis, Archiereus Asias, Asiarch (*IvE* 674, 858, 1500, 2047, 3033, 3034, 4342)	∞ Fl. Myrthon: Gymnasi- arch of Artemis (*IvE* 1500, 3033, 3023)

T. Fl. Aristobulus: Grammateus, Prytan is Asiarch (*IvE* 670A, 1500, 1384, 3033, 3034)	T. Fl. Iulianus (the Elder): Archiereus Asias, Asiarch (*IvE* 674, 712B, 3033, 3034, 4342)	Fl. Skapula (*IvE* 3033, 3034)	Fl. Pythia (*IvE* 3033, 3034)
C. Fl. Furius Aptus: Alytarch, priest of Dionysos *pro poleos*, Neokoros?[100] (*IvE* 502, 502A, 675, 1267, 834, 1099, 3064)	T. Fl. Iulianus (the Young- er): Grammateus, Prytane is Ergepistates (*IvE* 674A, 4342)		
T. Fl. Lollianus Aristobulus: senator (*IvE* 675, 864)			

Chart 1: Family Tree of the Owner Family of Dwelling Unit 6 (by Elisabeth Rathmayr)

---

[98] This Python from SEG 241 cannot be identically equal with a Python, son of a Python, which is listed in SEG 37:976 from Kolophon, because the here named person, a προφήτος, should be the same as the Python in SEG 37:968, a text dated "just before 147/148 AD."

[99] From T. Fl. Perigenes to T. Fl. Lollianus Aristobulus the ancestral chart is assured; ↓ is used for "father of."

[100] BURRELL, *Neokoroi*, 60: "Very soon after (i. e., the Neronian/Claudian period), the title 'neokoros' was to become part of official civic titulature in Asia, identified exclusively with the provincial imperial cult, not the possession of the temple of Artemis."

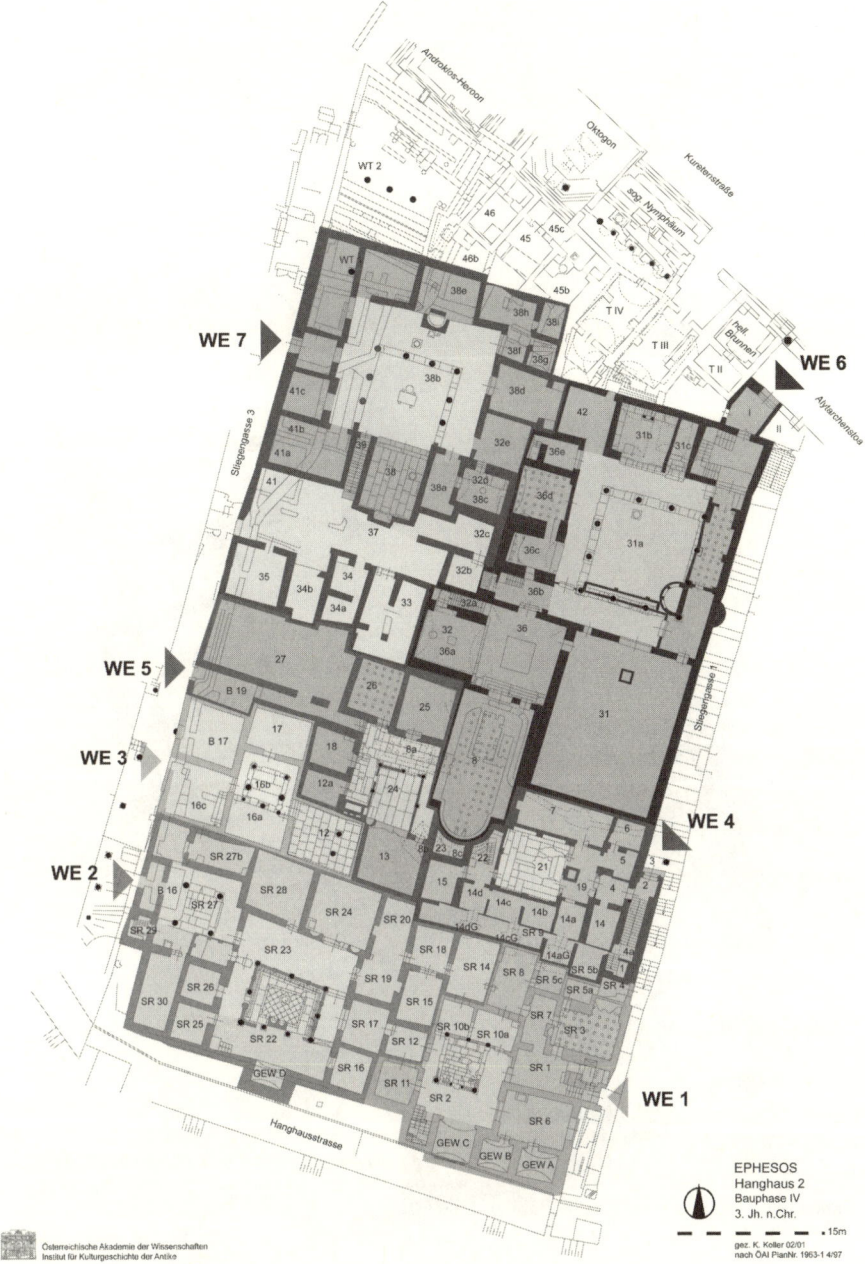

Figure 1: Ephesos, Terrace House 2. © Karin Koller ÖAW/ÖAI

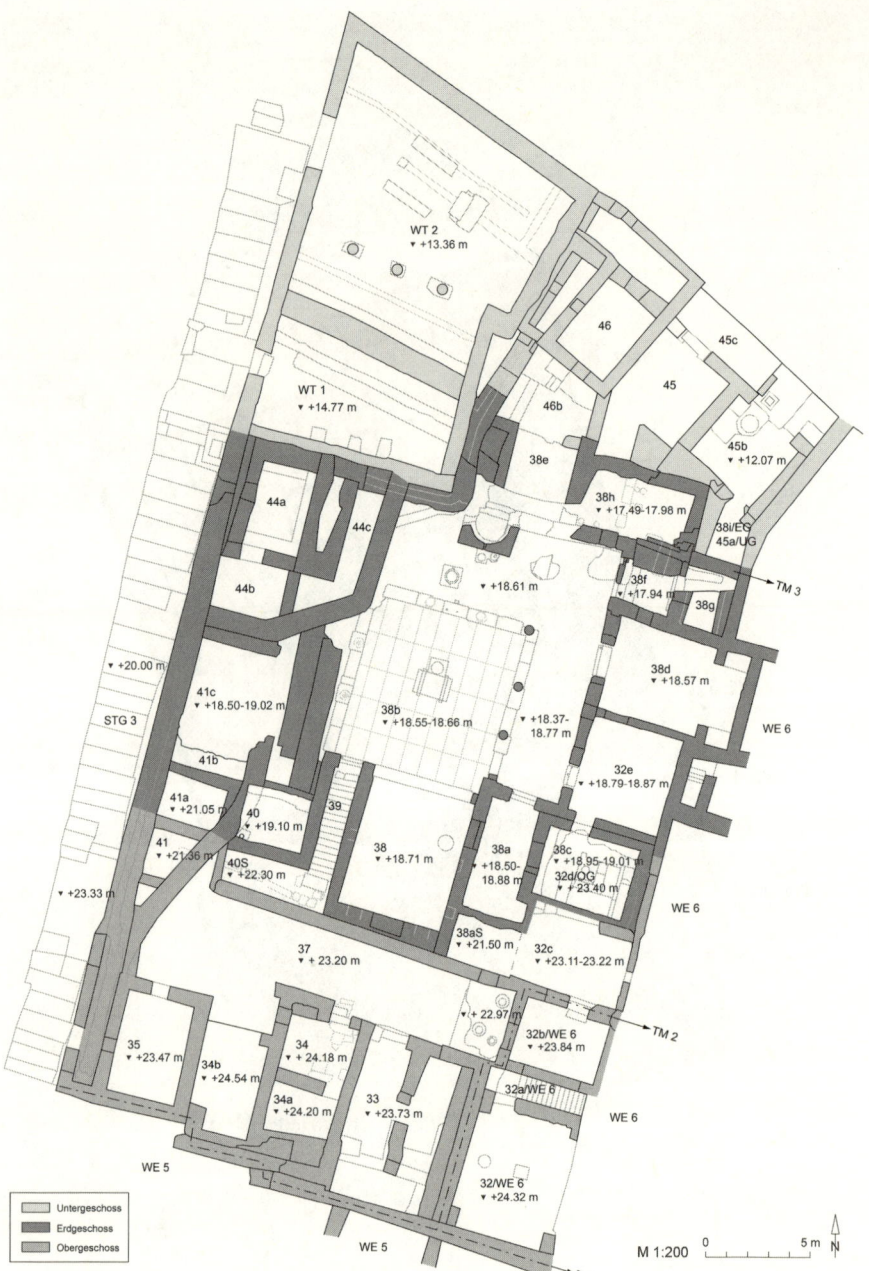

Figure 2: Unit 7, Reconstruction. © Ingrid Adenstedt, ÖAW, and Robert Kalsek,
TU Vienna

Figure 3: Unit 7, Peristyle Court 38b, Altar and Table. © Niki Gail, ÖAI

Figure 4: Unit 7, Room 38d, South Wall with Sacrificial Scene. © Niki Gail, ÖAI

Figure 5: Unit 7, Peristyle Court 38b and Room 38. © Niki Gail, ÖAI

Figure 6: Unit 7, Room 38, Find Context of the Portrait Busts of Tiberius and Livia and the Bronze Snake. © ÖAI, archive, DIA-006131

Figure 7: Unit 7, Efes Müzesi presentation of the Portrait Busts of Tiberius and Livia and the Bronze Snake. © Niki Gail, ÖAI

Figure 8: Unit 7, Peristyle Court 38b, Find Context of the Fountain on the North Stylobate. © ÖAI, archive, DIA 006267

Figure 9: Unit 7, Peristyle Court 38b, Wall Painting of Victoria found in the Eastern Hall.
© Norbert Zimmermann, ÖAW

The House of C. Fl. Furius Aptus in Ephesos: Clubhouse of a Dionysiac Association?

Hilke Thür

A. Introduction

In 1979, an important inscription was discovered in the city of Ephesos (*IvE* 4.1267). It was discovered on a barrier wall (fig. 1) in the area of Dwelling Unit 6 of Terrace House 2.[1] The inscription indicates that the homeowner, C. Flavius Furius Aptus, was a priest of Dionysus Oreios.[2] His name also appears in another inscription[3] and in a *dipinto* (painted inscription).[4] This information confirms the ownership of C. Flavius Furius Aptus during building phase 2,[5] dated to the early Hadrianic period.[6]

---

[1] Terrace House 2 was excavated from 1967 to 1985 by HERMANN VETTERS. The preliminary reports were published in: *AAWW* 105 (1967) to *AAWW* 123 (1986). For a new summary of the results see HILKE THÜR, "Art and Architecture in Terrace House 2 in Ephesus: An Example of Domestic Architecture in the Roman Imperial Period," in *Contested Spaces: Houses and Temples in Roman Antiquity and the New Testament*, ed. DAVID L. BALCH and ANNETTE WEISSENRIEDER, WUNT 285 (Tübingen: Mohr Siebeck, 2012), 237–59, fig. 1–23; see also ELISABETH RATHMAYR, "New Evidence for Imperial Cult in Dwelling Unit 7 in Terrace House 2 in Ephesos," *Ephesos as a Religious Center under the Principate*, ed. ALLEN BLACK, CHRISTINE THOMAS, and TREVOR W. THOMPSON, WUNT (Tübingen: Mohr Siebeck, 2019). For the final publication of Dwelling Unit 1 and 2 see FRIEDRICH KRINZINGER, ed., *Das Hanghaus 2 in Ephesos: Die Wohneinheiten 1 und 2: Baubefund, Ausstattung und Funde*, FiE 8.8 (Vienna: ÖAW, 2010); for Dwelling Unit 4 see HILKE THÜR, *Hanghaus 2 in Ephesos: Die Wohneinheit 4: Baubefund, Ausstattung, Funde*, FiE 8.5 (Vienna: ÖAW, 2005). For Dwelling Unit 6 see HILKE THÜR and ELISABETH RATHMAYR, ed., *Das Hanghaus 2 in Ephesos: Die Wohneinheit 6: Baubefund, Ausstattung, Funde*, FiE 8.9 (Vienna: ÖAW, 2014). Dwelling units 3 and 5 will be edited by SABINE LADSTÄTTER. For Dwelling Unit 7 see ELISABETH RATHMAYR, *Das Hanghaus 2 in Ephesos: Die Wohneinheit 7: Baubefund, Ausstattung, Funde*, FiE 8.10 (Vienna: ÖAW, 2016).

[2] The inscription is written on the top moulding of a barrier between the south columns of peristyle courtyard 31a and reads: Διόνυσος Ὄρειος Βάκχιος πρὸ πόλεως / οὗ ἱερᾶται Γάϊος Φλάβιος Φούριος Ἄπτος. DIETER KNIBBE translated it: "Dionysos Oreios (vom Berge) Bakchios (vom Heiligtum) vor der Stadt, für den C. Flavius Furius Aptus Priester ist" in HERMANN VETTERS, "Ephesos: Vorläufiger Grabungsbericht 1979," *AAWW* 117 (1980): 259; HANS TAEUBER, "Graffiti und Steininschriften," in THÜR and RATHMAYR, *Wohneinheit 6*, 342–43.

[3] See n. 57.

[4] TAEUBER, "Graffiti und Steininschriften," 331–46 (esp. 338–39).

[5] See ELISABETH RATHMAYR, "Das Haus des Ritters C. Flavius Furius Aptus: Beobach-

Shortly after the discovery and publication of this inscription (*IvE* 4.1267) in the excavation report in 1980, Reinhold Merkelbach wrote that Aptus not only held the office as a priest of the god Dionysus Oreios but was probably the patron and priest of one of the Dionysiac associations in Ephesos. Merkelbach assumed that his house served as a space for banquets and meetings.[7] The excavator Hermann Vetters and most scholars interpreted Dwelling Unit 6 simply as the luxurious townhouse of a high status Ephesian who rose to senatorial rank. In the following paper, I want to present new archaeological evidence for the use of Dwelling Unit 6 as the clubhouse of a Dionysiac association.

B. Dwelling Unit 6 in Terrace House 2

The Aptus House 6 occupies the northeast corner of the *insula* of Terrace House 2 (fig. 2). This complex of seven peristyle houses is located in the city center of Ephesos. It was built in the second quarter of the first century CE[8] and destroyed by an earthquake in the third quarter of the third century CE.[9] The house occupies 950 m² and was very spacious. It could be accessed from the south portico of the so-called *embolos* (modern "Kouretes Street"), the main east-west thoroughfare of the city.[10] The floor plan follows the layout of large peristyle houses, which were widespread in the eastern Mediterranean.

Dwelling Unit 6 was excavated by Vetters from 1973 to 1987.[11] The house was filled with rubble. The archaeological evidence – destroyed walls and badly damaged architectural pieces from the multi-storied peristyle courtyard – demonstrates destruction by an earthquake. This natural catastrophe can be con-

---

tungen zur Einflussnahme von Hausbesitzern an Architektur und Ausstattung in der Wohneinheit 6 des Hanghauses 2 in Ephesos," *MDAI (I)* 59 (2009): 307–36.

[6] See below.

[7] REINHOLD MERKELBACH, *Die Hirten des Dionysos: Die Dionysos-Mysterien der römischen Kaiserzeit und der bukolische Roman des Longus* (Stuttgart: Teubner, 1988), 23.

[8] The dating of building phase 1 differs slightly in the single dwelling units; for Dwelling Unit 1 and 2 see ELISABETH RATHMAYR, "Rekonstruktion der Bauphasen," in KRINZINGER, *Wohneinheiten 1 und 2*, 81–100 and 426–42. For Dwelling Unit 4 see THÜR, *Wohneinheit 4*, 9–40.

[9] SABINE LADSTÄTTER, "Die Chronologie des Hanghauses 2," in *Das Hanghaus 2 von Ephesos: Studien zu Baugeschichte und Chronologie*, ed. FRIEDRICH KRINZINGER, AF 7 (Vienna: ÖAW, 2002), 9–39.

[10] See ELISABETH RATHMAYR, "Auswertung: Eingangssituation und Peristylhof," in THÜR and RATHMAYR, *Wohneinheit 6*, 837–38.

[11] HERMANN VETTERS, "Ephesos: Vorläufiger Grabungsbericht 1973," *AAWW* 111 (1974): 211–24; HERMANN VETTERS, "Ephesos: Vorläufiger Grabungsbericht 1979," *AAWW* 117 (1980): 249–66; HERMANN VETTERS, "Ephesos: Vorläufiger Grabungsbericht 1980," *AAWW* 118 (1981): 137–68; HERMANN VETTERS, "Ephesos: Vorläufiger Grabungsbericht 1981," *AAWW* 119 (1982): 62–102; HERMANN VETTERS, "Ephesos: Vorläufiger Grabungsbericht für die Jahre 1984 und 1985," *AAWW* 123 (1986): 75–161.

nected to an earthquake around 262 CE during the reign of Gallienus, which is known from literary sources.[12]

In building phase 1,[13] the house had a footprint of 650 m² and a remarkably huge peristyle court (31a), which was surrounded by rooms on three sides. Several rooms are of the "broad room" type,[14] opening along more or less their full width to the porticoes of the peristyle court. In the southwest of Dwelling Unit 6 existed a second smaller courtyard (36). On its west side an *exedra* (36a) was situated, and in the northwest corner a stairway led up to the upper floor and the area of the neighboring Dwelling Unit 7 (fig. 2).[15] Service and storage rooms may have been placed in the spandrel between the north rooms and Kouretes Street, or in a housekeeping area in the upper floor west of Dwelling Unit 6, and in the southern part of the upper floor of Dwelling Unit 7. Building Phase 1 is dated to the second quarter of the first century CE on the basis of the small finds and the type of capital on the columns in the peristyle court (31a).[16] The building type follows the tradition of the *basileia*,[17] the residences of Hellenistic rulers and aristocrats with large peristyle houses and several banqueting rooms.

In building phase 2 (fig. 3),[18] room 31 was enlarged to 180 m² floor space, which is twice its original size. The room, now measuring 11.5 by 15.7 m, had a long rectangular floor plan, and its walls and floor were richly furbished with marble;[19] the wooden coffered ceiling was decorated with a maritime *thiasos* including hippocampuses.[20] In the rear wall a fountain was installed with an apse;[21] perhaps a statue was displayed in it (fig. 16).[22] Additionally, the peristyle

---

[12] HILKE THÜR, "Zerstörung und Aufgabe," in THÜR and RATHMAYR, *Wohneinheit 6*, 137. In general see LADSTÄTTER, "Chronologie des Hanghauses 2."

[13] See HILKE THÜR, "Rekonstruktion der Bauphase I," in THÜR and RATHMAYR, *Wohneinheit 6*, 123–27.

[14] WOLFRAM HOEPFNER, "Zum Typus der Basileia und der königlichen Androne," in *Basileia: Die Paläste der hellenistischen Könige: Internationales Symposium in Berlin vom 16.12.1992–20.12.1992*, ed. WOLFRAM HOEPFNER and GUNNAR BRANDS (Mainz: von Zabern, 1996), 29–31.

[15] Compare RATHMAYR, "New Evidence."

[16] HILKE THÜR, "Zur Datierung der Bauphasen: Anmerkungen zur Methodik," in THÜR and RATHMAYR, *Wohneinheit 6*, 13–15.

[17] HOEPFNER and BRANDS, *Basileia*; INGE NIELSEN, *Hellenistic Palaces: Tradition and Renewal*, Studies of Hellenistic Civilization 5 (Aarhus: Aarhus University, 1994).

[18] More details in THÜR, "Rekonstruktion der Bauphase II," 127–30.

[19] KARIN KOLLER, "Bauphase I: Marmorsaal 31," in THÜR and RATHMAYR, *Wohneinheit 6*, 228.

[20] HILKE THÜR, "Sonstige Ausstattung: Decken," in THÜR and RATHMAYR, *Wohneinheit 6*, 175–77; HILKE THÜR, "Zur Dach- und Deckenkonstruktion des Marmorsaales der Wohneinheit 6 im Hanghaus 2 in Ephesos," in *Holztragwerke der Antike*, ed. ALEXANDER VON KIENLIN, Byzas 11 (Istanbul: Ege, 2011), 235–45.

[21] HILKE THÜR, "Wasserwirtschaftliche Einrichtungen: Wandnischenbrunnen WB-A2 im sogenannten Marmorsaal 31," in THÜR and RATHMAYR, *Wohneinheit 6*, 204–6.

[22] ELISABETH RATHMAYR, "Skulpturenfunde: Marmorsaal 31," in THÜR and RATHMAYR, *Wohneinheit 6*, 389–90.

court 31a, court 36, *exedra* 36a, and the rooms 36b and 36c were furnished with
marble revetment;[23] the floors were covered with mosaics[24] and marble. In the
east portico of the peristyle court, a bath consisting of three rooms (M1–M3)
was installed.[25] Because of this alteration, the entrance into the ground floor
had to be rearranged. Now visitors entered the newly separated vestibule (31c),
situated in the middle axis of the peristyle court (31a), and continued on into
the north portico.[26] The spaces between the columns of the south colonnade
were closed with a barrier serving as the rear wall of a newly built fountain
(fig. 4). In the east and west porticoes, large marble door frames (fig. 8) separated the northern part of the peristyle court (31a) from the southern area of
Dwelling Unit 6. In building phase 2, two more fountains were installed: one in
the marble hall (31), the other in room 36a.[27] These building conversions can be
assigned to the owner of the dwelling during phase 2, C. Flavius Furius Aptus;
the above mentioned inscription (*IvE* 4.1267) was engraved on the central pillar
of the rear wall of the fountain (fig. 1); a portrait bust of Furius Aptus was probably placed above it.[28]

Building phase 2 can be dated – according to the design of the pilaster capitals in the marble hall (31) – to the first quarter of the second century CE.[29] This
date is confirmed by inscriptions found during the recent restoration work in the
marble hall (31). On the back sides of two Pavonazetto plates from the imperial
quarries in Dokimeion, two inscriptions name the third consulate of Hadrian in
119 CE and Cn. Arrius Augur, who was consul in 121 CE.[30] Through these texts
the building and decoration of phase 2 can be dated precisely to the early Hadrianic period. A *dipinto* on another plate is addressed to "Furi Apti."[31] It thus
constitutes an additional proof that Furius Aptus was the homeowner of Dwelling Unit 6.

---

[23] KARIN KOLLER, "Marmor: Bauphase II," in THÜR and RATHMAYR, *Wohneinheit 6*, 228–
43.

[24] VERONIKA SCHEIBELREITER-GAIL, "Mosaiken," in THÜR and RATHMAYR, *Wohneinheit 6*, 255–71.

[25] HILKE THÜR, "Baubeschreibung: Ostportikus 31 aO," in THÜR and RATHMAYR,
Wohneinheit 6, 51–60; HILKE THÜR, "Auswertung: Badeanlage," in THÜR and RATHMAYR,
Wohneinheit 6, 842–45.

[26] RATHMAYR, "Auswertung: Eingangsituation und Peristylhof."

[27] HILKE THÜR, "Wasserwirtschaftliche Einrichtungen: Bodenwasserbecken WB-A4 im
sogenannten Marmorsaal 31," in THÜR and RATHMAYR, *Wohneinheit 6*, 208–9 and HILKE
THÜR, "Wasserbecken WB-A1 in Raum 36a," in THÜR and RATHMAYR, *Wohneinheit 6*, 203–4.

[28] RATHMAYR, "Das Haus des Ritters C. Flavius Furius Aptus. "

[29] KARIN KOLLER, "Die Pilasterkapitelle aus dem 'Marmorsaal' der Wohneinheit 6: Bemerkungen zu Dekoration und Zeitstellung," in KRINZINGER, *Hanghaus 2 von Ephesos*, 119–36.

[30] TAEUBER, "Graffiti und Dipinti auf Verkleidungsplatten aus dem Marmorsaal 31," 339.

[31] TAEUBER, "Graffiti und Dipinti," 338.

In building phase 3 (fig. 5),[32] a second huge banquet hall was set up in the south part of the house, west of the marble hall. This new hall (8) was covered with a barrel vault and had a large apse in the south (fig. 12).[33] The decoration of this hall is badly preserved, but from the remains it can be reconstructed with a decor similar to the marble hall (31); the uppermost parts of the walls and the vault were covered with frescoes[34] and the half dome with a colorful glass mosaic.[35] A large water basin was installed in the northern area of the floor.[36] On the west side of this apsidal hall (8) another, smaller vaulted room (8a) was carved into the rock and equipped with a spectacular stucco ceiling.[37] In the lunette of the back wall the silhouettes of a couple are preserved, accompanied by two cupids (fig. 6). Elisabeth Rathmayr convincingly interpreted them as Dionysus and Aphrodite.[38] The medallions of the ceiling are filled with members of the *thiasos* of Dionysus and the sphere of Aphrodite (fig. 13). Two statues of the goddess – of the Anadymene type – were placed beside the broad stairway (fig. 12) leading from the entrance (36) up to the apsidal hall (8). In the epigram on one of the two preserved statue bases Gaius (Aptus) is named once more. In building phase 3, the former courtyard 36 is now covered with a cross vault. Because the inscription mentioned above,[39] set up in building phase 3, names Furius Aptus, he was not only responsible for the alterations in building period 2, but also for those in building period 3, in the middle of the second century CE.[40]

In building phases 1 to 3, a staircase (32a) led to an upper floor on the west side of the house; but with the exception of rooms 32, 32b and 36b. 1, the rooms in the upper floor could not be accessed from Dwelling Unit 6. Past staircase 32a and room 32b, a door led to the upper floor of Dwelling Unit 7, the courtyard 32c–d, and the surrounding rooms, as well as the service rooms 33–35 and 37.

---

[32] More details in THÜR, "Rekonstruktion der Bauphase III," 131–34.

[33] THÜR, "Baubeschreibung: Apsidensaal 8," 85–89; HILKE THÜR, "Auswertung: Repräsentationsräume," in THÜR and RATHMAYR, *Wohneinheit 6,* 838–42.

[34] NORBERT ZIMMERMANN, "Wandmalerei: Apsidensaal 8," in THÜR and RATHMAYR, *Wohneinheit 6,* 292–94.

[35] SCHEIBELREITER-GAIL, "Mosaiken: Apsidensaal 8," 262.

[36] HILKE THÜR, "Wasserwirtschaftliche Einrichtungen: Bodenwasserbecken WB A–5 in Apsidensaal 8," in THÜR and RATHMAYR, *Wohneinheit 6,* 209–10.

[37] ELISABETH RATHMAYR, "Stuckdekorationen der Räume 8a und 36c," in THÜR and RATHMAYR, *Wohneinheit 6,* 324–29; THÜR, "Auswertung: Repräsentationsräume."

[38] RATHMAYR, "Stuckdekorationen der Räume 8a und 36c."

[39] TAEUBER, "Steininschriften," 343; see also SEG 31.962, 963.

[40] See also ELISABETH RATHMAYR, "Die Besitzerfamilie," in THÜR and RATHMAYR, *Wohneinheit 6,* 846–49.

While in building phase 4,[41] only minor alterations on the ground floor can be attested, two more upper floors were constructed above the porticos of the peristyle court (31a).[42]

The dating of this building and decoration phase 4 around 230 CE[43] is confirmed from archaeological evidence in Dwelling Unit 1 and by other criteria as well. Dwelling Unit 6 was destroyed by a series of earthquakes. Immediately before the final destruction at the end of the third quarter of the third century CE, restoration work took place in certain rooms like the marble hall (31). Although after this destruction the house was not restored anymore, some rooms in the north area of the house and two of the former bath rooms, which were accessible from the Kouretes Street, stayed in use as storage. Later structures were built 3 to 4 m above the original ground floor of Unit 6. Through these fortunate circumstances, Dwelling Unit 6 and its architectural material finds have been very well preserved up to modern times.

C. The Homeowner, C. Flavius Furius Aptus

The family of C. Flavius Furius Aptus is documented in inscriptions from Ephesos during the first and second centuries CE. According to Elisabeth Rathmayr,[44] the earliest known member is a Perigenes who lived during the time of Augustus.[45] His son T. Flavius Perigenes might have been a Roman citizen. The next generation includes T. Flavius Python[46] who was alive in the time of Domitian and Trajan. He was married to Flavia Myrthon.[47] They had three sons, T. Fl. Aristobulus,[48] T. Fl. Iulianus (the elder),[49] Fl. Skapula,[50] and a daughter named Fl. Pythias.[51] T. Fl. Aristobulus had the son C. Fl. Furius Aptus.[52] His brother T. Fl. Iulianus (the elder) had a son T. Fl. Iulianus (the younger).[53] The last

---

[41] Thür, "Rekonstruktion der Bauphase IV," 134–47.

[42] Hilke Thür, "Architekturausstattung," in Thür and Rathmayr, *Wohneinheit 6*, 153–70.

[43] Norbert Zimmermann, "Wandmalerei: Zusammenfassung," in Thür and Rathmayr, *Wohneinheit 6*, 311–13.

[44] Rathmayr, "Haus des Ritters"; Rathmayr, "Die Besitzerfamilie"; see also Rathmayr, "New Evidence."

[45] *IvE* 6.905A.

[46] *IvE* 1578A.

[47] *IvE* 6.1500; 7.1.3033, 3034.

[48] *IvE* 3.670A; 4.1384; 5.1500; 7.1.3033, 3034.

[49] *IvE* 3.712B; 7.1.3033, 3034; 7.2.4342.

[50] *IvE* 7.1.3033, 3034.

[51] *IvE* 7.1.3033; 7.1.3034.

[52] *IvE* 2.502, 502A; 3.670A, 3.834; 4.1099 (1), 1099 (2); 1267; 7.1.3064; Dieter Knibbe and Bülent İplikcioğlu, "Neue Inschriften aus Ephesos 8," *JÖAI* 53 (1981–1982): 132–34 no. 140.

[53] *IvE* 3.674, 674A; 7.2.4342.

known member of the family is the son of C. Fl. Furius Aptus. The son, T. Fl. Lollianus Aristobulus,[54] was the first member of the family to become a member of the *ordo senatorius*. Therefore C. Fl. Furius Aptus should have been of equestrian rank.

According to the aforementioned inscriptions, one *dipinto* and a *graffito* on a pottery fragment from Dwelling Unit 6, C. Fl. Furius Aptus is attested as the homeowner. The most important piece of evidence is the above mentioned inscription (*IvE* 4.1267)[55] on the barrier wall (fig. 1) in the south portico of peristyle court 31a. Placed in the central axis of the courtyard and surmounted by a portrait bust of Aptus (fig. 4), it presented the owner of the house to every visitor.[56] The second important stone inscription[57] is the westernmost of the two statue bases placed alongside the monumental stairway from room 36 into the apsidal hall (8). An epigram naming Gaius (Fl. Furius Aptus) and an unidentified Perikles is asking Aphrodite to protect them as guest and host.

The third attestation of Aptus is a *dipinto* 'Furi Apti'[58] written on the backside of a slab of Pavonazetto originally placed in the middle area of the revetment of the marble hall (31). Aptus was the addressee and customer of the delivery of precious Pavonazetto slabs from the quarry in Dokimeion;[59] the production of marble blocks is dated by a stamp and a *graffito* in the year of the third consulate of Hadrian (119 CE) and the consul Cn. Arrius Augur (121 CE). The last piece of evidence for Aptus was found on a fragment of a ceramic bowl with a *graffito* saying "I belong to someone else other than Aptus."[60]

From this epigraphic evidence we not only know the homeowner of Dwelling Unit 6, but also the exact date of building phase 2. The name of Aptus on the statue base in front of the apsidal hall (8), placed there in building phase 3, shows that he was still alive and responsible for the further enlargement of the house with the apsidal hall (8) and the rooms 8a, 8b, and 8c. With the ascent of his son T. Fl. Lollianus Aristobulus into the senatorial rank, he would have had to be in Rome most of the year. Building phase 4 with the construction of two more sto-

---

[54] *IvE* 3.675, 864.

[55] See n 2.

[56] RATHMAYR, "Skulpturenfunde: Peristylhof 31a," 384–86; RATHMAYR, "Auswertung: Eingangssituation und Peristylhof."

[57] KNIBBE and İPLİKÇİOĞLU, "Neue Inschriften 8," 132–34 no. 140; TAEUBER, "Steininschriften," 343; see also SEG 31.962, 963.

[58] TAEUBER, "Graffiti und Dipinti," 338.

[59] JOSEF RÖDER, "Bericht über Arbeiten in den antiken Steinbrüchen von İscehisar (Dokimeion)," *TAD* 18.1 (1969): 109–16; AURELIO PADILLA MONGE, "Notas sobre la explotación de las cantoas imperiales hasta al reinado des Hadriano: El caso de Dokimeion," *Habis: Filología clasíca, historia antiqua, arquelogía clasíca* 33 (2002): 433–46.

[60] TAEUBER, "Kleininschriften," 342; ALICE WALDNER and SABINE LADSTÄTTER, "Keramik: Katalog," in THÜR and RATHMAYR, *Wohneinheit 6*, 567.

reys above the peristyle court porticoes, and also the living rooms in the upper floor newly accessible from the west portico show changes in the use and function of Dwelling Unit 6.

D. Interpretation of Dwelling Unit 6

Vetters interpreted Dwelling Unit 6 – in accordance with the other houses of the *insula* – as the house of an aspiring and wealthy politician of the Ephesian elite, who received guests and clients, administered justice in private cases, and gave banquets in the apsidal hall (8), which Vetters – according to Vitruvius – interpreted as a private basilica.[61] Due to Vetters's assessment, the team of archaeologists and architects working since 2000 on the final publication of Dwelling Unit 6 classified this house at the beginning also as the town residence of a member of the upper class, who strove after senatorial rank and furnished his house after imperial models.[62] However, already in 1988, Merkelbach emphasized C. Fl. Furius Aptus's role not only as a priest of Dionysus but also as a patron and chairman of a Dionysiac association.[63] His interpretation was accepted and followed by other specialists in religious studies, such as Alfred Schäfer.[64]

In the following section the question of the interpretation of Dwelling Unit 6 shall be discussed: First, was Dwelling Unit 6 the very well and expensively embellished town house of one of the leading Ephesian families demonstrating their ability and capacity to rise into the senatorial rank? Or does the naming of the owner C. Flavius Furius Aptus as priest of Dionysus Oreios rather give proof for the use of the house as the clubhouse of a Dionysiac association? Or, third, was the use multifunctional, and did the owner Aptus also use his "private" dwelling for the meetings, banquets and religious ceremonies of a Dionysiac association in which he presided as priest and patron?

---

[61] HERMANN VETTERS, "Basilica privata," in *Classica et provincialia: Festschrift Erna Diez*, ed. GERDA SCHWARZ and ERWIN POCHMARSKI (Graz: Akademische Druck- und Verlagsanstalt, 1978), 211–15; HERMANN VETTERS, "Nochmals zur Basilica privata," *RHM* 23 (1981): 209–12.

[62] HILKE THÜR, "Zum Stadtpalast des Dionysospriesters C. Flavius Furius Aptus im Hanghaus 2 in Ephesos: Ein Zwischenbericht," in *Thiasos: Festschrift für Erwin Pochmarski zum 65. Geburtstag*, ed. CHRISTIANE FRANEK (Vienna: Phoibos, 2008), 1057–72; NORBERT ZIMMERMANN and SABINE LADSTÄTTER, *Wandmalerei in Ephesos von hellenistischer bis in byzantinische Zeit* (Vienna: Phoibos, 2010), 69–70.

[63] MERKELBACH, *Die Hirten des Dionysos*, 23.

[64] ALFRED SCHÄFER, "Dionysische Gruppen als Phänomen der römischen Kaiserzeit," in *Gruppenreligionen im römischen Reich: Sozialformen, Grenzziehungen und Leistungen*, ed. JÖRG RÜPKE, STAC 43 (Tübingen: Mohr Siebeck, 2006), 161–80.

E. The Worship of Dionysus and Dionysiac Associations in Ephesos

To answer the questions a short overview of the evidence for the worship of Dionysus and religious communities in Ephesos is helpful.[65] The worship of Dionysus included mystery initiations similar to those for Demeter and Isis,[66] and the myths of Dionysus also had Orphic features.[67] Attributes of the mysteries and symbols of Dionysus are the *thyrsus*, the *narthex*, the *cista mystica*, the *liknon* and above all the *phallus*. During the course of the religious ceremonies the wine miracle symbolized by the crater played an important role. The mysteries ended with the holy marriage of the god with Ariadne. Because Dionysus was the god of theater plays, dramatic performances and plays had a fixed place in the mysteries.[68]

During Dionysiac festivities processions were an important element. In ancient sources two of these processions are attested. During the rule of Marc Antony in the east, the Ephesians dressed as Bacchantes, Pans, Satyrs and Maenads. They revered Marc Antony as the New Dionysus and decorated the city with ivy and *thyrsus,* and played flutes and cymbals.[69] The second episode took place when St. Timothy opposed the wild feast of the Katagoge in the lower *embolos* and was beaten and stoned to death by the *mystai.*[70]

---

[65] Dionysos as one of the oldest Greek gods was a god of nature and vegetation and therefore linked to the seasons. His cult places and sanctuaries were mostly situated outside the cities. He often was worshipped in grottos or wine summerhouses – together with his companions and attendants, such as Pan, the Nymphs, the Satyrs, Silenus, and shepherds, but also animals such as rams, he-goats and donkeys. Religious activity always included offerings, a festive dinner, and a symposium, that is, a drinking orgy. A. LEY, "Dionysos," *KlPauly;* FRIEDRICH WILHELM HAMDORF, *Dionysos-Bacchus: Kult und Wandlungen des Weingottes* (Munich: Callwey, 1986); MERKELBACH, *Hirten des Dionysos.*

[66] The core of the mysteries – which was of course secret – was the myth of the different stages in the life of the god, whereby an important aspect of his life was that he was born twice: then the nurture of Dionysus as a small boy by the nymphs, the return of the god from India, the punishment of certain enemies, the kidnapping by pirates, the wine miracle and the marriage with Ariadne and other goddesses and human women. In the course of the initial rites the *mystai* had to pass through the different stages in the life of the god, which meant birth and death, bathing and baptism, examination and punishment, binding and freeing, horror scenes, the pledge of secrecy, and the making of an oath. WALTER BURKERT, *Antike Mysterien* (Munich: Beck'sche Verlagsbuchhandlung, 1994); MARION GIEBEL, *Das Geheimnis der Mysterien: Antike Kulte in Griechenland, Rom und Ägypten*, 3rd ed. (Düsseldorf: Patmos, 2003).

[67] MERKELBACH, *Hirten des Dionysos*, 130–34; GIEBEL, *Geheimnis der Mysterien*, 55–65.

[68] The context between Dionysiac communities and the *technites* is discussed in HOLGER SCHWARZER, "Die Bukoloi in Pergamon: Ein dionysischer Kultverein im Spiegel der archäologischen und epigraphischen Zeugnisse," in *Zwischen Kult und Gesellschaft*, ed. INGE NIELSEN, Hephaistos Themenband 24 (Augsburg: Camelion, 2006), 153–67.

[69] Plutarch, *Ant.* 24.

[70] HERMANN USENER, *Acta Sancti Timothei* (Bonn: Georgi, 1877), 11 line 45 ff; JOSEF KEIL, "Zum Martyrium des heiligen Timotheus in Ephesos," *JÖAI* 29 (1935): 82–92.

During the period of Hadrian, the more widespread manner of worshipping Dionysus developed. The mystery initiations were performed in private circles.[71] Numerous epigraphic attestations for this practice are found throughout the Roman Empire in the imperial era. For example, in Athens we know the statutes of the association of the Iobakchoi.[72] The patron and priest of this organization during the middle of the second century CE was the well-known and wealthy Sophist T. Claudius Herodes Atticus.[73] The initiation rites and mysteries of these communities or clubs were not bound to a sanctuary; they were organized by religious communities and took place in public meeting houses and also in private dwellings.[74] In Italy the wealthy priestess Poppeia Agrippinilla was patroness of a Dionysiac association with more than 400 members in her villa near Rome.[75]

Religious associations for the god Dionysus are mentioned in several inscriptions found in Ephesos.[76] In addition to the inscription in the peristyle court (31a) in Dwelling Unit 6 in Terrace House 2, another inscription names Gaius Iulius Epagathus as president of a similar Ephesian association; he too was very wealthy and held high offices within the city administration;[77] M. Antonius Drusus is similarly attested.[78] Fragments of a list from the time of Hadrian also name *mystai* who took part in banquets.[79]

Despite these references to the religious activities of Dionysiac associations in private houses, in most cases it has not been possible to identify the relevant houses from the archaeological record. Dwelling Unit 6, with its floor plan, inscriptions, decoration, sculpture, and small finds may serve as the "missing link."[80]

---

[71] SCHÄFER, "Dionysische Gruppen."

[72] The clubhouse has been newly reviewed by ALFRED SCHÄFER, "Raumnutzung und Raumwahrnehmung im Vereinslokal der Iobakchen von Athen," in *Religiöse Vereine in der römischen Antike*, ed. ULRIKE EGELHAAF-GAISER and ALFRED SCHÄFER, STAC 13 (Tübingen: Mohr Siebeck, 2002), 173–220.

[73] PAUL GRAINDOR, *Un milliardaire antique: Hérode Atticus et sa famille* (Cairo: Misr, 1930); WALTER AMELUNG, *Herodes Atticus* (Hildesheim: Olms, 1983).

[74] Ley, "Dionysos," *KlPauly* 656; BURKERT, *Mysterien*, 39. For banquets of priests see JÖRG RÜPKE, "Collegia sacerdotum: Religiöse Vereine in der Oberschicht," in *Religiöse Vereine*, ed. EGELHAAF-GAISER and SCHÄFER, 41–67.

[75] *IGUR* 160. Editio princeps: ACHILLE VOGLIANO and FRANZ CUMONT, "La Grande Iscrizione Bacchica del Metropolitan Museum," *AJA* 37 (1933): 215–63.

[76] Short summery in: GUY M. ROGERS, *The Mysteries of Artemis of Ephesos: Cult, Polis and Change in the Roman-Greek World* (New Haven: Yale University, 2012), 295–98.

[77] C. Iulius Epagathus (*IvE* 14.1061 and 15.1600).

[78] M. Antonius Drusus (*IvE* 12.275, 14.1129 und 15.1601).

[79] Inscriptions from Ephesos with lists of *mustai* taking part in banquets (*IvE* 12.275, 14.1267; 15.1595, 1600–1602).

[80] See HILKE THÜR, "Die Wohneinheit 6: Vereinshaus eines dionysischen Kultvereins?" in THÜR and RATHMAYR, *Wohneinheit 6*, 849–53.

F. Clubhouses in the Eastern and Western Mediterranean

A general study on clubhouses situated in the eastern part of the Roman world is still missing. Holger Schwarzer has analyzed the clubhouses in Hellenistic and Roman Pergamon;[81] the clubhouses of the Iobakchoi in Athens and Melos are also more or less well known.[82] The architectural layout of these locations is either a peristyle house or a banquet hall – often with dining couches. Examples of peristyle houses in Pergamon are the "temenos for the imperial cult,"[83] the "House of the Bukoloi," both from the Hellenistic period,[84] and "building Z,"[85] and, in Athens, the "House of the Iobakchoi,"[86] both from an earlier period. Apsidal rooms for religious activity are found in Pergamon in the "building with a niche on the theater terrace,"[87] in the "temenos for the imperial cult," and in "building Z," and, in Greece, in the Houses of Iobakchoi in Athens and in Melos.[88] Podia as substructures for dining couches are found in Pergamon in the "Podium Hall," in the Hestiaion,[89] in the podium room in the long hall in the Asklepieion,[90] in the rock sanctuary in Kapıkaya,[91] and in the hall of the *mys-*

---

[81] Holger Schwarzer, "Vereinslokale im hellenistischen und römischen Pergamon," in *Religiöse Vereine*, ed. Egelhaaf-Gaiser and Schäfer, 221–60.

[82] Schäfer, "Raumnutzung."

[83] Erich Boehringer and Friedrich Krauss, *Das Temenos für den Herrscherkult*, AvP 9 (Berlin: de Gruyter, 1937); Wolfgang Radt, *Pergamon: Geschichten und Bauten einer antiken Metropole* (Darmstadt: Primus, 1999), 245–47; Holger Schwarzer, "Untersuchungen zum hellenistischen Herrscherkult in Pergamon," *MDAI* (I) 49 (1999): 249–300; Schwarzer, "Vereinslokale," 225–28; Holger Schwarzer, "Der Herrscherkult der Attaliden," in *Pergamon: Panorama der antiken Metropole: Begleitbuch zur Ausstellung*, ed. Ralf Grüssinger, Volker Kästner, and Andreas Scholl (Petersberg: Imhof, 2011), 110–17.

[84] Schwarzer, "Vereinslokale," 231–35; Schwarzer, "Bukoloi"; Holger Schwarzer, *Die Stadtgrabung: Teil 4: Das Gebäude mit dem Podiensaal in der Stadtgrabung von Pergamon*, AvP 15.4 (Berlin: de Gruyter, 2008), 1–103, 193–313.

[85] Schwarzer, "Vereinslokale," 228–31; Radt, *Pergamon*, 104–10; Ulrike Wulf-Rheidt, *Die Stadtgrabung: Die hellenistischen und römischen Wohnhäuser von Pergamon*, Altertümer von Pergamon 15.3 (Berlin: de Gruyter, 1999), 165–68; Martin Bachmann, "Bau Z in Pergamon – Analyse einer Langzeitnutzung," in *Städtisches Wohnen im östlichen Mittelmeerraum 4. Jh. v. Chr. – 1. Jh. n. Chr.*, ed. Sabine Ladstätter, Dimitra Andrianou, and Veronika Scheibelreiter, AF 18 (Vienna: ÖAW, 2010), 172–92. Martin Bachmann and Wolfgang Radt, *Die Stadtgrabung Teil 5, Bau Z, Architektur und Wanddekor*, AvP XV,5 (Berlin: de Gruyter, 2017)

[86] Schäfer, "Raumnutzung," 173–220 (with more references).

[87] Richard Bohn, *Die Theater-Terrasse*, AvP 4 (Berlin: Spemann, 1896), 18–20; Radt, *Pergamon*, 193–6; Schwarzer, "Herrscherkult," 249–300; Schwarzer, "Vereinslokale," 223–25.

[88] Robert Carr Bosanquet, "Excavations of the British School at Melos: The Hall of the Mystae," *JHS* 18 (1898): 60–80; Schäfer, "Raumnutzung," 181–84.

[89] Wolfgang Radt, "Pergamon: Vorbericht über die Kampagne 1985," *AA* (1986): 422–25; Wolfgang Radt, "Pergamon: Vorbericht über die Kampagne 1986," *AA* (1987): 520; Schwarzer, "Vereinslokale," 235–38.

[90] Radt, *Pergamon*, 220–42; Schwarzer, "Vereinslokale," 238–40.

[91] Klaus Nohlen and Wolfgang Radt, *Kapıkaya: Ein Felsheiligtum bei Pergamon*, AvP 12 (Berlin: de Gruyter, 1978); Schwarzer, "Vereinslokale," 240–3.

tai on Melos.[92] Another feature in some of the locations mentioned above is a small side room near the apse of the main religious assembly hall. Such a space can be observed in the House of the Iobakchoi in Athens, in the "building with a niche on the theater terrace" in Pergamon and in the Askleipieion. In most cases the clubhouses were dedicated to one main god or goddess, but also statues and small format sculptures of other deities have been found. In his article on the clubhouse of the Iobakchoi, Alfred Schäfer lists attestations of Artemis (A 2, A12, A13), Aphrodite (B1), Cybele (B2-B4), Hecate (B5), Athena (B6, B 13) and the ruler cult (A15, B8), alongside sculpture and inscriptions of the Dionysiac *thiasos* (A2 – A 11, A 16, B9)[93]; in the Bakcheion of Melos, in addition to the sculpture of a hierophant, a woman as founder, and a child, reliefs of the Tyche of Melos and of Athena were found.[94]

Schäfer summarizes the function of the Bakcheia in Athens and Melos. According to the inscription from Athens, the word *bakcheia* names the association, but also the location of the clubhouse itself. *Bakcheia* is also a term for Dionysiac festivities. Another word, *stibas*, describes the banquet hall and the meal of the members of the association. Also *hestiaterion* refers to the banquet hall. The room served several functions, also as the meeting place for the final assembly, where old statutes were read and confirmed, new resolutions were passed, speeches were held, and decisions by lots and votes took place. Banquets and symposia were organized for the festivals and other occasions. In connection with the banquets, other religious activities such as animal sacrifice and libations were performed. In addition to offerings, there were theatrical performances, which are documented by the lots by which roles in such plays were distributed to the members.[95]

The clubhouses in the eastern Mediterranean have parallels with the *scholae* collected by Beate Bollmann for Italy.[96] According to her, the floor plan of a clubhouse is defined by the tasks and duties performed by the members of the associations. These assemblies discussed and determined matters that concerned their own group, the religious activities of the association, and the organization and celebration of banquets on several occasions. For religious activities, an altar, a podium or an apse could be used. Assemblies and banquets needed enough space in houses; with portable dining couches, banquets could be organized in large halls, courtyards and porticoes.[97] Fixed installations for *triclinia* are rarely found in the *scholae* of the western part of the empire. In Ostia it is a curious fact

---

[92] SCHÄFER, "Raumnutzung," 181–84.

[93] SCHÄFER, "Raumnutzung," 175–81, 189–202 fig. 1–3; pl. 1–8.

[94] SCHÄFER, "Raumnutzung," 181–84, 202–5 fig. 4.5.

[95] SCHÄFER, "Raumnutzung," 184–88.

[96] BEATE BOLLMANN, *Römische Vereinshäuser: Untersuchungen zu den Scholae der römischen Berufs-, Kult- und Augustalen-Kollegien in Italien* (Mainz: von Zabern, 1998).

[97] BOLLMANN, *Römische Vereinshäuser*, 47–57.

that kitchens and restrooms necessary in this context are missing, so clearly public restrooms and kitchens would have been used. Another important feature for such "clubhouses" is the lack of rooms for private life. Criteria for the identification of a schola according to Bollmann are inscriptions, mosaics representing professions, sculptures, and installations for worship and other religious activities. From the house types observed for scholae in Italy, Dwelling Unit 6 in Terrace House 2 follows the "clubhouse type with a portico courtyard and a room for religious activities."[98]

G. Special Installations in Dwelling Unit 6

Dwelling Unit 6 has several special features and details of equipment and construction which can be connected very well with the demands of a society performing mystery initiations. First, there are several barriers to interpret. The barrier wall built in phase 2 between the columns of the south colonnade in the peristyle court (31a)[99] was mentioned above. It is built up to a height of 1.35 m (fig. 7). On its upper surface a bevel served for fixing an upper part in a lightweight construction, possibly a wooden lattice. The installation created a background for three sculptures set up on the pillars and blocked the view into the south portico. In the fountain in front of the portico water was flowing continuously and created an atmosphere of nature and gardens (fig. 4). The only access from the peristyle court (31a) to the south and to the area with the banqueting halls 31 and 8 was a marble door (fig. 8) in the west portico.[100] The closed door panels could be bolted with a horizontal bar on the south side. Through this installation persons who were not welcome or not invited – such as non-initiates – could be prohibited from the celebrations and activities in the south rooms. In the same building phase 2 a bath was built into the eastern portico, which was exclusively accessible from the southern hall of the peristyle 31a and the marble hall 31.[101] The use of the bath before or during banquets and celebrations of the *mystai*[102] – and perhaps also purification rituals – is obvious.

---

[98] BOLLMANN, *Römische Vereinshäuser*, 58–67.

[99] THÜR, "Baubeschreibung: Peristylhof 31a: Schrankenwand und Brunnen vor der Südkolonnade," 42–43; THÜR, "Architekturausstattung: Säulenstellung und Architektur im Erdgeschoss," 141–43; RATHMAYR, "Auswertung: Eingangssituation und Peristylhof."

[100] THÜR, "Baubeschreibung: Peristylhof 31a: Schrankenwand und Brunnen vor der Südkolonnade"; THÜR, "Architekturausstattung: Säulenstellung und Architektur im Erdgeschoss"; THÜR, "Türen," 179–90.

[101] THÜR, "Baubeschreibung: Ostportikus 31 aO"; THÜR, "Auswertung: Badeanlage."

[102] Bathing during banquets came into use in the first century CE, see JENS-ARNE DICKMANN, *Domus frequentata: Anspruchsvolles Wohnen im pompejanischen Stadthaus*, Studien zur antiken Stadt 4 (Munich: Pfeil, 1999), 256–67; Also in "Bau Z" in Pergamon a bathing complex was installed; see MARTIN BACHMANN, "Bau Z in Pergamon: Analyse einer Langfristnutzung,"

Worth mentioning are also two other barriers in the rooms 31b and 36c. In the *exedra* 31b, which is directly adjacent to the north of courtyard 31a, a very wide door opening could be shut by two systems of a sliding door and a sliding lattice (fig. 9).[103] We have reconstructed the second system, with a sliding bronze lattice, which could be closed when the inner sliding door was open (fig. 10). The system prevented persons from entering the room (31b), but allowed them to look into it through the lattice. The room had a peculiar form with an *aedicula*, niches in the north wall, a wooden closet in front of the north wall, and a bench along the west wall. It may have served for storing items such as religious statuary, books and archival materials. Items such as the *cista mystica*, the hidden *phallus*, the *liknon* and the *thyrsos* could have been preserved here safely. The room might also have been used for meetings in small groups. The special features and installations can be interpreted as equipment connected with the practice of mystery initiations.

A similar barrier can be observed in the traces of the threshold of room 36c from building phase 3 onwards.[104] A small groove seems to have served for permanent fixtures such as a lattice or a grid in a material such as wood or metal. Again, the room was separated from and not accessible from the courtyard (31a), but a view into the room was possible, and perhaps intended. Room 36c was richly decorated with marble revetment and had a central niche for sculpture in the back (fig. 11). In phase 4 the neighboring room 36d had a large window opening onto the peristyle court (31a), but no door connected it with the court. Both rooms 36c and 36d could only be entered from the corridor (36b).

In summary, it can be stated that only the north and west hall as well as the court and the rooms 36e and 42 were open to "normal" visitors such as clients. All other rooms (31b, 36d and 36c) and the whole southern part with the banqueting halls 31 and 8, their antechambers, and the bath, could only be entered by selected persons because of the barriers discussed above.

The southern part of the house has other unusual architectural features. The construction of the apsidal hall (8)[105] is worth noting (fig. 12): the room had a barrel vault, a huge apse in the south, a spacious water basin in the floor,[106] and a hypocaust heating system,[107] which were peculiar elements for a banque-

---

in Ladstätter, Andrianou, and Scheibelreiter, *Städtisches Wohnen*, 183–84; Bachmann and Radt, *Bau Z*; Wulf-Rheidt, *Wohnhäuser von Pergamon*, 203–6. For baths connected with clubhouses see Ulrike Egelhaaf-Gaiser, "Religionsästhetik und Raumordnung am Beispiel der Vereinsgebäude von Ostia," in Egelhaaf-Gaiser and Schäfer, *Religiöse Vereine*, 155–57.

[103] Thür, "Baubeschreibung: Raum 31b," 33–36; Thür, "Türen"; Thür, "Vereinshaus."
[104] Thür, "Baubeschreibung: Raum 36c," 64–65; Thür, "Türen"; Thür, "Vereinshaus."
[105] Thür, "Baubeschreibung: Apsidensaal 8"; Thür, "Vereinshaus."
[106] Thür, "Wasserwirtschaftliche Einrichtungen: Bodenwasserbecken WB A-5 in Apsidensaal 8."
[107] Hilke Thür, "Heizungsanlagen: Heizung in Apsidensaal 8, Stuckraum 8a, und Nebenraum 8c," in Thür and Rathmayr, *Wohneinheit 6*, 221–23.

ting hall. The hall was embellished with a marble floor, marble revetment on the walls,[108] painting in the vaulted ceiling,[109] and a glass mosaic in the half dome of the apse.[110] Additionally the room was illuminated by a large window in the north wall.[111] The water basin may have been used for bathing during religious ceremonies but it also may simply have been the central element of a water or garden *triclinium*; both functions are possible. A sculpture most likely stood in the large apse; it may have been an honorary portrait statue, but more probably it was a statue of a divinity.[112]

The adjacent room is also unusual (8a),[113] with its spectacular stucco ceiling.[114] It is covered with a barrel vault, and the walls have three central niches, and it was possible to heat it with a hypocaust system.[115] Because the room did not have any source of direct daylight, it would have been very dark. Nevertheless the ceiling was decorated with stucco medallions (fig. 13) depicting figures and animals belonging to the company of Dionysus and Aphrodite.[116]

Puzzling is the dark annex room 8c behind the apse (fig. 5).[117] This cellar, a cave-like room, could have been kept nicely warm with a floor heated by a system of hypocausts, and with walls heated by *tubuli*.[118] The room could only be entered by crawling through an opening from the next room 8b that was 50 cm wide by 90 cm high. This window could be closed or bolted. The room was nearly totally dark aside from a hole in the apse measuring 17 by 20 cm, through which a small ray of light could come in. The adjacent room 8b has a similar opening for light above the door.[119] Through these small holes certain items of worship may have been lit by moonlight or at dawn at the end of the initiatory ceremonies. Room 8c with its difficult access may have had a particular function during the ceremonies of the mysteries or initiations. It could have been used to create a symbolic situation of birth and rebirth. By using hot stones, vapor, and hemp seeds, intoxicating effects could also have been created in this small cave-like room.

---

[108] Karin Koller, "Marmor: Apsidensaal 8," in Thür and Rathmayr, *Wohneinheit 6*, 245.

[109] Zimmermann, "Wandmalerei: Apsidensaal 8."

[110] Scheibelreiter-Gail, "Mosaiken: Apsidensaal 8."

[111] Hilke Thür, "Fenster," in Thür and Rathmayr, *Wohneinheit 6*, 191–92.

[112] Thür, "Auswertung: Repräsentationsräume," and Thür, "Vereinshaus."

[113] Thür, "Baubeschreibung: Gewölberaum 8a," 89–92.

[114] Rathmayr, "Stuckdekorationen der Räume 8a und 36c."

[115] Thür, "Heizungsanlagen: Heizung in Apsidensaal 8, Stuckraum 8a, und Nebenraum 8c."

[116] Rathmayr, "Stuckdekorationen der Räume 8a und 36c."

[117] Thür, "Baubeschreibung: Raum 8c," 94–96.

[118] Thür, "Heizungsanlagen," 222–23.

[119] Thür, "Baubeschreibung: Raum 8b," 92–93.

Mystery celebrations and initiation rites might also explain another feature, the unusual combination of the fountain in the apsidal niche in the marble hall (31)[120] and its connection to a water channel crossing the rock behind the wall, whereby the *mystai* might have been brought to stand in the flowing water of the channel.

In my opinion the particular features of Dwelling Unit 6, and above all the remarkable restriction of access from the courtyard (31a) into the southern part of the house that contained the banqueting and festival halls and the bath, can best be explained by the needs and requirements of a Dionysiac association, as can the barriers in the door openings of the rooms 31b and 36c. Also some unusual and uncommon installations find a reasonable interpretation as elements that could be used during the celebration and the practice of mysteries and initiations.

H. Evidence for Religious Activity in Dwelling Unit 6

The installations mentioned above are complemented by the additional evidence of numerous features connected with Dionysus, the Orphic mysteries and remarkably, also with Aphrodite. Dionysus and Aphrodite seem to have been worshiped together in this residence. They are shown together as a couple in the lunette (fig. 6) in the rear wall of room 8a.[121] Furthermore both gods are named or addressed in inscriptions: Dionysus on the cornice of the barrier wall in the peristyle court (31a),[122] Aphrodite on the statue bases (fig. 12) on both sides of the entrance to apsidal hall (8).[123] Fragments of a statue of Dionysus S 9 (fig. 14) have been found in the peristyle court (31a),[124] and the torso of a less than life size statue of Aphrodite S 46 (fig.15) from the apsidal hall (8) can be reconstructed on one of the bases in room 36. An Eros, the son of Aphrodite, riding on a dolphin, completes the ensemble in this room (36).[125]

The hippocampuses on the coffered ceiling in the marble hall (31)[126] and other sea creatures on a fountain bowl[127] show an additional connection with a marine *thiasos,* and also belong to the circle of Aphrodite and Dionysus. Above all, the designs in the stucco decoration in room 8a are linked to these gods as well.

---

[120] THÜR, "Wasserwirtschaftliche Einrichtungen: Wandnischenbrunnen WB-A2 im sogenannten Marmorsaal 31."

[121] RATHMAYR, "Stuckdekorationen der Räume 8a und 36c."

[122] TAEUBER, "Steininschriften," 342–43.

[123] TAEUBER, "Steininschriften," 343.

[124] RATHMAYR, "Skulpturenfunde: Peristylhof 31a."

[125] RATHMAYR, "Skulpturenfunde: Raum 36," 386–87.

[126] THÜR, "Decken: Holzbalken- oder Kassettendecke im Marmorsaal 31," 175–77.

[127] URSULA QUATEMBER, "Funde aus Marmor und anderem Gestein: Ziergefäße," in THÜR and RATHMAYR, *Wohneinheit 6,* 714–15.

The lost glass mosaic in the half dome of the apse in the apsidal hall (8) may have been decorated similarly to the vaulted *exedra* GEW D in Dwelling Unit 2 in Terrace House 2,[128] which shows a colourful glass mosaic of Dionysos and Ariadne in a vineyard, and *erotes* bringing in the harvest. The better preserved allusion to Dionysiac symbolism in Dwelling Unit 6 is the ceiling in the adjacent vaulted room (8a), and above all the stucco relief on the rear wall with Dionysus and Aphrodite surrounded by *erotes*.[129]

All in all, the overall scheme of the house and its general design, several extraordinary installations in particular rooms, decorations connected with Dionysos and Aphrodite, and the epigraphic evidence, demonstrate beyond doubt that the house of Aptus was used by a Dionysiac association. The worship of *Dionysos pro poleos* and the celebration of his mysteries included Aphrodite as the female representative of the sea and as a divine associate of Dionysus.[130]

I. Conclusions

The topographic situation of Dwelling Unit 6 was the most privileged in the *insula* of Terrace House 2. The house was located immediately to the south of the main thoroughfare of the city, the *embolos,* and urban life and frequent religious processions passed by on it. Dwelling Unit 6 could be entered directly from the street through the south portico of the *embolos,* which was paved with mosaics. The large peristyle house was constructed on a higher level, so that the inhabitants and their guests had to climb up a staircase four meters high. The original floor plan (second quarter of the first century CE) was altered heavily in building phases 2 and 3 (121–150 CE) when C. Flavius Furius Aptus was the homeowner and responsible for the layout, function and decor of the house. In this paper only these two building phases (2 and 3) are of interest.

The spacious house 6 had a large peristyle courtyard and large halls for assemblies, festive occasions, reception of guests, and banquets. These rooms were embellished with marble revetments, wall paintings, mosaics, and marble floors, stucco ceilings in rooms 8a and 36c, a wooden coffered ceiling in the marble hall (31) with gilded reliefs, an advanced lighting system, numerous fountains, sculptures, and other decorations. These are of extremely high value and outstanding quality (fig. 16). On the other hand there is a lack of smaller rooms such as *cubicula*, which could serve as bedrooms, and for the other needs of private life. Nor-

---

[128] WERNER JOBST, *Römische Mosaiken aus Ephesos 1: Die Hanghäuser am Embolos* (Vienna: ÖAW, 1977).

[129] RATHMAYR, "Stuckdekorationen der Räume 8a und 36c."

[130] Evidence for cult connections of Dionysos with Aphrodite are documented in the clubhouse of the Iobakchoi in Athens. According to the mythology Aphrodite and Dionysos have a son together, Priapos.

mally these kinds of rooms are located on an upper floor, which here existed only in the west part of the house, but had no access from Dwelling Unit 6.

The two spacious banquet halls, one (8) with a big apse, the other (31) with very peculiar decoration and a central fountain niche with sculpture (fig. 16) represent a room type devoted to religious activities. Their use and function as the clubhouse of a private Dionysiac association is attested by an inscription, the decor of the house, and the sculptural program. Many of the adorning elements are connected with Aphrodite, as e. g. the numerous fountains and water basins, hippocampuses on the ceiling, and other sea creatures on a marble bowl and on the stucco ceiling, and a sculpture and stucco relief of Eros, the son of Aphrodite. The goddess was honored and worshipped together with Dionysus, they were associates in the religious ceremonies. The worship of Dionysus includes mystery initiations. Rooms for assemblies, festive occasions, and, of course, banquets for the members were requirements for the clubhouse. Moreover the location had to be equipped for the celebration of initiation rites, religious ceremonies and theater performances. In Dwelling Unit 6 several structures and installations might have served in the context of mysteries and religious ceremonies. Some of the barriers and door constructions are unusual; they organized access and visibility between the south part of the house and the peristyle courtyard and the northern rooms. The function and use of the small room (8c) behind the apse of hall (8) is also strange and enigmatic. But if they are considered as part of a clubhouse of a Dionysiac religious association, both elements make sense.

Dwelling Unit 6 presents in Ephesos – in my opinion – a unique attestation of a dwelling house used by a religious association. The rebuilding and decoration of the structure for a religious purpose was initiated by the owner C. Flavius Furius Aptus, a priest of Dionysus and an alytarch. He is known from several inscriptions as an important person. According to the latest evidence he can be dated exactly in the first half of the second century CE. The use of house 6 as a place for meetings, festive meals, mysteries and initiations of a Dionysiac society does not exclude the possibility that the patron and owner also used the place in the network of his social and political interests; a multifunctional use of rooms and even of entire buildings was quite common in antiquity.

Figure 1: Inscription on Barrier of South Portico in Peristyle Court (31a). ©Niki Gail ÖAW/ÖAI

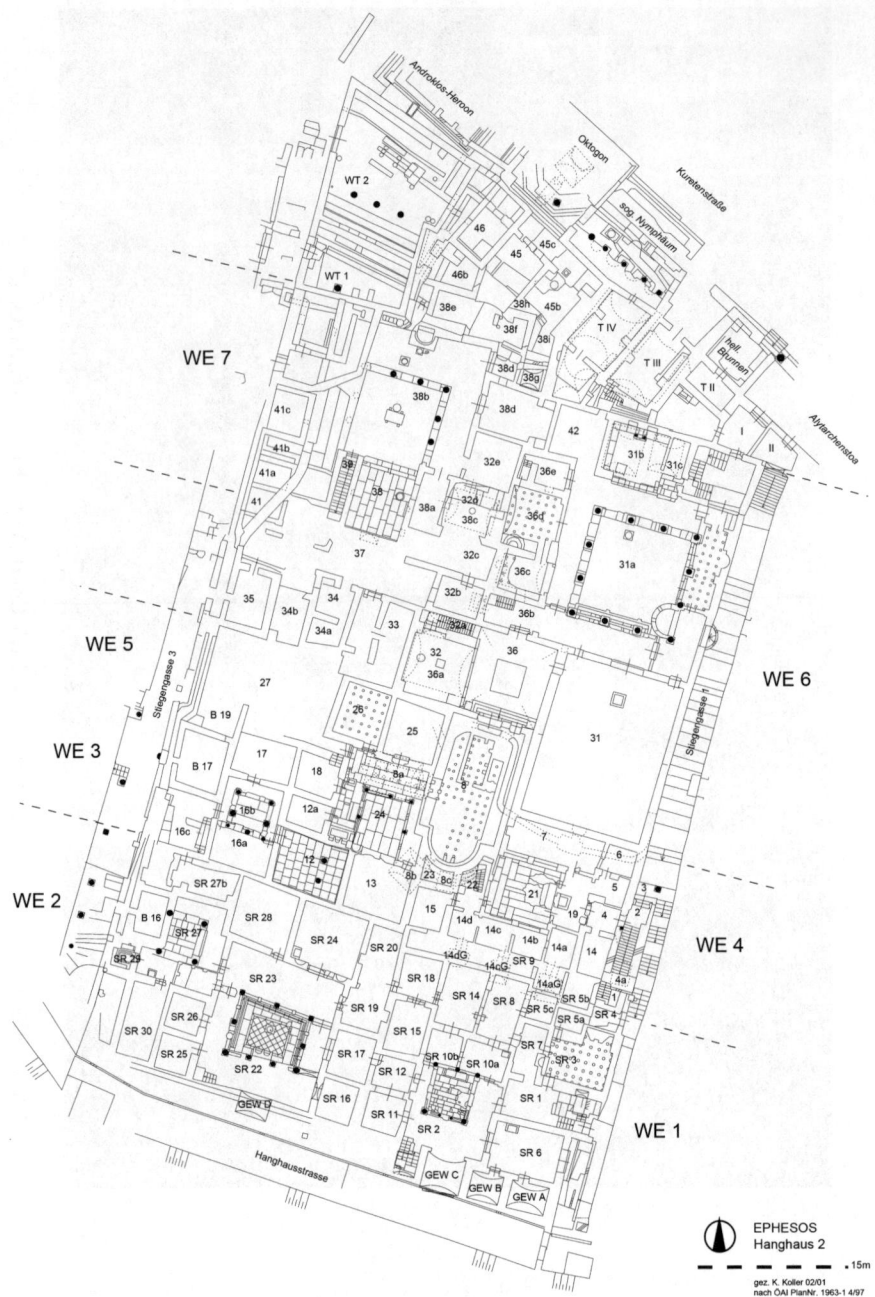

Figure 2: Floor Plan of Terrace House 2. ©Karin Koller ÖAW

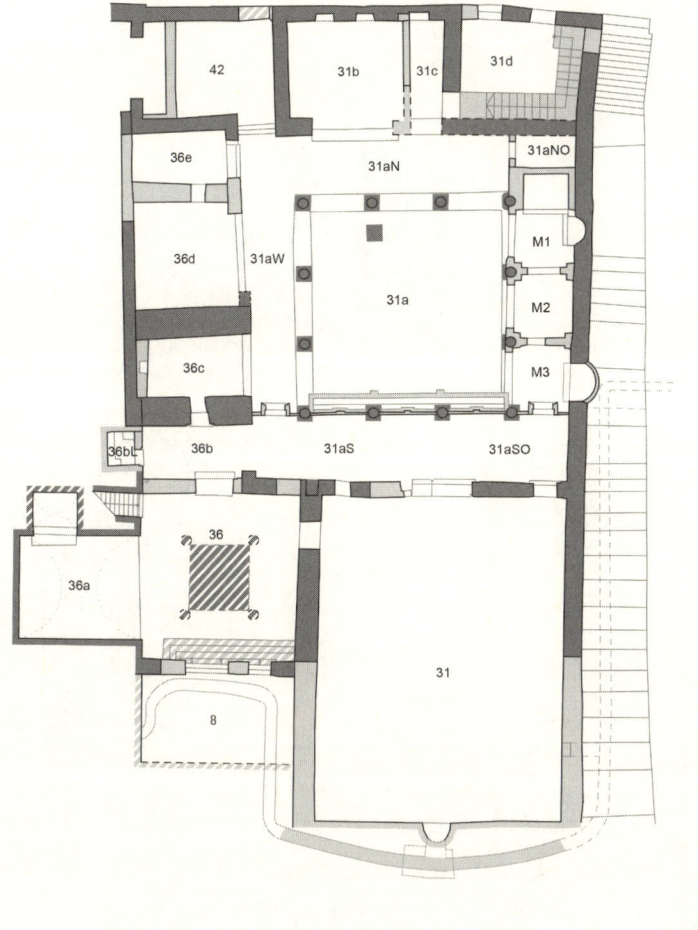

Figure 3: Floor Plan of Dwelling Unit 6, Building Phase 2. ©Hilke Thür and Ingrid Aden-stedt ÖAW

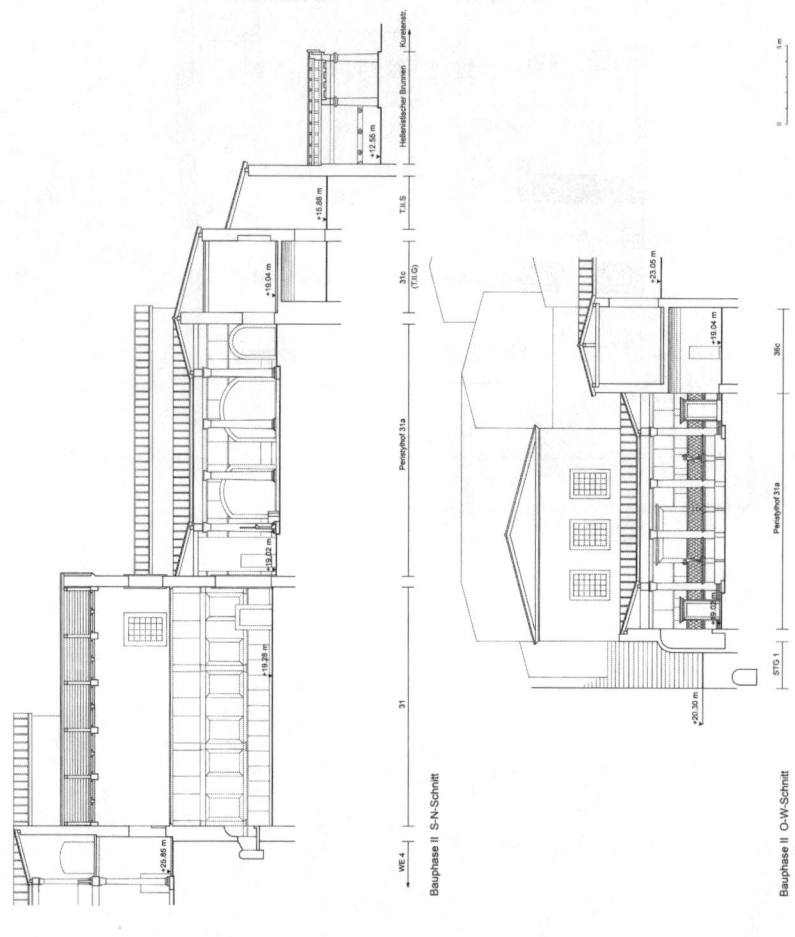

Figure 4: Reconstructed Sections of Dwelling Unit 6, Building Phase 2. ©Hilke Thür and Anna Pyszkowski-Wyszikowski ÖAW

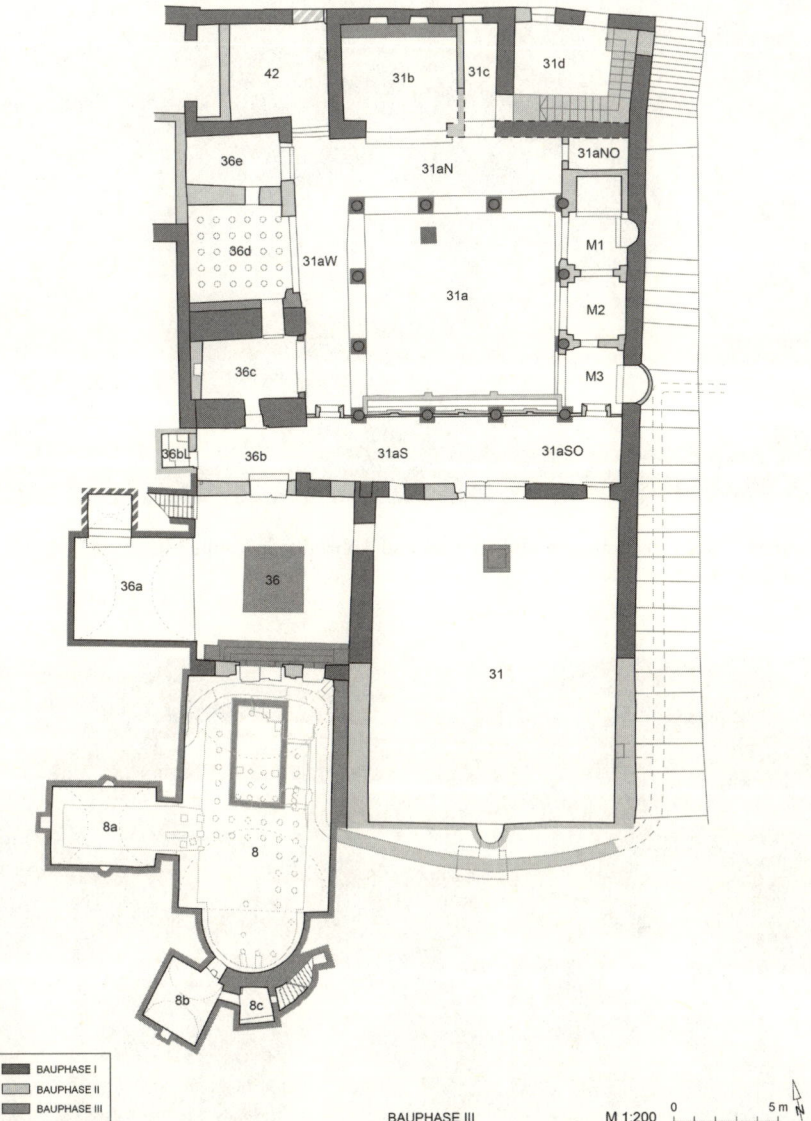

BAUPHASE I
BAUPHASE II
BAUPHASE III

BAUPHASE III

M 1:200   0   5 m

Figure 5: Floor Plan of Dwelling Unit 6, Building Phase 3. ©Hilke Thür and Ingrid Aden-stedt ÖAW

Figure 6: Stucco Decoration with Dionysos and Aphrodite in Vaulted Room (8a). ©Niki Gail ÖAW/ÖAI

Figure 7: Peristyle Court (31a), South Portico with Barrier and Fountain. ©Hilke Thür ÖAW/ÖAI

Figure 8: Peristyle Court (31a), Marble Door Frame in West Portico. ©Niki Gail ÖAW/ÖAI

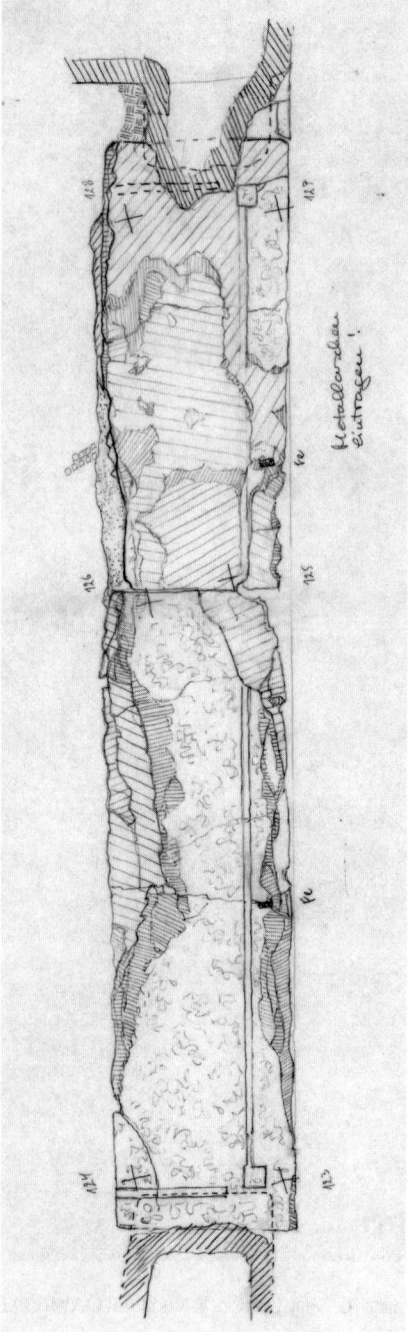

Figure 9: Room (31b), Threshold with Traces of Sliding Door. ©Andrea Sulzgruber ÖAW

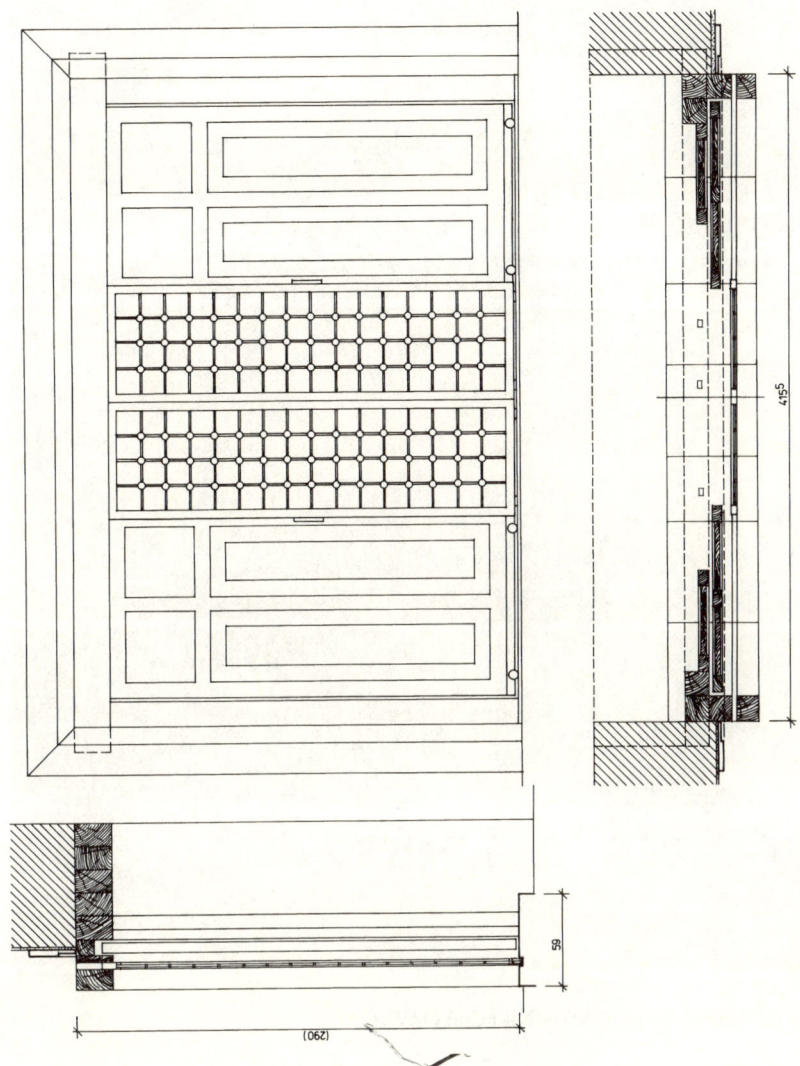

Figure 10: Room (31b), Reconstruction of Sliding Door and Lattice. ©Hilke Thür and Anna Pyszkowski-Wyszikowski ÖAW.

Figure 11: Vaulted Room (36c). ©Niki Gail ÖAW/ÖAI

Figure 12: Entrée (36) and Apsidal Hall (8). ©Niki Gail ÖAW/ÖAI

Figure 13: Stucco Ceiling in Vaulted Room (8a). ©Niki Gail ÖAW/ÖAI

Figure 14: Fragment of Dionysos Statue (Cat. pg. 9). ©Niki Gail ÖAW/ÖAI

Figure 15: Torso of Aphrodite Statue (Cat. pg. 46). ©Niki Gail ÖAW/ÖAI

Figure 16: Visualisation of Marble Hall (31). ©Ivan Iliev ÖAW

The Artemision of Ephesos in the Imperial Period

Ulrike Muss

A. Introduction

Literary sources and inscriptions from the Artemision and from Ephesos preserve information in numerous places concerning Artemis and her sanctuary in the imperial period. These references concern the right of asylum,[1] its religious institutions,[2] its rituals,[3] the bank – well-known throughout the entire ancient world[4] – and the wealth of the sanctuary in arable land and pasturage as well as in vineyards, salt mines, and fishing rights in the Kaystros Valley (fig. 1).[5]

In contrast to the abundance of this data, much less evidence has survived concerning the appearance and the furnishing of the sanctuary in the imperial period. This evidence comes from epigraphic and literary sources and from archaeological remains that survived in the temenos of the sanctuary.[6]

---

[1] Cicero, *Verr.* 21.33.85; Achilles Tatius 7.13.3; 8.2.2; Plutarch, *Mor.* 828D.

[2] Achilles Tatius 7.12; Diogenes Laertius 2.51; Xenophon, *Anab.* 5.3.6; Plautus, *Bacch.* 312; RICK STRELAN, *Paul, Artemis and the Jews in Ephesus*, BZNW 80 (Berlin: de Gruyter, 1996), 42, 77.

[3] O. JESSEN, "Ephesia," *RE* 5.2 (1905): 2753–71 (esp. 2761); JOHN ANTHONY CRAMER, ""Εφεσος," *Anecdota græca e codd. manuscriptis bibliothecarum oxoniensium descripsit* 2:435.

[4] DIETER KNIBBE, RECEP MERIÇ, and REINHOLD MERKELBACH, "Der Grundbesitz der ephesischen Artemis im Kaystertal," *ZPE* 33 (1979): 139–48. GUY M. ROGERS, "From the Greek Polis to the Greco-Roman Polis: Augustus and the Artemision of Ephesos," in *Regionalism in Hellenistic and Roman Asia Minor: Acts of the Conference Hartford, Connecticut (USA), August 22–24 August 1997*, ed. HUGH ELTON and GARY REGER (Paris: Ausonius, 2007), 141.

[5] RECEP MERIÇ, *Das Hinterland von Ephesos: Archäologisch-topographische Forschungen im Kaystros-Tal*, in Ergänzungshefte zu den JÖAI 12 (Vienna: Phoibos, 2009), esp. 29ff, 88 with fig. 91. See fig. 2 with indication of the sacred space of Artemis in the Kaystros Valley. For the general questions of properties of sanctuaries in earlier times see MARIETTA HORSTER, *Landbesitz griechischer Heiligtümer in archaischer und klassischer Zeit* (Berlin: de Gruyter, 2004).

[6] ULRIKE MUSS, "The Artemision at Ephesos: Paul, John and Mary," in *Contested Spaces: Houses and Temples in Roman Antiquity and the New Testament*, ed. DAVID L. BALCH and ANNETTE WEISSENRIEDER, WUNT 1.285 (Tübingen: Mohr Siebeck, 2012), 495–511; ULRIKE MUSS, "Republik und Kaiser im Artemision von Ephesos," in *Neue Zeiten, Neue Sitten: Zu Rezeption und Integration römischen und italischen Kulturguts in Kleinasien*, ed. MARION MEYER (Vienna: Phoibos, 2007), 243–50; HELMUT ENGELMANN, "Inschriften und Heiligtum," in *Der Kosmos*

During the imperial period, the sanctuary had already lost its location at the seacoast; it was situated in swampy land and between fields used for farming.[7] The footpaths to the sanctuary went through vineyards surrounded by dry stone walls, and went past the irrigation channels that lined the streams, bypassing the Artemision. This picture can be drawn from the reports of the field survey-ors during their work in the area around the sanctuary.[8] The vast land belonging to the sanctuary in the Kaystros valley was remeasured in the time of Augustus after the troubles of the civil war.[9] Under the emperors Domitian and Trajan, the land was assessed again.[10] The archaeological evidence – in the form of inscribed boundary stones – permits the reconstruction of the extent of this property.[11] The center of the town of Ephesos is about two kilometers away from the Arte-mision in the imperial period.

From epigraphic and literary sources, we know about other buildings in the sanctuary, in the temenos or the immediate vicinity of the fourth-century tem-ple and its altar that were erected in the imperial period.[12] An Augusteum area was dedicated to Augustus, as a new god, in the Artemision.[13] The Augusteum existed in 6/5 BCE, but when it was built remains unknown.[14] Other references for the Augustan period in the Artemision are a monumental architrave found

---

der Artemis von Ephesos 2001, ed. ULRIKE MUSS, Sonderschriften ÖAI 37 (Vienna: Phoibos, 2001), 33–44; ULRIKE MUSS, "Das Artemision von Ephesos in römischer Zeit," in *Festschrift für Ramazan Özgan*, ed. MUSTAFA ŞAHİN and İ. HAKAN MERT (Istanbul: Ege Yayınları, 2005), 249–63.

[7] Achilles Tatius 7.13.2.

[8] DIETER KNIBBE, HELMUT ENGELMANN, and BÜLENT İPLİKÇİOĞLU, "Neue Inschriften aus Ephesos XII," *JÖAI* 62, (1993): 113–50 (no. 59).

[9] *IGSK* Vol. 15 (1980): 1523–25; *IGSK* Vol. 17.2 (1981): 3513, 3516; DIETER KNIBBE, HELMUT ENGELMANN, and BÜLENT İPLİKÇİOĞLU, "Neue Inschriften aus Ephesos XI," *JÖAI* 59 (1989): 162–238 (no. 59); HELMUT ENGELMANN, "Inschriften aus Metropolis," *ZPE* 125 (1999): 143–46; ENGELMANN, "Inschriften und Heiligtum," 36, 40; MERIÇ, *Hinterland,* 23, 25–27, 130–31.

[10] *IGSK* Vol. 17.2 (1981): 3506–12; ENGELMANN, "Inschriften und Heiligtum," 41.

[11] MERIÇ, *Hinterland,* 24, 29 *et passim.*

[12] ENGELMANN, "Inschriften und Heiligtum." For the time of the Republic see MUSS, "Re-publik und Kaiser."

[13] *IGSK* Vol. 12 (1979): 412. The damaged surroundings of the new sanctuary were restored under emperor Titus (79/80 CE) at the cost of the temple treasury.

[14] *IGSK* Vol. 15 (1980): 1522, 1523, 1524 bilingual, known in six copies which come from the theatre and a wall east of the Panayırdağ, and by boundary stones, found by Wood in the so called "peribolos wall," according to the inscriptions of the ancient surveyors surveying the Selinus. For the peribolos wall see J. T. WOOD, *Discoveries at Ephesus: Including the Site and Re-mains of the Great Temple of Diana* (Boston: James R. Osgood and Co., 1877), 132–33; LILLI ZA-BRANA, "Vorbericht zur sogenannten Tribüne im Artemision von Ephesos – ein neues Odeion im Heiligtum der Artemision," *JÖAI* 80 (2011): 341–63; FRANCOIS KIRBIHLER and LILLI ZA-BRANA, "Archäologische, epigraphische und numismatische Zeugnisse für den Kaiserkult im Artemision," *JÖAI* 83 (2014): 102–4. For the problem of the localization of the Augustea at Ephe-sus see HELMUT ENGELMANN, "Zum Kaiserkult in Ephesos," *ZPE* 97 (1993): 279–83; PETER SCHERRER, "Augustus, die Mission des Vedius Pollio und die Artemis Ephesia," *JÖAI* 60 (1990): 87–101. ROGERS, "From the Greek Polis to the Greco-Roman Polis: Augustus and the Artemi-

at the site with an inscription naming a building as a donation of Augustus and Lucius Caesar[15].

In the imperial period, there was at least one gymnasium inside the sanctuary: an "agoronomos" is attested, who donated a certain amount of anointing oil to be distributed in the gymnasium of the sanctuary of Artemis.[16] A stoa, which originated in the sanctuary, is mentioned in the Trajanic period,[17] and Pausanias mentions a *pinakotheke* (a hall with paintings).[18] Philostratus mentions a *hestiatorion* (a banqueting hall), which Flavius Damianus funded and which was apparently furnished with every luxury.[19]

The reports of J. T. Wood provide information about the archaeological remains belonging to the imperial period. Near the "peribolos wall" he found remains of some mosaics and remains of hypocausts, first interpreted by him as "dwellings of the priests."[20] Wood describes these remains as located west by southwest of the temple.[21] He traced the buildings for about 700 ft (= 231.36 m) in a straight line, running eastward. One of the mosaic pavements, representing a triton and aligned with this long trench, seems to be marked on his map, just north of the temple (fig. 2, no. 1; fig. 3). Wood notes further that he had imagined that the long line of Roman buildings, where he had found the mosaic pavements, must flank either the temple itself – not yet found at the time of his writing – or an open space in front of it.[22] He therefore sank a number of deep test trenches southward, and found at a distance of 445 ft (= 135.64 m) the remains of another Roman building, which he describes as a small temple mounted on a stylobate of three marble steps. Here he found the head of a Minerva (Athena) and a torso which he left at the site.[23] Wood then found the remains of another building close to this Roman building described above, which was also mounted on a stylobate of three steps. He supposed that this building was probably the Augusteum mentioned in the inscriptions he had found in the "peribo-

---

sion of Ephesos." Further there exists an inscription with a reference to the restoration of a building about 160 CE. *IGSK* Vol. 17.2: 4327.

[15] *IGSK* Vol. 12 (1979): 408; Kirbihler and Zabrana, "Kaiserkult im Artemision," fig. 10.

[16] *IGSK* Vol. 13 (1980): 938.

[17] *IGSK* Vol. 15 (1980): 1545.

[18] Pausanias, *Descr.* 10. 38. 6–7.

[19] VS II 23, 2; Suidas s. v. "Damianos."

[20] Wood, *Discoveries at Ephesus*, 132–33, 149. A corner of the peribolos wall had been drawn in 1871 by F. Adler. Zabrana, "Tribüne im Artemision," 341–63, fig. 1. Kirbihler and Zabrana, "Kaiserkult im Artemision," fig. 3.

[21] Wood, *Discoveries at Ephesus*, 132–33 and 149–55.

[22] Wood, *Discoveries at Ephesus*, 152.

[23] Wood, *Discoveries at Ephesus*, 153: "As I came across no remains of buildings in the ground between these two roman buildings (mosaic and small temple) I concluded that it was an open space in front of the Temple which must now be sought for beyond it, and I therefore put a number of men to work in that direction."

los wall" (fig. 3).[24] "Amongst the debris of this building were found a small seated figure of Jupiter, with an eagle in bas-relief on the side of a chair,[25] a curious bas-relief of Pan as a warrior, a headless statue of Minerva, and other fragments of statuary, together with a number of inscriptions, chiefly of thanksgiving to Artemis."[26]

B. Visible Buildings of the Imperial Period in the Artemision and Its Surroundings

1. An odeion, known as the so-called tribune of which a substructure constructed of vaults was always visible. This building can be seen on the general Wood's plan inside the "peribolos wall," but it was not described by him (fig. 2, no. 3). The building lies exactly 180 m southwest of the temple at the edge of the temenos, which was 1 stadium (= 180 m) at the time of Strabo. The orientation of the odeion conforms generally to that of the temple; the west-east incline of its long side implies an orientation to the temple (fig. 3). Dieter Knibbe first identified this building as a "cult theatre" and as the starting point for processions to Ephesos,[27] whereas Anton Bammer, who first called the place a tribune, later believed this to be the place where the so called Parthian Monument, reconstructed as a huge u-shaped altar, was originally located.[28] This building, which has a rectangular ground plan, and measures approximately 40 × 22 m, consists of a complex system of substructures with underground chambers. During recent investigations carried out by Lilli Zabrana, the upper structure has turned out to belong to an odeion; parts of the rows of seats for the audience and furnishings of the building have been detected (fig. 4).[29] As odeia functioned as the venues for musical contests, it seems that this place was used during the sacred games in honor of Artemis attested at Ephesos as the *Ephesia* (later called *Ephesia Sebasta*) according to the inscriptions of the victors.[30] After the recent investigations,

---

[24] Wood, *Discoveries at Ephesus*, 132–33.

[25] Today in the British Museum.

[26] Wood, *Discoveries at Ephesus*, 153.

[27] Dieter Knibbe and Gerhard Langmann, *Via Sacra Ephesiaca I*, BerMat 3 (Vienna: Schindler, 1993), 19–20; Josef Keil, *Ephesos: Ein Führer durch die Ruinenstätte und ihre Geschichte* (Vienna: Alfred Hölder, 1915), 52–3.

[28] Anton Bammer, "Zum Standort des Parthermonuments," *Anatolia/Anadolu* 26 (2004): 11–24; Wolfgang Oberleitner, *Das Parthermonument von Ephesos* (Vienna: Phoibos, 2009), 420–23; Anton Bammer, "L'Architecture héllenistique en Asie minuere et ses concepts rétrospectifs et anticipants," in *Images et modernité héllenistiques. Appropriation et représentations du monde d'Alexandre à César*, ed. Françoise-Hélène Massa-Pairault and Gilles Sauron, Collection de l'Ecole Fr. De Rome 390 (Rome: École française de Rome, 2007), 91–101; Anton Bammer, "Zu kleinasiatischen Monumentalaltären," in *Festschrift für Ramazan Özgan*, 15–27.

[29] Zabrana, "Tribüne im Artemision," 347–58.

[30] Zabrana, "Tribüne im Artemision," 346–47, 361.

Zabrana proposed a date in the second half of the first century CE. Also, a later building phase has been attested and dated to the third century CE. It appears the original use as an odeion was abandoned at that time.[31]

2. The Damianus Stoa: at the end of the second century CE, the well-known Ephesian sophist T. Flavius Damianus – who was also the donor of the above-mentioned banqueting hall – created a roof over the processional way connecting the Artemision with the Hellenistic-Roman city with a covered colonnade. Remains of this stoa are visible today at the south side of the Panayırdağ.[32]

3. To the northwest of the Artemision area, three Roman – or late Hellenistic/ early imperial – structures have been excavated or partially brought to light (in fig. 3; fig. 5, 6, 7).

First, a small rectangular building of about 9×11.5 m with longitudinal walls of 2.4 m and crosswalls about 1.0 m size. For the construction of the building, unworked stones have been used; for the exterior, a socle provides a base for marble orthostats standing on a profile. On its southern side, one can detect remains of an exedra (?) which probably was added later. The workmanship of the orthostats shows high quality and may point to a date in the first century CE. North of the building, a small foundation is visible, completely made out of spolia. This is a north-south oriented altar or a base for (a) statue(s). It is 1.10 m wide and 2.90 m long and is not positioned along the axis of the building (fig. 8).

Second, west of the rectangular building, parts of a larger podium building have been excavated (fig. 5, 6, 7, 9). The foundation and the masonry use worked stones, but on the inner surface bigger stone blocks were used for the construction. On the south side the walls measure 2.5 m, on the east side 3 m. The podium lies on four steps which lead to a courtyard in the south. In the courtyard a rectangular foundation of 3.5×2 m is preserved – perhaps an altar – but this foundation is not positioned along the axis of the podium building. On its eastern side this rectangular building made use of a third building, an older, stepped marble structure (fig. 6, 9). The building technique is of outstanding quality.

The ground plan of the podium building cannot be exactly reconstructed due to the status of the excavation; the building formed an inner angle of which one wing lies parallel to the east side of the podium building, and the other one extended to the east in a right angle.[33] The remains of the earlier stepped structure

---

[31] See ZABRANA, "Tribüne im Artemision," 358, for the later uses of the odeion. ANTON BAMMER and ULRIKE MUSS, "Continuity and Discontinuity of Cults in the Artemision at Ephesus," in *The Land of the Crossroads: Essays in Honor of R. Meriç*, ed. SERDAR AYBEK and ALI KAZIM ÖZ (Istanbul: Ege Yayınları, 2010), 63–76.

[32] DIETER KNIBBE and HILKE THÜR, *Via Sacra Ephesiaca II*, BerMat 6 (Vienna: Schindler, 1995); DIETER KNIBBE, "Via Sacra Ephesiaca: New Aspects of the Cult of Artemis Ephesia," in *Ephesos: Metropolis of Asia*, ed. HELMUT KOESTER, HTS 41 (Valley Forge, PA: Trinity Press International, 1995), 144–55.

[33] Another eastern part of the foundation ends shortly before the rectangular structure but

probably date to the first century BCE. For the podium building we postulate a date at the end of the first or beginning of the second century CE. From the debris above these two structures comes a female head, belonging to about the end of the first century BCE, and pieces of architecture that probably belonged to the end of the first or the beginning of the second century CE. The head was found 67 m north of the south edge of the altar (labelled ASK on the plan) and 7 m west of the eastern edge of the altar (labelled AOK on the plan; fig. 6, 10) and thus inside the coordinate of the trench.[34] The preliminary reconstruction drawings of the buildings (fig. 11) show a podium temple, whose length has been calculated to about 25 m. In front of this building two altars are visible, one of which was found during excavation (fig. 6, 9). The building was oriented towards the great altar of Artemis and is situated very close to its northern side, but not exactly located on its axis. The first, rectangular building to the east of the podium temple is oriented towards the north and does not open to the temple and the altar area. That both – the rectangular structure and the podium building – were religious in nature can be supposed by the fact that they were both dismantled and destroyed almost down to their foundations, most probably during the Christian era.[35]

These buildings are the only visible testimonies still in situ in the sanctuary of Artemis that point to an imperial cult. The podium temple stood on the remains of a stepped structure of late Hellenistic or early Roman date. The form and function of the stepped structure cannot be determined at the moment, but the proposed date for this building fits well with the proposed date of the female head (fig. 10). The head is 48 cm high and wore a bronze helmet. It belongs to a statue of about 3 m. Most probably it represents Dea Roma.[36]

At this point, I would like to return to the Augusteum in the Artemision. The introduction of the imperial cult into a traditional sanctuary generally belongs to a process of socio-cultural change/exchange or "Romanization" related to the coming of Rome and subsequent changes in religious life.[37] In the early Empire, sanctuaries and shrines of the ruler cult came to dominate the most prestigious

---

originally extended further to the east – it was destroyed by the construction of the rectangular structure.

[34] The architecture is stored in the 'Steingarten' west of the Artemision. The head is in the Efes Müzesi in Selçuk, Inv. No. 68/68/89 (Art. 89/K 2075). She thereby weakens KIRBIHLER's arguments for the worship of Dea Roma in the Artemision.

[35] This attitude toward imperial cult buildings is known from other places at Ephesos as well, such as the temple in the Upper Agora and the Temple of Domitian; see under these entries in PETER SCHERRER, ed., *Ephesus: The New Guide* (Istanbul: Ege Yayınları, 2000). MUSS, "Paul, John and Mary," 502. ZABRANA suggests that they originally may have belonged to WOOD's "dwellings of priests"; KIRBIHLER and ZABRANA, "Kaiserkult im Artemision," 111.

[36] For further arguments of the identification of the head as Dea Roma see U. MUSS, "Römischer Zeit," 252–54; MUSS, "Republik und Kaiser," 243–50.

[37] DIRK STEUERNAGEL, "Synnaos Theos: Images of Roman Emperors in Greek Temples," in *Divine Images and Human Imaginations in Ancient Greece and Rome*, ed. JOANNIS MYLONO-

locations. One of the first suggestions for a location of the Augusteum came from Wood who thought that one of the stepped buildings he had found may be the Augusteum.[38] Ernst Curtius not only drew the remains of the peribolus wall but also considered the so called tribune (odeon) to be the Augusteum.[39] In 1990, Peter Scherrer hypothesized that the altar of Artemis was the place where a cult for Augustus had been established.[40] This is interesting in respect of the fact that the imperial cult was often attached to the most prominent sanctuary of the city.[41] The owner of the sanctuary is in most cases that same deity who was associated with the emperor.[42] Augustus instructed the Roman citizens to set up temples to the goddess Roma and the Divus Julius; later, by 7 BCE, this worship became more related to his persona.[43] As a prominent example for the establishment of the ruler cult in Asia Minor during the early imperial period, one can mention the sanctuary of Athena Polias at Priene, rededicated to house the cult of the emperor Augustus. There, statues of the divine Augustus and his successors were allegedly placed in the temple, making the emperors synnaoi (temple sharing gods) of the goddess.[44] Nothing has been preserved in the altar or the temple of Artemis to allow this suggestion for Ephesos. But traditional sanctuaries were altered to include the emperor also by putting up separate buildings or monuments within the sanctuary. So the evidence of the stepped building and the head of a statue of Dea Roma points to the possibility that this might have been a precinct dedicated to Augustus and Dea Roma. That the veneration of Dea Roma and Divus Iulius at Ephesos actually can be traced back to an early date between 41–38 BCE has recently been shown by François Kirbihler.[45] From epigraphic sources we know that the Augusteum in the Artemision existed in

---

POULOS, *Religions in the Graeco-Roman World* 170 (Leiden: Brill, 2010), 241–53 (esp. 248–50 Priene); PETER TALLOEN, "One Question, Several Answers: The Introduction of the Imperial Cult in Pisidia," in *Neue Zeiten, Neue Sitten: Zu Rezeption und Integration römischen und italischen Kulturguts in Kleinasien*, ed. MARION MEYER (Vienna: Phoibos, 2007), 233–42.

[38] WOOD, *Discoveries at Ephesus*, 153. This cannot be identified with the so called "tribune." See ZABRANA, "Tribüne im Artemision," 343.

[39] ERNST CURTIUS, *Beiträge zur Geschichte Kleinasiens: Abhandlung der königlich preußischen Akademie der Wissenschaften* (Berlin: G. Vogt, 1872). ZABRANA, "Tribüne im Artemision," 342, fig. 1.

[40] SCHERRER, "Augustus."

[41] ANDREAS BENDLIN, "Peripheral Centres – Central Peripheries: Religious Communication in the Roman Empire," in *Römische Reichsreligion and Provinzialreligion*, ed. HUBERT CANCIK and JÖRG RÜPKE (Tübingen: Mohr Siebeck, 1997), 56. STEUERNAGEL, "Synnaos Theos." The owner of the sanctuary is in most cases that same deity who was associated with the emperor.

[42] Augustus was mostly associated with Apollo.

[43] Then he established the worship of the Lares Augusti (his household gods) and the Genius Augusti (his spirit) in Rome and all colonies: Ovid, *Fast.* 5.129, 147 f. Suetonius, *Aug.* 31.4.

[44] STEUERNAGEL, "Synnaos Theos."

[45] KIRBIHLER and ZABRANA, "Kaiserkult im Artemision," 121–25.

6/5 BCE. Kirbihler suggests that in the Artemision a sacred space for the veneration of Dea Roma and Divus Iulius already existed before that – probably with the stepped structure,[46] later reused as a podium temple, this time with a western architectural concept. The adjacent rectangular building could also have served as a "Heroon" for one of the Emperors.[47]

Besides the altar, it is the temple that retained the continuity of the worship of Artemis throughout the centuries. The excavation report of Wood reveals much about the temple in the imperial period. Wood describes the following: "Within the cella was found an elliptical Corinthian capital, which I presume had been used in the upper tier of the columns decorating the cella in the time of Marcus Aurelius, when probably great alterations were made in the interior. This emperors' name, with that of his wife Faustina and his daughter Fadilla, were found carved in large characters on the lintel of the door at the west end."[48]

Wood further comments: "As the water in the excavations now stood at a remarkably low level, we were able to clear out the cella, where we found a number of fragments of some interest – these were part of an enriched Roman frieze."[49] He further notes, "In some of the upper strata and indeed in the lowest stratum of the excavations, were found an immense number of Roman enriched fragments; these I ordered to be carried up to the top, and they made a large heap, to which I in future referred those of my visitors who wanted a fragment. I was fortunately never asked what they were, or whether they came from the temple."[50] He also writes, "At the distance of thirty feet ten inches [= 9.40 m] from the lowest step of the [temple] platform was found the kerb of a portico twenty-five feet two inches wide [= 7.60 m], remains of which were found on both flanks of the temple, and which probably surrounded it on all sides" (fig. 3).[51] These remarks of Wood let us suggest that the temple during the imperial period had perhaps a forum-like conception.

Paullus Fabius Persicus (mid-first century CE) wrote that the sanctuary was the gem of the province: its fame was based on the great antiquity of devotion to the goddess, the impressive scale of the temple, and the abundance of wealth which Augustus had restored to the goddess. Pausanias later reports the veneration of Artemis during the imperial Period.[52] In the second century CE, other gods and goddesses who appeared to be more popular than Artemis received the

---

[46] Kirbihler and Zabrana, "Kaiserkult im Artemision," 123.

[47] Titus, Hadrian or Marcus Aurelius are possible candidates.

[48] Wood, *Discoveries at Ephesus*, 57.

[49] Wood, *Discoveries at Ephesus*, 65.

[50] Wood, *Discoveries at Ephesus*, 61–62.

[51] Wood, *Discoveries at Ephesus*, 249–50. This is visible on his general plan. See also Zabrana, "Tribüne im Artemision," Fig. 1, above right.

[52] *IGSK* Vol. 11.1a (1979): 24b; Pausanias, *Descr.* 4.31.8. Engelmann, "Inschriften und Heiligtum," 33. Helmut Engelmann, "Ephesos und die Johannesakten," *ZPE* 103 (1994): 297–302.

right to reside in the prytaneion, the official religious center of the city. These include Demeter and Kore, the oracular sanctuary of Clarian Apollo, and others.[53] Together they attest to the decline of Artemis, who now also assumed functions that she did not have in earlier times.[54] At that time, the worship of Artemis had not only lost its single location in the Artemision, it had been linked to the city of Ephesos, and to the entire empire, where statues of the goddess have been found.[55] Also "mass production" of the statue of Artemis in terracotta and bronze and on a smaller scale points to the "globalization" of her veneration.[56] But the worship of Artemis Ephesia not only survived the early Christian controversy in the mid-first century CE, the Apostle John was also directly connected with the temple of Artemis. The probably second century Acts of John (19.27) reports his visit to the Artemision. According to the narrative, during a festival he, through prayer, destroyed the altar, numerous offerings, statues of the divinity, and elements of the architectural structure.[57] An illustration of this destruction found its way into a French manuscript of the thirteenth century CE which today is in the Trinity College Library at Cambridge.[58] Even if this event cannot be historically verified, it at least provides a clear message that was handed down in Christian circles. It stands for the victory of John over Artemis as a symbol for the conquest of Christian belief and the defeat of paganism.

The Artemision seems to remain the religious center of the city also during the second and third centuries CE.[59] Although the exact scope and impact of the plundering by the Goths in 263 CE are not precisely known, this did not signal

---

[53] KNIBBE, *Via Sacra*, 144–6.

[54] KNIBBE, *Via Sacra*, 147–8.

[55] ROBERT FLEISCHER, *Artemis von Ephesos und verwandte Kultstatuen aus Anatolien und Syrien*, EPRO 35 (Leiden: Brill, 1973); ROBERT FLEISCHER, "Artemis von Ephesos und verwandte Kultstatuen aus Anatolien und Syrien – Supplement," in *Studien zur Religion und Kultur Kleinasiens: Festschrift für Friedrich Karl Dörner*, ed. SENCER ŞAHIN, ELMAR SCHWERTHEIM, and JÖRG WAGNER, EPRO 66 (Leiden: Brill, 1978); 324–58; ROBERT FLEISCHER, "Artemis Ephesia," in *LIMC* 2.1.755–63 (esp. 757–62).

[56] JAŚ ELSNER, "The Origins of the Icon: Pilgrimage, Religion, and Visual Culture in the Roman East as 'Resistance' to the Centre," in *The Early Roman Empire in the East*, ed. SUSAN E. ALCOCK, Oxbow Monographs 95 (Oxford: Oxbow Books, 1997), 178–99 (esp. 180–85). RICHARD E. OSTER, "The Ephesian Artemis: 'Whom All Asia and the World Worship' (Acts 19:27)," in *Transmission and Reception: New Testament Text-Critical and Exegetical Studies*, ed. J. W. CHILDERS and D. C. PARKER, TS 3rd series 4. (Piscataway, N. J.: Gorgias, 2006), 212–31.

[57] TREVOR W. THOMPSON, "Claiming Ephesus: Pauline Legacy in The Acts of John," in *The Rise and Expansion of Christianity in the First Three Centuries of the Common Era*, ed. CLARE K. ROTHSCHILD and JENS SCHRÖTER, WUNT 301 (Tübingen: Mohr Siebeck, 2013), 379–400; RAMSAY MACMULLEN, *Christianizing the Roman Empire A. D. 100–400* (New Haven: Yale University, 1984), 26.

[58] BLUMA L. TRELL, "The Temple of Artemis at Ephesos," in *The Seven Wonders of the Ancient World*, ed. PETER CLAYTON and MARTIN PRICE (London: Routledge, 1988), 97 fig. 48.

[59] RICHARD E. OSTER, "The Ephesian Artemis as an Opponent to Early Christianity," *JAC* 19 (1976): 29–44.

the end of the worship of Artemis. Measures for the preservation of the "historical substance" of the building are for example attested in the form of a repair to the cella door. Wood found six stones inside the cella; five of them display the incomplete profile of the frame of the cella door (fig. 12).[60] The profile of the door frame is best preserved with stone I (nos. after Benndorf) giving the name of Fadilla, daughter of Marcus Aurelius (fig. 13, 14);[61] stone II preserves the word daughter, θυγάτηρ (fig. 15),[62] stone III the wife of Marcus Aurelius, Faustina (fig. 16),[63] stone IV is without inscription,[64] and on stone V which is very much destroyed there is also no inscription left.[65] Stone VI without profile of the door gives remains of the inscription (fig. 17, 18), and three joining stones were found later (fig. 18).[66] Besides VI, all show the profile of the door. Stones VII and VIII give the name of Fausteina(n), another daughter, and stone IX gives the *subscriptio* (the description of the monument, with the dedicators and occasion, appearing beneath the individual inscriptions of the statues).[67]

Thus from the original monument, nine stones are known. The monument included eight statues – showing Marcus Aurelius, his wife Fadilla, his son Commodus and five daughters – each with a separate honorary inscription standing on a long base with an inscription of two lines. The beginning of the long *subscriptio* which was positioned under these is not preserved,[68] so the motive and the occasion of the dedication remains unknown. Where the monument was originally located is also unknown, but the fact that it has been used for the door lintel, points to a location in the temple or close to it. The conclusion however seems strange, that at a time when the worship of the Roman emperors still existed, the monument would have been used for a repair. Therefore another suggestion would be to interpret the repair of the cella door as a much later inter-

---

[60] Wood, *Discoveries at Ephesus*, 128. The texts are reproduced in Wood, *Discoveries at Ephesus*, "Appendix III: Inscriptions from the Site of the Temple of Diana," 18 n. 16. Otto Benndorf, "Studien am Artemision," *FiE 1*, ed. Otto Benndorf (Vienna: A. Hölder, 1906), 214–20; *IGSK* Vol. 12.2 (1979): 287, no. 1–9; Muss, "Republik und Kaiser," fig. 4.

[61] *IGSK* Vol. 12.2 (1979): 287, no. 2; Benndorf, "Artemision," fig. 163–5; Muss, "Republik und Kaiser," fig. 1b, 3a.

[62] *IGSK* Vol. 12.2 (1979): 287, no. 8; Benndorf, "Artemision," fig. 166–8; Muss, "Republik und Kaiser," fig. 2.

[63] *IGSK* Vol. 12.2 (1979): 287, no. 4; Benndorf, "Artemision," fig. 169–71; Muss, "Republik und Kaiser," fig. 2.

[64] Benndorf, "Artemision," fig. 174–77; Muss, "Republik und Kaiser," fig. 2.3b.

[65] Benndorf, "Artemision," fig. 173–78; Muss, "Republik und Kaiser," fig. 3b.

[66] *IGSK* Vol. 12.2 (1979): 287, no. 7; (= 6 plus a–c); Benndorf, "Artemision," fig. 179; Muss, "Republik und Kaiser," fig. 3b. Today in the "Steingarten" of the Artemision.

[67] *IGSK* Vol. 12.2 (1979): 287, no. 9. Stone I can be found in the ancient Agora in Izmir, stones VI (Benndorf, "Artemision"; Muss, "Republik und Kaiser," fig. 3a) and joining fragments can be seen in the 'Steingarten' in the Artemision. I do not know the location of the other stones.

[68] *IGSK* Vol. 12.2 (1979): 287, no. 9.

vention from the time when the temple was converted into a church in the sixth century CE.[69]

In the fourth century, when Christianity acquired the status of a *religio lici-ta* in 313 CE and eventually was elevated to the position of state religion in 391 CE, consequences seem to have been inevitable for the Artemision itself. John Chrysostom, during his stay in Ephesos in 401 CE, attempted to prohibit the further practice of pagan religion at the Artemision, in that he stripped the cult statue of Artemis down to the xoanon, that is, robbed it of its jewelry, and allowed it to be burned.[70] Even if this event cannot be confirmed historically, the tradition suggests, at the very least, that at the beginning of the fifth century, the temple was finally closed and the cessation of religious practices took place.[71]

---

[69] Muss, "Paul, John and Mary," 505–8. Two other monuments for Marcus Aurelius and his family (*IGSK* Vol. 12.2 [1979]: 288–89) have been reused in the byzantine aqueduct, passing by the modern town of Selçuk.

[70] Richard C. Kukula, "Literarische Zeugnisse über den Artemistempel von Ephesos und inschriftliche Zeugnisse über das Artemision," in FiE 1, ed. Otto Benndorf (Vienna: A. Hölder, 1906), 237–82 (esp. 269, no. 405). Procopius, *Orat.* 20.

[71] Ortwin Dally, "Pflege und Umnutzung heidnischer Tempel in der Spätantike," in *Die spätantike Stadt und ihre Christianisierung: Symposion vom 14. bis 16. Februar 2000 in Halle-Saale*, ed. Gunnar Brands and Hans-Georg Severin (Wiesbaden: Reichert, 2003), 98–114. On the Demeas inscription see Angelos Chaniotis, "The Conversion of the Temple of Aphrodite at Aphrodisias in Context," in *From Temple to Church: Deconstruction and Renewal of Local Topography in Late Antiquity*, ed. Johannes Hahn, Stephen Emmel, and Ulrich Gotter (Leiden: Brill, 2008), 243–44. Ulrike Muss, "The Artemision in Early Christian Times," *EC* 7.3 (2016): 293–312.

Figure 1: General View of the Artemision. ©Anton Bammer

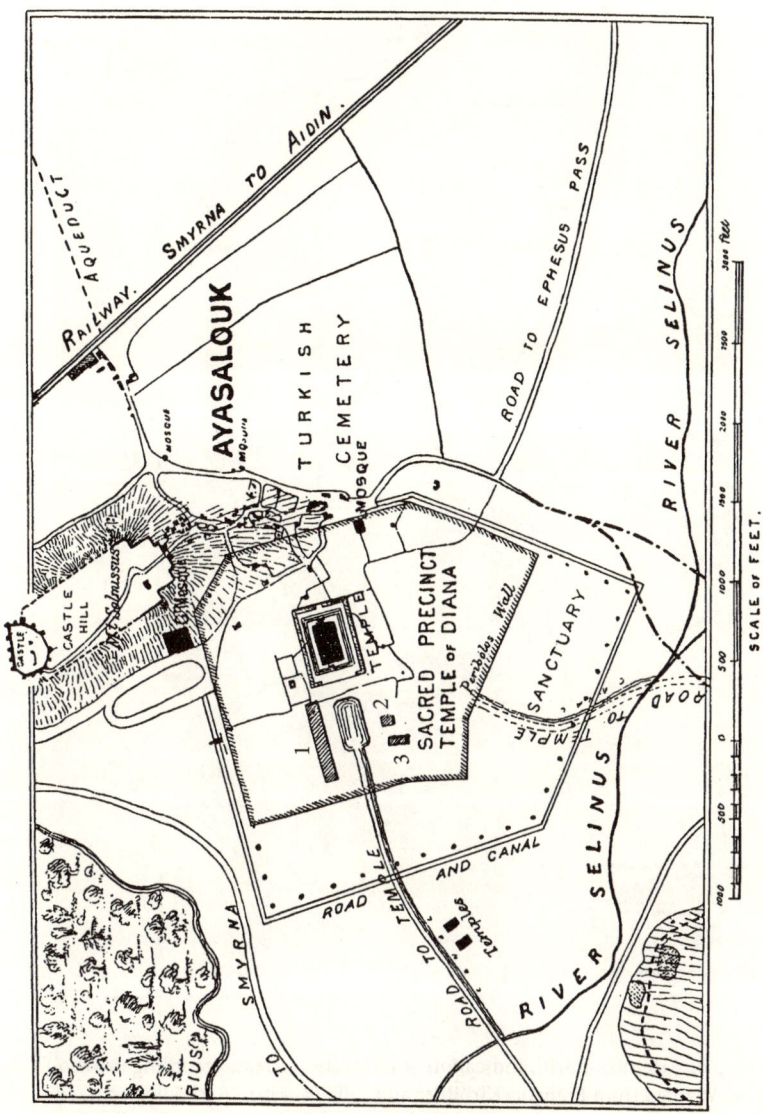

Figure 2: General Map of Artemision Area by J. T. Wood, *Discoveries at Ephesus: Including the Site and Remains of the Great Temple of Diana.* (numbers added by author).

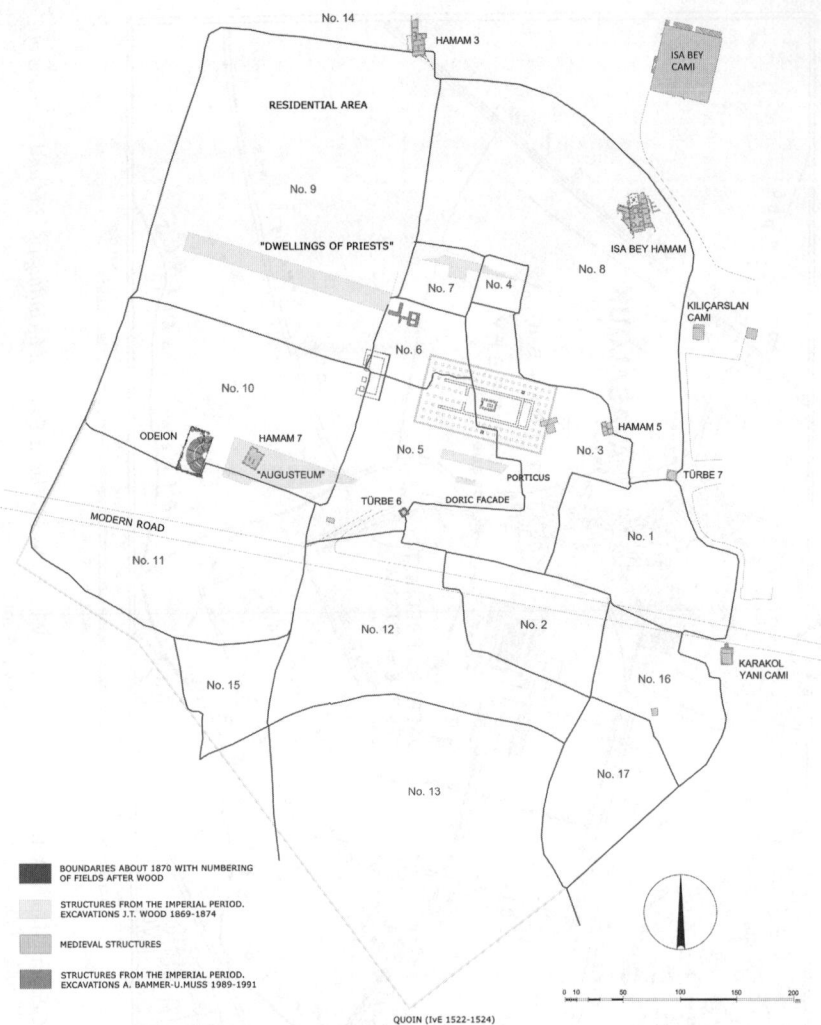

Figure 3: Map of Artemision with Indication of Excavation Areas, according to Wood's Field Notes. Adapted from François Kirbihler and Lilli Zabrana, "Archäologische, epigraphische und numismatische Zeugnisse für den Kaiserkult im Artemision." *JÖAI* 83 (2014): 105, fig. 3.

Figure 4: View of West Façade of Odeion and Parts of the Cavea. After Lilli Zabrana, "Vorbericht zur sogenannten Tribüne im Artemision von Ephesos: Ein neues Odeion im Heiligtum der Artemision." *JÖAI* 80 (2011): 351, fig. 5; 353, fig. 8.

Ulrike Muss

Figure 5: View of Artemision Area with Roman Buildings in the North (Marked with a Ring). ©Anton Bammer.

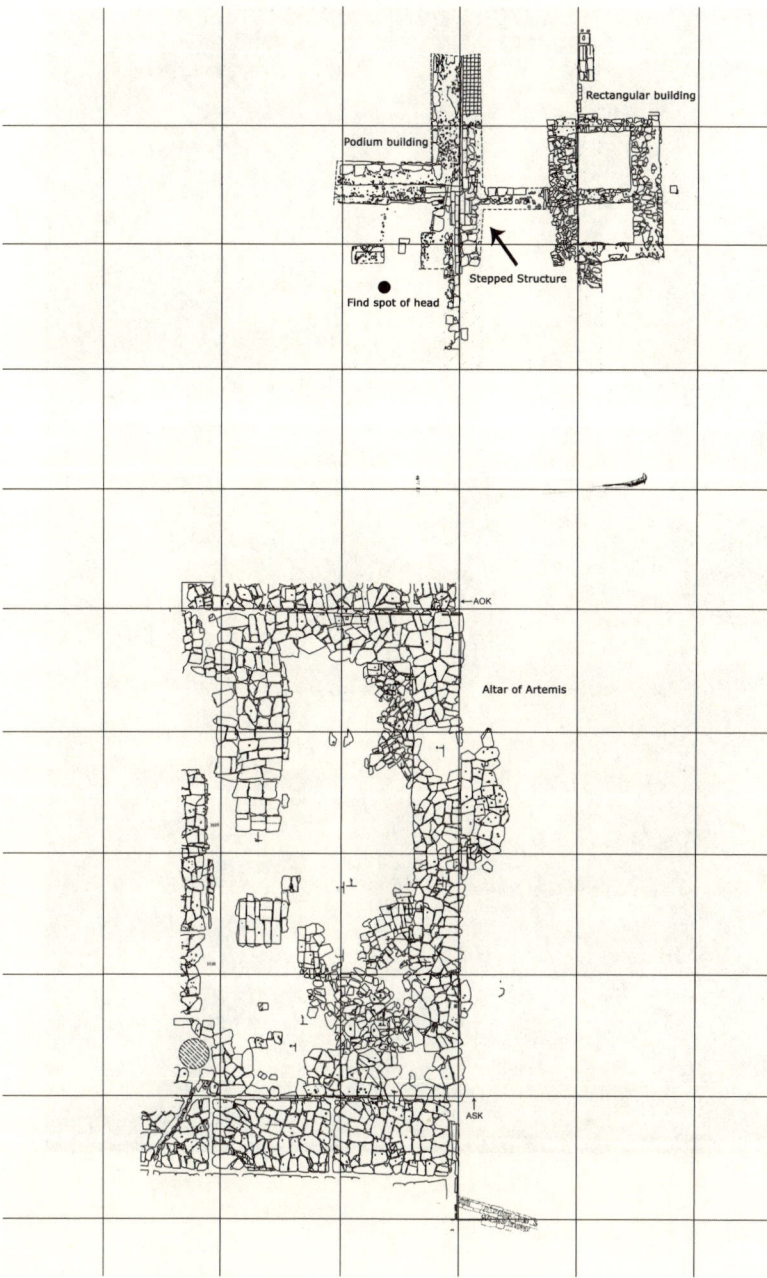

Figure 6: Artemision Altar Structures North of It with Indication of Find Context of Female Head. ©Anton Bammer

Figure 7: View of Rectangular Building and Podium Building from the Northwest.
©Anton Bammer

Figure 8: View of Rectangular Building from the North. ©Anton Bammer

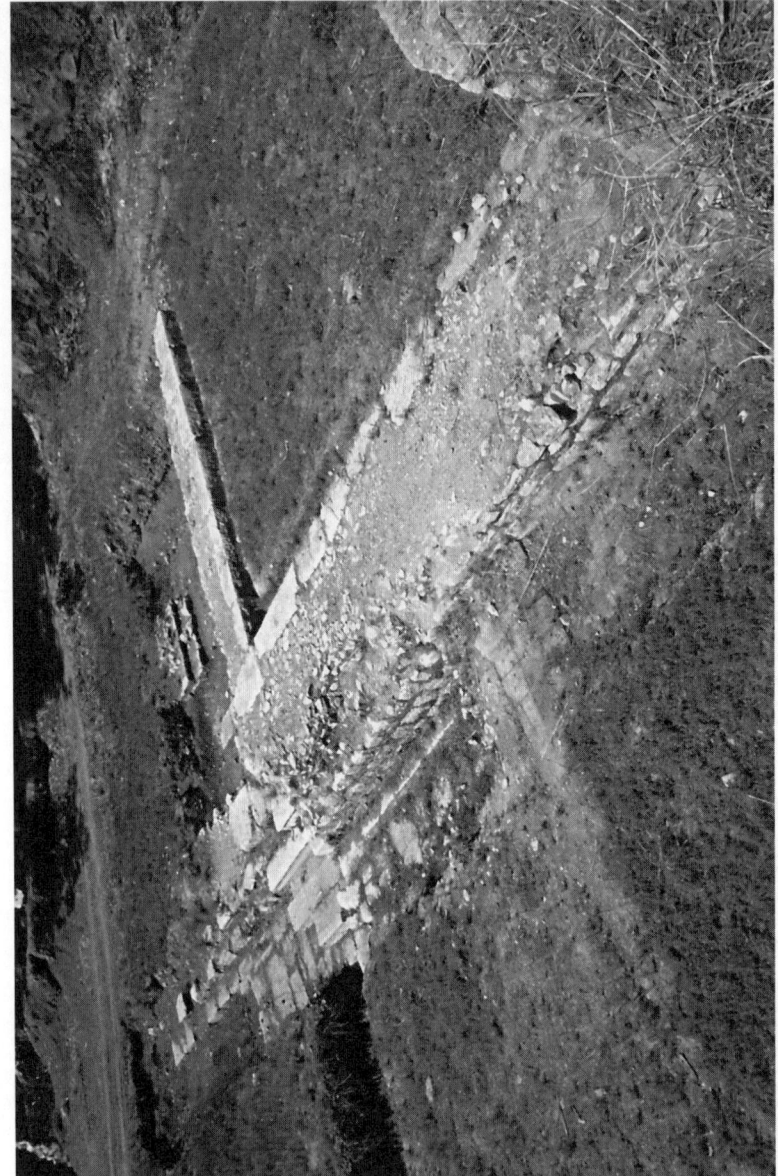

Figure 9: View of Podium Building and Stepped Structure from the Northwest.
©Anton Bammer

Figure 10: Female Head, Likely Representing Dea Roma. ©Anton Bammer

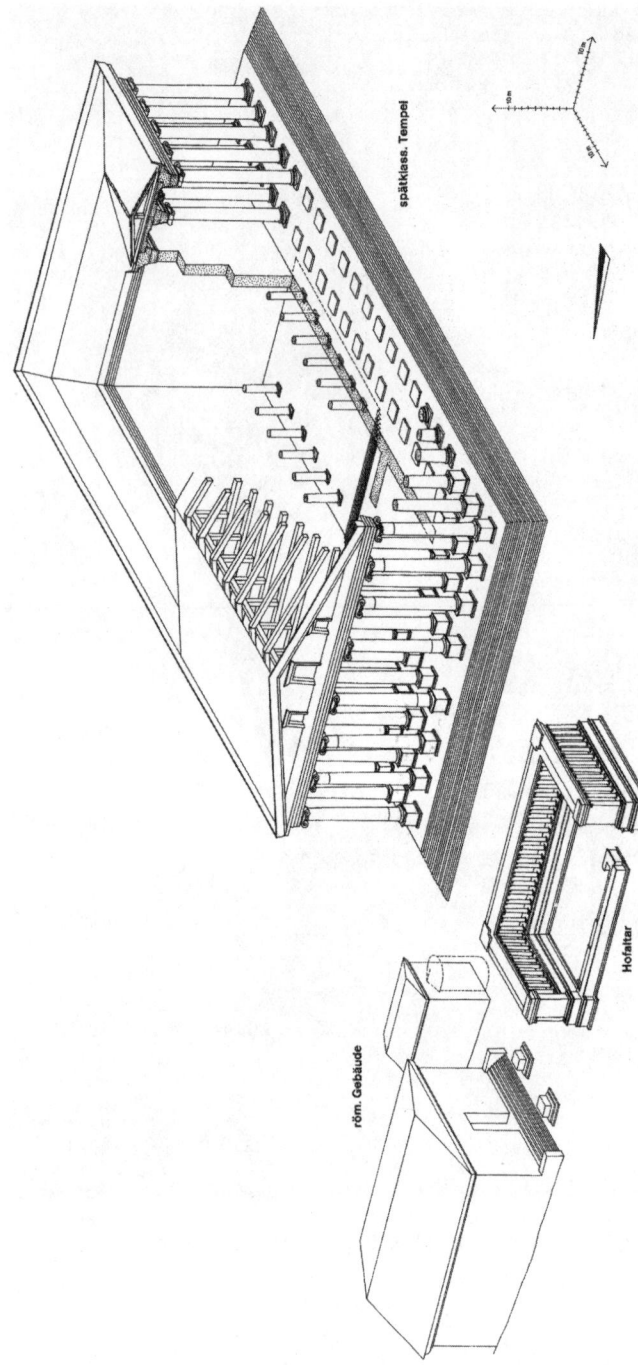

Figure II: Reconstruction Drawing of Roman Buildings and Late Classical Temple of Artemis and Its Altar. ©Anton Bammer

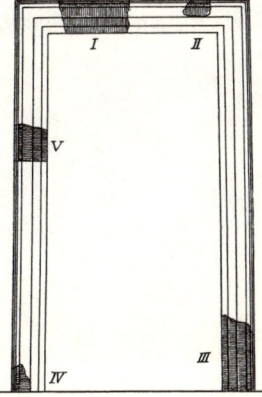

Figure 12: Schematic Pattern of Cella Door of the Temple of Artemis Indicating Stone Positions. Otto Benndorf, *Forschungen in Ephesos*. FiE 1 (Vienna: A. Hölder, 1906), Figure 162.

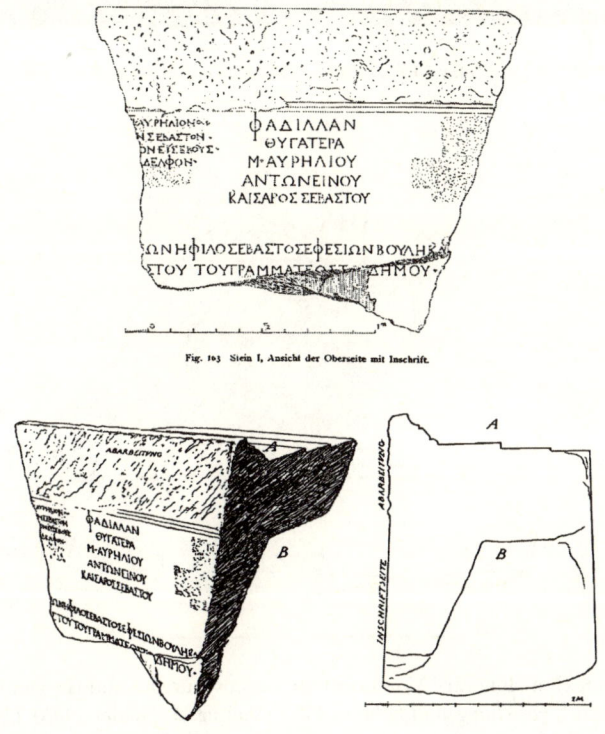

Figure 13: Stone I of Monument for Marcus Aurelius and His Family, Otto Benndorf, *Forschungen in Ephesos*. FiE 1 (Vienna: A. Hölder, 1906), Figure 163. View of Upper Surface.

Figure 14: Stone I of Honorary Monument for Marcus Aurelius and His Family.
©Ulrike Muss.

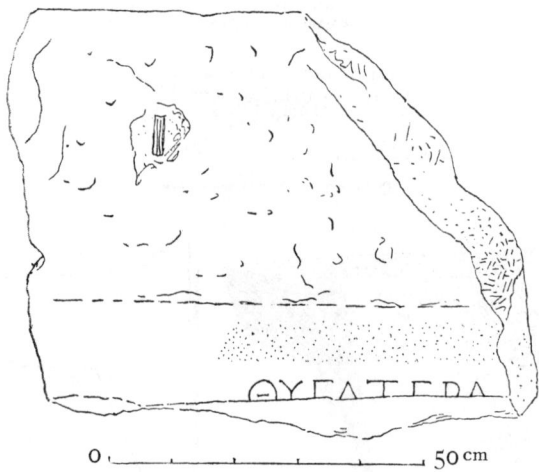

Figure 15: Stone II of Honorary Monument for Marcus Aurelius and His Family.
© Otto Benndorf, *Forschungen in Ephesos.* FiE 1 (Vienna: A. Hölder, 1906), Figure 166.
View of Upper Surface.

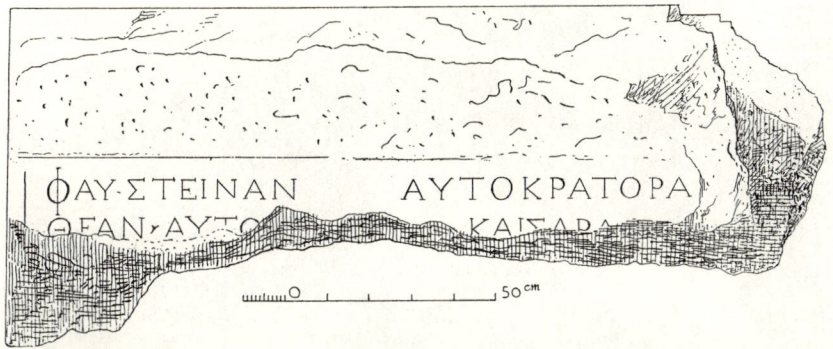

Figure 16: Stone III of Honorary Monument for Marcus Aurelius and His Family. ©Otto Benndorf, *Forschungen in Ephesos*. FiE 1 (Vienna: A. Hölder, 1906), Figure 172. View of Right Side of Surface.

Figure 17: Stone VI of Honorary Monument for Marcus Aurelius and His Family. ©Otto Benndorf, *Forschungen in Ephesos*. FiE 1 (Vienna: A. Hölder, 1906), Figure 179.

Figure 18: Stone VI and Three Joining Fragments from Honorary Monument for Marcus Aurelius and His Family. Artemision. Steingarten. ©Ulrike Muss.

Some Prytaneis of Ephesos

Guy MacLean Rogers

The prytaneis of Ephesos have never been the subject of a comprehensive epigraphical study, though recently their involvement in the celebration of the mysteries of Artemis of Ephesos has been reviewed.[1] Inscriptions found at the site of Ephesos however provide many references to the Ephesian prytaneis from which we are able to make many important inferences about the office and its holders from the Hellenistic period into the third century CE at least, above and beyond their supervision of Artemis's mysteries.

The following chart of references to the prytaneis of the city is based upon a review of the epigraphical corpus of inscriptions from Ephesos. There are only a few cases where we have enough evidence to date the prytany of individual prytaneis precisely; in the vast majority of cases it is contextual or circumstantial evidence that led the editors of *Die Inschriften von Ephesos* and/or the author to make educated guesses about the dates when individuals held the *prytaneia*. Inevitably, however, there are controversies and instances where we cannot be sure because of the fragmentary nature of so much of the evidence. At the end of the chart there are a number of cases cited where it simply is not possible to place the prytanis within this chronological chart.

The short summary below describes the major trends that emerge from analysis of the attested prytaneis. The overall purpose of the chart and the summary is to provide readers with a broader framework within which they may understand who the prytaneis were in Ephesos who helped to supervise the celebration of Artemis's mysteries after the Kouretes were moved to the prytaneion, and also where they fit into the political and socio-economic organization of the polis. Where it may be helpful to the conclusions of this article, I have provided short comments under entries. Under the column "office" are listed other known offices held by the individual prytaneis.

---

[1] See GUY ROGERS, *The Mysteries of Artemis of Ephesos: Cult, Polis and Change in the Graeco-Roman World* (New Haven: Yale University Press, 2013), 491–92, for a comprehensive index of references.

A. Summary

Since the time of Barclay Head's publication of the *On the Chronological Sequence of the Coins of Ephesus* in 1880 it has been assumed by some scholars that the office of the prytanis in Ephesos can be traced back to the fifth century BCE or even before, based upon the appearance of the names of a series of magistrates on various coins of the city dated from at least 407 BCE.[2] None of the coins that Head used to draw this inference, however, explicitly mentions the *prytaneia,* and no prytaneion pre-dating the Augustan-era building has been identified at the site thus far.

The explicit epigraphical evidence for the prytany nevertheless extends from the fourth century BCE into the middle of the third century CE.[3] For the period roughly between 300 and 1 BCE we have evidence for ca. 47 (and possibly 49) prytaneis; one epigraphical source alone however accounts for 30 of the holders.[4] On the other hand we have information about ca. 125 prytaneis from 1 CE to the mid-third century CE, and our sources of evidence for the imperial era prytaneis are both richer and more varied than those for the early Macedonian period officers. Overall, we know far less about the prytaneis from 300 to 1 BCE than about the prytaneis from the Roman imperial era.

As we should expect of an office that at least later required that its holder expend large sums of money to subsidize public sacrifices, virtually from the beginning of our evidence we find family members succeeding each other in the office down generations.[5] Before the Roman imperial era many of the prytaneis served as agonothetes of the Dionysia, and at least some were priests of deities including Dionysos Phleus Poimantrios,[6] but also of Apollo Pythios and Asclepius.[7] Some of the early prytaneis held civic offices as well, such as Herophilos, secretary of the demos in 38 BCE,[8] and others were wealthy enough to sponsor acts of public euergetism, such as Apollonios who dedicated a statue of Augustus and a temenos.[9] With one exception, C. Iulius Nikephoros, the freedman of Augustus, all of the prytaneis before ca. 1 BCE were non-Roman citizens[10] and all of them were men.

---

[2] BARCLAY V. HEAD, *On the Chronological Sequence of the Coins of Ephesus* (Chicago: Obol International, 1880), 85.

[3] *IvE* 4.1389; 7.1.3071.

[4] *IvE* 1a.9.

[5] E.g., Mandrylos, prytanis of c.66 BCE (3004.4–6) succeeded in the next generation by his son Glaukon in 36/5 BC (9N.43).

[6] *IvE* 3.902.6, 15.

[7] *IvE* 1a.9Nb.21–22.

[8] *IvE* 4.1387.5.

[9] *IvE* 3.902.1–5.

[10] *IvE* 3.859.1–5.

From the end of the reign of Augustus into the first-century CE we begin to find a steady stream of Roman citizens holding the office (c.13 out of 23, including four women). Three out of the four known first-century CE prytaneis (Curtia Postuma, Claudia Trophime, and Iulia Helias) appear in the lists of Kouretes without reference to any male relatives;[11] if women once had been excluded from the office and/or physical space of the prytaneion, that clearly was no longer the case from the end of the reign of Augustus.[12] It is difficult to believe that Curtia Postuma, Claudia Trophime and Iulia Helias held one of the most important offices in the polis but were not allowed inside the walls of the sanctuary.

Among the first-century CE holders of the office we find men such as Tiberius Claudius Nysios and Publius Vedius Antoninus, whose acts of euergetism and record of civic offices indicate that they were wealthy.[13]

From the epigraphically rich second century CE we know the names of ca. 68 prytaneis. Roughly 88% of the second-century CE prytaneis were Roman citizens. More than one in four were women; in more than half of those cases the husbands, fathers, and sons of the women prytaneis are not mentioned. From these facts a re-thinking of how women were represented publicly in the most important city in Asia should follow. Service in the office was passed down through the generations. For instance, C. Flavius Iustus was prytanis c.95 CE and his son was prytanis c.125.[14]

Included among the second-century CE prytaneis were some of the wealthiest and most prominent individuals in the history of the Graeco-Roman polis, such as C. Licinius Maximus Iulianus, Tiberius Claudius Aristion, M. Claudius P. Vedius Antoninus Phaedrus Sabinianus, and M. Claudius Publius Vedius Papianus Antoninus.[15] During the reigns of Marcus Aurelius and Commodus, P. Vedius Papianus Antoninus, the so-called "Erblasser," was a member of the senatorial order and was honored as a euergetes and founder of the fatherland; suitably enough, he ended up making Artemis Ephesia his heir.

Our information about the prytaneis of the third century CE is less rich. It extends from the first few years of the century until roughly 250 CE and includes the names of 23 prytaneis. Of these 18 bore Roman names, including, of course, Caesar. Eight were women – or goddesses, including Artemis. In three out of eight instances the fathers, brothers, husbands, or other male relatives of the prytaneis are not named – including in Artemis's case. It may have become more important for women prytaneis to name their male relatives in these inscriptions

---

[11] RIET VAN BREMEN, *The Limits of Participation: Women and Civic Life in the Greek East in the Hellenistic and Roman Periods* (Amsterdam: J.C. Gieben, 1996).

[12] SUSAN GUETTEL COLE, *Landscapes, Gender and Ritual Space: The Ancient Greek Experience* (Berkeley: University of California Press, 2004), 79–85.

[13] *IvE* 4.1010, 1016.

[14] *IvE* 4.1013; 3.955.

[15] *IvE* 4.1022.1–2; 2.425.6; 3.728.13; 1a.47.8.

at the time. Because our sample of prytaneis is smaller during the third century CE it is difficult to compare general levels of wealth across the centuries; nevertheless there certainly were very wealthy men among the prytaneis during the third century, such as C. Iulius Epagathus and M. Fulvius Publicianus Nikephorus.

To judge by the criteria of offices (*archai*) held in whatever sphere and level of authority,[16] liturgies (*leitourgiai*),[17] priesthoods, public acts of euergetism, as well as positions within the Roman military and administration, we can conclude that the prytany of Ephesos during the Roman imperial period represented the apex of the hierarchical pyramid of the political, economic, and sacred order of Ephesos. At least some of the holders of that office belonged to the senatorial or equestrian orders, and we know that the vast majority of the imperial prytaneis must have been of the decurial class. They truly were an elite within the civic elite.[18]

B. The Office of the Prytanis

Register Name	Date	IvE[19]	Office
	300–200 BCE		
Demagoras	300–299	4.65; 76; 79; 83; 98	prytanis
Mantikrates	?	4A.98	prytanis
Apollas	ca. 297	4A.69; 72; 98	prytanis
Danaos	297/296	4A.93	prytanis
Pu[ ]	fourth century	1389.3	prytanis
Zo[ ]	fourth century	1421.3–4	prytanis
Histiaios	fourth century	1423.1 1424.3 1425.2 1426.2	prytanis
Badromios	fourth century?	1390.1; 6	prytanis

---

[16] Sviatoslav Dmitriev, *City Government in Hellenistic and Roman Asia Minor* (Oxford: Oxford University Press, 2005), 13–17.

[17] "Service for the people performed at one's own expense"; see Dimitriev, *City Government in Hellenistic and Roman Asia Minor*, 18.

[18] Arjan Zuiderhoek, *The Politics of Munificence in the Roman Empire: Citizens, Elites and Benefactors in Asia Minor* (Cambridge: Cambridge University Press, 2009), 63.

[19] In the following references, the numbers before the decimal point refer to the number of the inscription in the collection of the *Inscriften von Ephesos*, letters between the inscription number and the decimal refer to the face or fragment of the inscription in question, and the numbers after the decimal point refer to the line number in that inscription.

Register Name	Date	IvE	Office
	200–100 BCE		
Herakleitos	second century	6A.7	prytanis
Lykos	second century	6B.1	prytanis
[　]on	second century	4102.1	prytanis

Register Name	Date	IvE	Office
	100–50 BCE		
Athenagoras	ca. 100	901.1	prytanis
Seleukos	98/97 or 94/93	711.34	prytanis
Mandrylos	ca. 66	3004.4–6	prytanis

Mandrylos's son, Glaukon, was prytanis in 36/35 BCE.

Register Name	Date	IvE	Office
	50–51 BCE		
Herophilos	51/50	9S.3	prytanis
Boiotios	50/49	9S.7	prytanis
Dionysios	49/48	9S.11	prytanis
Aratos	48/47	9S.17	prytanis
Agathenor	47/46	9S.19	prytanis
Glaukon	46/45	9S.21	prytanis
Themistios	45/44	9S.22	prytanis
Memnon	44/43	9S.26	prytanis
Proteas	43/42	9S.29	prytanis
*Artemon	?	Josephus, *Ant.* 14.10.11, 12	prytanis
*Menophilos	43/42	Josephus, *Ant.* 14.10.25	prytanis
Poseidonios	42/41	9S.31	prytanis
Proxenos	41/40	9S.34	prytanis
Agathenor	40/39	9S.37	prytanis
Aratos	39/38	9N.31–33 1387.2	prytanis
		9N.31–35	agonothete Dionysia ephebos?
		905A.3	

Register Name	Date	IvE	Office
Moschos	38/37	9N.36–38	prytanis?
		9N.36–38	agonothete Dionysia athlete
		1126.2	
Herophilos	37/36	9N.39–40	prytanis
		9N.39–41	agonothete Dionysia secretary in 38
		1387.5	
Glaukon	36/35	9N.43	prytanis
		9N.43–44	agonothete Dionysia
Memnon	35/34	9N.45	prytanis
		9N.45–46	agonothete Dionysia
Protogenes	34/33	9N.47	prytanis
		9N.47–48	agonthete Dionysia
Agathenor	33/32	9N.49–50	prytanis
		9N.49–50	agonothete Dionysia
Asclepiades	32/31	9N.51–52	prytanis
		9N.51–52	agonothete Dionysia
Artemon	30/29	9N.27–29	prytanis
		9N.27–30	agonothete Dionysia
Aga[ ]	27/26	9Nb.9–10	prytanis
		9Nb.9–12	agonothete Dionysia
Presbon	25/24	9Nb.17–18	prytanis
		9Nb.17–20	agonothete Dionysia
		9Nb.17–18	priest of Dionysos
		902.6; 15	priest of Dionysos Phleus Poimantrios
Eubios	24/23	9Nb.21–23	prytanis
		9Nb.21–23	agonothete Dionysia priest of Apollo Pythios
		9Nb.21–22	priest of Asclepius
		9Nb.21–22	
[ ] B]oiot[iou	23/22	9N.8–10	prytanis
		9Nb.8–10	agonothete Dionysia
Apollonios	22/21	9N.11–13	prytanis
Dionysios	21/20	9N.14–15	prytanis
		9N.14–17	agonothete Dionysia
Archidemos	20/19	9N.18–21	prytanis
		9N.18–21	agonothete Dionysia
Apollonios	19/18	9N.1–2	prytanis
		9N.1–4	agonothete Dionysia
Demetrios	18/17	9N.5–6	prytanis
		9N.5–7	agonothete Dionysia

Register Name	Date	IvE	Office
C. Iulius Nikephorus (freedman of Caesar, changed to Augustus)	Augustan	859.1–5	prytanis for life
Hieron Aristogiton	c. 1 BCE	1848.2 2033.1–2	prytanis

Register Name	Date	IvE	Office
	1–50 CE		
Alexandros Passalas	4–14	257.4 2018.1	prytanis for the second time (4–14) prytanis for the second time (4–14)
Nikomachos Theudas	14–37	1001.1–2	prytanis
Artemidoros	14–37	1002.1–3	prytanis
Lucius Staidios Attalos	14–37?	1002A.1–5	prytanis
Curtia Postuma	1–50?	1004.1–2	prytanis
Dionysios	36/7	614B.6	prytanis
Kreios		3023.3–7	
C. Minucius	41–68	1005.1–2	prytanis
Charidemos	41–68	1006.1–2	prytanis
Nikomachos Theudas	14–37	1001.1–2	prytanis
Artemidoros	14–37	1002.1–3	prytanis

Apollonios dedicated a statue of Augustus and a temenos (902.1–5); he also appears in no. 257.4. Nikephorus endowed the celebration of the Romaia (859A.1–5). Aristogiton subsidized the building of one of the entry-ways into the theatre (2033.2–3). Alexandros Passalas was responsible for setting up an honorary statue for Q. Haterius, the suffect consul of 5 BCE, or perhaps Q. Haterius Asiaticus (3031.1–8).

Register Name	Date	IvE	Office
	50–100 CE		
Tiberius Claudius Hermias	54–59	1008.1–4	prytanis
Diognetos neoteros	50–100	999A.1	prytanis
Dionysodoros	50–100	1009.5–6 1009.5–6	prytanis koures

Register Name	Date	IvE	Office
Dionysodoros	50–100	1009.1–3	prytanis
C. Licinnius	–65/66	987.25–26	prytanis
Iulius Carus	80?	650.9–10	prytanis twice
Tiberius Claudius Nysios	–92	1010.1–2 1114.4–5 1115.3–5 1116.5–7 1117.5–7 1118.3–5 1120.3–4 4113.5–6	prytanis agonothete for life
Claudia Trophime	92/93	508.4 1012.1 1062.1 508.4 1012.1–2 1062.1	prytanis priestess
C. Flavius Iustus	93–6	1013.1	prytanis
Iulia Helias	–95	1047.1	prytanis
Publius Vedius Antoninus	96–9	1016.1–3 726.4–6 726A.3 726A.2 429.2 429.3	prytanis tribunus militum Legio I Italica praefectus cohortis secretary (twice) asiarch
Artemidorus	98–101	1018.1	prytanis
T. Flavius Perigenes	81–117	1270.2–3 1270.2–3	Prytanis asiarch
Vedia Marcia	97–100	1017.1–3 1017.2 1017.2–3	prytanis priestess archiereia

Tiberius Claudius Nysios endowed a statue group dedicated to Domitian and the demos of Ephesos in no. 518; and some kind of altar for a draw in the Ephesian Olympics pankration for boys in no. 1115; another for a victor in the pankration of men in no. 1116; another for a victor in boxing in no. 1117; another for a victor in the ring in no. 1118; another for a draw in no. 1120; and possibly no. 1121A; and for a victor in the stadion in no. 4113. Claudia Trophime is also famous for her epigram to Hestia (1062), which gives some poetic sense of what was expected of the prytanis. That could be compared to *IvE* 10. She is also known to have set up a statue dedicated to Artemis Ephesia and to the emperor and to the neokorate demos of the Ephesians. P. Vedius Antoninus (1, the adoptive father) adopted M. Claudius Sabinus (2, the adoptive son) after 128. Vedia Marcia was the sister of P. Vedius Antoninus, prytanis from probably the year before.

Register Name	Date	IvE	Office
	100–150 CE		
T. Claudius Tuendianus Magnus	c. 100?	650.3–6 1049.3–5 650.2–6 650A.2–3 1049.3–4	prytanis tribunus militum three times
T. Peducaeus Canax	c. 100?	702.2–6 702.4–5 702.6–8	prytanis gymnasiarch of gerousia priest of priest of Rome and Isauricus
Iulia Polla	c. 100?	980.16–18 989A.4–5 980.17? 980.17 980.17	prytanis priestess kosmeteira archiereia
Tiberius Claudius Romulus	100–3	1020.1–3 275.8–9 1020.1–3	prytanis priest priest for life
Tiberius Claudius Antipater Iulianus	104	1021.1–4 1384.11 27.1–2, 333–4, 370–71, 414, 431, 449 1053.6? 27.417–18, 433–35 1385.4–5 1499.9–13	prytanis koures secretary for the second time secretary for the third time? secretary
C. Licinius Maximus Iulianos	c. 105	1022.1–2 1385.1 3066.3–5 3066.6–7 3066.8 3066.9 3066.9 3066.9–10	Prytanis Priest of Rome and Isauricus gymnasiarch neopoios strategos ambassador to the emperor

Register Name	Date	IvE	Office
Tiberius Claudius Prorosius Phretorianus	104+	477.1+4?	prytanis
		27.426	secretary
		1024.2	
		1023.3–4	koures
		1023.3	bouleutes
Tiberius Flavius Phretor Skymnos	104+	1023.1	prytanis
Dionysodoros	104+ CE	1024.3	prytanis
Attalis [ ] tou Euthu[	120–30	992.8	prytanis
		1026.1–3	
		992.9	priestess
		1026.4	
		1026.4	kosmeteira?
T. Flavius Vestricianus	105–20	1028.1–4	prytanis
Q. Cerrinius Cimber	105–20	1029.1–3	prytanis
T. Flavius Aristoboulos	116/17	1384c.18	prytanis
Iulia Pisonis	120+	1030.1–3	prytanis
		1030.3	archiereia
Tiberius Claudius Aristion	early second century	425.1–6	prytanis
		427.1	
		638.1–5	
		234.13–15	archiereus
		235.15–16	
		239.10–11	
		424.1	asiarch three times
		425.1–3	three times archiereus three times archiereus?
		425A.(4)	asiarch asiarch
		508.5–6	archiereus
		638.1–3	asiarch
		1498.17	three times asiarch
		5101.4	secretary
		5113.24	
		461.1	
		508.5	
		1128.4	
		1129A(1).2	neokoros
		1129A(2).1	
		237.17–18	
		241.18	

Register Name	Date	IvE	Office
		424.1	
		638.6	gymnasiarch
		4105.5?	epimeletes
		638.4	
		5101.3	
		5113.21	
Iulia Lydia Laterane	early second century	424.2–3	prytanis
		1601e.1	
		424.2	archiereia
		424A.1	
		424.2	Daughter of Asia
		424A.1	
T. Claudius Tuendianus Neoteros Charidemos	Hadrian	650.10–15	prytanis
		1049.1–3	
		650.12–14	agonothete
C. Claudius Titianus	Hadrian	1213.1–2	Prytanis
		1213.3	archiereus
Tiberius Claudius Demostratus Titianus	Hadrian	643.1–2	prytanis
		1503.14	
C. Flavius Iustus	c. 125	955.1–2	prytanis
Flavia Voconia [ ]	c. 128	2913.2	prytanis
		1579B.4	
A. Larcius Iulianus	?	985.9–10	prytanis
		985.10–11	gymnasiarch
		985.12–13	hierokeryx
		1040.7–8	koures
		1040.9	Bouleutes
Larcia Theogenis Iuliane	128+	985.4–5	prytanis gymnasiarch of all gymnasia
		985.6–7	priestess of Artemis
		985.7–8	
		1579B.6	
L. Cerrinius Paetus	125–50	635.3–4	prytanis
		1034.1–3	
		211.10; 34	secretary
		635.5–6	gymnasiarch of all gymnasia
		925.4	agoranomos

Register Name	Date	IvE	Office
[ ]a Marcellina	132+	893.5–6	prytanis
		893.7	priestess
		893.7	theoros
C. Terentius Flavianus	130–40	1032.1–4	prytanis
		1035.8–9	
		338.5–6	secretary
		720A.1	
		1035.8	koures
		1035.8	bouleutes
		720A.1	secretary of the Boule
P. Carsidius Epiphanes	130–40	1033.1–4	prytanis
		21.13	secretary 138/9
		924A.3	agoranomos?
		1048.12?	bouleutes
L. Cerrinius Paetus	130–40	1034.1–3	prytanis
		635.1–4	secretary
		211.34	gymnasiarch of all gymnasia
		635.5–6	agoranomos
P. Carsidius Pamphilo	137/138-	633.2	Prytanis
		924A(IV).4	
		1033.9–10	
		1048.1–3	
		633.3	gymnasiarch of the gymnasium of the emperor (Vedius gymnasium)
		633.4	panegyriarch
		1033.11	bouleutes
Dionysios	ca. 140	661.7–9	prytanis
		661.9–10	paraphylax
		1034.10	
		661.10	neopoios
		661.11	secretary of Boule
		661.11	bouleutes
		1034.9	koures
C. Terentius Veratius	c. 140	984.6–8	prytanis
		720A.preamble?	
		1035.4–5	
		1032.7–8	koures
		1032.9	bouleutes
C. Servilius Menander	138–61	1036.1–3	prytanis
		3072.10–11	

Register Name	Date	IvE	Office
P. Aelius Pontius Attalianos	138–61	1040.1–5	prytanis
Flavia Paula	138–61	1044.1–2 1044.2 1044.3	prytanis priestess gymnasiarch
T. Flavius Iulianus	138–61	4342.8–9 4342.16	prytanis secretary
Claudius Modestos	?	215.15	prytanis

In the year after his prytany, Canax supplied citizens with oil and made monetary donations to the Boule and Gerousia and displayed most fully his piety with regard to the mysteries, and also gave money for public spectacles (702.8–16). Iulia Polla was the sister of the suffect consul of 94 CE and consul II of 105, and proconsul of Asia, c.109/110, C. Antius A. Iulius Quadratus. Claudius Romulus appears as a priest in an honorary inscription for Hadrian *synthronon* with Dionysos set up by the *mystai pro poleos* (275.7–9). In 1020.1–3 he is priest for life and also *philosebastos*; this is the first use of this epithet for a prytanis in the lists of Kouretes. In 1385.4–5 Tiberius Claudius Antipater Iulianus is called *philopatris* and *philosebastos*. During his prytany, Iulianos gave 10,000 denarii on behalf of the spectacles into the perpetual gymnasiarchy and gave 2,500 denarii for the construction of the harbor. He also gave for the construction of a new gymnasium and arranged feasts in the time of his prytany and when he was neopoios the citizens by lot according to tribe (3066.12–9). Iulia Lydia Laterane was the wife of Tiberius Claudius Ariston. The office of the prytanis was apparently held in in Tiberius Claudius Tuendianus's name by his mother, as mentioned in lines 18–19. The father of the man just below. While Flavia Voconia was prytanis the mysteries were completed successfully. His brother, Q. Cerrinius Cimber, was prytanis in 1029. Modestos was prytanis during the time of the proconsul's letter about the bakers' strike; see NAPHTALI LEWIS, ed., *Greek Historical Documents on The Roman Principate 27 BC–285 AD* (Toronto: Hakkert, 1974), 45 no. 13; REINHOLD MERKELBACH, "Ephesische Parerga (18): Der Bäckerstreik," *ZPE* 30 (1978): 164–65.

Register Name	Date	IvE	Office
	150–200 CE		
C. Iulius Princeps	150+	1037.1	prytanis
Titus Flavius	first to second century	1051.2	prytanis
Basilides Iulianos		450.1–2 936C.1–3?	agoranomos

Register Name	Date	IvE	Office
M. Claudius	mid-second century	728.13	prytanis
P. Vedius		4110.4–5	XXvir
Antoninus		4110.6–7	tribunus militum
Phaedrus			legio IV Scythica
Sabinianus		4110.8	quaestor
		732.2–3	senatorial order
		4110.4	
		728.14	secretary twice
		1489.17	
		728.15–16	panegyriarch
		728.21–22	gymnasiarch
		728.17	alytarch
		728.14	asiarch
		2065.3	
		728.18–20	ambassador to the Senate and emperors
		727.1–4	ktistes of the polis
		3075.4–5	
		2065.5	ktistes of the fatherland
		3274.5–6?	ktistes of Ephesos
		2065.1–5	euergetes of the professors
		727.1–4	ktistes of the polis
		3075.4–5	
		2065.5	ktistes of the fatherland
			ktistes of Ephesos
		3274.5–6?	euergetes of the
		2065.1–5	professors
		3075.1–7	euergetes of the hand-workers
C. Laberius	162/63 or 163/64	1055A.1–5	prytanis
Amoenus		1557.2–3	
		24B.5–6	secretary
		1557.3	
		2911.1?	
Tullia	c. 170	1063	prytanis
		1064	

Famous for the two prayers to Hestia for herself, giving thanks after her service that the gods would grant her health, a long life, and children that looked like their mother.

Register Name	Date	IvE	Office
Vedia Phaedrina	180–92	47.9 733.1–2	prytanis
Klaudia Antonia	–180–92	47.13	prytanis
Tiberius Claudius Kleoboulos	–180–92	47.14	prytanis
Cornelia Polla	–180–92	47.15	prytanis
Vedia Papiane	–180–92	47.16	prytanis
Fabius Faustinianus	–180–92	47.17 666A.8 1041.1–2 3424.1 4107.5–7 666A.9 666A.11–12 940A(b).11–12 666A.13	prytanis gymnasiarch hierokeryx of Artemis agonothete
Terentia Flaviana	–180–92	47.18 720A.2? 1135A.1	prytanis
Terentia Ailiane	–180–92	47.19 720A.1	prytanis
Iulia Damiane Polla	mid-second century	47.20 980.14 980.14? 980.14?	prytanis priestess kosmeteira
Vedia Iusta	–180–92	47.21 3072.16 3072.15 3072.15	prytanis (162 or 64) priestess kosmeteira
Antonia Frugilla	–180–92	3072.16	prytanis
Alexandros	–180–92	47.22 613.8–11 613A (hollow groove, left side)	prytanis
Dies	–180–92	47.23 613.10 613A (hollow groove, right side) 1055B.2 1600.10	prytanis

Register Name	Date	IvE	Office
Hekatonumos III Baros	–180–92	47.24 1135A.2	prytanis
Kokas III	–180–92	47.25	prytanis
M. Aurelius Menemachos	Commodus	47.1; 26 293.9–10 1075.7	prytanis
		293.9	archiereus
		1075.7–8	asiarch
		1075.7	ekdikos (lawyer)
Claudia Crateia Veriane	–180–92	47.27–28 980.3–4	prytanis
		47.27–28 980.3	senatorial order
		980.5	gymnasiarch of all gymnasia
		980.7	priestess of Artemis?
		980.8	kosmeteira of Artemis
M. Claudius Publius Vedius Papianus Antoninus	ca. 160–92	47.8	prytanis
		47.8	senatorial order
		502.8–12 730.4 732.1 3078.8–9	
		730.4–6	agonothete
		730.7	euergetes
		730.8	ktistes
Vedia Phaidreina	ca. 180–92	47.9 733.1–2	prytanis
Asiaticus Charetos	180–92	1042.1–2	prytanis
		1042.3	gymnasiarch
		1042.3	neopoios of Artemis
		1042.4–5	secretary of Boule
M. Aurelius Septimius Marinus	Commodus	629.1–6 1135A.10–12	prytanis
		629.1–5	masseur of the Emperors
Hostius Metrodorus	Commodus	982.12 1135A.4	prytanis
Iulius Artemas	Commodus	983.5–7	prytanis
		983.6	asiarch
		983.7–8	secretary
		938.11–12	ambassador to the Emperors

Register Name	Date	IvE	Office
M. Aurelius Metrodorus	Commodus	1106A.2	Prytanis
		3058.7–8	Secretary
		991.4–5	
		991.6	argurotamias
		991.6	eirenarch
		991.7	strategos
		991.7	agoranomos
] Eutuchion Faustus	second century	1570A.7–8	prytanis
Demetrios	second century	1578A.3–4	prytanis
T. Claudius Attalos Melior Kle[	198–210	4109.8–9	prytanis
		4109.9	asiarch
		4109.9	secretary

Prytanis already during the reign of Marcus; appears as prytanis on list of Kouretes; his mother was a priestess of Leto during the mid-second century. See REINHOLD MERKELBACH, "Ephesische Parerga (13): Der Prytanis und Hierokeryx Fabius Faustinianus," *ZPE* 28 (1978): 82–83. Vedia Phaedreina was the daughter of Marcus Claudius Publius Vedius Antoninus Phaedrus Sabinianus and the wife of Titus Flavius Damianus; see DIETER KNIBBE, "Private Euergetism in the Service of the City-Goddess: The Most Wealthy Ephesian Family of the 2nd Century CE Supports Artemis in Her Struggle Against the Decline of Her Cult after the Meteorological Catastrophe of 186 CE," *Mediterraneo Antico* 5.1 (2002): 49–62.

Register Name	Date	IvE	Office
	200–250 CE		
T. Claudius	second/third cent.	1065.1–2	prytanis
Plutarchos	second/third cent.	3.	gymnasiarch
M. Aurelius Agathopous	second/third cent.	1069.3–4	prytanis
		8.	secretary of gerousia
			gymnasiarch
		1587.9	
Aurelia	early third cent.	1066.2–3	prytanis
[Aris]tonos tou Ar[	early third cent.	1067.1	prytanis?
M. Aufidius	212+	1070.1–2	prytanis
		1070.2	bouleutes

Register Name	Date	IvE	Office
C. Iulius Epagathus	214	1061.2–3	prytanis
		1600.4	
		1061.2	gymnasiarch
		1061.4	hymnodos
		1600.5	
		1061.4	secretary
		1600.5?	
		1061.4–5	boularchos
		1600.6?	
		1061.5	eirenarchos
		1061.5	strategos
		1061.5–6	agoranomos
			commissioner of the
		1061.7–8?	works
			of the goddess in the
		1600.6–7	prytaneion
		1600.1–2	priest of the founder god Dionysos and Zeus Panhellenios and Hephaistos
Favonia Flaccilla	214/15+	1060.1	prytanis
		1060.1	gymnasiarch
		1060.2	archiereia
Marcus Fulvius Publicianus Nikephorus	c. 220–40	444.2–7	prytanis
		445.7 = *AE* (1929) 122	
		= *SEG* IV (1929) 539	
		679.3	
		679A.4	
		739.13	
		1087A.4	
		3063.5	
		444.6	
		445.6	asiarch
		679.3	
		679A.3–4	
		739.12	
		1087A.4	
		2076.3–4	
		2077.3	
		2078.3	
		2080.3?	
		2082.9–10	
		3063.3	
		3086.2	
		679.4	

Register Name	Date	IvE	Office
		3049.13–14	secretary
		679.5	
		679A.5	agonothete
		1087A.5–6	
		3063.7	
		632.10	
		1080.3–4	advocatus fisci protokoures
M. Aurelius Statilius Stratonicus	218–22	476.1–2	prytanis
		625.16–18	
		1135A.13?	
Tiberius Flavius Lucius Hierax	210+?	435.3–4	prytanis
		436.2–3	
		801.3–4	
		3062.11	
		801.4?	secretary of demos
		3062.9–10	
		3062.11	gymnasiarch
prytanis (female?)	early third cent.	1059.1	prytanis?
Caesar	early third cent.	1057.(1)	prytanis?
Artemis	early third cent.	1078.1–4	prytanis
Aurelius Telephus	212+	1071.2–3	prytanis
		1071.4	boularchos
Aelia Severa Bassa	212+	1072.2–3	prytanis
		488.2	
		488.2–3	gymnasiarch ofall gymnasia
Lollia	third cent.	1074.2	prytanis
M. Aurelius Artemidorus Metrodorianus	222–35 or 235–38	3071.16–7	prytanis
		3071.17	equestrian order
		3071.18	gymnasiarch of all gymnasia
		3071.19	agonothete
		3071.19	eisagogeus
Claudia Caninia Severa	mid-third cent.	892.9	prytanis
		892.6	of consular rank
		635C.4	
		639.6	
		648.7	
		892.7	priestess of Artemis
		892.7	kosmeteira of Artemis
		892.10–1	sacred envoy to the Olympic games

Register Name	Date	IvE	Office
Claudia Severa	third cent.	956.2–3 956.3	prytanis senatorial order

M. Aurunceius
  Vedius Myron
  (father)
	–238–44	724.7
		724.8
		724.8–9
		724.10
		724.10
			prytanis
			secretary
			panegyriarch
			ephebarch
			leitourgos

M. Aurunceius
  Vedius Mithridates
  (son)
	238–44	724.2
		724.1–2
		
		724.5
		2042.7–9
		4336.8
			prytanis
			hierokeryx of Artemis
			gymnasiarch of all
			gymnasia continually
			secretary

For M. Fulvius Publicianus Nikephorus see MARGARETE ROSSNER, "Asiarchen und Archiereis Asias," *Studii Clasice* 16 (1974): 101–42 (130). Her nephew T. Claudius Artemidorus was proconsul.

Register Name	Date	IvE	Office
Tiberius Claudius Diodorus Romulus	?	950.2	prytanis
T[ ] Routilius Lo[ ]	?	715A.5 715A.5	prytanis secretary?
Stertinius?	?	1601G.4 981.5	prytanis

L. Septimius Aurelius
  Achilleides
  neoteros
	?	3246.2–3	prytanis

Apoleia Fausteina	?	3247.2	prytanis twice
Apollonios	?	3317.3–5	prytanis
Dionysodoros	?	999A.5–6	prytanis

The Customs House Inscription from Ephesos: Exchange, Surplus, Ideology, and the Divine

*Steven J. Friesen**

In September of 1929, Josef Keil and his excavation team engaged in a system-atic surface survey at Ephesos to search for exposed artifacts.[1] During the first half of the month they found a piece of finished marble protruding from the ground near the southeast corner of the ancient harbor.[2] As they cleared around the stone, they discovered that it was the top of a stele that appeared to be on its original base *in situ* and that it stretched nearly 2 meters straight down into the soggy soil. They removed the stele and its base from the mud, and cleaned and documented the stones (fig. 1).[3] The inscription on the stele contained a donor list for the construction of a customs house to tax the fishing industry, but the excavators could not ascertain any information about the building where the in-scription was displayed because of the high water table. The marble stele is now on display in the courtyard of the Efes Museum in Selçuk,[4] and its inscription has been published as *IvE* 1a. 20.

This text and stone provide us with an opportunity to address an unresolved issue in New Testament studies and more broadly in the study of ancient relig-ion. That issue is the mismatch between our modern category "religion" and the ancient phenomena we study. The problem lies in our tendency to treat religion as an autonomous phenomenon separated from politics, economics, and other

---

* Earlier versions of this material were presented at the Colloquium on Material Culture and Ancient Religion (2008), the Early Christianity in Ephesos and Asia Minor seminar spon-sored by the Network for the Study of Early Christianity in its Greco-Roman Context (2009), the Ephesos as a Religious Center under the Principate conference (2012), and a Department of Religious Studies Colloquium at the University of Texas at Austin. I thank the participants in those meetings for their discussions of this work, and I also thank G. ANTHONY KEDDIE and DEBORAH JOHNSON for their assistance with the research.

[1] JOSEF KEIL, "XV. Vorläufiger Bericht über die Ausgrabungen von Ephesos," *JÖAI* 26 (1930): 48–49.

[2] See KEIL's excavation notebook for 1929, 31 and 52–53. I thank HANS TAEUBER for his as-sistance with access to the relevant materials.

[3] KEIL copied the text between September 19 and 22.

[4] Inv. 2389.

forms of social action, even though the ancient evidence exhibits no such auto-
nomy or separation.[5]

In this paper, I develop an alternative approach. After a critique of the ways in
which the customs house inscription has entered the specialist literature in New
Testament studies, I examine the inscription rather in terms of the exchanges
among humans, the natural world, and divine beings. Those ancient exchanges
defy our modern distinctions (religion, economy, government, etc.) because any
particular transaction may be described with any number of these labels.[6] So instead of asking whether these activities were religious or not, I examine the objects and benefits exchanged, and the ideologies that framed these exchanges.
The analysis leads to two observations: relations with the divine realm were invoked where surpluses were generated, and where there was a pronounced gap
between ideology and practice. These observations are based on this case study,
and they provide a hypothesis about exchanges that should be tested against
other materials from the Roman Empire and elsewhere.

A. The Stele, the Inscription, and the Donors

The blue marble stele found by Keil and his team was roughly worked in the
production process.[7] After the intervening centuries, most of the stele was still
in good condition except for general wear and some damage at the top corners.[8]
Much of the inscription is found on the broad front side of the stele, which is
known as side A. Lines 1–11 on side A contain a dedication formula, lines 12–66
provide the names of most of the donors in two columns (columns a and b), and
lines 67–71 record the donation and name of the man who oversaw the construction of the customs house. The reference to the donor in ll. 67–71 gives the impression that the inscription ends at the bottom of side A, but the list of donors
resumes on the small right side of the stele ("side B") with 48 more lines that are
heavily damaged.

---

[5] For critiques of our tendency to employ this anachronism, see WILFRED CANTWELL
SMITH, *The Meaning and End of Religion* (New York: Harper & Row, 1978), 15–50; and BRENT
NONGBRI, *Before Religion: A History of a Modern Concept* (New Haven: Yale University Press,
2013).

[6] In this analysis, "transaction" is a technical term for one part of an exchange. Thus, if an
exchange involves two parties, the contributions of one party comprise one transaction in the
bilateral exchange.

[7] The maximum height of the stone is 191 cm, maximum width is 82 cm, and maximum
depth is 31 cm. The height of the letters varies from 1 to 3 cm, with the largest letters in the damaged first line.. The measurements are from *IvE* 1a. 20, but the excavation notebook (31) gives
the maximum height as 186 cm. The back of the base has a semicircular groove to the left of the
central axis, perhaps to fit around an obstacle in its original location.

[8] There are also eight holes in the stone that suggest secondary usage of the stone *in situ* at
the customs house. This probably reflects a later phase in the use of the whole building.

The opening dedication (ll. 1–11) provides important information about the customs house and its donors. The opening makes explicit reference to the goal of the project – the construction of a customs house in order to tax commercial fishing (l. 9) – and it makes a point of noting that the *polis* (city) of Ephesos provided the land. Thus, it is appropriate that the Ephesian δῆμος (people) is one of the five dedicatees. The other dedicatees are the emperor Nero, his mother Agrippina, his wife Octavia, and the δῆμος of the Romans. The dedication to members of the imperial family allows us to calculate a secure date for the inscription in the late 50s of the first century CE, for Nero only became emperor in the year 54, and he had his mother Agrippina murdered five years later in 59. So the inscription comes from the years 54–59 CE.

We can also deduce the type of taxation that went on at this customs house. Greg Horsley's suggestion that the funds went to the Artemision has been correctly rejected by Pleket,[9] but I question Pleket's alternative assertion that the taxes were part of an Ephesian municipal taxation.[10] It is much more likely that they were part of the imperial taxation system.[11] The dedication provides some of the supporting evidence for my conclusion: the project is dedicated to the imperial family and to the city of the Romans, suggesting that the project went beyond Ephesian taxation.[12] The dedication also mentions the Ephesian *polis*, but there is no reference to any Ephesian official, as one would expect if the taxation was a municipal institution.[13] Thus, the evidence of the inscription itself points toward a customs house for imperial taxation at the harbor.

---

[9] So G. H. R. HORSLEY, "A Fishing Cartel in First-Century Ephesus," *NewDocs* 5 (1989): 105. HORSLEY also argued that this tax was actually a fee for the rights to fish in the area, but MARZANO's dissent is correct: the tax was a customs fee for bringing fish into the area and not a fee for fishing rights; ANNALISA MARZANO, *Harvesting the Sea: The Exploitation of Marine Resources in the Roman Mediterranean* (Oxford: Oxford University Press, 2013), 243–6.

[10] SEG 39 (1989) no. 1211.

[11] HELMUT ENGELMANN and DIETER KNIBBE, eds., *Das Zollgesetz der Provinz Asia: Eine neue Inschrift aus Ephesos*, EA 14 (Bonn: Habelt, 1989), 1–206; MICHEL COTTIER, MICHAEL H. CRAWFORD, C. V. CROWTHER, JEAN-LOUIS FERRARY, BARBARA LEVICK, and MICHAEL WÖRRLE, eds., *The Customs Law of Asia* (Oxford: Oxford University Press, 2008).

[12] There may, however, have been a reference to Ephesian Artemis. See below.

[13] In fact, the only references to individuals who play a role in a taxation system are two guards (side A, col b, l. 32–35), which does not help us determine whether the taxation system was municipal or imperial. *IvE* 5.1503 (mid second century) also mentions this customs house by name, but it refers to officials who could work in any sort of taxation institution: τοῖς ἐπὶ τό τελώνιον τῆς ἰχθυϊκτῆς πραγματευομένοις, "those working in the customs house for fishing taxes." *Pragmateutai* was a term used for assistants in a taxation institution when their superior was not a slave; ONNO VAN NIJF, "The Social World of Tax Farmers and their Personnel," in *The Customs Law of Asia*, 288–89. Note also that while free cities were theoretically free from imperial taxation, free cities were nevertheless subject to some taxation, and harbors in free cities were taxed since the revenues were generated from activities on the sea and not in the city; STEPHEN MITCHELL, "Geography, Politics, and Imperialism in the Asian Customs Law," in *The Customs Law of Asia*, 183–84.

Further support for the argument that the customs house collected an imperial tax on fishing comes from another inscription from Ephesos known as the
lex portorii Asiae (law about customs taxes of Asia).[14] This long legal inscription was erected in 62 CE, and it was preserved because the massive stone was
reused in the Church of St. John. The reuse involved extensive modification of
the stone, but the extant portion of the text still runs more than 150 lines. The inscription enumerated regulations for imperial taxation, including the required
locations for customs houses, and the location required by the *lex portorii* inscription about imperial taxation fits the find context of the customs house inscription precisely.

Whatever place of this province [there is, wherever it is necessary to declare, if in] these
[places] a harbor lies by the sea, [they are to have] by each harbor in these (places) up to
one guard-post in sequence, if [they wish, for the sake of exaction of *telos*]; and also on
the coast by the sea; and around the boundaries of the province, where it is lawful to go
or drive (animals), if they wish; [provided that] they have (a building) within [… (feet) of
wherever it is necessary to declare], built or fenced, one in each place, thirty feet from front
to back, ⟨thirty feet from side to side⟩, and provided that it is not [built in a temple or *temenos*] or sacred place or with (another) building nearer than ninety feet.[15] (ll. 32–36, §13)

So the customs house inscription most likely involved imperial taxation rather
than municipal taxation.[16]

---

[14] The editio princeps is ENGELMANN and KNIBBE, *Das Zollgesetz*. An English translation
based on reexamination of the stone and squeezes is provided in COTTIER, CRAWFORD, CROW-
THER, FERRARY, LEVICK, and WÖRRLE, *Customs Law*, along with five chapters that reflect developments in scholarship since the editio princeps was published. High resolution images are
available at http://www.csad.ox.ac.uk/lex-portorii/.

[15] L. 32–36, §13. The translation is from COTTIER, CRAWFORD, CROWTHER, FERRARY,
LEVICK, and WÖRRLE, *Customs Law*, 37, 39. Immediately preceding the quote is the following
text: "Whoever has accepted the contract for the (exaction of the) *telos*, in whatever cities and
places [it is written (?) and laid down] in the [*lex*] of the *locatio*, [is to see that whoever] imports
or exports by sea or land declares to and registers with the collector. If he wishes, he is to have
up to one building [in all these cities and places] for the sake of [declaration (?)] or registration
or habitation, provided that [it is] not in a temple or *temenos* or [sacred place; and at (?) – – –]
they are to have [???] guard-posts, and (in any case) one guard-post on the River Rhyndacus"
(ll. 29–31, §12). The lacunose ll. 36–38 suggest that it is not the imperial responsibility to construct customs houses.

[16] EPHRAIM LYTLE argues that Roman law did not permit taxation of marine fishing ("A
Customs House of Our Own: Infrastructure, Duties and a Joint Association of Fishermen and
Fishmongers [*IK*, 11.1a-Ephesos, 2]," in *Tout vendre, tout acheter: Structures et équipements des
marchés antiques: Actes du colloque d'Athènes, 16–19 juin 2009*, eds. Véronique CHANKOWSKI
and Pavlos KARVONIS [Bourdeaux-Athènes: Diffusion de Boccard, 2012], 216–19). While the details of imperial taxation of marine fishing are not well-established, TØNNES BEKKER-NIELSEN
has cited probable examples of regulation and taxation: "Fishing in the Roman World," in *Ancient Nets and Fishing Gear: Proceedings of the International Workshop on "Nets and Fishing Gear
in Classical Antiquity: A First Approach,"* eds. TØNNES BEKKER-NIELSEN and DARÍO BERNAL-
CASASOLA (Cádiz [Spain] and Aarhus [Denmark]: Servicio de Publicaciones de la Universidad
de Cádiz and Aarhus University Press, 2010), 197–98.

The donors mentioned in the customs house inscription have entered New Testament scholarship in two ways, and both of these are mistaken. The first is the assertion that the donors were members of a trade-related guild, which would mean that they were part of a group that could have institutional parallels with Pauline assemblies.[17] But the assertion that the people listed in this inscription comprised a trade association is wrong for several reasons. First, the building was commissioned by the fishers and fish vendors of Ephesos (οἱ ἁλιεῖς καὶ ὀψαριοπῶλαι, l. 7), but that phrase does not necessarily describe all of the donors. It certainly did not describe the guards mentioned in lines A(b)32–35. Second, the inscription contains no references to the organizational structures, gatherings, or ritual practices characteristic of an association, for there are no technical terms for associations or association members (such as κοινόν, κολλήγιον, οἱ θιασῖται,[18] etc.), nor are any association officers named (e. g., ἄρχων, γραμματεύς, or ἱερεύς).[19] Finally, fishing associations tended to be organized much more narrowly, such as the tuna fishers of Odessos,[20] or the σωλήν fishers of Miletos (perhaps a razorfish or some type of shellfish),[21] and they would not include both producers and vendors. So this is not an association inscription but rather a list of donors who helped members of the fishing industry at Ephesos pay for the construction of a customs house.[22]

The second misconception about this inscription is that the list of donors has a socio-economic profile that was similar to the profile of a normal Pauline assembly. Greg Horsley concluded, "this group of fishermen and traders from Ephesos provides the first really comparable evidence known to me from a group contemporary with the NT in which we encounter a social 'mix' closely akin to that represented in the Pauline congregations."[23] This conclusion is unwarranted, however, for Horsley's argument relies on selective use of onomastic evidence.

---

[17] So HORSLEY, "Fishing Cartel," 101–2. This is also assumed in the other secondary literature on the inscription, including MARZANO, *Harvesting*, 47.

[18] *IByz* 37.

[19] For common terms, see Indices VI–VII in JOHN S. KLOPPENBORG and RICHARD S. ASCOUGH, *Attica, Central Greece, Macedonia, Thrace*, vol. 1 of *Greco-Roman Associations: Texts, Translations, and Commentary* (Berlin: DeGruyter, 2011), 432–42.

[20] *AE* (1928) 42 no. 146.

[21] *OGIS* 756.

[22] PHILIP HARLAND asserts that this is an association inscription and then notes that it is an exception to the tendency for associations to be relatively homogenous in terms of socio-economic status; *Associations, Synagogues, and Congregations: Claiming a Place in Ancient Mediterranean Society* (Minneapolis: Fortress, 2003), 4–5, 43–44. PHILIP HARLAND, *Dynamics of Identity in the World of the Early Christians* (New York: T&T Clark, 2009), 33 and fig. 3. However, since this is the only exception cited and since the inscription does not refer to any association institutions or activities, it is more likely that the inscription is a list of donors who do not form an association. In other words, the range of socio-economic statuses is actually an argument against the association hypothesis.

[23] HORSLEY, "Fishing Cartel," 110.

Horsley's main support is twofold. First, he cites an overlap in names: up to eighteen names from the donor list are names also associated with Paul. This alleged overlap, however, demonstrates nothing because most of the names found both in the inscription and in literature about Paul are quite common – Alexandros, Apollonios, Dionysios, Eutychos, Hermas, Cornelius, Felix, Gaius, Lucius, Marcus, Rufus, Secundus. These are not startling overlaps, given that the inscription preserves names from more than one hundred twenty individuals, some of whom are listed with more than one of their names (Table 1).[24]

Second, Horsley argues that the ratio of Latin names to Greek names is very close to the ratio found in names associated with Paul in New Testament texts. There are many problems with this argument, but the most important one is that individuals often had more than one name for use in different situations (e. g., Saul/Paul, Mary/Mariam, Priscilla/Prisca, or Simon/Cephas/Peter), and usage varied according to context. So comparisons made on this basis from diverse contexts are not reliable. Another problem with this argument is that Semitic names and female names were excluded from Horsley's calculation, and without Jews or women, we are only comparing an unrepresentative subset (i. e., Gentile men) from the Pauline assemblies.

When we turn Horsley's questions around, however, and compare differences, we see the stark contrasts between the participants mentioned in the donor list and in the Pauline epistles. For example, the inscription commemorated approximately ninety-seven donors to the building project, some of whose names are now lost. If we include names of family members, there are one hundred twenty-three named individuals in the donor list.[25] From Paul's undisputed letters, on the other hand, we have thirty-eight named individuals, and on this basis we can make at least four significant distinctions.

First distinction: Roman citizenship. The Res Gestae text implies that about 6 %–8 % of the imperial population held Roman citizenship in the late Augustan period,[26] but it is impossible to be precise about the percentage of an urban population in the eastern Mediterranean that held citizenship in the mid-first century CE. It is clear, however, that Roman citizenship is overrepresented in

---

[24] The argument is also weakened because Horsley treats non-Pauline texts such as Acts and the Pastoral Epistles as though these certainly reflect actual individuals in the Pauline assemblies. The inclusion of these non-Pauline texts inflates Horsley's number of reliably overlapping names.

[25] I omit names too damaged for analysis. Many of the donors also listed unnamed wives or children (without stipulating how many), which would raise the number of attested individuals to around one hundred forty-eight. If we include the fathers who appear only in patronymic formulas, the total number of individuals mentioned in the original inscription would have been approximately one hundred eighty-eight.

[26] For a discussion of the issues and estimates, see Walter Scheidel, "Progress and Problems in Roman Demography," in *Debating Roman Demography*, ed. Walter Scheidel (Leiden: Brill, 2001), 1–81 (esp. 52–55).

Pu. Hordeonius Lollianos	Pu. Corn. Philistion	Demetrios	Antiochos Psychas	Thiasos
Pu. Corn. Alexander	L. Octavius Rufus	Xanthos	Chares	[ ]mos
Ti. Cl. Metrodoros	Tryphon	Pythio	Chares (father)	Philon
Pu. Gerelanus Melleitos	Artemidoros	Phorbos	L. Fabricius Vitalius	Apollonios
Euporos	Isas	Secundus	[ ]ymenos	[ ]laos
Artemidoros	Attalos Hamaxas	M. Ant. Bassos	Hermesianax	Diophantos
Philokrates	Charixenos	Syneros	Antimedes	L. Staccius Graphikos
Apellas	Eikrates Krykras	Kleanax	Metrodoros	Pomponius Stateri[ ]
L. Octavius Macer	Antiochos	Vetulanus Primus	Philonas	Onesimos
Publius Anthestios	Isas	Cn. Corn. Eunous	Idas	Hermesianax
Publius (father)	Isidoros	Attalos	Hordeonius Lainos	Valerius Anaktos
Onesimos	Hesperos	Attalos (father)	[ ]alius Montanus	M. Oneris
Apollonios	Demetrios	Kassiades	Polybios	Herennius Kallinikos
Dionysios	Quintus Laberius Niger	Diogenes	Tryphon	Clodius Tyrannos
Charesios	Isas	Diogenes (father)	[ ]aelius Lesbios	Ant. Ruf[us?]
Pu. Corn. Felix	Hermocharios	Vettidius Nikandros	[D]ionys[ios]	[ ]ourius[ ]
Cornelia Ision	Gaius Furios	Gaius Roscilius	Lollius Arruntius	Ph[ilo]n
Septimius Trophimos	M. Valerius Fronto	Zosimos	Licinnius Naukleros	Philonides
Herakleides	Artemisios	Bacchios	[ ]is Epaphras	Onesimos
Herakleides (father)	Lesbios	Euphrosynos	Popilius Hermas	[P]aulinus
Herakleides (grandfather)	Pu. Sabidius Amethystos	L. Vitellius	[ ]cius Koliotheras	Pomponius Epaphroditos
Epaphras	Hierax	L. Consius Epaphroditos	[Tyra]nnos	Eutychos
Tryphonas	Hermokrates	Aristeas	Tryphon	Phygelos
Pu. Naevius Niger	Didymos	Aristoboulos	[ ]eros	Corn. Pius
Pu. Vedius Verus	Theudas	Ruficius Faustus	Sekos	
L. Fabricius Tosdies	Demetrios Kenartas	Pu. Livius	[ ]as	

Table 1: Named Individuals in *IvE* 1a. 20. Underlined names appear in Acts of the Apostles as assembly participants. Double underlined names appear in undisputed Pauline letters as assembly participants.

the customs house inscription: about 34 % of the donors were Roman citizens. Among the named individuals from Paul's undisputed letters, the percentage is likely no more than 5 %, and it is possible that none of them were citizens.[27]

Second distinction: gender ratios. In the donor inscription over 99 % of the named individuals are male,[28] while in the Pauline letters 74 % are male. If we include all the unnamed sons, wives, relatives, and friends from the inscription, the comparison is 95 % male in the inscription and 75 % male in the letters.

Third distinction: slavery. A comparison of the two groups of names cannot claim much accuracy in this regard. In the donor inscription, slaves or freedpersons account for 2 %–8 % of the names, while in the Pauline epistles they account for anywhere from 3 %–26 %.[29] These ranges are too broad to have analytic value.

Fourth distinction: Semitic names. There are no Semitic names in the donor list, but Semitic names are available for 11 % of the individuals named in Paul's letters.[30]

	Inscription	*Undisputed letters of Paul*
Roman citizens, named individuals	34 % (42/123)	0 %–5 % (0–2)
Male/female, named individuals	99 % male (127m/1f)	74 % male (28m/10f)
Male/female, all individuals	95 % (157m/9f)	75 % male (39m/13f)
Slaves	2 %–8 % 3–10 of 123	3 %–26 % 1–10 of 38
Semitic names	0 % (0/123)	11 % (4/38)

Table 2: Names Found in the Customs House Inscription and in the Undisputed Letters of Paul: Comparison by Legal Status, Gender, and Ethnicity.

These contrasts should not be taken as straight demographic information, for they do not give us hard data for the supporters of the fishing industry in Ephesos nor for the members of the Pauline assemblies. Moreover, comparisons of the two discourses are complicated by the fact that we are dealing with two different

---

[27] I count Julia (Rom 16:15) and Herodion (Rom 16:11) as possible Roman citizens, but neither is certain. I do not include here data about citizens from Acts: Sergius Paulus and Publius (Malta); and perhaps Paul's sister and nephew.

[28] The number of named individuals in this comparison is one hundred twenty-seven rather than one hundred twenty-three because of four fragmentary names that can be gendered even though we cannot determine citizenship.

[29] One slave (Onesimos), and ten possibly slave or freed (Herodion, Achaicus, Ampliatus, Fortunatus, Hermes, Nereus and sister, Persis, Tryphaena, Tryphosa).

[30] Barnabas, Cephas, Jacob, John; Mary/Mariam (?).

genres of communication – a private letter to a small group, and a public monument. Nevertheless, the contrasts do permit the following conclusions about the people institutions, and discourses.

1. The citizenship evidence suggests that the participants in the customs house discourse were heavily biased in favor of Roman rule. The discourse of the Pauline correspondence is silent about the citizenship of its participants.
2. The discourse of the customs house inscription was overwhelmingly patriarchal. The discourse of the Pauline letters was 'only' heavily patriarchal.
3. With regard to slavery, it is impossible to distinguish between the discourses due to lack of accurate information.
4. In the customs house epigraphic discourse, Semitic ethnicity was either nonexistent, irrelevant, or suppressed. In the Pauline epistolary discourse, Jewish ethnicity was openly discussed and was sometimes of great importance.

So the customs house inscription found near the Ephesian harbor does not provide an example of a group with structural similarities to Pauline congregations nor does it provide an example of a group with a similar social profile. Even the communicative genres suggest the contrast, for a public honorific monument like the customs house inscription was not an option for Paul's assemblies in the mid-first century. These differences in social structure and discourse create a challenge for us: the task of developing methodologies and conceptual frameworks that recognize the fundamental connections between religious, economic, and political activities without erasing all distinctions between them. Such methods and theories need to be usable both for the first century assemblies and also for the broader first century networks of social, economic, and religious relationships. The next section lays out one response to this challenge.

B. Examining Exchanges

My starting point is the observation that the customs house inscription records or implies various kinds of exchanges. The donor list names over a hundred transactions of money, building supplies, and furnishings for the customs house, and there are many more reciprocal transactions that are unnamed but necessary in order to sustain the larger social networks of exchange in which this donor list participates. In this study, I analyze those exchanges for three purposes. First, I want to understand what sort of reciprocity took place – who got what, and why. Second, I want to examine the meanings attached to those exchanges. Third, I want to determine which exchanges involved the divine realm and what functions these exchanges with supernatural beings fulfilled.

In order to pursue those three questions, I poach some concepts from Pierre Bourdieu, and then customize them to apply to the analysis of a pre-modern society like that of the Roman Empire. My interest in Bourdieu is not so much theoretical as practical; i. e., I am interested in his work to the extent that it helps me think about particular phenomena and problems. Bourdieu's work draws my attention because it offers possibilities for the analysis of society and religion, because it requires us to position actors in relation to each other, and because it pushes us to consider the ways in which those actors are constrained by external factors without expunging the phenomenon of personal agency. So I appropriate his notions of *field* and *social formation* as technical terms for this discussion.

Bourdieu defined *field* as a set of social positionings that are both the product of ongoing struggles and the continuation of those struggles.[31] His more elaborate descriptions of *field* tend to be opaque,[32] so Johnson's summary is helpful. He described Bourdieu's concept of field as:

a structured space with its own laws of functioning and its own relations of force independent of those of politics and economy, except, obviously, in the cases of the economic and political fields. Each field is relatively autonomous but structurally homologous with the others. Its structure, at any given moment, is determined by the relations between the positions agents occupy in the field. A field is a dynamic concept in that a change in agents' positions necessarily entails a change in the field's structure.[33]

There are at least two urgent problems to resolve in this definition of *field* in order to make the concept useful for the analysis of religious phenomena in the Roman Empire. The first problem is that Bourdieu assumes a modern western organization of social life with distinct fields for religion, for economy, for government, and so on. This style of social organization is foreign to the ancient world (and is perhaps not completely appropriate for the analysis of the modern world either). For the customs house inscription is simultaneously a part of the relationships that Bourdieu would segregate either into a religious field, an economic field, or a political field. So in order to avoid imposing that artificial separation onto the ancient phenomena, I will define fields by specific clusters of exchanges rather than by rationalized categories of social action. To be specific, in this paper I discuss the customs house field as a set of positioned relations, rather than trying to disentangle its religious elements from the economic or political ones.

---

[31] PIERRE BOURDIEU, *The Field of Cultural Production: Essays on Art and Literature*, ed. RANDAL JOHNSON (New York: Columbia University Press, 1993), 30, 34.

[32] For example, PIERRE BOURDIEU and LOÏC J. D. WACQUANT, *An Invitation to Reflexive Sociology* (Chicago: Chicago University Press, 1992), 97, write, "a field may be defined as a network, or a configuration, of objective relations between positions. These positions are objectively defined, in their existence and in the determinations they impose upon their occupants, agents or institutions, by their present and potential situation (*situs*) in the structure of the distribution of species of power (or capital) whose possession commands access to the specific profits that are at stake in the field, as well as their objective relation to other positions (domination, subordination, homology, etc.)."

[33] JOHNSON in his introduction to BOURDIEU, *Field of Cultural Production*, 6.

The second problem is that Bourdieu uses *relations* for the internal structure of a field in a way that is not sufficiently precise for the analysis of specific
phenomena like the customs house field. His description is useful at the level of
theoretical formulation, but for analysis of my specific materials I need something more descriptive. So I examine the relations within a field in terms of the
exchanges of material (sometimes called "objects" in this paper) and non-material resources (sometimes called "benefits"). These exchanges define the relationships by directing and redirecting objects and benefits from one actor to another.
This process of exchange thus generates, confirms, or revises a *network*, by which
I mean the relational hierarchies that are manifest in the patterns of exchanges
and that structure a field.[34]

Bourdieu's concept of *social formation* is useful for describing larger social
structures that involve more than one field, so in this paper I treat social formation as a hierarchical ordering of fields.[35] Bourdieu at times included the categories of *group* and *class* as intermediate concepts between *social formation*
and *fields*,[36] but that level of conceptual stratification is difficult when we deal
with the fragmentary ancient evidence, so I will conceptualize the task simply in
terms of clusters of fields that comprise a social formation.

While I am defining my terms, I should also note that I find *habitus* to be
frustratingly vague when I attempt to use it as an analytical tool for pre-modern
topics.[37] So rather than looking for the "structured and structuring dispositions"
of a *habitus*, I examine my topics in terms of discourse,[38] ideology,[39] and practice.[40]

---

[34] I have in mind here the kind of analysis advocated for modern topics by MANUEL A. VÁS-
QUEZ in "Studying Religion in Motion: A Networks Approach," *Method and Theory in the Study
of Religion* 20 (2008): 151–84; MANUEL A. VÁSQUEZ, *More than Belief: A Materialist Theory of
Religion* (Oxford: Oxford University Press, 2011), 291–319. My approach is in some ways sim-
ilar to that used by ARJAN ZUIDERHOEK in *The Politics of Munificence in the Roman Empire:
Citizens, Elites and Benefactors in Asia Minor* (Cambridge: Cambridge University Press, 2009).
However, I am interested in developing a method that is useful for a wider range of specific exchanges, and in examining the religious aspects of such exchanges.

[35] JOHNSON, in BOURDIEU, *Cultural Production*, 6. PIERRE BOURDIEU and JEAN-CLAUDE
PASSERON, *Reproduction in Education, Society, and Culture*, 2nd ed. (London: Sage, 1990), 5–7.

[36] BOURDIEU and PASSERON, *Reproduction in Education, Society, and Culture*, 5–7.

[37] BOURDIEU defined habitus as the system of principles by which the objects of knowledge
are constructed in a particular historical cultural context. It is "the system of structured, structuring dispositions ... which is constituted in practice and is always oriented toward practical
functions"; PIERRE BOURDIEU, *The Logic of Practice* (Stanford: Stanford University Press, 1990),
52, and more broadly 78–87; see also PIERRE BOURDIEU, *Outline of a Theory of Practice*, Cambridge Studies in Social Anthropology 16 (Cambridge: Cambridge University Press, 1977), 72.

[38] I use a broad definition of discourse: the range of things that are thought or spoken on a
particular topic in a particular setting.

One final problem with Bourdieu is that I do not grant his assumption of the primacy of economic relations in the operation of society. I do find his concept of misrecognition helpful since it names an important and regularly occurring sleight of hand in social intercourse – relations of domination and dependence "disguised under the veil of moral relations."[41] But I am not sure how one would establish that "the conversion of economic capital into symbolic capital" is the central operation of that process.[42] It seems to me, rather, that an implication of misrecognition – "an alienated cognition that looks at the world through categories the world imposes, and apprehends the social world as a natural world"[43] – is that we cannot ourselves claim to have passed through the veil to some sort of unalienated cognition with true knowledge of the nature of things. I think it more honest to accept the existence of misrecognition and apply it to my own cognition as well: I see signs of "social alchemy" at work but for the purposes of this analysis I do not claim privileged insight into the alleged reality that generates the process.[44]

With those amendments in place, I examine how some humans engaged in various material and nonmaterial exchanges in the customs house field, as manifest through the inscription. In particular, I am interested in how they connected those exchanges to divine beings in hopes that this might help us better understand the interactions of religious, economic, and political facets of life in the ancient world.

C. Redirection through the Customs House

One way to understand the customs house building is as an architecturally defined focal point for a network of structured relationships that were dedicated to the redirection of material and non-material resources. That network of structured relationships established the expectations for exchanges of certain objects and benefits, indicating how those objects and benefits should move among actors in a field.

---

[39] I treat ideology as a subcategory of discourse, specifically, as legitimating discourses that provide justification for the things that *should* be done, thought, or spoken.

[40] In this study, 'practice' simply indicates actions, whether or not these conform to discourse and ideology.

[41] BOURDIEU, *Logic of Practice*, 123.

[42] BOURDIEU, *Logic of Practice*, 114–15, 122–130.

[43] BOURDIEU, *Logic of Practice*, 140–41.

[44] Thus, I also avoid applying the label "capital" for all forms of human interaction since I think it unfairly predisposes us to assume economic primacy. I think "resources" is somewhat less prejudicial. Note, however, that PIERRE BOURDIEU claimed he was not reducing all interactions to economic transactions, and that he hoped also to relativize economic theory; "The Genesis of the Concepts of Habitus and Field," *Sociocriticism* 1.2 (1985): 19–20.

Those exchanges were neither neutral nor equitable. On the contrary, the exchanges worked to the advantage of some actors and to the disadvantage of others, and this formalized inequity required the inscription not to tell the whole story. The stele engaged in a process of misrecognition – a redirection of human attention that correlated with the redirection of objects and benefits. In order to understand what the customs house donor list revealed and concealed, we need to examine the explicit, implicit, and suppressed transactions in the inscription.[45]

The primary explicit exchange – the occasion for this text – involved money, land, and a building. The city of Ephesos gave land to the fishers and vendors; donors gave money and goods to the fishers and vendors; the fishers and vendors gave money to Vitalis; Vitalis used the money to construct a building for them on the land provided by the city;[46] and the fishers and vendors dedicated the land and building to the imperial family, to Rome, and to Ephesos. Thus, the inscription opens with a typical formula, which in this case focuses on the actions of the donors and dedicators.

The inscription almost certainly named Ephesian Artemis also as a dedicatee in the first line of this inscription, but this is obscured by damage to the top of the stone and by the official publication of the text. The transcription of the damaged first line should probably be emended to read [ ]ΕΦΕΣΙ[ ] rather than the published [ ]ΕΦΙΣΙ[ ]. This emendation allows the reconstruction of an opening line that read [Ἀρτέμιδι] Ἐφεσί[η καὶ], "[To] Ephesi[an Artemis and]", which would be in line with standard epigraphic practice at Ephesos in the early imperial period.[47] If this revised reconstruction is correct, then Artemis was also named as part of the primary explicit exchange in the customs house field.[48]

These named dedicatees in the opening formula provide us with at least four exchanges with implicit transactions, i. e., aspects of exchanges to which the inscription only alludes or aspects that are mentioned but only partially described. These implicit transactions give us some idea of what the discourse conceals. The most important implicit transaction is the reference to taxation because this introduces a crucial unacknowledged party in the exchanges – the *publicani*, or tax

---

[45] Explicit transactions are those overtly named in a given text. Implicit transactions are those to which the text alludes without discussion. Suppressed transactions are not named in the text but are a necessary part of the practice.

[46] There is some ambiguity regarding to whom Vitalis dedicated the two columns with bases (A 67–71): were his own columns included in the fishing industry's dedication of the building to the imperial family, the city of Rome, and the city of the Ephesians; or were the columns his own dedication to the imperial family and to the cities? For the purposes of this analysis, the columns are treated as part of the building.

[47] For example *IvE* 2.404 (Augustan), 411 (Neronian), 424a (Trajanic); 7.1.3005 and 3008 (both Domitianic).

[48] Lytle also suggested such an emendation ("A Customs House of Our Own," 215).

farmers.[49] The fishing industry did not give money directly to the city of Rome
because the Romans outsourced the implementation of the taxation in the mid-
first century CE. Ephesians paid the tax farmer who in turn paid Rome his con-
tractual amount and then kept the rest of the funds as his profit. The inscription
alludes to this relationship by mentioning taxation, and so these transactions
should be added to the diagram.

The addition of the *publicanus* and his staff to the network reminds us that
Rome's ownership of the customs house building was more complicated than the
dedication suggests, and so the building is a second point at which we can detect
implicit transactions. The dedication of this building – a crucial part of the ideology of the discourse – was to the imperial family, to the Roman δῆμος, and to
the Ephesian δῆμος. The actual practice, however, turned the building over to the
Roman Senate, and not to the emperor, to his family, to the *populus* of Rome, or
to the city of Ephesos (hence the dotted lines in figs. 2–5), and the Senate oversaw
an administrative bureaucracy that leased the taxation rights out to *publicani*. So
actual use of the building was in the hands of the *publicanus* and his staff for the
term of the lease, who were the agents of taxation at the Ephesian harbor.[50] The
publicanus received use of these buildings at the beginning of his contract, and
at the end of the contract he had to certify that they were in good condition and
ready for the next contract.[51]

This misrepresentation of the building's ownership leads us to transactions
that are suppressed by the inscription. What did the Romans and the *publicani*
offer in exchange? The Roman contribution to this exchange is a suppressed
transaction, but is easy to reconstruct: the Romans offered enforcement of the
transactions that allowed tax farmers to collect money and to turn a profit. The
publicani in turn also offered something to the fishing industry that is not mentioned in the inscription – control of the production of commodities. The taxation regulated who could fish in the sea off the Ephesian coast and sell the catch
legally, and thus it protected authorized fishing.[52] However, this system of control was not designed primarily for the benefit of the fishers and vendors, and it
was not benign. In this system, the *publicani* came out ahead in their dealings
with the fishers and vendors, and the Roman Senate came out ahead of the *publicani*. This system for extraction and accumulation of wealth through the *publi-*

---

[49] The *publicanus* is not mentioned in this inscription, but I treat the exchange as implied
rather than as suppressed because taxation is mentioned and two members of his staff appear as
donors – the guards in side A lines 32–35b.

[50] The reference to the two guards who would have been members of his staff reminds us
of this fact.

[51] MIREILLE CORBIER, "The *Lex Portorii Asiae* and Financial Administration," in *The Customs Law of Asia,* 217; VAN NIJF, "Social World," 287–89.

[52] HORSLEY, "Fishing Cartel," 103. In addition, the official *publicani* network clarified for
fishers and vendors whom to bribe when they needed a favor.

cani is made invisible and concealed in the inscription. Our attention is redirected instead toward Artemis, Nero and his family, Rome, and Ephesos.

A third set of implicit exchanges in this inscription has a different quality, for the relationship with the sea was one of pure extraction. This relationship was fundamental to the whole system because the sea provided the fish that became the commodity around which the system was organized. Fishers extracted the fish, and vendors sold the fish to Ephesians and to others for money, which helped define the relationships between producers, consumers, tax-farmers, and Rome. No material objects were returned to the sea, and so it was the original source of surplus for this commodity chain,[53] made possible by the labor of the fishers.

There were, however, exchanges related to the sea, and this alerts us to a fourth implicit aspect in this system of exchanges – the Samothracian deities (fig. 5). In ll. A 68–71 the reference to the contractor's gift of two columns with bases alludes to the existence of a small shrine to the Samothracian deities in the customs house.[54] This is one point in the inscription where religious practices surface, and it begins to elucidate the religious aspects of this system of exchange.

The inscription does not name the benefits expected from the Samothracian deities, but other sources provide that information. The ancient mysteries of the Great Gods of Samothrace[55] included cult stories and rituals with structural similarities in the Roman period to Demeter mythology and practice. The Great Gods were also associated with – and sometimes equated with – the Kabieroi or the Dioskuroi. But the primary benefits promised by the Samothracian deities were "salvation from drowning at sea and successful voyages."[56]

Thus, the customs house field can be mapped in terms of three types of major exchanges.[57] One type includes those explicitly named: the bequest of land, the

---

[53] By "commodity chain" I mean "a network of labor and production processes whose end result is a finished commodity"; TERENCE K. HOPKINS and IMMANUEL WALLERSTEIN, "Commodity Chains in the World-Economy prior to 1800," *Review* 10.1 (1986): 157–70. For a broader description of the history of the concept, see JENNIFER BAIR, "Global Commodity Chains: Genealogy and Review," in *Frontiers in Commodity Chain Research*, ed. JENNIFER BAIR (Stanford: Stanford University Press, 2009), 1–34.

[54] Thus, the contractor and his family were the fourth largest donor unit in the fundraising project.

[55] SUSAN GUETTEL COLE, *Theoi Megaloi: The Cult of the Great Gods at Samothrace* (Leiden: Brill, 1984), 1–20. There was always a non-Greek element to these institutions that cannot be traced back with certainty to any specific area or group. For a discussion of this in terms of hybridity, see PETYA ILIEVA, "Samothrace: Samo- or Thrace?" in *Material Culture and Social Identities in the Ancient World*, eds. SHELLEY HALES and TAMAR HODOS (Cambridge: Cambridge University Press, 2010), 138–70.

[56] WALTER BURKERT, *Greek Religion* (Cambridge: Harvard University Press, 1985), 282–85; the quote is from 284.

[57] I refer to 'major exchanges' because there are myriad other exchanges in this system. The major exchanges are those that play a role in the discourse and those that are required to explain them. It is important to note that this mapping of the transactions is highly schematized and

donations of money, and construction of a building. There are also implicit trans-actions which are not explicitly named but to which the discourse alludes. In this case, the inscription hints at transactions with the administration of taxation by the *publicanus* and his staff, with the Samothracian deities, and with the sea. Fi-nally, there are transactions that are thoroughly suppressed. These involve the coercion that requires people to participate in the institutions of taxation – the control of production through the *publicanus*, the threat of Roman punishment for those who violate these laws for exchanges, and the issue of what the imperial line contributes to this system.

As a result of this approach four observations are in order. First, the mapping highlights the ways in which these exchanges form relationships of asymmet-rical reciprocity, for the reciprocal exchanges do not involve equivalent goods or services: Ephesos contributes land but receives the fulfillment of the legal re-quirement that the harbor must have a customs house; Vitalis accepts money, but returns a building and adds two columns with bases; the *publicanus* receives use of a building and a monopoly from the Roman Senate but returns money to their coffers; etc. These asymmetries affected both the quantity of the goods ex-changed and the quality of the goods exchanged – material objects, commodi-ties, money (the commodity *par excellence*), legal requirements, ritual actions, threats of punishment, promises of payment. The reproduction of this system of asymmetrical exchanges in turn contributed to ongoing inequalities in Roman imperial Ephesos and beyond.

The second observation touches on transactions with deities, which only sur-face in two places in the extant text. One reference to exchanges with the divine occurs where a surplus is generated and there is no other reciprocity. This ref-erence comes as part of the record of the donation of two columns to the Sam-othrakeion in the customs house. This shrine to the Samothracian deities put exchanges with divine powers at a central node of the whole network, where fishermen were taxed for the fish extracted by their labor from the sea, thereby generating the system's fundamental commodity.

This extraction was a dangerous enterprise, not just because of the exposure to the elements but also because it was a violation of reciprocity: the transaction gave nothing to the sea in return. The sea provided the material surplus (fish), and the labor of the fishermen provided the production surplus that generated the commodity chain for profit and consumption. The fishermen received some payment, but the sea received none. So one function of the exchanges with the Great Gods of Samothrace was to protect those engaged in this exploitation of the sea by completing the reciprocity through worship offered to the deities of

selective. The mapping is influenced first of all by the goals of the donor inscription and then by my goals as the analyst. Statements about the discourse using other analytic goals could produce different mappings of the interactions that made up this discourse.

the sea. Because the Samothrakeion was located inside the customs house, the transactions with the gods comprised one crucial part of the larger system of exchanges with the publicanus, his staff, the Roman Senate, and the imperial family.

The only other extant Ephesian inscription that refers explicitly to this customs house comes from the mid-second century CE and assumes the same divine contribution to the customs house exchanges, but with a different deity. The text – now damaged at beginning and end – was carved into a round base for a statue of Isis and reads:

[To Ephesian Artemis], to em[peror T(itus) Aeliu]s Hadrian Antoninus Caesar Sebastos Pius, and to the first and greatest metropolis of Asia and twice neokoros of the Sebastoi city of the Ephesians, and to those working in the customs house for the fishing taxes. Cominia Junia dedicated the (statue of) Isis with the altar from her own funds, when the prytani[s was Tib. Cl. D]em[os]t[r]at[us].[58]

With this inscription, the wealthy female Roman citizen who donated the Isis statue and altar dedicated them to the emperor, to the city of the Ephesians, to the staff of the customs house, and probably to the city's patron deity Ephesian Artemis.[59] Like the Samothracian gods, Isis was associated with safe passage on the sea.[60] The reference to an altar is an explicit indication of sacrificial activity in the customs house. So this inscription, commissioned about a century later than the customs house donor list, continues to affirm the need for divine assistance at the point where extraction of resources by workers becomes the starting point for a system of taxation, circulation, and consumption.[61]

---

[58] *IvE* 5.1503; found near the harbor.

[59] The first line of the inscription is missing, as is the case also with the customs house inscription. But this part of the Isis statue base inscription is formulaic in the second century, and the reconstructed dedication to Ephesian Artemis is secure.

[60] For example, an aretalogy from Memphis (1st century BCE–1st century CE) includes these statements: "I divided earth from heaven. I appointed the paths of the stars. I regulated the passage of sun and moon. I invented fishing and seafaring … I am mistress of rivers, winds and sea …"; MARY BEARD, JOHN NORTH, and SIMON PRICE, *A Sourcebook*, vol. 2 of *Religions of Rome* (Cambridge: Cambridge University Press, 1998), 298 #12.4a. R. E. WITT, *Isis in the Graeco-Roman World* (Ithaca, NY: Cornell University Press, 1971; repr., *Isis in the Ancient World* [Baltimore: Johns Hopkins, 1997]), 165–84; JAMES BRERESFORD, *The Ancient Sailing Season* (Boston: Brill, 2013), 40–42; and more broadly, LAURENT BRICAULT, MIGUEL JOHN VERSLUYS, and PAUL G. P. MEYBOOM, eds., *Nile into Tiber: Egypt in the Roman World: Proceedings of the IIIrd International Congress of Isis Studies* (Leiden: Brill, 2007).

[61] The Isis inscription alludes to divine exchanges at three points. First, the damaged first line certainly included a dedication to Ephesian Artemis. Second, the title Sebastos ("the revered one"; parallel to *Augustus* in Latin) is used for the emperor. Third, the inscription is dated by a reference to the prytanis, the official in charge of the annual round of municipal sacrifices sponsored by the city; GUY M. ROGERS, *The Mysteries of Artemis of Ephesos: Cult, Polis, and Change in the Graeco-Roman World* (New Haven: Yale University Press, 2012), esp. 7–14. All three references are formulaic, but the small changes suggest that the public invocation of the divine

A third observation is based on the only other reference to divine beings in the customs house inscription. The dedication to Ephesian Artemis in the inscription's damaged first line is an example of misrecognition that redirects attention away from Roman coercion. I label it misrecognition because the importance of Ephesian Artemis for the city was used to focus attention away from the fact that the Romans established imperial taxation, owned the customs house, and collected the revenues from the taxation on fishing. The taxation system was a Roman imposition that financed Roman imperialism through myriad customs houses like this one throughout the areas it controlled.

The misrecognition was necessary because of a pronounced gap between ideology and practice. The ideology is enshrined in any major Ephesian inscription in the formulaic opening that normally consisted of a dedication to Artemis, the reigning emperor, and the city. This formula is so frequent in Ephesian epigraphy that is easily overlooked, which is a characteristic of effective ideology. It misleads without effort, its efficacy enhanced by the predictability of the formula. The reason that the redirection of attention was necessary was that Roman taxation did not benefit Ephesos; rather, it gave Rome the means for subjugating Ephesos. The formulaic opening recast this hegemonic practice as a positive transaction, a gift to the emperor and imperial family, the city of the Romans, and the city of the Ephesians.

As a fourth observation, I note that religious language is not employed to promote misrecognition in the case of the emperor, for Nero is not treated as divine in this inscription. Our attention is redirected instead by two additions that are not required by the formulaic Artemis/emperor/Ephesos dedication. The two additions are dedications to the emperor's mother Julia Agrippina and to his wife Claudia Octavia (A 3–5). Here the ideological redirection turns our attention not toward divine approval for the customs house field, but rather toward the reproduction and continuity of the imperial dynasty by invoking the woman who gave birth to Nero and to the woman who was expected to produce his heir to the throne. The distance of this dynastic ideology from actual practice is dramatic. In less than ten years after the creation of the customs house donors list, Nero ordered the execution of both his mother and his wife. In 68 CE his own suicide brought an end to the Julio-Claudian dynasty. But none of the imperial exchanges were couched in religious language,[62] and so we are reminded that invocations of the divine are only one method for ideological misrecognition.

One final observation: for the most striking example of ideological redirection we must return to the primary explicit exchange, where at least one hundred forty-eight individuals are categorized according to the monetary amount of their donations. Most of this inscription – 103 out of 119 lines – is devoted to

---

became more pronounced in such contexts during the century between the customs house inscription and the Isis inscription.

[62] There are mild religious overtones to the title *Sebastē* (the Greek form of the Latin *Augusta*) used for Julia Agrippina, but the more important fact is that no divine language is used for the emperor in this context.

this list, which is organized in a nearly relentless hierarchy of economic value. There are only two places where this criterion of monetary value is violated. One is the reference to Vitalis the contractor. His family's donation would have placed them in fourth place on the list, but Vitalis's service as project manager earned them the honored position at the bottom of the stele where special recognition was often awarded.[63]

The other violation of economic valuation is more surprising. Lines A 32b–35b document the gifts of two guards from the customs house, Phorbos and Secundus, who each contributed one thousand bricks. A gift of one thousand bricks each should have consigned them to Side B, but their donation was instead listed after Xanthos son of Pythion who gave two thousand bricks. Apparently, these customs house guards received special treatment and were moved up to Side A, as if their contributions counted as one combined donation. In the process, their case reminds us of the competition and favoritism that had a corrupting influence on the taxation system itself.

The point of discussing the relentless ranking by value, however, is to point out not the minor exceptions but rather the major ones – the dedicatees in the opening formula whose donations to the populace were ambivalent. The list subjects the many donors to rigorous scrutiny and ranking, taking note of variations of five drachma and perhaps less (near the end of Side B). In contrast to this hierarchy by size of donation, the inscription requires no accountability from Artemis, the emperor, his mother, his wife, the δῆμος of the Romans, or the δῆμος of the Ephesians. The ideology of the customs house field redirected attention away from the opaque practices of deities, emperors, and elites, encouraging members of the δῆμος and other readers instead to honor those who redirected objects and benefits upward toward those dedicatees.

From the customs house donor inscription, then, we get a glimpse of one of the many systems of exchanges in Roman imperial Ephesos. This customs house field – the taxation of the fishing industry at one of the largest harbor cities in the empire – included various kinds of reciprocity involving deities, money, goods, and services. The explicit and implicit exchanges in the donor inscription discourse focused primarily on the movement of resources from the Ephesians toward the imperial center. The donor inscription, however, drew attention away from this bias of the system by portraying the wealthy as the biggest donors rather than as the biggest accumulators. Both were true – the wealthy were large-scale donors and large-scale accumulators.[64] However, the ideology

---

[63] Technically, the end of an inscription is a place for special recognition. Since this inscription spilled over onto the small Side B, however, the bottom of Side A was more visible and served as the honored position. The list then resumed on Side B with donors who gave fifteen drachma or less.

[64] The donations were not particularly burdensome. ZUIDERHOEK calculated that civic

of the customs house discourse highlighted one and concealed the other. The Isis inscription, on the other hand, did not conceal the practice of elite accumulation, but rather redirected attention from the practice by associating these imperial and municipal relationships with religious transactions. This mystification breaks down, however, when we reach the Romans near the top of the hierarchy, for Rome – one of the biggest accumulators in the system – gave nothing to the project that could be named in the inscription. Rather than draw attention to the record of Rome's actual contribution – a mandatory tax system for extraction of money from the provinces with coercive enforcement – both inscriptions remained silent on Rome's donation to the customs house field.

D. Conclusions

Throughout his career Richard Oster has encouraged those of us who work on early Christianity to engage archaeological materials in a sophisticated manner in our research, and he focused especially – but not exclusively – on Ephesian materials to suggest how this might be done. In this study I have taken up his challenge by examining a donor list from the mid first century CE that is inscribed on a stele of blue marble found near the Ephesian harbor. I argued that earlier attempts to relate this Ephesian inscription to the Pauline assemblies of the New Testament have not been sufficiently rigorous. The inscription was not produced by a trade guild, and the individuals in the text do not match the general profile of Pauline assemblies. The earlier misuse of the archaeological artifact contributed to an inaccurate portrait of Paul's assemblies with too many Roman citizens, too much wealth, and too few women.

In order to provide an alternative approach, I used the large inscribed donor list as an occasion to develop a method of analysis of ancient religious phenomena that does not automatically treat such phenomena as though they comprised an autonomous sector of social activity. The analysis focuses instead on the exchanges of material and non-material resources that are explicit, implicit, or suppressed by the text.

Two patterns emerged from this case study that can be tested against other materials from the Roman Empire and from other times and places in order to see whether they are idiosyncratic features of the data under consideration, or whether they might be more widespread features of human religiosity. I suspect that the patterns can at least be found in other religious phenomena from the Roman world, including those associated with the followers of Jesus.

---

benefactions from elites in this region of the Empire averaged only about 3%–5% of their annual income; *The Politics of Munificence in the Roman Empire Citizens, Elites and Benefactors in Asia Minor*, 26–27.

One pattern is that the divine realm was invoked in relation to surplus. The customs house inscription recorded donations for a building devoted to taxation of one commodity chain. The surplus was generated by the sea at the chain's point of origin, and so divine figures associated with safety at sea were recognized there. A second pattern is that invocations of divine beings occurred where there were significant gaps between ideology and practice. In the customs house field we see this in the damaged opening line of the donor list inscription and in the later Isis statue base inscription. In both texts the religious language of the text obscured severe ideological gaps related to the alleged generosity of imperial and local elites.

Examination of the New Testament and other ancient sources will certainly bring other patterns to light, and surplus and ideological misrecognition could provide possible starting points for that search. But whatever the eventual results, this is the sort of robust engagement with archaeological materials that Oster has advocated throughout his career, and it is a path that holds great promise for the future of New Testament studies.

Figure 1: The Stele and Base of the Customs House Inscription (*IvE* 2389). ©ÖAI, Negative II 423.

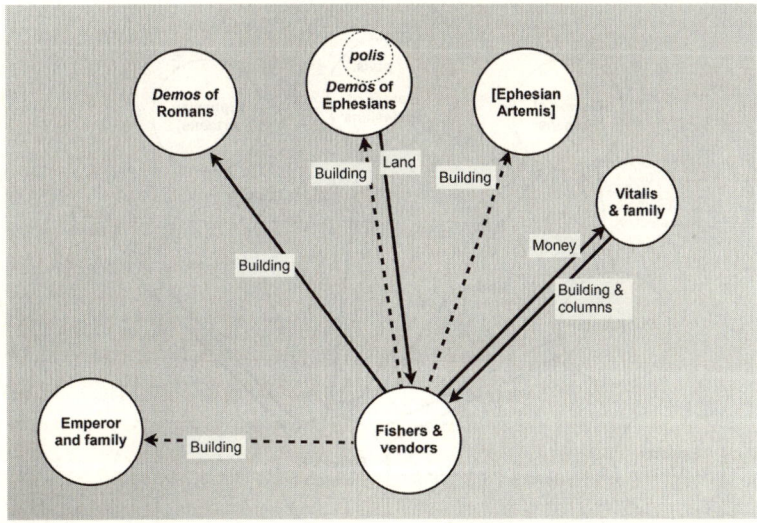

Figure 2: Explicit Transactions in the Customs House Exchanges.

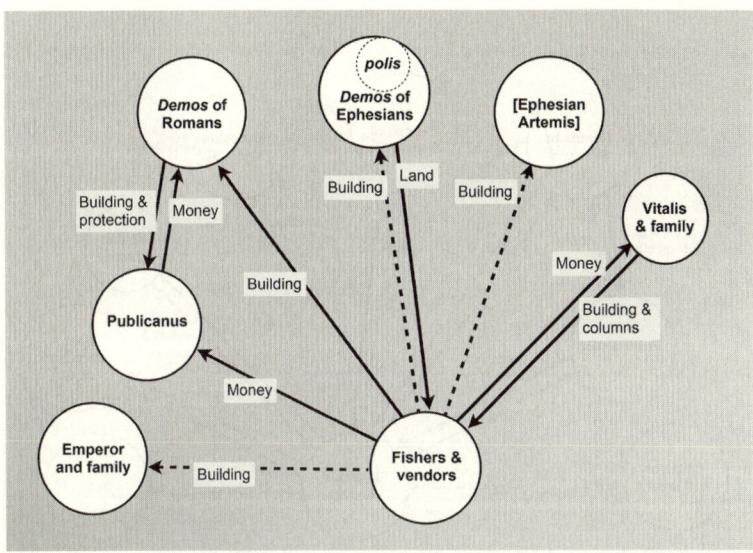

Figure 3: Implicit Transactions in the Customs House Exchanges: *Publicanus.*

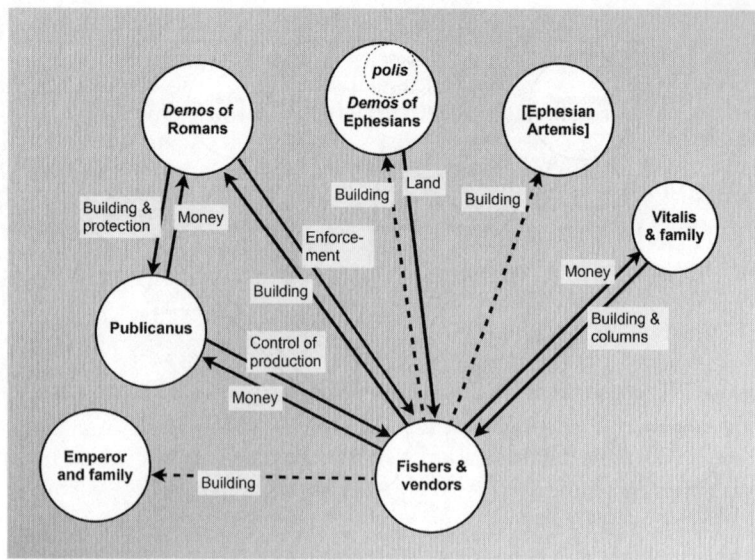

Figure 4: Implicit Transactions: Rome.

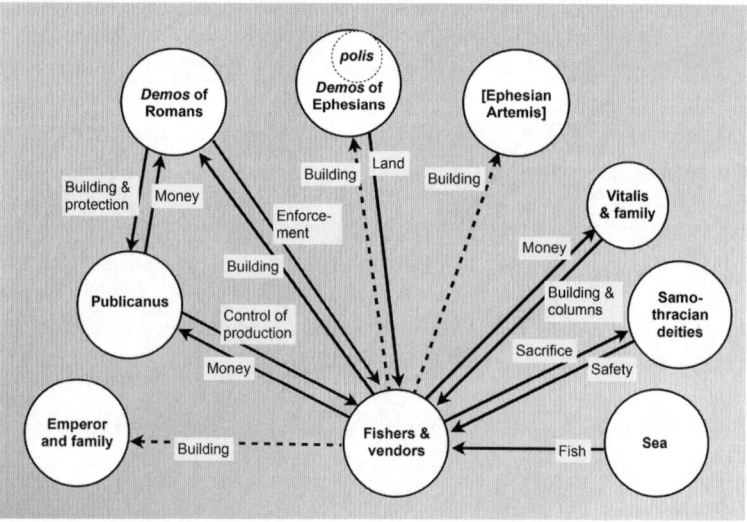

Figure 5: Implicit Transactions: The Sea and the Divine.

Ephesos under the Flavians

The Domitiansplatz as a Marker of Local and Imperial Identity

Daniel Schowalter

Compared to other areas of the ancient city of Ephesos, the irregular square known by modern excavators as the Domitiansplatz ("Domitian Square") receives relatively little attention from visitors. Given its location below the Upper Agora and above Kouretes Street, the Celsus Library and the Terrace Houses, one cannot blame tourists for moving quickly through the Domitiansplatz on their way to someplace else. Given the busy tour schedule, there is rarely enough time to begin deciphering the collection of poorly preserved monuments assembled there (fig. 1). In this paper, I would like to unpack these puzzle pieces and try to visualize what the area looked like at the turn of the second century CE. The result yields a picture of an architectural, artistic, and hydrological wonderland that would have been a stunning feature for ancient visitors and an important space for ritual activity in the early second-century city.

In recent years, the area of the Domitiansplatz and especially its component parts have received a fair amount of attention from scholars of ancient Ephesos, although certainly not an excessive amount when compared to other, more popular neighborhoods.[1] The area has been mentioned peripherally in analyses of developments in the immediate surroundings, especially in studies that have discussed and debated the Temple of the Flavian Emperors.[2] In addition, Anton Bammer has studied several of the monuments in detail and has provided both drawings and on-site reconstructions.[3] Wilhelm Alzinger focused on the Augustan monuments, and Ulrike Outschar has added her reconsideration

---

[1] Among the over one hundred essays in the volume celebrating the centenary of the Austrian excavations, none address monuments in this area directly. HERWIG FRIESINGER and FRITZ KRINZINGER, eds., *100 Jahre österreichische Forschungen in Ephesos: Akten des Symposions Wien 1995* (Vienna: ÖAW, 1999).

[2] STEVEN J. FRIESEN, *Twice Neokoros: Ephesus, Asia, and the Cult of the Flavian Imperial Family* (Leiden: Brill, 1993); BARBARA BURRELL, *Neokoroi: Greek Cities and Roman Emperors* (Leiden: Brill, 2004), 59–85.

[3] WILHELM ALZINGER and ANTON BAMMER, *Das Monument des C. Memmius,* FiE 7 (Vienna: ÖAI, 1971); ANTON BAMMER, "Die politische Symbolik des Memmiusbaues," *JÖAI* 50 (1972–1973): 220–22; ANTON BAMMER, "Das Denkmal des C. Sextilius Pollio in Ephesos," *JÖAI* 51 (1976–1977): 77–92.

of the Memmius Monument.[4] In his important study of the Salutaris inscription, Guy Rogers mentions several of the monuments that would have been visible in the area as the procession sponsored by Salutaris in the early second century passed through the square.[5] Dominick Maschek has raised significant theoretical questions about the history of interpretation for both the Flavian temple and the Domitian Fountain.[6]

Recently, Brenda Longfellow has discussed one feature of the square, the so-called Domitian Fountain, in a larger study of monumental Roman fountain complexes. Longfellow sees the Domitian Fountain in Ephesos as an architectural and artistic statement by the donor Calvisius Ruso, proconsul of Asia, in which Ruso celebrates his Roman connections in tandem with the Hellenic background of Ephesos, the lead city of his province. Longfellow compares the Domitian Fountain to the Fountain of Trajan built further down Kouretes Street in the early second century, and sees both monuments as part of a nearly three hundred year development of monumental fountains in Rome and the provinces.[7] In this paper, I will consider how the Fountain of Domitian fits into its immediate surroundings on the Domitiansplatz, and how the fountain and other Domitianic additions contributed to a built environment that was already rich in history and powerfully symbolic architecture.

In order to understand this unique public space in Ephesos, this paper will first review the buildings that would have been standing or under construction around the Domitiansplatz in the early second century CE, then consider the impact of the Temple of the Flavian Emperors and the terrace on which it stood, and finally make some suggestions about how the meaning of this assemblage of architecture as a whole would have depended on the perspective from which one viewed it, an idea that is especially suggestive for ritual activity in the area.

The overview begins on the north side of the Domitiansplatz, with the oldest monument constructed there. Ulrike Outschar describes the Memmius Monument (fig. 1, item A) as "one of the few remaining architectural monuments from the late Hellenistic times," and dates the monument to the third quarter of the

---

[4] WILHELM ALZINGER, *Augusteische Architektur in Ephesos*, Sonderschrift 16 (Vienna: ÖAI, 1974); ULRIKE OUTSCHAR, "Zum Monument des C. Memmius," *JÖAI* 60 (1990): 57–85.

[5] GUY ROGERS, *The Sacred Identity of Ephesos: Foundation Myths of a Roman City* (London: Routledge, 1991), 86–91. ROGERS focuses more on what happens in the procession earlier at the Magnesian Gate and in the Upper City, and later on what happens at the Embolos, at the theater, and at the Koressos Gate.

[6] DOMINIK MASCHEK, "Domitian und Polyphem: Kritische Anmerkungen zur hermeneutischen Methode in der antiken Kunstgeschichte am Beispiel Ephesos," *JÖAI* 76 (2008): 279–99.

[7] BRENDA LONGFELLOW, *Roman Imperialism and Civic Patronage: Form, Meaning, and Ideology in Monumental Fountain Complexes* (Cambridge: Cambridge University Press, 2011), 61–76. In her study of the Peirene Fountain in Corinth, BETSEY ANN ROBINSON also mentions the fountain built in Ephesos by Ruso and the nearby Hydrekdocheion built a decade earlier by C. Laecanius Bassus (*Histories of Peirene: A Corinthian Fountain in Three Millennia* [Princeton: American School of Classical Studies in Athens, 2011], 246–47).

first century BCE,[8] while Alzinger dates this tribute to Memmius to the Augustan period.[9] This tower-like marker stands at the point where the road from the lower city (Kouretes Street) meets the Domitiansplatz. The monument has been reconstructed on paper by Anton Bammer along with his partial reconstruction on site (fig. 2), and was also re-drawn by Ulrike Outschar.[10] Outschar's reconstruction includes the cylindrical tympanum assemblage with garland and boucrania repositioned in the plaza just to the south of the Memmius Monument (fig. 3).[11] Alzinger points out how the structure is reminiscent of the Hellenistic tower tombs common in the eastern Mediterranean.[12]

Epigraphic evidence on the monument indicates that it was dedicated to Gaius Memmius and also built with his own funds.[13] Memmius was suffect consul in Rome in 34 BCE, but his exact connection to Ephesos is uncertain. The inscription also reveals that Memmius was the son of Gaius Memmius and the grandson of Sulla, here called Felix. The reference to Memmius as grandson of Sulla raises some interesting questions since Sulla's best known connection to Ephesos comes from trials he held there in 84 BCE to punish those from the province of Asia who supported Mithradates in the Pontic War (Appian, *Hist. rom.* 12.61–63). One would expect that Sulla's demands for retribution from the city would certainly not be remembered fondly, but somehow his grandson had gained status in the city that merited or at least allowed for the erection of this monument.

Outschar's reconstruction puts the height of the monument at nearly 4.5 m tall.[14] The tower would have been visible throughout much of the city. Its location would have insured that at the time it was built, it was the focal point for people coming from any direction. In spite of any residual negative feelings toward Sulla, this building was intended to serve as a very vivid reminder of the city's longstanding and complicated relationship with Rome.

The complications in this structure do not stop with the initial construction. At some point, the space of the Memmius Monument was encroached upon by the addition of a water facility to the west.[15] The Hydreion is almost 12 m long,

---

[8] ULRIKE OUTSCHAR, "The Memmius Monument," in *Ephesus: The New Guide*, ed. PETER SCHERRER, trans. LIONEL BIER and GEORGE M. LUXON, rev. ed. (Istanbul: Ege Yayınları, 2000), 96.

[9] ALZINGER, *Augusteische Architektur*, 19.

[10] BAMMER, "Die politische Symbolik"; ALZINGER and BAMMER, *Das Monument*; OUTSCHAR, "Zum Monument." ULRIKE OUTSCHAR calls BAMMER's physical reconstruction at the site an "architectural pastiche," and suggests that it is "more of a modern interpretation than an illustration of an ancient edifice" ("The Memmius Monument," 96).

[11] OUTSCHAR, "Zum Monument," 76–77; ALZINGER, *Augusteische Architektur*, 43–44.

[12] ALZINGER, *Augusteische Architektur*, 18.

[13] *C. Memmio C. f(ilio) Sullae Felicis n(epoti) ex pecunia[...* (IvE 2.403).

[14] OUTSCHAR, "Zum Monument," 69.

[15] HILKE THÜR ("Hydreion" in *Ephesus: The New Guide*, 96), argues that the fountain was

and featured a series of three basins. It was built on a different axis from the monument, but on its south side, the side facing the square, the new structure almost abuts the older one. This is striking considering that there seems to be ample space to avoid this kind of crowding. Either the builders of the water basins saw their work as a complement to the Memmius Monument, or they showed very little regard for it in their choice of location. While the dating for the Hydreion is uncertain, it is clear that it functioned as a water source. As will be seen, great effort was made to provide water for the area that would eventually become known as the Domitiansplatz.

One of the roads that met at this intersection enters the square just to the east of the Memmius Monument. This street, referred to as The Sacred Way, or Clivus Sacer, by Fikret Yegül,[16] rose up to the east along the north side of the upper agora (fig. 1, item B; fig. 4). After the construction of the Basilica Stoa ("Royal Stoa") during the Augustan period, the road would have run along the back side of this massive building ending just past the Bouleterion. Prior to construction of the Stoa, this path would have looked very different. Peter Scherrer mentions another ancient name for this road, the Kathodos,[17] which fits well with Guy Rogers's view that the Salutaris procession came down this road after crossing the Upper Agora and entering into the Basilica Stoa.[18] Scherrer points to two bases with relief sculpture at the point where the Kathodos enters into the Domitiansplatz, and suggests that this assemblage "might have indicated the end of fundamentally different realms of cult."[19] This is an interesting suggestion, but the architecture and activity both east and west of this point should be described as meeting a mix of religious, commercial, honorific and governmental needs.[20]

Immediately south of the Kathodos was a huge foundation structure built of rusticated blocks that served as supports for the Chalcidicum (fig. 1, item C), a name drawn from Vitruvius's term for an extension built onto a basilica (*de arch.* V 1.4). This huge base, extending almost 16 m eastward from the western terrace wall of the upper agora, is an obvious indicator of the size of the structure looming above (fig. 5).[21] While the Basilica Stoa above neatly defined the north side of the upper agora,[22] the Chalcidicum foundation intruded into the plaza space below and actually divided it somewhat awkwardly. While the Basilica Stoa is

---

"probably" added during the Augustan period, and that a further remodeling took place around 200 CE.

[16] FIKRET K. YEGÜL, "The Street Experience of Ancient Ephesus," in *Streets: Critical Perspectives on Public Space*, ed. ZEYNEP ÇELİK, DIANE FAVRO, and RICHARD INGERSOLL (Berkeley: University of California, 1994), 103–4.

[17] PETER SCHERRER, "Kathodos with Embasis," in *Ephesus: The New Guide*, 86.

[18] ROGERS, *Sacred Identity*, 88–89.

[19] SCHERRER, "Kathodos with Embasis," 86.

[20] Cf. ROGERS, *Sacred Identity*, 90–91.

[21] ANTON BAMMER, "Chalcidicum," in *Ephesus: The New Guide*, 88–90.

[22] ALZINGER, *Augusteische Architektur*, 26–37.

said to have been built in the last decade of the rule of Augustus,[23] the Chalcidicum with its massive foundation building was added later. A monumental dedicatory inscription would have faced the square, and an erasure in that inscription seems to indicate construction during the time of Nero (fig. 6).[24]

The colossal addition of the Chalcidicum foundation would have dwarfed
and partially obscured the structure that for some time previous had stood immediately to the south (fig. 1, item D). That monument was dedicated to Sextilius Pollio whose family contributed the funds to build an important aqueduct
and the massive (almost 2700 square meters) Basilica Stoa mentioned above, on
the north side of the Upper Agora (fig. 1, item G).[25] Pollio was honored by his
stepson with this monumental tomb located across the square from the Memmius Monument (fig. 7). According to Longfellow, the west side of the marble-
faced monument originally included a fountain installation.[26] The dedicatory
inscription mentions that the demos of the city contributed the land, presumably out of gratitude for Pollio's many benefactions.[27] Prior to the intrusion of
the Chalcidicum foundation, this would have been a prime location, and the
building took maximum advantage of it. The Pollio Monument was uphill from
the Memmius Monument and stood out against and above the background of
the terrace retaining wall for the upper agora. In all, this would have been a very
prominent tribute to Pollio's benefactions, but it did not stand unobstructed for
long.

In addition to being affected by the foundation for the Neronian Chalcidicum, which impinged on the space of the Pollio Monument and dominated sight
lines to the north, the Pollio Monument was later incorporated into a new fountain structure built to the south (fig. 8). This may sound similar to the fate of the
Memmius Monument, but in this case the builder did a much more thorough job
of overwhelming and enveloping the tribute to the earlier benefactor. The new
fountain monument was constructed in honor of the emperor Domitian by Calvisius Ruso, proconsul of Asia in 92/93 CE (fig. 1, item E; fig. 8). Ruso's fountain
complex extended to two stories, and the second level incorporated a fountain
court – shaped like the Greek letter pi – which opened to the Upper Agora above
(fig. 9). There is some uncertainty about the decoration of the fountain court,
but Longfellow describes "recumbent statues of the source rivers, Marnas and
Klaseas, as well as a statue of Zeus." The statue was over life-sized and "may have
been modeled on the chryselephantine statue that Domitian commissioned for
the Capitolium in Rome after his father's temple and statue were destroyed in the

---

[23] *IvE* 404; ALZINGER, *Augusteische Architektur*, 36–37.
[24] *IvE* 410.
[25] ROGERS, *Sacred Identity*, 89.
[26] LONGFELLOW, *Roman Imperialism*, 225 n. 7.
[27] *IvE* 405.

fire of AD 80."[28] Longfellow argues that the inclusion of the Zeus statue is a clear indication of Ruso's desire to make visual and symbolic connections to Domitian and the imperial court.[29]

This intent is also obvious for the lower fountain, facing west to the square, where two identical inscriptions clearly dedicate the fountain to Ephesian Artemis and the Emperor Domitian.[30] Another inscription states that "the people of Ephesos introduced the water [probably of the Aqua Domitiana] during the proconsulship of Calvisius Ruso, who took care of bringing in [the water] and setting up [the fountain]." Like Pollio eighty years before, Ruso clearly spent an enormous amount of money to bring water to the city.[31] Longfellow argues that he did so to "mark his attainment of the proconsulship of Asia, the pinnacle of a senatorial career."[32] In contrast to the Pollio Monument, Ruso set up his own marker of achievement and honor, and was not buried within it. Apparently the city had no scruples about having two fountains built around the tomb of Pollio, who was himself remembered as a bringer of water. Longfellow describes the fountain as follows:

> An apsidal settling basin and linear architectural façade resting on a three-stepped krepidoma … A tall podium, which supported the sculptural group … follows the apsidal curve of the settling basin's rear wall. The basin is closed off in front by a parapet approximately 9.5 meters long, which is made up of vertical orthostat blocks 1.67 meters tall and topped by a crowning element.[33]

The most striking feature of the monument on site today is the reconstructed arch spanning the front of the basin (fig. 10). Longfellow notes that the use of a female head projecting from the keystone of the arch is an unusual feature "that primarily was limited to the western provinces." Along with the apsidal settling basin and the visual accessibility of the water, the head feature is said to mark "the Ephesian Fountain of Domitian as western, and particularly Italian, in inspiration."[34] The supporting columns are mostly reconstructed of concrete now, but originally were richly decorated with acanthus leaves. These along with column fragments featuring mythological figures (Acteaon and Eros) give the impression of the very lush and non-traditional nature of the monument. This character is further enhanced by the sculptural display lining the back of the apse surrounding the retrieval basin. This ensemble, now on display in the Efes Mu-

---

[28] LONGFELLOW, *Roman Imperialism*, 65, citing VOLKER MICHAEL STROCKA, "Zeus, Marnas und Klaseas: Ephesische Brunnenfiguren von 93 n. Chr.," in *Festschrift für Jale İnan*, ed. NEZİH BAŞGELEN and MİHİN LUGAL (Istanbul: Arkeoloji ve Sanat Yayınları, 1989), 92 n. 58.

[29] LONGFELLOW, *Roman Imperialism*, 65.

[30] LONGFELLOW, *Roman Imperialism*, 65; IvE 2.413.

[31] *IvE* 2.419.

[32] LONGFELLOW, *Roman Imperialism*, 65.

[33] LONGFELLOW, *Roman Imperialism*, 65–66.

[34] LONGFELLOW, *Roman Imperialism*, 68.

seum in Selçuk, depicts Odysseus offering wine to Polyphemus while his companions prepare the stake that will blind the creature's eye. As Longfellow points out, the images in this scene "were deemed appropriate for residential settings in Italy and were particularly well suited for grotto settings where water played an active role in the aesthetic effect of the display."[35] If the reconstruction of a vault in front of the apsidal basin is correct, it appears that Ruso had brought the grotto-fountain motif with him from Italy, and, for certain elite Romans, had created a little slice of home right in this public plaza in Ephesos.[36]

Longfellow points out that the total effect of the fountain would have had a special meaning for only a few viewers, those who would recognize the connections to imperial villas in Italy:

Ruso honored Domitian with the public display of a scene previously limited to interior spaces of the wealthy, if not exclusively to those of the imperial family. In this way, the first known monumental fountain dedicated to an emperor honored him with a display that was truly imperial in nature.[37]

Longfellow's excellent chapter focuses on the meaning of this display for Ruso as an elite Roman in Ephesos, and for a few of his wealthy friends. How this structure and its decoration would have been received or understood by average Ephesians on the street is harder to gauge. Longfellow mentions a general Hellenic and mythological connection to the imagery that would have been familiar to most passersby, but it would seem that the meaning would have been impacted by the built environment around the square that would have created a closed-in, subterranean feeling that made Ruso's grotto fit right in.

To the right of Ruso's "grotto," the Domitiansgasse ("Domitian Lane") ascends to the south (fig. 11). As with the Kathodos to the north, the road built between two terraces back to back made walking up the path seem like climbing out of a chasm to get to one's destination. The modern view of this way is much more open, due to the partial collapse of both terraces, but Yegül describes how the street known as the Domitiansgasse was "compressed by the aggressively textured and lofty masses of the two artificial terraces facing each other." He comments that "the southern continuation of the Embolos must have felt like an

---

[35] LONGFELLOW, *Roman Imperialism*, 73.

[36] I will not address the question of the origin of the statuary used in this group. Casts of the figures are on display as a pediment group in the Selçuk museum courtyard, reflecting the argument of BERNARD ANDREAE that these statues were originally intended for the pediment of the temple in the center of the state agora, which he sees as a Dionysus temple built by order of Mark Antony ("Vorschlag für eine Rekonstruktion der Polyphemgruppe von Ephesos," in *Festschrift für Frank Brommer*, ed. URSULA HÖCKMANN and ANTJE KRUG [Mainz: von Zabern, 1977], 1–11). LONGFELLOW reviews ANDREAE's theory and more recent analysis that has raised serious questions about the reconstruction and the point of origin for the statue group (*Roman Imperialism*, 68–72). MASCHEK ("Domitian und Polyphem," 293–98) also challenges the interpretation of ANDREAE and its influence.

[37] LONGFELLOW, *Roman Imperialism*, 74.

urban canyon."[38] One can imagine that it would have been a significant spatial change in leaving the Domitiansplatz and climbing to the less-enclosed spaces of the Upper Agora. To the west of the Domitiansgasse stand the reconstructed façade elements on the north face of the Flavian temple terrace (fig. 12).[39] Discussion about the final design and even the dating of the façade continues,[40] but there can be no argument with Maschek's assessment that the terrace and façade formed, "an exceptionally prestigious architectural design" (eine außergewöhnlich repräsentative architektonische Formgebung).[41]

Given that this was the main pedestrian entrance to the temenos of the Flavian Emperors, it is safe to assume that from the beginning there would have been some kind of decorative façade to mask the vaulting of the platform and the side of the terrace. The 10 m high reconstructed elements offer a possible view of what that covering might have been like (fig. 12), but as Maschek concludes, "in the final analysis, the question of appearance and dimensions of the north façade … remains unclear."[42]

This brings us back to the question of how the space of the Domitiansplatz would have been perceived by the people who occupied it. In part, the answer to this question depends on both the physical approach to the space, and the circumstances of use. With these factors in mind, the geophysical position of the square combined with the built environment would have produced some obvious and unavoidable consequences.

The Domitiansplatz stands near the central point of the valley pinched between Bülbül Dağ and Panayır Dağ, and the great height of the built architecture of the square serves to make that sense of enclosure feel even more severe. The

---

[38] YEGÜL, "Street Experience," 105.

[39] The Flavian Temple and its massive platform would have been most remarkable, both for its size and for the huge area of the town that must have been demolished to enable its construction. While examining the history of scholarship by which the terrace and temple came to be associated with Domitian and the Flavians, MASCHEK notes that the project would have required an inordinate amount of cooperation among the civic authorities (MASCHEK, "Domitian und Polyphem," 285).

[40] HILKE THÜR, "Domitian's Terrace with Imperial Temple and Altar," in *Ephesus: The New Guide*, 92. BURRELL (*Neokoroi*, 63–64) mentions several times that the façade may date as late as the mid-second century, but does not discuss the evidence for this claim.

[41] MASCHEK, "Domitian und Polyphem," 284.

[42] MASCHEK, "Domitian und Polyphem," 284. The suggestion that the façade represents a line of captive figures (THÜR, "Domitian's Terrace," 92) brings up comparisons with other such monuments in Corinth and Rome, as well as the much more elaborately decorated, multi-storied entryway to the Sebasteion in Aphrodisias. As the anastylosis work shows so well, when people approached the monument at Aphrodisias, they saw a visual account of the mythological and historical greatness of Rome lining the porticoes on either side of them. Captive figures were also included as part of a display of subject nations. Cf. R. R. R. SMITH, "The Imperial Reliefs from the Sebasteion at Aphrodisias," *JRS* 77 (1987): 88–138. If the figures lining the south side of Domitiansplatz are meant to represent similar captive images, their lofty perch above the square would have likewise advertised the sweeping power of Rome and the emperor.

Memmius Monument as reconstructed by Outschar is nearly 4.5 m tall. On the uphill side of the square, the fountain of Domitian/Pollio checks in at 14 m, and it would have been dwarfed by the even more massive Chalcidicum to the north. The terrace on the south side of the square was faced with the aforementioned façade approximately 10.4 m high, and above that stood the northern colonnade of the temenos of the Temple to the Flavian Emperors. The western side of the square has not been excavated, but the terrace to the south would have continued to the west until it blended into the slopes of Bülbül Dağ. Everyone would have been slight of stature compared to this built environment. Since all of these components were not developed at the same time, it cannot be seen as an intentional design scheme, but certainly the builders of the Flavian terrace and façade understood that their design was taking advantage of a very special piece of real estate. When they replaced whatever structures stood on the side of the hill with the massive terrace and northern colonnade, they basically extended the slope of Bülbül Dağ and made it vertical. Peter Scherrer includes the Domitiansplatz in his study of "Die Stadt als Festplatz," and certainly this area fits his description of how civic officials could "create an all embracing network from seemingly different buildings … to blend newer and more politically current construction programs with those of the former emperor," leading to "awe-inspiring priorities." As a result of these efforts, citizens and visitors to the city "constantly held the presence and concern of the Emperor before their eyes, not just during imperial festivals but in everyday life as well."[43]

Finally, it remains to consider three different views of the Domitiansplatz, based on the route taken to approach the space: one way coming up the Embolos from the west, one coming down from the east on the sacred road behind the Basilica Stoa, and one coming down the hill from the south on the Domitiansgasse.

The first perspective, heading east up the Embolos, is one possible route for the procession of the Artemisia Festival. In this very plausible reconstruction, the procession would enter through the Koressos Gate, stop at the theater, and then take a left on the Embolos, pass through the Domitiansplatz, and ascend on the Kathodos to the area that eventually becomes the upper agora, eventually passing out of the city through the Magnesian Gate. This path is described quite vividly by Yegül in his chapter on the streets of Ephesos. Yegül describes the view straight up the Embolos and the "exceptionally prominent position" given to the Memmius Monument which features a "remarkable layering of urban history."[44] He then heads up the Kathodos, or as he calls it the Clivus Sacer, to the Upper Agora without comment. He returns later to the square which he describes as follows:

---

[43] Peter Scherrer, "Die Stadt als Festplatz: Das Beispiel der ephesischen Bauprogramme rund um die Kaiserneokorien Domitians und Hadrians," in *Festrituale in der römischen Kaiserzeit*, ed. Jörg Rüpke, STAC 48 (Tübingen: Mohr Siebeck, 2008), 35–65.

[44] Yegül, "Street Experience," 103.

The clearing at the east end of the Embolos, dubbed the Plaza of Domitian, represents a very different kind of space and a different kind of experience from the open space of the State Agora above. The area is relatively low. In antiquity it was closed in by the towering terrace of the Temple of Domitian on the south and west, and the rising embankment of the agora terrace on the east. The advancing visitor's glance … would have been arrested by the projecting bulk of the rusticated ashlar substructure supporting the west end of the basilica.

Yegül also describes the "deep, cavelike opening" of the Domitian fountain "carved into the mass of the agora terrace," and he suggests:

The sound of the falling water, echoing in the shadowy depths of the artificial cavern, the cool spray filling the air, and the shimmering and distorted reflections of the statuary on the water's surface must have left an impression on a hot summer day, inviting every citizen into this memorable theater of the street.[45]

After some equally flowery speculation on the design and function of the non-extant Niche Monument that he locates at the approximate center of the "irregular and richly articulated periphery of the square," he concludes by talking about the canyon-like appearance of the Domitansgasse mentioned above. While Yegül's language here is a bit over the top, I think he does a good job of describing the experience of someone entering the square from the west. In fact, I would take his language of "urban canyon" and extend it to the entire area of the Domitiansplatz. As one would have come up into the square the perception would have been of great height all around and a growing sense of confinement. By the time someone reached the tight spaces of either the Kathodos, the cave-like fountain, or the Domitiansgasse, he or she would have become somewhat acclimated to the canyon effect. Of course people coming down the hill would have had the opposite experience of leaving behind the ominously tall buildings and terraces and seeing the relatively open space in front of them.

The second perspective follows someone who descends on the Kathodos from the Upper Agora, follows the road behind the Basilica Stoa, and arrives at the square from the east. According to Guy Rogers, this is the route taken by participants in the multiple processions prescribed by the Salutaris inscription in the early second century. Rogers sees the parade of statues entering from the Magnesian Gate, cutting across the Upper Agora, going through the Basilica Stoa and passing by the Prytaneion before descending to the square. Once there, Rogers suggests that the Roman monuments would have served to underline the broader purpose of the endowment of Salutaris, namely to show an appreciation for the mythical and historical traditions of the city while at the same time not forgetting about the new founding figures who were represented in the monuments around the Domitiansplatz.[46]

---

[45] Yegül, "Street Experience," 105.
[46] Rogers, *Sacred Identity*, 83–86.

Of course, by the time of the Salutaris endowment in 104 CE, Domitian's place in the cityscape and in the empire would have been largely obliterated. Even though the big temple up on the terrace was known more generically as the Temple of the Flavian Emperors, it would have been less than ten years since the end of Domitian's reign. The current emperor Trajan was of course represented in the procession. The Domitian Fountain would have been largely out of sight from this perspective, unless people walked around the Chalicidicum foundation to get to it, or turned around to look back at it as they left the square. It would not be surprising, however, if the Salutaris procession avoided that strange artificial grotto with the bizarre statuary display, even after the name of Domitian had been scratched off of it. The terrace of the Flavian temple was, of course, unavoidable, and recognition of the emperors was an important part of the endowment. After acknowledging the previous dynasty, however, the Salutaris procession could carry statues of the current emperor, Trajan, along with Artemis, past the Memmius Monument and down the hill to the lower city center.

Finally, the third path to the square would be down the hill from the south. Yegül's reference to the urban canyon feeling of this road has already been mentioned. This route between the Upper Agora terrace to the east and the terrace for the Temple of the Flavian Emperors on the west is not usually associated with any of the known festivals of Ephesos, but a case can be made for its use in processions celebrating the cult of the Flavian Emperors. If victims were led in through the Magnesian Gate, they would have presumably marched in straight from the gate, and directly through the southernmost entrance on the east face of the terrace. The question then becomes, what about the people participating in the procession. Did they follow the cattle in through the opening in the East Stoa of the Flavian terrace, or did they take a right, and follow the Domitiansgasse down to the plaza, and then enter through the stairway leading up to the terrace from the north. The use of this route cannot be proven, but it certainly would have contributed to a very dramatic processional way.

The sharp decline of the Domitiansgasse would have led to a feeling of descent into the increasingly canyon-like and dark space of the square below. At the bottom of this path, the participant encountered the sights and sounds of Ruso's pseudo-underground grotto, the Fountain of Domitian. The fantastic statuary group of the fountain could speak to the participants in a number of ways. On one level, Odysseus was also known for a subterranean journey, and encountering him in this dark, wet place made perfect sense. At the same time, these images of ancient Greek heroes would have been complemented by the memorials to notable, deceased Romans who had brought water and other benefactions to the city.

After this encounter, the processants would turn and recognize that they stood under the gaze of the figures on the terrace façade, before stepping into the even darker space of the portico in front of the stairway. Torches would have been necessary for this part of the journey, in order to negotiate the stairway and begin the ascent. The fact that the stairway splits into two could have been necessary in order to break the procession according to cultic hierarchy or social position. After this division, both lines of worshippers would have come out into the light of the temenos, and experienced a sudden revealing of the temple and most importantly the altar with the victims patiently waiting for the ceremony to begin.[47]

While this reconstruction of the procession and the routing through Domitiansplatz must remain hypothetical, it does take advantage of the physical layout of the square and its surroundings. The most compelling argument for some kind of ritual procession from the square below is the existence of the staircase. If the procession came right through the entrance on the southeast corner of the Flavian terrace, why spend the time and money to build the entry from the square? It can also be argued that moving worshippers through the descent into the relative darkness of the square and into the very dark space inside the portico before climbing the dim staircase and emerging into the light of the courtyard would highlight the "awe-inspiring priorities" mentioned by Scherrer,[48] a kind of first century special effects. The fact that the stairway opens to the temenos on axis with the altar would make the effect complete.

Ascent to worship at a high place is, of course, a common part of ancient cultic practice from Jerusalem, to Athens, to Rome. Descent to a subterranean (or pseudo-subterranean) space is less common but is found in places like the Asklepieion and the Red Hall in Pergamum, Mithras sanctuaries in Rome and elsewhere, the Serapis sanctuary in Thessalonike, and the Nekyomanteion in western Greece. The proposed route for the procession to the Flavian temenos takes advantage of the topography and the built environment to include both a descent and then a dramatic approach to, and revelation of, the sacred space.

Viewing the city with Scherrer as "Festplatz," allows for a reconsideration of the Domitiansplatz and how it functioned as an important intersection in the city, as a collection of monuments commemorating important historical and mythological figures, and as a ceremonial space within specific ritual contexts.

---

[47] A similar scenario would also work in the (to me) less likely case that the procession for the Flavian Emperors came through the entire city and up the Embolos from the west. The victims could then proceed south up the Domitiangasse to the entrance at the southeast corner of the temenos, while the human participants could go through the façade and ascend the staircase into the temple compound.

[48] SCHERRER, "Stadt als Festplatz," 35–65.

Figure 1: Composite View of the Domitiansplatz, View from the Southwest.
©James Walters.

Figure 2: Partially Reconstructed Memmius Monument from the South.
©Daniel Schowalter

Figure 3: Tympanum from Memmius Monument Superstructure from North.
©Daniel Schowalter

Figure 4: Sacred Way or "Kathodos" with Two Sculpted Bases at Entrance to the
Domitiansplatz. ©Daniel Schowalter

Figure 5: Chalcidicum from Southwest. ©Daniel Schowalter

Figure 6: Inscription Blocks from Chalcidicum. ©Daniel Schowalter

Figure 7: Pollio Monument from West. ©Daniel Schowalter

Figure 8: Fountain of Domitian Incorporating Pollio Monument. ©Daniel Schowalter

Figure 9: Fountain of Domitian, Second Story Fountain Court from East.
©Daniel Schowalter

Figure 10: Fountain of Domitian, Reconstructed Pillars and Arch from West.
©Daniel Schowalter

Figure 11: Domitiansgasse from North. ©Daniel Schowalter

Figure 12: Partially Reconstructed Façade from Flavian Temple Platform from North.
©Daniel Schowalter

II. Ephesos in Christian Memory

Reading Ephesians in Ephesos

A Letter to Pauline *and* Johannine Christ-followers?[1]

Paul Trebilco

A. Introduction

Evidence from the book that we call *The Epistle to the Ephesians* has often been excluded from discussions about the life of the early Christ-followers in Ephesos because of the difficult issue of determining the original provenance for this letter.[2] However, in his commentary on Ephesians, John Muddiman has suggested that Ephesians was written to Pauline *and* Johannine Christ-followers *in* Ephesos.[3] In Muddiman's view, one of the reasons that Ephesians was written

---

[1] I am enormously grateful to RICHARD E. OSTER for his scholarly writing, particularly his work on Ephesos, from which I have learned so much. I am delighted to have the opportunity to write this essay in his honor, as a small token of my appreciation.

[2] HELMUT KOESTER, "Ephesos in Early Christian Literature," in *Ephesos, Metropolis of Asia: An Interdisciplinary Approach to its Archaeology, Religion, and Culture*, ed. HELMUT KOESTER, HTS 41 (Valley Forge: Trinity Press International, 1995), 122, 124; MATTHIAS GÜNTHER, *Die Frühgeschichte des Christentums in Ephesus*, Arbeiten zur Religion und Geschichte des Urchristentums 1 (Frankfurt am Main: Peter Lang, 1995), 68–70; STEPHAN WITETSCHEK, *Ephesische Enthüllungen 1: Frühe Christen in einer antiken Grossstadt: zugleich ein Beitrag zur Frage nach den Kontexten der Johannesapokalypse*, BTS 6 (Leuven: Peeters, 2008), 208–20; MIKAEL TELLBE, *Christ-believers in Ephesus: A Textual Analysis of Early Christian Identity Formation in a Local Perspective*, WUNT 1.242 (Tübingen: Mohr Siebeck, 2009), 54, exclude Ephesians from their discussion of Christ-followers in Ephesos. RICK STRELAN, *Paul, Artemis, and the Jews in Ephesus*, BZNW 80 (Berlin: Walter de Gruyter, 1996), 155–62, 291–93; WERNER THIESSEN, *Christen in Ephesus: Die historische und theologische Situation in vorpaulinischer und paulinischer Zeit und zur Zeit der Apostelgeschichte und der Pastoralbriefe*, Texte und Arbeiten zum neutestamentlichen Zeitalter 12 (Tübingen: Francke Verlag, 1995), 348–50; JEROME MURPHY-O'CONNOR, *St. Paul's Ephesus: Texts and Archaeology* (Collegeville: Liturgical Press, 2008), 231–33, draw on Ephesians in their studies.

[3] As JOHN MUDDIMAN, *The Epistle to the Ephesians*, BNTC (London: Continuum, 2001), 37, notes, this is not a new suggestion since J. MOFFATT, *An Introduction to the Literature of the New Testament* (Edinburgh: T&T Clark, 1911), 385, called attention to what he regarded as similarities between Ephesians and John's Gospel and went on to say "These links of thought and language have led one critic to remark that 'it would be a tenable view that the writer [of Ephesians] was the author of the Fourth gospel, writing in the name of St. Paul' (Lock, *DB*. i. 717), but the likelihood is that the unknown *auctor ad Ephesios* was a Paulinist who breathed the at-

was to appeal to Johannine Christ-followers and to assure them that "unity with the Gentile churches of Paul's foundation will not dilute or compromise their [Johannine] faith or reduce them to second-class citizens. On the contrary, they will contribute more to the union than they receive."[4] Accordingly, Ephesians "is intended to enlist the authority of Paul to enlarge the scope of Pauline Christianity in order to accommodate new members from the Johannine circle."[5] For Muddiman, the author of Ephesians, who was a Pauline disciple, interacted with and was influenced by Johannine literature when writing the letter. The author has incorporated Johannine language and imagery in his letter, both to appeal to these Johannine readers and to show them that their particular Johannine emphases are currently valued and will continue to be valued.

In this paper I hope to show that this view is plausible, although because of the nature of the evidence, it cannot be confirmed as more than that. I also hope to argue for this view in a more thorough-going way than Muddiman was able to do in his commentary.[6]

---

mosphere in which the Johannine literature afterwards took shape." J. O. F. MURRAY, *The Epistle of Paul the Apostle to the Ephesians*, CGTSC (Cambridge: Cambridge University Press, 1914), lxxxviii–xci, also argues for an affinity between Ephesians and John's Gospel. JOHN C. KIRBY, *Ephesians: Baptism and Pentecost: An Inquiry into the Structure and Purpose of the Epistle to the Ephesians* (London: SPCK, 1968), 166–68, does likewise, but thinks (167–68) that "John is not copying from Ephesians here, nor vice versa; both authors are copying from the liturgical tradition" of the Ephesian church. C. K. BARRETT, *The Gospel According to St. John: An Introduction with Commentary and Notes on the Greek Text*, 2nd ed. (London: SPCK: 1978), 62, noted that "Ephesians, though in form entirely different, reveals a number of points of contact with John," and went on to list the areas dealt with here, along with others (62–63). He thought these revealed (62 n. 3) "a common background of thought." URBAN C. VON WAHLDE, *The Gospel and Letters of John*, 3 vols., ECC (Grand Rapids: Eerdmans, 2010), 1:392–93, cites these connections between John and Ephesians with approval, as evidence for Ephesos as the place of composition of what he regards as the third edition of John. MURPHY-O'CONNOR, *St. Paul's Ephesus*, 231–33, agrees with the view of MUDDIMAN. Cf. ERNEST BEST, *A Critical and Exegetical Commentary on Ephesians*, ICC (Edinburgh: T&T Clark, 1998), 18, who considers some "similarities of thought but not wording" between Ephesians and the Johannine literature but comments that "lack of verbal similarity compels the rejection of literary dependence." But in my view a consideration of thematic connections in detail leads to a different conclusion.

[4] MUDDIMAN, *Ephesians*, 39.

[5] MUDDIMAN, *Ephesians*, 37.

[6] Of course there have been numerous suggestions relating to why the author of Ephesians wrote the letter. See for example, BEST, *Ephesians*, ICC, 63–75; CLINTON E. ARNOLD, *Ephesians*, Zondervan Exegetical Commentary on the New Testament (Grand Rapids: Zondervan, 2010), 41–46; STEPHEN E. FOWL, *Ephesians: A Commentary*, NTL (Louisville: Westminster John Knox Press, 2012), 28–30.

B. Does Ephesians Belong in Ephesos?

Clearly some New Testament data indisputably relate to Ephesos. Here we can think of 1 Cor 15:32; 16:8; Acts 18:18–20:38; Rev 2:1–7. In my view, strong arguments can be made that 1 and 2 Timothy were written to Ephesos around 80–100 CE,[7] and that Ephesos was the location of the writer of John's Gospel and the recipients of the Johannine Letters, around 80–100 CE.[8] But can Ephesians be located in Ephesos? Can we use it in our discussions about Christ-followers in the city?

With Ephesians, both Pauline authorship and Ephesos as the original destination are disputed. Some of the pertinent data here are that the phrase ἐν Ἐφέσῳ is omitted from some manuscripts of Eph 1:1,[9] that Eph 1:15 and 3:2–4 speak of Paul "having heard" of the faith of the addressees but not knowing it directly and of the addressees having heard of Paul's mission,[10] and also the lack of greetings to a church Paul knew well. None of this seems to fit Ephesos, where, according to Acts, Paul worked among the Christ-followers for over two years and three months (Acts 19:8, 10).

This means that, if the letter was by Paul, then it is unlikely to have been sent to Ephesos originally,[11] and the omission of ἐν Ἐφέσῳ in some manuscripts of Eph 1:1 is the original reading. Other explanations of the location of its original addressees are then sought – that it was originally sent to some other place or places,[12] or that it was a circular letter.[13]

---

[7] See 1 Tim 1:3; 2 Tim 1:18; 4:12; see further PAUL R. TREBILCO, *The Early Christians in Ephesus from Paul to Ignatius*, WUNT 1.166 (Tübingen: Mohr Siebeck, 2004), 197–236.

[8] See section C.II below. Although not explored in detail here, the Church of St. John towers over the site and is built from the spolia of the Temple of Artemis. Of note, there were predecessor structures before the present Justinianic building. These earlier structures reflect ancient and strong oral traditions about the burial of John in Ephesos.

[9] See ERNEST BEST, *Essays on Ephesians* (Edinburgh: T&T Clark, 1997), 2–9; ROGER L. OMANSON, *A Textual Guide to the Greek New Testament: An Adaptation of Bruce M. Metzger's Textual Commentary for the Needs of Translators* (Stuttgart: Deutsche Bibelgesellschaft, 2006), 384–85. The words ἐν Ἐφέσῳ are missing from P[46], א*, B*, 6, 424c, 1739, and the texts used by Origen, Basil, and Tertullian do not explicitly quote the words. Marcion's text probably also omitted the reference to Ephesos. Further, the position of ἐν Ἐφέσῳ in the vast majority of manuscripts makes the text difficult to understand grammatically. However, even those texts that omit ἐν Ἐφέσῳ retain the reference to Ephesos in the superscription; see further BEST, *Ephesians*, ICC, 98; MUDDIMAN, *Ephesians*, 35.

[10] See also Eph 4:21.

[11] Although some scholars do argue for Pauline authorship to Ephesos.

[12] For example, that it was sent to Hierapolis and Laodicea; see ANDREW T. LINCOLN, *Ephesians*, WBC (Dallas: Word Books, 1990), 3–4.

[13] This theory was propounded by E. J. GOODSPEED, *The Meaning of Ephesians* (Chicago: University of Chicago Press, 1933). For convincing rebuttals of Goodspeed's view see JAMES I. COOK, *Edgar Johnson Goodspeed: Articulate Scholar*, BSNA 4 (Chico, CA: Scholars Press, 1981), 9–21; BEST, *Ephesians*, ICC, 66.

However, I agree with many other scholars who argue on other grounds that the letter was not by Paul, but rather was written by a Pauline disciple.[14] The options then become two-fold. Firstly, that the letter was written to Ephesos (and so ἐν Ἐφέσῳ is the original reading in Eph 1:1), and we must explain the omission of ἐν Ἐφέσῳ in some manuscripts of Eph 1:1 and how a Paulinist could have written Eph 1:15 and 3:2–4. *Or* secondly, that the letter was written to somewhere other than Ephesos, which explains the omission in Eph 1:1 and the contents of Eph 1:15 and 3:2–4, but we need to explain how the letter became connected to Ephesos.

In his recent commentary, Muddiman has argued that the letter was originally written by a Pauline disciple, writing in Paul's name, *to* Christ-followers in Ephesos. Why then has the author written Eph 1:15 and 3:2–4? Muddiman argues that the author of Ephesians used an authentic Pauline Letter to Laodicea as the basis for Ephesians, a letter the author has edited and expanded, and that Eph 1:15 and 3:2–4 "belong to the source he [the author] is using, i. e., the letter of Paul from Ephesus to Laodicea [and so] it is much easier … to explain their retention in the letter"[15] of Ephesians, which Muddiman thinks is presented as written from Rome to Ephesos.

Further, for a letter written after Paul's time by a Pauline disciple some specified destination would be needed, and Muddiman thinks the best explanation of the manuscript evidence is that it was to Ephesos. After all, *only* the reading ἐν Ἐφέσῳ as the original address has support in the great majority of Greek manuscripts, versions, and most early Fathers, with the only exception being Marcion's claim that the letter was addressed to the Laodiceans. Further, even though ἐν Ἐφέσῳ is missing from key manuscripts as we have noted, the texts with superscripts all have "to the Ephesians" as that superscript.[16] Muddiman

---

[14] Of course, this is greatly debated. For the case that Ephesians is not by Paul, see for example, LINCOLN, *Ephesians*, lix–lxxiii; BEST, *Ephesians*, ICC, 6–40; MUDDIMAN, *Ephesians*, 2–47. For the case that Ephesians is by Paul see for example, HAROLD W. HOEHNER, *Ephesians: An Exegetical Commentary* (Grand Rapids: Baker Academic 2002), 2–61; ARNOLD, *Ephesians*, 46–50. FOWL, *Ephesians*, 9–28, discusses the issue and concludes: "As a matter of historical interest, I find the arguments so finely balanced that my decisions about this could vary from day to day" (28).

[15] MUDDIMAN, *Ephesians*, 35; see also 20–31, 298. On 1:15 he writes: "The later writer was not intending to create a coherent literary fiction, or he would have avoided the mistake (1.15) of having Paul address the saints at Ephesos as though he had never met them. He has simply shaved off some specifics at the beginning and end of the letter to make it more universally applicable and built on the remainder" (24). Accordingly, MUDDIMAN does not think that Colossians is a source for Ephesians. That Marcion called his version of Ephesians "Laodiceans" is taken as supporting this view; see MUDDIMAN, *Ephesians*, 27–29. But note that the argument pursued in this paper – that it is plausible that Ephesians was written to Pauline and Johannine readers – does not depend on accepting MUDDIMAN's view that an authentic Pauline Letter to Laodicea was the basis for Ephesians, since other explanations have been offered for Eph 1:15 and 3:2–3, particularly by those who argue Ephesians is Pauline and to Ephesos. Such arguments can also be relevant if the letter is understood to be by a Pauline disciple.

[16] See MUDDIMAN, *Ephesians*, 59–62; see also ARNOLD, *Ephesians*, 27.

can then give a range of explanations as to why ἐν Ἐφέσῳ was omitted in some manuscripts.[17] He argues then that it remains possible for us to think that Ephesians was written to Ephesos – but by a Pauline disciple rather than by Paul. A number of other scholars also argue that the letter was written to Ephesos.[18]

As noted above, it has often been argued that Ephesians is a circular letter, partly because of its general nature.[19] However, although Ephesians is much more general than, for example, Galatians, Muddiman contends that it still contains quite specific material. Firstly, in 1:15 Paul is said to have heard of their faith, which implies that he did not know a particular group personally. Secondly, in 3:2–4 it is said that there was an earlier document that the readers will soon be able to read. Thirdly, in 6:21–22, it is said that Tychicus, who has been sent with the letter, will add a verbal report about Paul. These points "are unlikely to be true of all the possible destinations of a circular letter."[20]

Given these indications of a *specific readership*, other points in the letter can be seen as being more focused on the concerns and issues of a particular audience than is often thought. Note Eph 4:14, 17, 19–20; 5:3, 6–7:

4:14We must no longer be children, tossed to and fro and blown about by every wind of doctrine, by people's trickery, by their craftiness in deceitful scheming. ... 17Now this I affirm and insist on in the Lord: you must no longer live as the Gentiles live, in the futility of their minds. ... 19They have lost all sensitivity and have abandoned themselves to licentiousness, greedy to practice every kind of impurity. 20That is not the way you learned Christ! ... 5:3But fornication and impurity of any kind, or greed, must not even be mentioned among you, as is proper among saints. ... 6Let no one deceive you with empty

---

17 MUDDIMAN, *Ephesians*, 62. The most likely explanation is that a scribe omitted the place name to make the text more relevant to his own context. This is comparable to the omission of "in Rome" from Rom 1:7 in several manuscripts. Or it could be that a scribe perceived the tension between "in Ephesos" in 1:1 and Eph 1:15 and so omitted the former. Muddiman adds two other possibilities. See also DAVID A. BLACK, "The Peculiarities of Ephesians and the Ephesian Address," *Grace Theological Journal* 2 (1981): 67–69; ARNOLD, *Ephesians*, 28. Cf. ERNEST BEST, "Recipients and Title of the Letter to the Ephesians: Why and When the Designation 'Ephesians'?" *ANRW* 2.25.4: 3247–79.

18 See HANS CONZELMANN in JÜRGEN BECKER, HANS CONZELMANN, and GERHARD FRIEDRICH, *Die Briefe an die Galater, Epheser, Philipper, Kolosser, Thessalonicher und Philemon*, 3rd ed., NTD 8 (Göttingen: Vandenhoeck & Ruprecht, 1985), 89; JOACHIM GNILKA, *Der Epheserbrief*, 3rd ed., HTKNT 10.2 (Freiburg: Herder, 1982), 7; HOEHNER, *Ephesians*, 144–48; FRANK THIELMAN, *Theology of the New Testament: A Canonical and Synthetic Approach* (Grand Rapids: Zondervan, 2005), 393 and n. 1; FRANK THIELMAN, *Ephesians*, BECNT (Grand Rapids: Baker Academic, 2010), 11–16; JOHN PAUL HEIL, *Ephesians: Empowerment to Walk in Love for the Unity of All in Christ*, SBLStBL 13 (Atlanta: SBL, 2007), 6–9; ARNOLD, *Ephesians*, 27–29; RAINER SCHWINDT, *Das Weltbild des Epheserbriefes: Eine religionsgeschichtlich-exegetische Studie*, WUNT 1.148 (Tübingen: Mohr Siebeck, 2002), 55–62.

19 This view has numerous problems; see for example BLACK, "The Peculiarities of Ephesians," 61–62.

20 MUDDIMAN, *Ephesians*, 61. See RALPH P. MARTIN, "An Epistle in Search of a Life-Setting," *ExpTim* 79 (1968): 297: "the author does have a certain group of persons in mind and speaks to them in the second person of the verbs he uses." See also FOWL, *Ephesians*, 28–30.

words, for because of these things the wrath of God comes on those who are disobedient. [7]Therefore do not be associated with them.[21]

If there were *no* indications at all that the letter was addressed to a particular group, then these verses might be able to be regarded as general paraenesis. But given the other indications of specificity in 1:15; 3:2–4; 6:21–22, these additional verses can be seen to involve mention of or polemic against certain issues of life-style and theology that the readers were facing.[22]

This evidence suggests then that the letter was written to one destination – and it is most likely that this is Ephesos.

C. Pauline and Johannine Christ-followers in Ephesos

If we grant that the original recipients of Ephesians were in Ephesos, then what is the author's message to these Christ-followers? A range of scholars have suggested that there were a number of different groups of Christ-followers in Ephesos from a comparatively early stage in the growth of the movement. For example, Koester argues that in Ephesos at the end of the first century there were followers of John the Baptist, a group of Christ-followers owing allegiance to Apollos, a Pauline church, a prophetic conventicle to which John wrote the Revelation, and the Nicolaitans.[23]

---

[21] Translations are from the NRSV unless otherwise noted.

[22] See MARTIN, "Epistle," 297–99; WILLIAM S. CAMPBELL, "Unity and Diversity in the Church: Transformed Identities and the Peace of Christ in Ephesians," *Transformation: An International Journal of Holistic Mission Studies* 25 (2008): 23. It is also possible that the stress on unity of Jew and Gentile in one body in Christ is because of the specific issue of animosity of Gentile Christ-followers towards Jewish Christ-followers among the readers. Hence the letter emphasizes that Gentile believers need to appreciate fully the Jewish heritage of their new-found faith. See further ARNOLD, *Ephesians*, 44, and the literature referred to there; but on this view see also BEST, *Ephesians*, ICC, 68–69. MUDDIMAN, *Ephesians*, 39, thinks that Paul's churches are mainly Gentile while Johannine Christianity is mainly Jewish; this would explain a passage like Eph 2:11–22. However, in my view we are unable to determine the ethnic composition of readers of John's Gospel or of 1–3 John, and so cannot say that Johannine Christ-followers were predominantly Jewish. This is because Gentiles could come to theological perspectives that reflected a strongly Jewish Christ-follower-perspective and Jews could come to theological perspectives that reflected a strongly Gentile Christ-follower-perspective. But Eph 2:11–22 would remain relevant to both Jewish and Gentile Christ-followers who were readers of John.

[23] See KOESTER, "Ephesos in Early Christian Literature," 119–40. TELLBE, *Christ-believers in Ephesus*, 3–22, gives a summary of the views of eight scholars. Others have argued for what can be called the "merger" or "takeover" model, which would involve there being only one community of Christ-followers in the city at any one time. However, this is very unlikely apart from the earliest period; on this see TREBILCO, *Early Christians*, 349–530. TELLBE, *Christ-believers in Ephesus*, 47–52, rejects the view that we can reconstruct groups (such as Pauline and Johannine communities) that are addressed by texts and prefers to discuss the ways that texts represent different perspectives.

As noted above, in Muddiman's view there were at least Pauline and Johannine Christ-followers in Ephesos, and Ephesians was written to both of these groups in the city. In the letter, the Pauline author includes Johannine imagery and language to appeal to these Johannine Christ-followers. Before considering this in more detail, I need to first put the case that there were both Pauline and Johannine Christ-followers in the city.

I. Pauline Christ-followers in Ephesos?

Paul informs us about at least two house churches in Ephesos in 1 Cor 16:19–20; at least in part these resulted from the "effective work" of which he writes in 1 Cor 16:8.[24] Our further information for the early period in Ephesos comes from Acts.[25] In my view, we learn from Acts 18:27 of a pre-Pauline group of Jewish Christ-followers of an unknown background and then from Acts 19:1–7 of the "Ephesian twelve" who seem to have previously been disciples of John the Baptist. We also learn of other conversions, amongst both Jews (Acts 19:9) and Gentiles (Acts 19:9–41). Paul worked in Ephesos for over two years and three months (Acts 19:8, 10), and by the end of this period the majority of the community of Christ-followers had probably been converted through his ministry, or through that of associates like Prisca and Aquila. We can suggest then that by around 55 CE most of the Christ-followers in Ephesos were "Pauline."

In my view, 1 and 2 Timothy are to be dated after Paul's life, probably between 80–100 CE, and are written to Christ-followers in the city of Ephesos who see themselves in the Pauline tradition, as is evident by the author of 1 and 2 Timothy writing in Paul's name, by what is said about Paul in the letters, and by their extensive use of Pauline tradition. These letters show that the Pauline tradition continued to be valued in Ephesos.[26] Between around 105–110 CE Ignatius wrote to Christ-followers who know of and value Paul.[27]

It is reasonable to think then that if Ephesians was written by a Pauline disciple to Ephesos, that at least some of those Christ-followers would think of themselves as in the Pauline tradition. That a Pauline disciple chose to write Ephesians in Paul's name shows that he thinks Paul still has significant influence and credibility in Ephesos among the readers.

---

[24] On the material relating to Ephesos in Paul's letters see TREBILCO, *Early Christians*, 53–103.

[25] On the Acts material relating to Ephesos see TREBILCO, *Early Christians*, 104–96. There I argue for it being broadly historical.

[26] On the Pastorals see TREBILCO, *Early Christians*, 197–236.

[27] See Ign. *Eph.* 12.2; see also TREBILCO, *Early Christians*, 628–47, where I suggest that Ign. *Eph.* 12.2 is compatible with seeing the addressees as all Ephesian Christ-followers, who in Ignatius' view can all trace their spiritual lineage back to Paul.

Further evidence of this vitality of Pauline tradition for the author and probably also among the readers can be seen in the use of Pauline expressions and the
prevalence of Pauline theology in Ephesians. For example, Eph 1:5 takes up Rom
8:29 with regard to adoption and predestination, Eph 2:8–9 speaks of salvation
by grace through faith and not works so that no one may boast, drawing on Rom
3:24–28; 4:2, and the imagery of the temple in Eph 2:20–22 is dependent on 1 Cor
3:6, 9–12, 16.[28]

Part of this connection between Ephesians and the Pauline tradition is also
the relationship between Colossians and Ephesians, although the nature of this
relationship is vigorously debated.[29] But for my purposes, the similarity of Colossians and Ephesians is primarily evidence for the strong connection between
Ephesians and the Pauline tradition, of which Colossians is so clearly a part.[30]

II. Johannine Christ-followers in Ephesos?

Although the matter is debated, it seems to me to be very likely that the Gospel
of John was written from Ephesos, probably in the 80s.[31] Our earliest evidence
from a range of sources links John's Gospel with the city. Arguments can be
made that Polycrates, bishop of Ephesos in the last decade of the second century, and Irenaeus both link John's Gospel with the city. It seems likely that Polycarp was the basis for the tradition of the link with Ephesos found in Irenaeus,
which strengthens the credibility of that tradition. We can also argue that Polycarp of Smyrna knew John, the author of the Gospel, which suggests that John

---

[28] See LINCOLN in ANDREW T. LINCOLN and ALEXANDER J. M. WEDDERBURN, *The Theology of the Later Pauline Letters* (Cambridge: Cambridge University Press, 1993), 88, who gives
other examples. See also C. L. MITTON, *The Epistle to the Ephesians: Its Authorship, Origin and
Purpose* (Oxford: Clarendon Press, 1951), 98–158; 279–338; BEST, *Ephesians*, ICC, 25–27. LIN-
COLN in LINCOLN and WEDDERBURN, *Theology*, 87, notes: "Above all, as indicated by his writing in Paul's name, the writer sees himself as a transmitter and interpreter of Pauline tradition."

[29] See for example, LINCOLN in LINCOLN and WEDDERBURN, *Theology*, 84–85. ERNEST
BEST, "Who Used Whom? The Relationship of Ephesians and Colossians," *NTS* 43 (1997): 72–
96, has argued with regard to Colossians and Ephesians that there are difficulties in arguing
that one writer used the letter of the other. He thinks that it is more likely that different authors
who were members of the same Pauline school both drew independently from tradition, which
would be Pauline tradition; see also BEST, *Ephesians*, ICC, 20–25.

[30] For example, πλήρωμα is used of Christ or God in John 1:16 and Eph 1:23; 3:19 (cf.
Eph 1:10; 4:13) but it is found in a similar sense in Col 1:19; 2:9. So this is a case where the relationship of Ephesians and Colossians is probably most significant (whatever that exact relationship might be), rather than the use of πλήρωμα being evidence for the relationship between
Ephesians and John.

[31] For a discussion of the likely date of John's Gospel see GRAHAM N. STANTON, *The Gospels and Jesus*, 2nd ed. (Oxford: Oxford University Press, 2002), 120. RAYMOND E. BROWN, *An
Introduction to the Gospel of John: Edited, Updated, Introduced, and Concluded by* FRANCIS
J. MOLONEY, AYBRL (New Haven: Yale University Press, 2003), 206–15, thinks the evidence
points to a date between 90 and 110 CE.

lived nearby; again this is compatible with Ephesos as John's home. The *Acts of John*, written around 150 CE, provides further evidence for the location of the Gospel in Ephesos. With some confidence then, we can locate John's Gospel in the city.[32]

The author of the Gospel of John[33] also demonstrates reliable knowledge of Galilee and Jerusalem.[34] Thus, it seems likely that John lived in Palestine for quite some time and later travelled to Ephesos. One suggestion here is that he moved to Ephesos around the time of the Jewish War (66–70 CE), perhaps with a group of other Christ-followers.[35] Although we have no direct evidence for the arrival of such a group in Ephesos, it remains a reasonable suggestion. Polycrates also gives evidence that Philip, who had left Jerusalem after the persecution of Stephen and had gone to Caesarea (Acts 8:40, where he was still living some time later, see Acts 21:8–10) emigrated at some point to Hierapolis with his daughters.[36] "John" may well have similarly emigrated to Western Asia Minor, specifically Ephesos, at this time and subsequently written the Fourth Gospel there. Somewhat after the Gospel was completed, and probably in the 90s, 1–3 John were written in the same location as the Gospel, and so are also to be connected to Ephesos and give evidence for a "Johannine movement" in and around the city, perhaps around 100 CE.[37] Accordingly, we have strong evidence that locates Johannine tradition in Western Asia Minor and argues that the Gospel of John

[32] See further TREBILCO, *Early Christians*, 241–63; see also for example CHARLES E. HILL, *The Johannine Corpus in the Early Church* (Oxford: Oxford University Press, 2004), 471–72; VON WAHLDE, *The Gospel and Letters of John*, 1:390–93. BROWN, *Introduction to the Gospel of John*, 206, writes "in my judgment the Ephesus region fits the internal evidence of John best of all the proposals, and is the only site that has ancient attestation."

[33] I would suggest the author was John the Elder, although the point is not critical for this discussion. In my view, John the Elder wrote the Gospel of John and 1–3 John, while a different John wrote Revelation; see TREBILCO, *Early Christians*, 246–67, 293.

[34] On the accurate knowledge in John's Gospel of Galilee and Jerusalem as it was before 70 CE, see RAYMOND E. BROWN, *The Gospel According to John: Introduction, Translation, and Notes*, 2 vols., AYB 29 (New Haven: Yale University Press, 1966) 1:xlii–xliii; BROWN, *Introduction to the Gospel of John*, 200–1.

[35] For evidence of Jewish migration at this time, see *Ant.* 20.256. Here, Josephus, speaking of the Procuratorship of Gessius Florus (64–66 CE), writes: "The ill-fated Jews [of the province of Judaea], unable to endure the devastation by brigands that went on were one and all forced to abandon their own country and flee, for they thought that it would be better to settle among gentiles, no matter where." It seems likely that some of these refugees went to Asia Minor, and Ephesos in particular. See also Josephus, *BJ* 7.410–19; see also THOMAS A. ROBINSON, *The Bauer Thesis Examined: The Geography of Heresy in the Early Christian Church* (Lewiston/Queenston: Edwin Mellen Press, 1988), 98; NILS A. DAHL, *Studies in Ephesians: Introductory Questions, Text- & Edition-Critical Issues, Interpretation of Texts and Themes*, WUNT 1.131 (Tübingen: Mohr Siebeck, 2000), 457; TREBILCO, *Early Christians*, 270–71. Cf. GÜNTHER, *Die Frühgeschichte*, 121, 211.

[36] See Eusebius, *Hist. eccl.* 3.31.3; 5.24.2.

[37] See TREBILCO, *Early Christians*, 263–90. While the Revelation is not written by the same person as the Gospel, it is clearly linked theologically to the Gospel and Letters and shows the ongoing impact of the broader Johannine movement in Western Asia Minor. On the relation-

and 1–3 John were written there. Further, although some modern scholars have argued that John's Gospel is to be located elsewhere, Ephesos is the only location for the Gospel in the traditions of the early Church.[38]

Given that we can make strong arguments for the presence of Pauline and Johannine Christ-followers in the city around the time that we think Ephesians was written,[39] the question then emerges whether Ephesians could have been written to both Pauline and Johannine readers in the city? Are there connections between Ephesians and John's Gospel?[40] But first we need briefly to discuss method.

D. Intertextuality

Can we establish criteria to assist us when seeking to discern whether the author of Ephesians might have known John's Gospel? Intertextuality is of some assistance here, since it gives a well-established method by which we might determine whether there are allusions to John's Gospel in Ephesians.

Intertextuality is concerned with the relationship between texts, particularly the way in which a later text refers to an earlier one, and how this generates meaning for each text. Of course, the author of Ephesians might have quoted John's Gospel directly,[41] or quoted a saying of Jesus in its Johannine form. However, NT letters rarely quote sayings of Jesus, and the author of Ephesians follows this pattern.

There is a broad range of possible ways in which a later text can refer to an earlier one. The clearest is a direct and acknowledged citation, but at times the relationship consists of allusion, echo, or indirect reference. Clearly we will have differing degrees of certainty when identifying such intertextual references. As Hays comments:

The volume of intertextual echo varies in accordance with the semantic distance between the source and the reflecting surface. Quotation, allusion, and echo may be seen as points along a spectrum of intertextual reference, moving from the explicit to the subliminal. As we move farther away from overt citation, the source recedes into the discursive distance, the intertextual relations become less determinate, and the demand placed on the reader's listening powers grows greater. As we near the vanishing point of the echo it inevitably

---

ship between the Revelation and John's Gospel see PIERRE PRIGENT, *Commentary on the Apocalypse of St. John* (Tübingen: Mohr Siebeck, 2001), 36–50.

[38] See RICHARD BAUCKHAM, "Papias and Polycrates on the Origin of the Fourth Gospel," *JTS* 44 (1993): 28.

[39] See section D.I below.

[40] For reasons of space, I do not consider possible connections between Ephesians and 1–3 John and Revelation.

[41] That is, if it had been written; see section D.I.

becomes difficult to decide whether we are really hearing an echo at all, or whether we are only conjuring things out of the murmurings of our own imaginations.[42]

Hays gives seven criteria for determining the presence and meaning of echoes: availability, volume, recurrence, thematic coherence, historical plausibility, history of interpretation, and satisfaction.[43] The crucial criteria in the sort of exercise involved here are availability, volume, and recurrence, and so I will concentrate on these three factors.[44]

I. The Criterion of Availability: Dating

This criterion concerns whether or not the supposed source document was available to the author and/or the original readers? We can give no definitive answer here, since the issue in part revolves around the complex matter of dating and authorship. If Ephesians is by Paul, then it must have been written around 60–62.[45] If this was the case, then any linguistic contact between Ephesians and the Gospel of John might be attributable to John having read the already-written Ephesians. In fact, Abbott suggested this in 1897.[46] However, as already noted, I think Ephesians is written by a Pauline disciple after his death, and can be dated between 80–90 CE.[47]

---

[42] RICHARD B. HAYS, *Echoes of Scripture in the Letters of Paul* (New Haven: Yale University Press, 1989), 23.

[43] See HAYS, *Echoes*, 29–32; see also RICHARD B. HAYS, *The Conversion of the Imagination: Paul as Interpreter of Israel's Scripture* (Grand Rapids: Eerdmans, 2005), 27–45. For another set of criteria see THOMAS L. BRODIE, *The Birthing of the New Testament: The Intertextual Development of the New Testament Writings*, New Testament Monographs 1 (Sheffield: Sheffield Phoenix Press, 2004), 43–49. On method see also THOMAS L. BRODIE, DENNIS R. MACDONALD, and STANLEY E. PORTER, "Conclusion: Problems of Method-Suggested Guidelines," in *The Intertextuality of the Epistles: Explorations of Theory and Practice*, ed. THOMAS L. BRODIE, DENNIS R. MACDONALD, and STANLEY E. PORTER, New Testament Monographs 16 (Sheffield: Sheffield Phoenix Press, 2006), 284–96.

[44] DAVID C. SIM, "Matthew and the Pauline Corpus: A Preliminary Intertextual Study," *JSNT* 31 (2009): 404, focuses on the first two criteria in his study. The criterion of thematic coherence focuses mainly on the question of whether the ideas of the precursor text illuminate the argument in the later text (see HAYS, *Echoes*, 30); since we are mainly considering themes rather than particular passages here, this is less relevant to this study.

[45] See ARNOLD, *Ephesians*, 50–52.

[46] THOMAS K. ABBOTT, *A Critical and Exegetical Commentary on The Epistles to the Ephesians and to the Colossians*, ICC (Edinburgh: T&T Clark, 1897), xxix: "The correspondence between Eph. and the Johannine writings is sufficiently accounted for by the supposition that 'St. John read and valued St. Paul's writings,' as Salmon remarks. This appears strongly confirmed by certain correspondences between the Apocalypse and the Ep. to the Colossians."

[47] See LINCOLN, *Ephesians*, lxxii–lxxiii; LINCOLN in LINCOLN and WEDDERBURN, *Theology*, 86. BEST, *Ephesians*, ICC, thinks there is "a fair possibility that Ignatius knew our Ephesians" and that "there seems little doubt that Polycarp knew our Ephesians" (16) and suggests that the letter was written towards the end of the period from 60–90 CE (35). RUDOLF SCHNACKEN-

In my view, John's Gospel is to be dated between 80–100. Given these tentative dates, the author of Ephesians might have written prior to John's Gospel being completed. However, we need to take note of oral traditions. Most scholars would argue that traditions that were eventually written down in John's Gospel circulated orally first and so were in existence for many years prior to the Gospel being written down, or completed.[48] Accordingly, it is quite likely that an author of a book like Ephesians would have known oral Johannine traditions prior to writing Ephesians, as well as or rather than knowing the actual written Gospel. Hence, the author of Ephesians could be influenced by oral Johannine traditions *prior* to the Gospel being written. Accordingly, dating does *not* solve the issue of the direction of connections or influence, nor does uncertainty about dates of composition undermine this overall discussion. Is it plausible that Ephesians was written to all Christ-followers in Ephesos, including Johannine Christ-followers, and that Ephesians incorporates Johannine traditions and language? Given our imprecision about dating for both documents, this seems a reasonable question to ask.

The probable existence of Johannine traditions in Ephesos prior to the writing of the Gospel also means that, rather than simply looking for allusions to actual passages in John's Gospel in Ephesians, we are rather looking for allusions to broader Johannine themes and theology.

II. *The Criterion of Volume*

This criterion investigates how loud the alleged echo of the earlier text is. It relates to "the degree of explicit repetition of words or syntactical patterns."[49] The "distinctiveness, prominence, or popular familiarity of the precursor text,"[50] and the amount of rhetorical stress given to an echo in the later text are also factors.

We have already noted that there are no clear quotations of John's Gospel in Ephesians, a point that is hardly surprising in itself given the paucity of actual quotations of the canonical gospels in New Testament letters. Accordingly, we are looking for the use of key words and for thematic similarities. When only thematic similarities are present, it becomes more difficult to posit an intertextual relationship.

BURG, *Ephesians: A Commentary* (Edinburgh: T&T Clark, 1991), 33, and MUDDIMAN, *Ephesians*, 35, see 90 CE as the most probable.

[48] See for example BROWN, *Introduction to the Gospel of John*, 62–69. Other scholars also argue for a first, second and sometimes third edition of the Gospel.

[49] HAYS, *Echoes*, 30; see also HAYS, *The Conversion of the Imagination*, 34–37; SIM, "Matthew and the Pauline Corpus," 405.

[50] HAYS, *Conversion of the Imagination*, 36.

In a study of the use of John's Gospel in the second-century churches, Charles Hill makes some important points that are relevant to this discussion.[51] Hill notes that scholars who discuss the use of John's Gospel normally look for clear or explicit quotations of that Gospel by later authors. However, studies of literary dependence or reception in the ancient world have shown that a later author was often *not* concerned with near-flawless reproduction of an earlier text. Rather a later author would introduce deliberate changes into the texts that they quoted. Further, such authors "often consciously adapted the material they quoted or borrowed, for varying reasons."[52] There is also evidence that an author was most scrupulous in quoting or alluding to texts that that author *disagreed with*, and borrowed *more freely* from authors with whom they agreed or felt a strong affinity.[53] What this means is that, if the author of Ephesians did draw on John's Gospel, and did fundamentally agree with much that was said in that Gospel, we should not expect Ephesians to quote the Gospel directly, but rather to allude to it or draw on its ideas quite indirectly. The "volume" then cannot be expected to be "loud."

III. The Criterion of Recurrence

This relates to how often a later text cites or alludes to an earlier text. This criterion could also be called "multiple attestation."[54] Where it is clear that an author regarded a text as particularly important, then "proposed echoes from the same context should be given additional credence."[55] Accordingly, the case presented here is cumulative. If it can be shown that *several* proposed allusions or echoes are reasonably likely, then the strength of the overall argument grows.

IV. Challenges and a Way Forward

This discussion faces some significant challenges. To be completely convincing with regard to our thesis that Ephesians is written to both Pauline and Johannine Christ-followers, we would need to be able to show that in Ephesians, alongside the unsurprising use of Pauline tradition, the author was *also* using concepts and language that could *only* have come from Johannine tradition. To show this we would need to be able to demonstrate that such new concepts and language in Ephesians (that is, new to the Pauline tradition) could *not* have been a natural development from the Pauline tradition, nor could they have come

---

[51] See HILL, *Johannine Corpus*, 67–71. He does not relate this to intertextuality, but his comments remain relevant.

[52] HILL, *Johannine Corpus*, 68.

[53] See HILL, *Johannine Corpus*, 70, and the references given there.

[54] HAYS, *Conversion of the Imagination*, 37.

[55] HAYS, *Echoes*, 30.

from the Jesus tradition, nor from other traditions about Christ which were "in the air" (such as Petrine traditions or those from James), nor could they have been adopted from a Jewish context, nor from the wider environment of Western Asia Minor. To be able to show that an idea *must* have come from a particular source – such as Johannine tradition – and *could not have come* from any other source – is clearly beyond us. But as Hays comments, "In the nature of the case, of course, it is difficult to *prove* things about sources and direct influences, given the paucity of evidence at our disposal."[56]

Further, and more generally, I do not think that the movement of early Christ-followers should be understood to be made up of hermetically sealed silos – a Marcan silo, a Matthean silo, a Pauline silo, a Johannine silo and so on. Rather, I think that the movement should be conceived of as a network of inter-related communities, in frequent communication with one another across space and time and exerting an influence on one another's ideas and development.[57] This makes the sharing of concepts and language proposed here *a priori* more likely. But given such a degree of networking, the identification of just one source for a particular idea is additionally challenging.

Perhaps then one way to proceed is to think of what might *undermine* the suggestion that Ephesians was written to both Pauline and Johannine Christ-followers. This hypothesis would be undermined if there were *no* conceptual or linguistic connections between Ephesians and John's Gospel. For if the author of Ephesians was writing to Johannine Christ-followers, and was interested in effective communication, we would expect him or her to include some language and adopt some concepts that were both well-known and congenial to Johannine Christ-followers. It is such connections or contact that I am looking for then. The *lack* of such connections would undermine this hypothesis. That such connections can be argued for does not, of course, prove this hypothesis (especially since I think there was a strong degree of commonality across the documents that would come to comprise the New Testament) but such proof is virtually always beyond us in any case, as Hays notes. Rather, such connections certainly take away the key factor that would undermine this hypothesis, as well as making it plausible. Accordingly, I will proceed to discuss what I see as the conceptual and linguistic connections between Ephesians and John's Gospel.

As part of his argument that the addressees of Ephesians included Johannine Christ-followers, Muddiman lists a whole range of what he calls "parallels be-

---

[56] See HAYS, *Conversion of the Imagination*, 31. Hays is commenting on what he calls the "stringent criteria for proof" that MORNA HOOKER applied with regard to the influence of the Servant Songs on the NT (*Jesus and the Servant: The Influence of the Servant Concept of Deutero-Isaiah in the New Testament* [London: SPCK, 1959]).

[57] For this general view, see RICHARD BAUCKHAM, *The Gospels for All Christians: Rethinking the Gospel Audiences* (Grand Rapids: Eerdmans, 1998).

tween Ephesians and the Johannine literature."[58] However, his list includes both strong and weak connections. A better argument can be made by concentrating on the strongest connections – those where a case can be made that particular language or concepts are new to the Pauline tradition, and that such new language can be seen to be strongly present in the Johannine tradition or, *as far as we know*, only found in the Johannine tradition up to this point in time.[59] Hence there may well be a connection between new language being found in the Pauline strand of traditions about Christ, as represented by Ephesians, and the Johannine tradition. That is what is argued for here.[60]

E. Are there connections between Ephesians and John's Gospel?

I. Realized Eschatology

Here I will argue that strongly realized eschatology – more strongly realized than elsewhere in the NT – is present in both Ephesians and John's Gospel.

In Ephesians, salvation can be spoken of as already achieved, even to the extent that Christ-followers are already ascended with Christ and enthroned in heaven. Thus Eph 2:4–6 reads: "But God, who is rich in mercy, out of the great love with which he loved us even when we were dead through our trespasses, *made us alive together with Christ* (συνεζωοποίησεν τῷ Χριστῷ) – by grace you have been saved – and *raised us up with him* and *seated us with him in the heavenly places in Christ Jesus* (καὶ συνήγειρεν καὶ συνεκάθισεν ἐν τοῖς ἐπουρανίοις ἐν Χριστῷ Ἰησοῦ)." Note the three aorist verbs here – made alive together with (συζωοποιεῖν) Christ,[61] raised up with (συνγείρειν) Christ,[62] and seated with (συγκαθίζειν) Christ.[63] Believers can be spoken of as corporately located *in the present* with Christ in the heavenly places then, where they already share in Christ's triumph and rule over the hostile cosmic powers. By contrast, in 1 Corinthians Paul chides the Corinthians for thinking that they are already kings

---

[58] MUDDIMAN, *Ephesians*, 37–38 (37). Other parallels that he lists which are not discussed in detail here since they are considered to be too weak include: truth and falsehood (John 8:44; Eph 4:25), the pre-existence of the Son of God (John 17:24; Eph 1:6); his descent and exaltation (John 3:13f; Eph 4:9f); the kingship of Christ (John 18:36; Eph 5:5); what is said about the Holy Spirit (John 14:26; Eph 4:30), and the language of fullness (John 14:20; 15:4, 8; 17:11–12; Eph 3:19).

[59] Of course, as noted above, we cannot rule out that such language or concepts may have come from the Jesus tradition, from traditions held by other Christ-followers, or may have been adopted from a Jewish context, or the wider environment of Western Asia Minor.

[60] Some scholars argue for a relationship between Ephesians and 1 Peter, but on this see the critical remarks of BEST, *Ephesians*, ICC, 5, 18–19.

[61] The verb is also found in Col 2:13.

[62] The verb is also found in Col 2:12; 3:1.

[63] The only other place in the NT where this verb is found is Luke 22:55.

(1 Cor 4:8) and speaks of the rule of the saints over the world and over angels as still in the future (1 Cor 6:2, 3).[64] As Lincoln notes:

A realized eschatology with its focus on the heavenly dimension can be found in Paul (cf. e. g., Gal. 4.26; 1 Cor. 15.48; 2 Cor. 12.2–4; Phil. 3.20), but not to the same extent as in Ephesians, where from the start of the letter the benefits of the age to come are regarded as having already become a present spiritual and heavenly reality for the believers. The opening eulogy blesses God because he "has blessed us with every spiritual blessing in the heavenly realms in Christ" (1.3).[65]

The use of οἱ ἅγιοι with the meaning of "the angels" in Eph 1:18 and 2:19 can also be connected to realized eschatology. In Eph 1:18 we read: "so that, with the eyes of your heart enlightened, you may know what is the hope to which he has called you, what are the riches of his glorious inheritance among *the holy ones* (τῆς κληρονομίας αὐτοῦ ἐν τοῖς ἁγίοις)." Whilst the meaning of ἐν τοῖς ἁγίοις here could be "among believers in Christ,"[66] a strong case can be made that οἱ ἅγιοι refers to "heavenly ones" or "angels" here. After the reference to "hope," "the riches of his glorious inheritance" seems to refer to heaven rather than the situation on earth, so it is immediately suggested that οἱ ἅγιοι are angels. Further, "the holy ones" is used extensively with this meaning of "angels" in the OT and intertestamental literature including at Qumran (especially 1QS 11:7–8 which is very similar to Eph 2:6),[67] and as we have noted in Eph 2:6 it is said that believers already sit in the heavenlies.[68] The meaning of Eph 1:18 is then that "the saints on earth share their inheritance with the angels. This sharing exists now and does not belong to the future … As the church is *already* blessed in the heavenly places (1:3) so it *already* partakes of its inheritance."[69] Given this usage in Eph 1, οἱ ἅγιοι in Eph 2:19 probably also refers to "heavenly ones" or "angels:" "So then you are no longer strangers and aliens, but you are citizens with *the holy ones* (συμπολῖται τῶν ἁγίων) [= angels] and also members of the house-

---

[64] In the Undisputed Paulines, ERNEST BEST, *Ephesians*, NTG (Shefffield: JSOT Press, 1993), 73, notes that Paul "places the death of believers with Christ in the past [but] he regards their resurrection with him as future (Rom. 6.3–5, 8; 8:17; 2 Cor 4.14; Phil. 3.21)."

[65] LINCOLN in LINCOLN and WEDDERBURN, *Theology*, 129. BEST, *Ephesians*, ICC, 52–53, prefers to speak of a "fully realized soteriology," since in BEST's view the author of Ephesians has little interest in eschatology and a lot of interest in soteriology. On eschatology in Ephesians see PETRUS J. GRÄBE, "'And He Made Known to Us the Mystery of His Will …': Reflections on the Eschatology of the Letter to the Ephesians," in *Eschatology of the New Testament and Some Related Documents*, ed. JAN G. VAN DER WATT, WUNT 2.315 (Tübingen: Mohr Siebeck, 2011), 256–68, and the references given there.

[66] See MUDDIMAN, *Ephesians*, 86.

[67] See PAUL R. TREBILCO, *Self-Designations and Group Identity in the New Testament* (Cambridge: Cambridge University Press, 2012), 122–28.

[68] BEST, *Ephesians*, ICC, 34, 168.

[69] BEST, *Ephesians*, ICC, 168 (emphasis added), see also 53 and 636; OTTO PROCKSCH, "ἅγιος, κτλ," *TDNT* 1:107 n. 61; SCHNACKENBURG, *Ephesians*, 75.

hold of God."[70] Accordingly, believers are *already* seen as fellow-citizens with the angels.

While some scholars argue that Paul uses οἱ ἅγιοι with the meaning of angels in three verses (1 Thess 3:13; 2 Thess 1:10; Col 1:12), it is more likely that the reference in these verses is to humans.[71] Using οἱ ἅγιοι with reference to angels in Ephesians is a new development within the Pauline tradition then.[72] This is another dimension of the realized eschatology of the author – believers already share in the inheritance of angels, and are already citizens with the angels in heaven.

Elements of this realized eschatology are present in Colossians, "where resurrection with Christ is set in the past (2.12; 3.1), and the lives of believers are said to be hidden with Christ in God (3.3)."[73] But I would argue that there is a greater degree of realized eschatology in Ephesians, even compared with Colossians,[74] particularly the idea of believers presently sitting together with Christ in heaven (Eph 2:6), which is absent from Colossians.[75] This line of thought is therefore a new development within the Pauline tradition.

The closest parallel to this strongly realized eschatology of Ephesians, whereby believers are currently seated with Christ in the heavenlies, is to be found in John's Gospel.[76] Note John 5:24–25: "Very truly, I tell you, anyone who hears my word and believes him who sent me *has* eternal life, and does not come under judgment, but *has passed from death to life* (ἀλλὰ μεταβέβηκεν ἐκ τοῦ θανάτου εἰς τὴν ζωήν). Very truly, I tell you, the hour is coming, *and is now here*, when the dead will hear the voice of the Son of God, and those who hear will live."[77] Note also John 10:10: "The thief comes only to steal and kill and destroy. I came that *they may have life*, and have it abundantly."

Further, in John's Gospel, judgment, which generally is a feature of the End, has already occurred, at least to some extent. Note John 3:18–19: "Those who be-

---

[70] This is supported by 3:10, 21 where it is said that the church has a cosmic dimension. In 2:19 Gentile readers (2:17) are probably described as fellow citizens with "the holy ones," that is, along with good supernatural beings; see further BEST, *Ephesians*, ICC, 278, 629; see also SCHNACKENBURG, *Ephesians*, 75; cf. LINCOLN, *Ephesians*, 150–51. The "holy ones" in 2:19 may also include glorified believers; see BEST, *Ephesians*, ICC, 278–79.

[71] See TREBILCO, *Self-Designations*, 132–33.

[72] It is however in keeping with the predominant sense of οἱ ἅγιοι in other Jewish literature and so in a sense is a reversion to a more common meaning.

[73] BEST, *Ephesians*, NTG, 73.

[74] See for example LINCOLN in LINCOLN and WEDDERBURN, *Theology*, 129; BEST, *Ephesians*, NTG, 76; MUDDIMAN, *Ephesians*, 82.

[75] Compare Col 3:1–4.

[76] See MUDDIMAN, *Ephesians*, 109. For discussions of Johannine eschatology see BROWN, *Introduction to the Gospel of John*, 234–48; JAN G. VAN DER WATT, "Eschatology in John: A Continuous Process of Realizing Events," in VAN DER WATT, *Eschatology*, 109–40, and the literature referred to in these studies.

[77] See also John 5:21.

lieve in him are not condemned; but those who do not believe *are condemned already*, because they have not believed in the name of the only Son of God. And this is the judgment, that the light *has come* into the world, and people loved darkness rather than light because their deeds were evil."[78]

It is not as if future eschatology has been done away with in either Ephesians or John's Gospel. In Ephesians, it is clear that believers are not presently perfect (even if they sit in the heavenly places),[79] the author also speaks of "hope" (1:12, 18; 2:12; 4:4), and in 1:14 the future element is explicit since believers are said to have received a down payment and so are awaiting the future inheritance.[80] And in John there remains a future hope of the parousia, for example.[81] But the stronger dimension of realized eschatology is clear in both cases. This greater sense of realized eschatology in Ephesians could be a natural development within the Pauline tradition (particularly given the mediating position of Colossians). But there is a strong parallel here between Ephesians and John's Gospel, and in both Ephesians and John's Gospel the emphasis is much more on realized eschatology than in the earlier Pauline tradition.

II. Unity

There is a key emphasis on unity in both Ephesians and in John's Gospel.[82] One element of the theme of unity in Ephesians is that in Christ the age-long hostility between Jew and Gentile has been ended, and the two groups have been reconciled to God and so to one another, breaking down the dividing wall of hostility, abolishing the law and thus creating one new humanity (2:14–22).

But there is much more to the theme of unity in Ephesians.[83] The unity of the Church as the body of Christ,[84] and its one faith and one baptism, is strongly

---

[78] See van der Watt, "Eschatology in John," 120–21, 134–35; see also John 12:31.

[79] Best, *Ephesians*, NTG, 74: "If they were, there would be no need for chs. 4–6 which are devoted to instructions in the nature of true behaviour."

[80] Further, Eph 5:5 refers to the future. Future reference is also found in Eph 4:30, where reference to the "day" suggests eschatological redemption is in view; see also Eph 1:9–10, 21; 5:16, 21; 6:8–9, 13; see Best, *Ephesians*, NTG, 75; Muddiman, *Ephesians*, 18.

[81] See for example John 5:28–29; 6:39–40, 44, 54; 12:25, 48; 14:2–3, 18, 28; 17:24; see also Muddiman, *Ephesians*, 109; Brown, *Introduction to the Gospel of John*, 240–41; van der Watt, "Eschatology in John," 124–25.

[82] See Ulrich Heckel, "Die Einheit der Kirche im Johannesevangelium und im Epheserbrief: Ein Vergleich der ekklesiologischen Strukturen," in *Kontexte des Johannesevangeliums: das vierte Evangelium in religions- und traditionsgeschichtlicher Perspektive*, ed. Jörg Frey and Udo Schnelle, WUNT 1.175 (Tübingen: Mohr Siebeck, 2004), 613–40, for a study of the similarities between John and Ephesians with regard to the unity of the church.

[83] On unity in Ephesians see Campbell, "Unity and Diversity," 15–31, and the references given there.

[84] On the theme of the Church as the Body of Christ, Muddiman, *Ephesians*, 182–83, notes: "the image of the Church as the one, indivisible Body of Christ had probably become so well established in and beyond Pauline circles that it might well be invoked in this abbreviated fashion

grounded in the unity of God in Eph 4:4–6: "There is one body and one Spirit, just as you were called to the one hope of your calling, one Lord, one faith, one baptism, one God and Father of all, who is above all and through all and in all." Because of this theological unity, readers are urged to make "every effort to maintain the unity of the Spirit in the bond of peace" (Eph 4:3).

The goal of the building up of the body of Christ, which is itself the goal of the work of ministry, is expressed in Eph 4:13–16:

> Until all of us come to the unity of the faith and of the knowledge of the Son of God, to maturity, to the measure of the full stature of Christ. … But speaking the truth in love, we must grow up in every way into him who is the head, into Christ, from whom the whole body, joined and knit together by every ligament with which it is equipped, as each part is working properly, promotes the body's growth in building itself up in love.

Thus, the unity of the body of Christ is seen as paramount.

In fact, the overall goal of Christ's work is focused on the unity of all things, as expressed in Eph 1:8–10: "With all wisdom and insight he has made known to us the mystery of his will, according to his good pleasure that he set forth in Christ, as a plan for the fullness of time, to gather up all things in him, things in heaven and things on earth (ἀνακεφαλαιώσασθαι τὰ πάντα ἐν τῷ Χριστῷ, τὰ ἐπὶ τοῖς οὐρανοῖς καὶ τὰ ἐπὶ τῆς γῆς ἐν αὐτῷ)." Muddiman summarizes: "The unity of the Church and of Christians is therefore the overarching theme of Ephesians, with special emphasis placed on the unity between the Gentile Christians whom Paul is supposedly addressing and their Jewish fellow-Christians, the heirs of God's covenants with Israel."[85]

The unity of believers is also a prominent theme in John's Gospel. Believers are to be united to Christ and to one another. This is clear in John 10:16: "I have other sheep that do not belong to this fold. I must bring them also, and they will listen to my voice. So there will be one flock, one shepherd." Jesus's intention is that the sheep of another fold will be brought into the one flock; these other sheep are Gentiles, and they will be united with Jewish followers of Jesus. As Lincoln notes, "Jesus, the one shepherd, will bring about the one flock of Jews and Gentiles, whose distinguishing mark is their willingness to listen to their shepherd's voice."[86] Similarly, in John 11:51–52, Caiaphas prophesies that Jesus will die for the nation "and not for the nation only, but to gather into one the dispersed children of God." Here the "dispersed children of God" who are gathered into one consist of the whole community of Christ-followers, and thus the text

---

(cf. also Rom 12.4; Col 3.15) and this is almost certainly how the author of Ephesians understood the material he was incorporating."

[85] MUDDIMAN, *Ephesians*, 36.

[86] ANDREW T. LINCOLN, *The Gospel According to John*, BNTC (London: Continuum, 2005), 298. See also HECKEL, "Die Einheit der Kirche," 614–15; J. RAMSEY MICHAELS, *The Gospel of John*, NICNT (Grand Rapids: Eerdmans, 2010), 588–90. MICHAELS argues that the "other sheep" are Gentiles, and not Diaspora Jews (588 n. 90).

speaks of the unity of Jewish and Gentile followers of Jesus.[87] Further, the Son, when he is lifted up from the earth, "will draw *all* people to myself" (John 12:32). "All people" will be drawn to Christ on the cross (John 12:32). He is the true Vine in whom all believers are united (John 15:1–10; see also 4:42).

These themes come to particular prominence in John 17,[88] where Jesus expresses his concern for the unity of believers. Note John 17:11, 20–23:

> [11]And now I am no longer in the world, but they are in the world, and I am coming to you. Holy Father, protect them in your name that you have given me, so that they may be one, as we are one … [20]I ask not only on behalf of these, but also on behalf of those who will believe in me through their word, [21]that they may all be one. As you, Father, are in me and I am in you, may they also be in us, so that the world may believe that you have sent me. [22]The glory that you have given me I have given them, so that they may be one, as we are one, [23]I in them and you in me, that they may become completely one, so that the world may know that you have sent me and have loved them even as you have loved me.

This unity is rooted theologically in the unity of the Father and the Son (John 17:21), and the Father-Son relationship provides both the basis for this unity and the pattern on which it is modelled (John 17:11).

Thus, according to John, "sinful men and women are able to participate in the holy fellowship within the Godhead, in the measure possible to human beings, and so a unity with fellow believers who also share in that same fellowship with God becomes possible."[89] Unity with God and unity with those who are also united to God become complementary. Again this is very similar to what we find in Eph 2:14–18, where we read that by reconciling both Jew and Gentile to God, the two groups that were formerly enemies have been reconciled to each other, and Christ has created "in himself one new humanity in place of the two, thus making peace" (Eph 2:15).

The stress on unity in Ephesians is compatible with our view that its addressees were not currently unified, and hence supports the hypothesis that the readers of Ephesians included Christ-followers in the Pauline and Johannine traditions. In addition, that *both* John's Gospel and Ephesians share this very prominent stress on unity is significant with regard to our view that Ephesians was in part written with readers of John's Gospel in mind.[90] Ephesians and what it says about unity, would certainly be a highly congenial document for readers of John's Gospel.

---

[87] See MICHAELS, *John*, 653–54.

[88] MUDDIMAN, *Ephesians*, 183, writes: "After Eph. 4.4–6, the passage in the New Testament that is most emphatic about the unity of the Church is undoubtedly John 17." He goes on to speak of "this extraordinary emphasis on unity in the Johannine community."

[89] GEORGE R. BEASLEY-MURRAY, *Gospel of Life: Theology in the Fourth Gospel* (Peabody: Hendrickson, 1991), 112; see also R. A. CULPEPPER, "The Quest for the Church in the Gospel of John," *Int* 63 (2009): 351–52.

[90] Note the comment by HECKEL, "Die Einheit der Kirche," 627 (emphasis original): "Nirgends im Neuen Testament wird die *Einheit der Kirche* so betont wie im Johannesevangelium und Epheserbrief."

III. The Church

The term ἐκκλησία is found nine times in Ephesians (1:22; 3:10, 21; 5:23, 24, 25, 27, 29, 32), and the church can be seen as a central theme of the letter, with a good deal of its content related to this topic.[91] For example, in Eph 1:22–23 we read: "And he has put all things under his feet and has made him the head over all things for the church, which is his body, the fullness of him who fills all in all."

The word ἐκκλησία is always used in Ephesians with the sense of "the universal church," rather than with reference to a congregation.[92] As Best notes, "In doing this he [the author] might have conceived of the whole church as the sum total of a number of local communities; instead he thinks of it as the sum total of believers."[93] This dimension of universality is also emphasized by the fact that the author always speaks simply of ἡ ἐκκλησία, and never adds a genitive or dative expression.

There is a very close association between Christ and ἡ ἐκκλησία in Ephesians, with the church being Christ's body (Eph 1:22–23; 5:29), Christ being the Head of the church (Eph 5:23) and also filling the church (1:23). In Eph 2:11–22, the church is conceived of as a "third people," consisting of believing Jews and Gentiles, reconciled to God in one body (2:16), which is the church (3:6). The church is also Christ's wife or bride (5:22–33), as well as a building (2:19–22). The Spirit is at work in the church and gives it its unity (1:13; 4:3–4; 4:30; 5:18–19).

It is through the church that "the wisdom of God in its rich variety might now be made known to the rulers and authorities in the heavenly places" (Eph 3:10). The church, which is an agent of revelation, has a cosmic dimension (see also 3:21),[94] and as we have already noted, in Eph 2:6 believers are said to be already sitting in the heavenly places in Christ. In Eph 1:18 and 2:19 we see that for the author, the membership of the church includes heavenly beings.[95]

Thus, there is considerable development here compared with the undisputed Paulines, with ἐκκλησία becoming a strongly theologically charged term. In particular, it emphasizes participation in a universal entity that has cosmic significance.

---

[91] See LINCOLN in LINCOLN and WEDDERBURN, *Theology*, 80; J. H. ROBERTS, "The Enigma of Ephesians: Rethinking Some Positions on the Basis of Schnackenburg and Arnold," *Neot* 27 (1993): 97–103; BEST, *Ephesians*, ICC, 623. On the church in Ephesians see KARL L. SCHMIDT, "ἐκκλησία," in *TDNT* 3.509–13; BEST, *Ephesians*, ICC, 622–41, and the literature referred to there.

[92] MUDDIMAN, *Ephesians*, 4.

[93] BEST, *Ephesians*, ICC, 625.

[94] See EDUARD SCHWEIZER, *Church Order in the New Testament* (London: SCM, 1961), 109.

[95] See BEST, *Ephesians*, ICC, 625, and section E.I above.

Although ἐκκλησία is not found in John's Gospel,[96] the *concept* of the church or community of believers occurs often.[97] Further, the community is regularly conceived of in terms consistent with the Church being understood as a universal entity. That is, the way in which the church is spoken of regularly transcends a particular community, and expresses the idea that the church is an over-arching, universal collectivity.[98]

The concept found in Ephesians of Christ as Head of the Church with believers being Christ's Body can be seen as highly comparable to the Johannine metaphor of Christ as the True Vine, with believers being the branches (John 15:1–2).

One dimension of this Johannine image of the vine and the branches is the idea of believers abiding in Christ, expressed in John 15:4: "You abide in me as I abide in you (μείνατε ἐν ἐμοί, κἀγὼ ἐν ὑμῖν). Just as the branch cannot bear fruit by itself unless it abides in the vine, neither can you unless you abide in me." As abiding-branches, Jesus's followers are conceived of as part of him, as organically connected. Hence John 15:2: "He removes every branch *in me* that bears no fruit (πᾶν κλῆμα ἐν ἐμοὶ μὴ φέρον καρπὸν αἴρει αὐτό)."[99] The idea of mutual inter-connectedness of Christ and believers, with one part co-inhering with or in the other, is present in both Ephesians and John's Gospel, via the Head-Body language of Ephesians and the Vine-Branches language of John. That Jesus is the Johannine vine gives him the key place or position in the Church, just as the metaphor in Ephesians of Jesus as head of the body does.[100]

A similar view is clear in John 10:1–18, with its presentation of Jesus as the Good Shepherd of the Flock. As with the Head-Body metaphor, this emphasizes *both* the on-going and intimate relationship of all believers to Jesus as Shepherd *and* the corporate dimensions of all believers as Flock. There are key similarities to the body metaphor here then.

---

[96] This in itself is not highly significant since ἐκκλησία is not found in Mark or Luke either; the only occurrences in the Gospels are Matt 16:18; 18:17 (twice).

[97] For discussions of the church in John see BROWN, *Introduction to the Gospel of John,* 221–9; CULPEPPER, "The Quest for the Church," 341–54, who argue that scholars who think John's Gospel lacks a significant emphasis on or interest in the church (such as e. g., RUDOLF BULTMANN, *Theology of the New Testament,* 2 vols. [London: SCM, 1955], 2:91) are mistaken. I am not denying that in John's Gospel there is a strong emphasis on the individual and on personal faith; see for example, John 3:3, 7, 16; RAYMOND E. BROWN, *The Churches the Apostles Left Behind* (New York: Paulist, 1984), 84–85.

[98] With regard to universality, see also John 12:32: "And I, when I am lifted up from the earth, will draw all people to myself."

[99] Note also John 15:7: "If you (pl.) abide in me, and my words abide in you (pl.) (ἐὰν μείνητε ἐν ἐμοὶ καὶ τὰ ῥήματά μου ἐν ἡμῖν μείνῃ)."

[100] BROWN, *Introduction to the Gospel of John,* 228, notes that the Johannine image of the vine puts no emphasis on the different functions of the various members of the community, which is found in the Pauline image of the body. But he notes that to go on to say that there is no church order in John (in contrast to Ephesians for example – see Eph 2:20; 3:5; 4:11) is an argument from silence, which must be used only with the greatest caution.

Further, in both John and Ephesians Jesus is understood to be the bridegroom or husband, and the community of believers is conceived of as the bride or the wife. In John 3:29 we read: "He who has the bride is the bridegroom. The friend of the bridegroom, who stands and hears him, rejoices greatly at the bridegroom's voice. For this reason my joy has been fulfilled." In Eph 5:23–25: "For the husband is the head of the wife just as Christ is the head of the church, the body of which he is the Savior. Just as the church is subject to Christ, so also wives ought to be, in everything, to their husbands. Husbands, love your wives, just as Christ loved the church and gave himself up for her."[101] Again then, although the use of the language is different, the way the relationship is expressed is almost identical.

There are also similarities between what The Good Shepherd is said to do for the sheep in John and what Christ as husband has done for the Church in Ephesians. In John 10:11, 15, 17–18 we read: "I am the good shepherd. The good shepherd lays down his life for the sheep (τίθησιν ὑπὲρ τῶν προβάτων) ... And I lay down my life for the sheep ... For this reason the Father loves me, because I lay down my life in order to take it up again. No one takes it from me, but I lay it down of my own accord. I have power to lay it down, and I have power to take it up again. I have received this command from my Father." Similarly, in Eph 5:25, 28–29 we read: "Husbands, love your wives, just as Christ *loved the church and gave himself up for her* (ἑαυτὸν παρέδωκεν ὑπὲρ αὐτῆς) ... In the same way, husbands should love their wives as they do their own bodies. He who loves his wife loves himself. For no one ever hates his own body, but he nourishes and tenderly cares for it, just as Christ does for the church." In both texts, Christ is said to lay down his life or give himself for his followers.[102]

Accordingly, I suggest that the presentation of the Church in Ephesians and in John is highly compatible.

IV. *Darkness and Light*

The language of darkness and light is found quite widely in the NT, so here we are not considering concepts or language that are only found in Ephesians and

---

[101] See also Eph 5:26–32.

[102] In both Ephesians and John glory is something that believers are to have or be given. In Eph 3:21 we read: "to him be *glory in the church* and in Christ Jesus to all generations, forever and ever. Amen" (see also Eph 1:18), and in John 17:22: "The glory that you have given me I have given them, so that they may be one, as we are one." In Eph 2:19–22 the church is understood as a temple ("In him the whole structure is joined together and grows into a holy temple in the Lord; in whom you also are built together spiritually into a dwelling place for God"), while in John 2:19–21 Jesus's body (rather than the group of believers) is the new temple, the place where the presence of God is, and hence where believers encounter God. However, since in Ephesians the Church is the *Body of Christ* (Eph 4:12; 5:23, 30), the two ideas (the Church as temple and Christ as temple) are not as different as they might at first appear.

John's Gospel. However, our two texts do share a notable concentration of this language.

In Ephesians 5 we have the contrast between darkness and light. Eph 5:8 reads: "For once you were darkness, but now in the Lord you are light. Live as children of light (ἦτε γάρ ποτε σκότος, νῦν δὲ φῶς ἐν κυρίῳ· ὡς τέκνα φωτὸς περιπατεῖτε)." Note that people were formerly "darkness" – that is, people themselves can actually be described as "darkness" rather than just being "in darkness." As Thielman notes: "They were not merely in darkness but were darkness, and so their entire existence was defined by it."[103] In Eph 5:11 ("Take no part in the unfruitful works of darkness [καὶ μὴ συγκοινωνεῖτε τοῖς ἔργοις τοῖς ἀκάρποις τοῦ σκότους], but instead expose them"), we have a genitive of source – the source of the unfruitful works is "darkness;"[104] this corresponds to the darkness of which believers were once a part, according to Eph 5:8.[105] John 3:19 is clear that people "loved the darkness": "And this is the judgment, that the light has come into the world, and people loved the darkness rather than the light (ἠγάπησαν οἱ ἄνθρωποι μᾶλλον τὸ σκότος ἢ τὸ φῶς) because their deeds were evil."[106]

What is said about darkness as a power in Ephesians is similar to John.[107] In Eph 6:12 we read: "For our struggle is not against enemies of blood and flesh, but against the rulers, against the authorities, against the cosmic powers of *this present darkness* (πρὸς τοὺς κοσμοκράτορας τοῦ σκότους τούτου), against the spiritual forces of evil in the heavenly places."[108] Similarly, this world is regularly described as "darkness" in John. John 12:35 reads: "Jesus said to them, 'The light is with you for a little longer. Walk while you have the light, so that the darkness may not overtake you. If you walk in the darkness, you do not know where you are going.'" Noteworthy also are John 1:5 ("The light shines in the darkness, and the darkness did not overcome it" [καὶ τὸ φῶς ἐν τῇ σκοτίᾳ φαίνει, καὶ ἡ σκοτία αὐτὸ οὐ κατέλαβεν]), John 8:12 ("Again Jesus spoke to them, saying, 'I am the light of the world. Whoever follows me will never walk in darkness but will have the light of life'"), and John 12:46 ("'I have come as light into the world, so that everyone who believes in me should not remain in the darkness'").[109]

---

[103] THIELMAN, *Ephesians*, 338.

[104] See HOEHNER, *Ephesians*, 678.

[105] ERNEST BEST, "Ephesians: Two Types of Existence," *Int* 47 (1993): 44–45, notes that although the author asserts Christ-followers are now "light," his injunctions in 4:25–30; 5:3, 5 and elsewhere show that "he realized that darkness still existed among them" (44). For a discussion of this language in Ephesians see BEST, "Ephesians: Two Types of Existence," 39–51. BEST notes the contrast between Ephesians and Paul's other writings in the way Ephesians shows little interest in "the world outside, except to depict it in the darkest of colors" (50).

[106] See also John 12:35.

[107] Darkness is also seen as a power in Luke 22:53 and Col 1:13.

[108] On this passage see CLINTON E. ARNOLD, *Ephesians: Power and Magic: The Concept of Power in Ephesians in Light of its Historical Setting*, SNTSMS 63 (Cambridge: Cambridge University Press, 1989), 65–68.

[109] See also 1 John 1:5–7; 2:8–11.

What is said about light in Eph 5:8 is also very similar to the emphasis in John's Gospel on Jesus as the light. Eph 5:8 says "but now in the Lord you are light," implying in context that "the Lord," that is Christ,[110] is himself light. This is made explicit in John 8:12: "Again Jesus spoke to them, saying, 'I am the light of the world. Whoever follows me will never walk in darkness but will have the light of life.'" John 9:5 ("'As long as I am in the world, I am the light of the world'") and 12:35 ("Jesus said to them, 'The light is with you for a little longer'") reiterate the point.[111] The christological focus of light is clear in both texts then.

Related to this, in John 12:36 believers are "light," as well as children of light,[112] ("'While you have the light, believe in the light, so that you may become children of light'" [ἵνα υἱοὶ φωτὸς γένησθε]), just as they are in Eph 5:8. Further, in both Eph 5:13–14 and John 3:21 we have an emphasis on light and visibility, with both texts using φῶς and φανεροῦν ("to make known or visible").[113]

We see then that the dualism of darkness and light is a noteworthy feature of both Ephesians and John's Gospel.[114]

F. Conclusions

A number of other connections can be suggested between Ephesians and John's Gospel, but in my view those dealt with here are the strongest.[115]

I have argued that the criterion of availability can be viewed as met – these writings are to be located in Ephesos, and even if the author of Ephesians did not have access to the written Gospel of John, the author could well have had access to oral Johannine traditions. With regard to the volume of the intertextual

---

[110] See LINCOLN, *Ephesians*, 327.

[111] See also John 1:9; 12:40, 46.

[112] τέκνα φωτός is found in the NT only in Eph 5:8; John 12:36 has υἱοὶ φωτός; the latter phrase is also found in Luke 16:8 and 1 Thess 5:5.

[113] See also MUDDIMAN, *Ephesians*, 237–38.

[114] ABBOTT, *Ephesians and Colossians*, xxix, notes: "The contrast between the light which Christ brings and the opposing power of darkness is expressed in both (Ephesians and John) with striking similarity (he cites Eph 5:8, 11, 13; John 12:35; 3:20–21). Here what comes close together in Eph. appears in the Gospel of John in two separate places." MUDDIMAN, *Ephesians*, 37, writes: "The dualism of light and darkness (John 1.5; cf. Eph. 5.8) and of truth and falsehood (John 8.44; cf. Eph. 4.25) is also a marked feature of both." The contrast between light and darkness is also present in other Pauline texts; see Rom 13:12; 1 Thess 5:4–5; Col 1:12. There is also of course similar language at Qumran. See also KIRBY, *Ephesians*, 167.

[115] For other suggestions see KIRBY, *Ephesians*, 166–68; BARRETT, *St. John*, 62–63; MUDDI-MAN, *Ephesians*, 37–39 and notes 58 and 100 above. I am not denying that Ephesians and John's Gospel disagree on some important matters, such as the issue of continuing Jewish unbelief, about which Ephesians is silent (see MUDDIMAN, *Ephesians*, 19) and John has much to say, or the significance of "apostles" in Ephesians (2:20; 3:5; 4:11) about which John is silent. Clearly on the hypothesis offered here, Ephesians is *not* simply agreeing with John, but rather is seeking to be congenial to Johannine readers on *some* key points.

links, in each case I have sought to argue that there is a *discernible* similarity of language, imagery or concepts between Ephesians and the Gospel of John. This relates to four very significant areas: realized eschatology, unity, the church, and darkness and light. There is also a recurrence of intertextual links here, which means that the case is cumulative.

I have noted that my suggestion that Ephesians was written to all Christ-followers in Ephesos would be disproved, or at least significantly undermined, if there were no connections between Ephesians and the Gospel of John. These connections between Ephesians and John mean then that it is plausible that the author of Ephesians wrote with an awareness of Johannine tradition, and sought to appeal to Johannine readers by using imagery and language that was congenial to them. Of course this is not the only reason the author wrote Ephesians – there are in fact a number of reasons the author wrote the letter.[116] But I suggest that this is one reason he wrote.

I have *not* been trying to show that there are *only* connections between Ephesians and the Gospel of John. I am not denying that there are multiple influences on Ephesians, and so some dimensions of the language and concepts that I have been discussing are found across a range of early texts written by Christ-followers. However, it is very significant that there are some elements that Ephesians and John's Gospel *alone* share (such as the degree or extent of realized eschatology and the highly prominent stress on the unity of the church). But the author of Ephesians is certainly not only thinking of Johannine tradition when writing. My point rather is that these connections between Ephesians and John are discernible and in fact are surprisingly strong.

In no cases have I been able to argue that the author of Ephesians *must* have known a particular passage in John. But we have also noted that Johannine traditions were almost certainly in existence for a number of years prior to the Gospel being written, so we are looking for broader links between Ephesians and Johannine Gospel traditions rather than only for allusions to a Johannine text.

That these connections and similarities can be detected, or argued for, does not of course prove my hypothesis (especially since I think there was a strong degree of commonality across the books that would later comprise the New Testament) but it certainly makes it plausible.[117] And the lack of these similarities would certainly undermine my view.

I conclude then that it is plausible that Ephesians was written in part with readers of the Gospel of John in mind. We cannot say that this is any more than plausible but in my view it is not less than plausible. Accordingly, as well as writ-

---

[116] See note 6 above.

[117] The comment of HAYS, *Conversion of the Imagination*, 34, about discerning the presence of intertextual echoes is helpful here: "precision in such matters is not attainable … We should also bear in mind that the use of such criteria will often yield only greater or lesser degrees of probability about any particular reading, especially where echoes are concerned."

ing to those in the Pauline tradition – as is clear from writing in Paul's name, and from the persistent use of Pauline tradition – it seems plausible that the author of Ephesians was also writing to Johannine Christ-followers, and was seeking to write a work that was both congenial to and compelling for them *too*, by incorporating a range of Johannine traditions into his work. We may suggest that the author's overall goal was harmony between the two groups. The author may not necessarily have been seeking to unite the two streams into one, and thus to encourage the Johannine stream to join with the Pauline stream. But the author is seeking to convince Johannine readers that they belong to the same movement as Pauline readers and are valued within that wider movement. Ephesos is perhaps a center of Christ-followers that not only demonstrates diversity, but also a city where there is an active concern for Christian unity.

"Do Not Harm the Suppliant"

Inviolability and Asylum at Ephesos and in the Book of Revelation[1]

Gregory Stevenson

"Now where are we to flee from violence? What is to be our refuge? To which of the gods are we to have recourse if Artemis cannot protect us?"[2] This statement, from a second century CE work by Achilles Tatius, illustrates the prominent role that the Temple of Artemis at Ephesos played in the history of Greek asylum. As a place where the unfortunate, the victim, and the oppressed could find protection and aid, the Temple of Artemis at Ephesos had few parallels. In exploration of the importance of asylum at Ephesos, this essay examines the history of asylum at Ephesos in the context of the broader historical development of the practice and then draws a few implications from this analysis for the interpretation of selected texts in Revelation.

A. Overview of Supplication and Inviolability

Technically, supplication and inviolability were two distinct institutions within Greek religion. The Greek term ἱκετεία, meaning "supplication" or "suppliant asylum," identifies the right of a sanctuary to receive suppliants (individuals seeking the protection or aid of the deity). The terms ἄσυλος or ἀσυλία, often translated as "inviolability" or even "place of asylum," refer to the declared or inherent safety of a place. A sanctuary, for instance, that has ἀσυλία is to be exempt from war, exempt from violent seizure of its property and individuals, and immune from the power of the state, in some ways not unlike the modern concept of a foreign embassy. But although ἱκετεία and ἀσυλία are separate institutions,

---

[1] I consider it a great privilege to contribute to this collection of essays honoring RICHARD E. OSTER. As a former student, I benefited greatly from his pedagogical wisdom and patient guidance. As a teacher, I continue to benefit from his scholarly output. In particular, his emphasis on the importance of engaging Graeco-Roman culture for New Testament interpretation has profoundly shaped my own academic agenda. In the case of Revelation, with its culturally evocative imagery and its setting in the rich environment of western Asia Minor, the perspective afforded by engagement with Graeco-Roman culture can be illuminating.

[2] Achilles Tatius, *Leuc. Clit.* 8.2.1 (Gasele, LCL).

there is a strong conceptual and practical overlap between them. When a suppliant seeks protection in a sanctuary, he or she takes part in the inviolability of the site.[3] Consequently, there can be a lack of distinction between the two institutions in ancient Greek literature, particularly by the first century CE, when they had become virtually indistinguishable.[4] For the purposes of this study, therefore, I use the term "asylum" to refer to the phenomenon as a whole, while distinguishing between supplication and inviolability where necessary.

The driving force of Greek asylum was the belief that the deity owned whatever was within its sanctuary. Any individual who was wronged, oppressed, or threatened could, therefore, find protection with the deity by establishing physical contact with the deity's space – most commonly altars and cult statues. Often individuals would come bearing suppliant branches, such as palm branches, that marked them as suppliants. Three concepts governed the ideology of this practice. The first was *protection*. Those who sought asylum gave themselves over to the deity and became, in essence, the deity's property and under his or her protection. Debtors, political refugees, slaves, the falsely accused, and victims of war could all find safety with the deity. A second concept was *justice*. In theory asylum was available only to the innocent and the wronged, thus creating a space where injustice could be rectified and the victim receive their due. The deity, in essence, became not only the protector of the suppliant but his or her advocate. Asylum often led to justice in a more practical sense as well as it frequently initiated a process of adjudication, with the priests and sometimes magistrates stepping in as mediators to bring resolution to the matter at hand. Seeking asylum at a temple or altar did not, for instance, remove the obligations that debtors owed or automatically set an oppressed slave free. Rather it created a safe environment where complaints could be heard and the matter worked out satisfactorily for all parties involved. The third concept that governed asylum was *vengeance*. Since the institution of asylum fell under divine law, one could not typically look to secular authorities for its enforcement. Instead what encouraged people to respect the laws of asylum was fear of divine vengeance. Any violation of a deity's suppliant was believed to incur the wrath of the deity who would exact vengeance on behalf of his or her suppliants. Although these concepts governed the institution of asylum theoretically, the reality of asylum, however, was at times very different.

Most Greek temples, by virtue of being sacred space, were considered inherently inviolable and as possessing the right to receive suppliants. Yet certain temples and deities (most notably Zeus, Apollo, Artemis, Poseidon, and Athena) dis-

---

[3] Rob W. M. Schumacher, "Three Related Sanctuaries of Poseidon: Geraistos, Kalaureia and Tainaron," in *Greek Sanctuaries: New Approaches*, ed. Nanno Marinatos and Robin Hägg (London: Routledge, 1993), 69.

[4] Clyde E. Billington, Jr., "Greek Suppliant Asylum and Its Adoption and Adaptation by the Early Western Christian Church" (PhD diss., University of Iowa, 1984), 36, 48, 53; John Gould, "Hiketeia," *JHS* 93 (1973): 77.

tinguished themselves in this regard and gained distinct reputations as providers of asylum.[5] The level of protection and aid afforded suppliants depended on the perceived holiness of the site and the power of the deity.[6] In essence, although all sanctuaries were sacred, some were more sacred than others, and so individuals would typically seek asylum where they were most likely to get the best help.[7] One of the most noteworthy of such sites was the Temple of Artemis at Ephesos. The role of asylum at the Temple of Artemis has a long and varied history, which we now examine in the context of the broader historical developments occurring within Greek asylum.

B. The Ephesian Artemis and Asylum in Historical Perspective

1. Pre-Classical Period

The origins of Greek sacred asylum are unknown, yet from at least the time of Homer on, asylum played a prominent role in Greek mythology, history, and tradition. The Ephesians witnessed to the antiquity of asylum when they traced the origin of asylum at the Temple of Artemis to mythological times; in particular, to the Amazons who fled there as suppliants seeking refuge in a time of war.[8] When appearing before the Emperor Tiberius to defend their rights of asylum, the Ephesians invoked the ancient Amazons as evidence for the antiquity of their claim.[9] By appealing to the mythological foundations of their temple's asylum, the Ephesians identified asylum as a vital and longstanding component of their temple's identity and function.[10]

One particular event involving asylum at the Temple of Artemis in the pre-Classical period highlights some interesting features regarding the expectation of protection. In the sixth century Croesus laid siege to the city of Ephesos. In response the Ephesians reportedly attached ropes from the gates and towers of the city to the columns of the Temple of Artemis, intending by this action to in-

---

[5] BILLINGTON, "Greek Suppliant Asylum," 81.

[6] BILLINGTON, "Greek Suppliant Asylum," 1.

[7] SCHUMACHER, "Three Related Sanctuaries," 76; ULRICH SINN, "Greek Sanctuaries as Places of Refuge," in *Greek Sanctuaries: New Approaches*, ed. NANNO MARINATOS and ROBIN HÄGG (London: Routledge, 1993), 97.

[8] Pausanias, *Descr.* 4.31.8; 7.2.6–8.

[9] Tacitus, *Hist.* 3.61.

[10] The Amazons seeking asylum at the altar of Artemis was a theme that found representation in the sculptural and architectural program of the temple during various stages of its history, and also elsewhere. See NADA SAPORITI, "A Frieze From the Temple of Hadrian at Ephesus," in *Essays in Memory of Karl Lehman*, ed. L. F. SANDLER (New York: Institute of Fine Arts, 1964), 270–73; FLORENCE M. BENNETT, *Religious Cults Associated with the Amazons* (New York: AMS Press, 1967), 30; CHRISTIAN PICARD, "Percées Tympanales ou Niches de Fronton?" *RAr* (1949): 31–39.

corporate the city itself within the temple's sphere of inviolability.[11] Their ploy essentially worked but raises the question, why did it work? To what does one attribute the success of asylum? When a person flees to an altar to escape a pursuing enemy, what keeps that person from being slain on the spot? Unfortunately, there is no universal answer to these questions, but rather ones that involve a variety of competing motivations and interests. Although supplication and asylum were quasi-legal maneuvers that could initiate legal procedures, "secular" legal enforcement in general was not a dominant factor in the success of Greek asylum, particularly in the earlier periods. The Greeks were reluctant to introduce clear and unambiguous laws that either enforced or restricted the practice of asylum, which they viewed as falling more under the purview of sacred authority. Instead they opted for "ad hoc reactions" to specific instances.[12] Consequently, as Chaniotis notes, "Until the Hellenistic age there is no evidence for a legal procedure against persons who had violated asylia."[13]

If the threat of legal or civic reprisals was not the primary motivating factor, what factors did contribute most commonly to the success of asylum? First was respect for the custom. Asylum and supplication created a sort of social contract whereby its enforcement came from public agreement to honor this established tradition. A second factor was piety towards the deity. The third factor was fear of divine retribution for violating a deity's asylum. In the case of Croesus, however, none of these factors appear to be determinative. As the leader of an invading force, Croesus betrays no concern for any legal consequences should he refuse asylum to the Ephesians. That he responds to the suppliant Ephesians with laughter, according to Aelian, suggests that he is neither moved by piety for Artemis nor fear of her wrath. A measure of respect for the custom of asylum may have played a role in his decision, though it may also be that he did not consider the Ephesians' ingenious attempt at supplication to be successful in placing themselves within the inviolable territory of the temple. According to Aelian, Croesus's willingness to accept the supplication of the Ephesians was motivated primarily by his good humor, perhaps generated by the cleverness and audacity of the Ephesians' actions. Regardless, what this event illustrates is that the inviolability of a temple was not an automatic guarantee of protection, but often depended upon the populace respecting the practice and willingly submitting to its restrictions.

---

[11] Aelian, *Var. hist.* 3.26; Herodotus, *Hist.* 1.26.

[12] ANGELOS CHANIOTIS, "Conflicting Authorities: Asylia between Secular and Divine Law in the Classical and Hellenistic Poleis," *Kernos* 9 (1996): 71, 79.

[13] CHANIOTIS, "Conflicting Authorities," 70.

2. Classical and Hellenistic Periods

In the Classical and Hellenistic periods, individuals continued to seek refuge from their troubles by appealing to Greek sacred asylum, particularly owing to the frequency of civic unrest and war. Thus, Aeschylus can write in the fifth century BCE, "Even for those who flee hard-pressed from war there is an altar, a shelter against harm through awe of the powers of heaven."[14] During this time two related themes begin to show up frequently in the available sources. First, from the fifth century on there appears an increasing emphasis on the idea that asylum should not be afforded unconditionally to suppliants, but must take into account their moral and legal status.[15] What is at stake is the very nature of Greek asylum itself. Should Greek temples and altars provide a common refuge to all regardless of what crimes they may have committed or should asylum be the privilege only of those who have been unjustly wronged? The earliest appearance of this debate in the literary record comes from Euripides in the fifth century who argued that the wicked should never be allowed to sit on altars (a standard posture for the suppliant) as it represents the height of injustice for the unrighteous and the righteous to receive the same benefit from the gods.[16]

This debate highlights the potential conflict between divine and secular law that is inherent in the practice of asylum. When the law courts have condemned to death one who has sought asylum at the temple, which law is to prevail? Although there were voices of dissent, and actual practice often deviated from the ideal, the dominant opinion was that asylum was a right only for the innocent so that the seeking of asylum did not absolve one from responsibility to the state. Consequently, Lycurgus, in the fourth century BCE, can praise the state for executing Callistratus even though he had sought asylum at the altar of the twelve gods.[17]

Due to its status as a premier site of asylum, the Temple of Artemis at Ephesos particularly garnered a reputation for harboring criminals and other unsavory characters, a reputation that continued well into the second century CE. In fact in the second century work, *The Adventures of Leucippe and Clitophon*, this debate over the proper function of asylum and its relation to the law courts played a prominent role in the plot of the story.[18] In the story Thersandros expresses outrage that Clitophon is allowed asylum in the Temple of Artemis, arguing that this right pertains only to those who have not yet received a guilty verdict on their crimes from a municipal court, which Clitophon had. He protests that those who

---

[14] Aeschylus, *Suppli.* 83–85.

[15] CHANIOTIS, "Conflicting Authorities," 83, 85.

[16] Euripides, *Ion* 1312–19; CHANIOTIS, "Conflicting Authorities," 65–66.

[17] Lycurgus, *Leoc.* 93.

[18] CHRISTINE M. THOMAS, "At Home in the City of Artemis: Religion in Ephesos in the Literary Imagination of the Roman Period," in *Ephesos: Metropolis of Asia*, ed. HELMUT KOESTER (Valley Forge, PA: Trinity Press International, 1995), 81–117.

are guilty have no right to asylum, stating that "the goddess has never loosed a criminal from his chains or rescued a condemned felon from his deserved fate; her altars are for the unfortunate, not for the guilty."[19] This protest by Thersandros, however, reveals a faulty understanding of the goddess's relationship to the city's law courts. Artemis is not bound by the verdicts of the civil court, for her interest is justice. Clitophon maintains his innocence despite the verdict of the court.[20] It is only the intervention of Artemis and the protection she affords that spares him an unjust fate and leads to his vindication. In this case the right of asylum trumped the unjust verdict of the civil court.

A second theme that permeates the literary record from the Classical period on is the lack of respect for the rights of asylum. If affording protection to criminals constituted one form of asylum abuse, the refusal to respect the protection of asylum counted as another. Several factors contributed to this phenomenon, including a general lack of concern for legal reprisals in the absence of consistent Greek laws governing asylum and a lack of respect on the part of some for the power of the deity. Another contributing factor, though, was the belief that asylum should be afforded only to the innocent. The unintended consequence of this belief was that some pursuers who viewed their prey as being guilty or deserving of punishment felt thereby justified in violating asylum to get at them. Classical and Hellenistic sources are full of examples of suppliants either being killed in temples or while clinging to altars, a theme that also finds artistic representation on many Greek vases.[21] In other instances suppliants were first dragged away from altars before being dispatched or even bricked in and left to die through starvation or exposure.[22] One notable example of such abuse at Ephesos occurred when an Ephesian military commander and his courtesan sought asylum in the Temple of Artemis around the middle of the third century BCE. Some Thracians who were pursuing them killed the commander in the temple and then murdered his courtesan as she clung to the knockers of the temple doors, splashing the altars with her blood.[23]

These examples of abuse, however, were often balanced by displays of respect for a temple's rights of asylum. On several occasions, Alexander the Great either supported asylum at the Temple of Artemis at Ephesos or guarded against abuses of it. In one instance, the Ephesians sought to kill some individuals who had failed to support the liberation of their city, even dragging them from the temple and stoning them. Alexander, however, intervened to keep the innocent from

---

[19] Achilles Tatius, *Leuc. Clit.* 8.8.9–11.

[20] Achilles Tatius, *Leuc. Clit.* 8.2.1–3.

[21] Apollodorus, *Epi.* E. 5.21; *Bib.* 1.9.8, 28; Diodorus Siculus, 13.62.4; 19.63.5; Herodotus, *Hist.* 1.160; 5.46; Lysias, *Erat.* 96; Polybius, *Hist.* 4.35.2–4; 9.29.4; *LIMC,* 1.1, no. 21; 2.1, no. 19–21; 7.1, no. 87–97.

[22] Lycurgus, *Leoc.* 128; Thucydides, *Hist.* 1.134.1–3; 3.81.5.

[23] Athenaeus, *Deipn.* 13.593a–b.

being killed along with the guilty.[24] On another occasion, Alexander wrote a letter to a priest of Artemis encouraging him not to lay hands upon a slave who had sought asylum there unless he could first entice him to leave the sanctuary.[25] This respect that Alexander showed for the asylum rights of the Temple of Artemis may also have contributed to his decision to extend the limits of the asylum area.[26]

One of the most significant developments relating to Greek temple asylum in the Hellenistic age is the appearance of *asylia* decrees. More than ninety such decrees have been discovered that date between 260 BCE and 22 CE.[27] These are decrees in which Greek states declared space in other Greek states to be inviolable.[28] Since, however, all temples were inviolable in theory, what was the purpose of a decree declaring inviolability for a temple that essentially already possessed it? Several factors provide some clues to the function of these decrees. First, many of these decrees declare inviolability not only for a renowned temple, but also for the *city* and/or the surrounding territory. In the decrees, temples are declared to be "inviolable" (ἄσυλον), while cities and territories are declared "sacred and inviolable" (ἱερὰν καὶ ἄσυλον).[29] In essence, the decrees represent an attempt to incorporate the city itself symbolically within the sacred space of the temple – the addition of the descriptor "sacred" when referring to the city supports this conclusion. Second, the frequent use of honorary language in the inscriptions and the practice by cities of trumpeting their title "sacred and inviolable" on their coinage suggests that these decrees functioned, at least in part, as honorary declarations extolling the deity and city.[30] Third, most of these decrees originate in the Hellenistic period during very turbulent and unstable times. They are, therefore, perhaps best understood as a tool of interstate relations designed to compensate in part for the lack of international law.[31] In other words, the decrees, which involve agreements between Greek states to honor the inviolability of a temple and/or city, were an attempt to create safety through mutual respect. In fact many of the decrees relate specifically to the presentation of Panhellenic games. They provide a measure of assurance for visitors, athletes, and merchants who cross interstate boundaries to attend the games that they will be able to do so in safety, though that assurance appears to have been based more

---

[24] Arrian, *Anab.* 1.17.12.

[25] Plutarch, *Alex.* 42.1; see also JEROME MURPHY-O'CONNOR, *St. Paul's Ephesus: Texts and Archaeology* (Collegeville, MN: Liturgical Press, 2008), 125.

[26] Strabo, *Geogr.* 14.1.23.

[27] KENT J. RIGSBY, *Asylia: Territorial Inviolability in the Hellenistic World* (Berkeley: University of California Press, 1996), 3.

[28] RIGSBY, *Asylia*, 3.

[29] RIGSBY, *Asylia*, 3.

[30] RIGSBY, *Asylia*, 22–25, 34–36; KEVIN BUTCHER, *Roman Provincial Coins: An Introduction to the 'Greek Imperials'* (London: Seaby, 1988), 112.

[31] SCHUMACHER, "Three Related Sanctuaries," 69; RIGSBY, *Asylia*, 5, 14.

on the mutual agreement to respect inviolability than on any legal or military enforcement.[32]

A noteworthy absence in the list of cities receiving these decrees is Ephesos. No Hellenistic decree granting recognition of the inviolability of the Temple of Artemis at Ephesos has been discovered. However, it is generally believed that the Temple of Artemis did receive a Hellenistic grant of inviolability based on the fact that by the Roman period it had achieved notoriety for its rights of asylum and could boast a history of foreign nations and city-states respecting its asylum.[33] If it had received a grant of inviolability, it likely would have been for the temple alone and not the city since, typically, inviolability was extended to cities only when the temple stood inside the city proper, which was not the case at Ephesos.[34] Rigsby also identifies the boundary stone that belonged to a perimeter wall of the Temple of Artemis as further evidence that the temple had received a Hellenistic grant of inviolability.[35] This boundary stone – which may date to the first or second century BCE, though likely incorporated into the wall at a later date – declares the sanctuary of Artemis to be inviolable and warns against violating the asylum (τὸ τέμενος τῆς ᾽Α[ρτέμιδος ἄσυλον] πᾶν ὅσον ἔσω π[εριβόλου· ὃς δ᾽ ἂν] παραβαίνηι, αὐτὸς [αὐτὸν αἰτιάσεται]).[36] Hicks, based on similar boundary stones elsewhere that warn against harming suppliants, reconstructs the Ephesian inscription with a similar warning (μὴ ἀδικεῖν).[37] Regardless of whether the temple had received a Hellenistic grant of inviolability, one thing is clear: by the time of the Roman period, the Temple of Artemis at Ephesos had become a standard by which rights of asylum were measured.

3. The Roman Period

In general the Romans did not practice temple asylum (at least until the time of Julius Caesar), but they did demonstrate a measure of respect for Greek asylum.[38] In one speech delivered at Corinth in 192 BCE, a Roman general, in an

---

[32] Schumacher, "Three Related Sanctuaries," 70, 90; Martin P. Nilsson, *Cults, Myths, Oracles, and Politics in Ancient Greece* (Göteberg: Paul Aströms, 1986), 120; Rigsby, *Asylia*, 22–23. See also Plutarch, *Arat.* 28; Polybius, *Hist.* 4.73.9–10.

[33] Rigsby, *Asylia*, 386–88; Tacitus, *Ann.* 3.61.

[34] Rigsby, *Asylia*, 20.

[35] Rigsby, *Asylia*, 387.

[36] *IvE* 5.1520. G. H. R. Horsley, "The Inscriptions of Ephesos and the New Testament," *NovT* 34 (1992): 156–57.

[37] E. L. Hicks, *The Collection of Ancient Greek Inscriptions in the British Museum* (Oxford: Clarendon Press, 1890), 3.176 (no. 520). An inscription from Tralles contains the following warning: τὸν ἱκέτην μὴ ἀδικεῖν μηδὲ ἀδικούμενον περιορᾶν; Margherita Guarducci, *Epigrafia Greca* (Rome: Istituto poligrafico dello Stato, 1978), 4.70–71, LL. 8–12.

[38] Billington, "Greek Suppliant Asylum," 182–88; Rigsby, *Asylia*, 2. Although apparently

attempt to curry favor with the Greeks, presented the Romans as "champions of the right of protection."[39] Nevertheless, they appeared willing to involve themselves in its regulation and adjudication, as an example from Ephesos illustrates. The slave of a Roman politician named Marcus Aurelius Scaurus sought asylum at the Temple of Artemis. When Scaurus attempted to remove his slave from the temple, an Ephesian named Pericles forcibly prevented him from doing so. As a result Pericles was summoned to Rome to stand trial for this act.[40]

In the first century BCE certain high-profile figures (Ptolemy XII and Chaeremon, an enemy of Mithridates) sought asylum at the Temple of Artemis, but this century is most notable for several important developments regarding Roman legal involvement with the temple's rights of asylum.[41] The first of these is the purge executed by Mithridates in 88 BCE when, after conquering the province of Asia, Mithridates ordered the murder of all Italians in the province. Many fled to the temples for asylum, including the Temple of Artemis at Ephesos; but when the appointed day for the purge came, asylum was not respected and thousands were slaughtered. At Ephesos the Ephesians dragged their suppliants out of the temple and killed them.[42] Following the war the Romans revoked the Hellenistic grants of asylum for many of the cities involved in these atrocities, although some of those rights appear to have been restored later by Julius Caesar.[43] Although the evidence is unclear as to whether the Temple of Artemis at Ephesos was one of those to have lost its privileges, certainly during the time of Julius Caesar the asylum function of the temple was operative, as evidenced by several events involving Mark Antony. Antony initially showed respect for Artemis and her asylum by doubling the distance of the asylum area, including a portion of the city within it, and by extending pardons to several high profile suppliants in the temple.[44] Later, though, under the influence of Cleopatra, Antony ordered the murder of one or more of her siblings while they were suppliants at the Temple of Artemis in Ephesos.[45] Appian adds that Antony's actions demonstrate his loss of respect for both divine and human laws.[46]

---

respecting the Hellenistic grants of asylum, the Romans understood asylum to be the prerogative of temples alone rather than cities and territories as mentioned in some of the grants.

[39] Diodorus Siculus, 29.1; SINN, "Greek Sanctuaries," 93–94.

[40] Cicero, *Verr.* 2.1.85.

[41] For Ptolemy see Dio Cassius, *Hist.* 39.16.3; MURPHY-O'CONNOR, *St. Paul's Ephesus*, 25. For Chaeremon see *SIG*, 741.4.

[42] DAVID MAGIE, *Roman Rule in Asia Minor: To the End of the Third Century after Christ* (Princeton: Princeton University Press, 1950), 1.216–17.

[43] RIGSBY, *Asylia*, 366, 389; STEFAN WEINSTOCK, *Divus Julius* (Oxford: Clarendon Press, 1971), 397.

[44] Appian, *Bell. civ.* 1.4; Strabo, *Geogr.* 14.1.23.

[45] The sources are a bit confused on the exact location and individuals involved in this event. Appian says it was Cleopatra's sister Arsinoe but that she was killed in the Temple of Artemis at Miletus, *Bell. civ.* 5.1.9. Dio Cassius states that Cleopatra's brothers were killed at the Tem-

Regardless of these violations, the Temple of Artemis at Ephesos continued to enjoy a reputation as one of the premier sites of asylum. Two inscriptions dating from the latter half of the first century BCE demonstrate that the temple had become a model against which rights of asylum were measured. Inscriptions from Sardis and Aphrodisias, in which the Romans confirmed the asylum privileges of their temples of Artemis and Aphrodite respectively, each contain a similar phrase that identifies the Temple of Artemis at Ephesos as the model of comparison for the asylum rights of these cities. The inscription from Sardis states: "The sanctuary of the Sardian Artemis … is to be an asylum (ἄσυλον εἶναι) by the same right (δικαίωι) which also belongs to the sanctuary of the Ephesian Artemis."[47] Likewise the inscription from Aphrodisias states that their temple is to be an asylum with the same "rights and the religious sanctity" (δεισιδαιμονίᾳ) of the Temple of Artemis at Ephesos.[48] Specifically what is involved in the "rights and the religious sanctity" of the Ephesian temple is unclear, though Rigsby suggests it may be an indication that the Temple of Artemis at Ephesos was the first temple to have its right of asylum reinstituted by Julius Caesar following the massacre under Mithridates and thus set the precedent for others.[49] Regardless, these invocations of the Ephesian Temple of Artemis highlight its status as the standard-bearer of asylum in the province of Asia.

These inscriptions also witness to Roman intervention in the establishment and governance of Greek temple asylum. As mentioned earlier, the Greeks were generally reluctant to establish broad and unambiguous laws governing asylum.[50] The Romans, by contrast, had no such qualms, particularly in the early imperial period. During Hellenistic times, interstate recognition of inviolabil-

---

ple of Artemis in Ephesos, *Hist.* 48.24.2. Josephus says it was Arsinoe who was killed at Ephesos, *Jewish Antiquities* 15.89–90. MURPHY-O'CONNOR argues that Josephus's account is likely the more accurate, *St. Paul's Ephesus*, 45–46, 61. HILKE THÜR discovered the skeleton of an 18-year-old woman in the Octagon at Ephesos, which is modelled after the Pharos in Egypt. These details and the dating of the monument lead her to identify it as the tomb of Arsinoe, which is further support for Josephus's account ("Arsinoe IV, Eine Schwester Kleopatras VII, Grabinhaberin des Oktogons von Ephesos? Ein Vorschlag," *JÖAI* 60 [1990]: 43–56.).

[46] Appian, *Bell. civ.* 5.1.9.

[47] PETER HERRMANN, "Rom und die Asylie griechischer Heiligtümer: Eine Urkunde des Dictators Caesar aus Sardeis," *Chiron* 19 (1989): 134.

[48] JOYCE REYNOLDS, *Aphrodisias and Rome,* JRS Monographs 1 (London: Society for the Promotion of Roman Studies, 1982), no. 8, LL. 55–58. See also RICHARD E. OSTER, "Holy Days in Honour of Artemis," *NewDocs* 4 (1983): 74–82.

[49] RIGSBY, *Asylia,* 389.

[50] One exception to this is runaway slaves. The process of handling slaves who have sought asylum is relatively consistent in the sources. When a runaway slave sought asylum, the priest or other officials intervened and heard the case. If an agreement of fair treatment for the slave could be reached, the slave was released to his or her master. If not, then the slave was sold to another. A variation on this theme occurred at Ephesos where the magistrates would hear the slave's case and if it was determined to be just, the individual would become the slave of Artemis; see Achilles Tatius, *Leuc. Clit.* 7.13.2–4.

ity was essential for a temple's security, but that became much less of a concern under the Roman peace.[51] The necessity of maintaining peace and control within the empire and guarding against potential threats to public order led the Romans to limit and restrict the practice in the light of growing abuses. At Ephesos the earlier extensions of the asylum area made by Alexander, Mithridates, and particularly Antony who included a part of the city in the asylum area, created a potentially volatile situation as it led to the influx of criminals into the city. Consequently, the emperor Augustus revoked these extensions, returning the asylum area to earlier limits.[52] This suggests that just as Ephesos set the standard for asylum rights in the period of the republic, it may have also set the standard for abuse and the need for restriction in the imperial period.

When we come to the reign of Tiberius this problem of criminal elements and other undesirables taking advantage of asylum generated the need for restrictions on a broader scale, and it may have been Augustus's earlier actions at Ephesos that set the precedent for this.[53] Due to this growing problem in Greek cities, the emperor Tiberius initiated a review of asylum rights in the year 22 CE that involved many cities in western Asia Minor. The cities under review sent representatives to Rome to plead the case for their asylum rights before the Roman senate. The first to make a defense were the Ephesians who pointed to the antiquity of their claim, including the suppliant Amazons who had sought refuge at the altar, and the respect shown to their right of asylum by others, including the Persians, Macedonians, and Romans. Reportedly the senate confirmed the asylum rights of the cities, but imposed limits on the practice.[54] What exactly those limits were is unknown, though it may have involved increased oversight, limiting the size of asylum areas, or the forbidding of new grants of asylum.[55] What is clear is that following the review of 22 CE, there are no certain new grants of asylum and fewer examples of individuals fleeing to temples in the available sources.[56] However, the decrease in examples of people fleeing to asylum probably has less to do with Tiberius's review and more to do with the fact that many of the earlier examples of asylum involved people fleeing for shelter in war or fleeing from political enemies, problems which were much less operative under Roman imperial governance.

If Ephesos is any indication, Tiberius' reforms ultimately had little effect on the overall persistence and viability of the practice, as it continued to play a prominent role in the life of Ephesos post-22 CE.[57] In the second half of the

---

[51] MAGIE, *Roman Rule,* 1.504.

[52] Strabo, *Geogr.* 14.1.23.

[53] RIGSBY, *Asylia,* 392–93, 580.

[54] Tacitus, *Ann.* 3.60–63.

[55] MAGIE, *Roman Rule,* 1.504; RIGSBY, *Asylia,* 584.

[56] RIGSBY, *Asylia,* 29, 584.

[57] Suetonius states that Tiberius "abolished the customary right of asylum in all parts of the

first century Josephus records a letter sent earlier by Herod Agrippa to Ephesos in which Agrippa asks that anyone who stole the sacred money earmarked for the temple in Jerusalem and then sought asylum in the Temple of Artemis be dragged from the temple and delivered to the Jews.[58] By the second century CE Plutarch can refer to asylum offered to debtors at the Temple of Artemis, Aelius Aristides can declare Ephesos to be "a refuge in time of need," and Achilles Tatius can employ asylum at the Temple of Artemis as a major plot device in his novel.[59] Furthermore, Tiberius's reforms apparently had little lasting effect also on the abuses of asylum at Ephesos, as Philostratus, writing in the early third century CE, records a letter of Apollonius of Tyana who declares the Temple of Artemis at Ephesos to be a "den of robbers" since it offers asylum to "thieves and robbers and kidnappers and every sort of wretch or sacrilegious rascal."[60] In fact, the practice of asylum at the Temple of Artemis continued at least into the middle of the third century CE where Ephesian coins tout the inviolability of Artemis of Ephesos.[61]

C. Summary of Major Themes

Despite persistent abuses, throughout the historical evolution of the practice, several consistent themes arise that governed the ideology of Greek asylum. First, the primary function of asylum was the providing of divine protection against a perceived threat, such as the dangers of war. Second, asylum afforded justice for the innocent and the wronged. Although there are some dissenting voices in the sources, the dominant viewpoint held that asylum existed to benefit the righteous, not the wicked. Third, what ultimately enforced Greek asylum was recognition of the power of the deity – both respect for a deity's power and fear of divine retribution for violation of a deity's asylum.

Greek temple asylum maintained a prominent presence in the area of western Asia Minor. Cities such as Pergamum, Sardis, Smyrna, Aphrodisias and others enjoyed temples with significant rights of asylum. Most notably, however, stood Ephesos whose Temple of Artemis was a beacon for justice and safety not only in western Asia Minor but throughout the world.

---

empire" (*Tib.* 37.3), but this is clearly incorrect. See MAGIE, *Roman Rule*, 2.1361, n. 30; MURPHY-O'CONNOR, *St. Paul's Ephesus*, 136; RIGSBY, *Asylia*, 584.

[58] Josephus, *Ant.* 16.167–68.

[59] Plutarch, *Vit. aere al.* 828D; Aelius Aristides, *Orat.* 24; Achilles Tatius, *Leuc. Clit.*

[60] Philostratus, *Ep.* 65.

[61] BARCLAY V. HEAD, *Catalogue of the Greek Coins of Ionia* (Bologna: Arnaldo Forni, 1964), 99, no. 344–45. An Ephesian inscription from the early third century BCE contains a reference to inviolability (ἀσυλίας), but is badly damaged and fragmentary, *IvE* 2.295.11.

D. Asylum and the Book of Revelation

In exploring areas of potential overlap between the book of Revelation and Greek asylum, the primary issue is not one of direct influence (though that may be present), but rather the issue of the broader conceptual world in which John writes and how his language functions within that world. For instance, how would the members of John's seven churches in western Asia Minor have heard his language of the righteous oppressed finding shelter from their enemies in the temple of God? How would Gentile Christians in Ephesos have received John's description of oppressed saints crying out for justice from an altar?

Within the narrative world of Revelation a war is raging. On the one side are God, the Lamb, and his righteous saints; on the other stand the dragon, the beasts, and their followers. The dragon has declared war on all those who keep God's commandments (12:17), and the beast has been given the power to make war against the saints and to conquer them (13:7). Within this narrative context, the saints appear as righteous victims, innocents caught in the crossfire. Due only to their faithful witness, they face suffering and oppression. This warfare theme permeates the text of Revelation and provides the structure for many of the events that unfold within it. Given that warfare was also a context in which Greek asylum functioned prominently, any language in Revelation that connects the concepts of shelter, violence, justice, or vengeance to sacred space should be explored as a potential manifestation of asylum.

War is an inherently violent endeavor. One terminological grouping used to express these violent actions in Revelation is ἀδικέω and its cognates. The term ἀδικέω means "to do harm" or "to wrong" another person. In Revelation this term and its cognates represents both the actions of the wicked who do harm (11:5; 18:5; 22:11) and God's actions of judgment upon the wicked (7:2; 9:4, 10, 19), perhaps as a representation of *lex talionis* whereby the wicked receive back upon themselves the very harm they do to others. The term ἀδικέω also appears frequently in literary sources and inscriptions involving supplication and asylum.[62] In these texts ἀδικέω identifies those who have been harmed or wronged, and that status of being on the receiving end of attempted harm is what qualifies them for asylum. Those from whom the suppliant seeks relief are the perpetrators of harm. At Ephesos the term is used of slaves who sought asylum from oppressive masters and appears in Hick's reconstruction of the asylum boundary stone as a warning not to harm suppliants – which is itself modeled on similar warnings elsewhere, such as the following example from Tralleis: τὸν ἱκέτην μὴ ἀδικεῖν μηδὲ ἀδικούμενον περιορᾶν.[63] In Revelation John employs the term in

---

[62] CHANIOTIS, "Conflicting Authorities," 83–84. See, for instance, Aristotle, *Rhet.* 3.11.5.

[63] Achilles Tatius, Leuc. Clit. 7.13.3; Hicks, 3.176 (no. 520). For the Tralleis inscription see *Die Inschriften von Tralleis und Nysa*, ed. Fjoder B. Poljakov, *Inschriften griechischer Städte aus Kleinasien*, 36,1 (Bonn: Rudolf Habelt, 1989), no. 3.

several passages depicting God's protection of his saints, both from the threatening actions of the wicked and from God's own judgment (2:11; 7:2–3; 9:4). All the
righteous in Revelation come under God's protection, in essence as his suppliants, and judgment is presented as God's wrath poured out on those who would
violate his suppliants (6:10–11, 16–17; 9:4; 11:5; 16:5–6; 17:6; 18:20, 24).

Although space does not allow for a detailed exploration, four texts in Revelation deserve mention for their conceptual overlap with the practice or ideology of asylum. The first is John's vision of the fifth seal where the souls of those
who have been slaughtered because of their faithful witness cry out from an altar
for justice and vengeance on their behalf (Rev 6:9–11). This scene contains within it all of the vital elements of Greek supplication: innocent victims in this war
with the dragon and the beast find shelter at an altar as they seek justice and rec-
ompense for what has been done to them.[64] The divine response is that wrath
will come in time against all who dare to violate God's suppliants (6:11–17). Elsewhere in Revelation the outpouring of divine judgment against the enemies of
God's people is often connected to the altar (8:3–5; 9:13; 14:18; 16:6–7). With the
fifth seal one thus finds the common themes of justice, protection, and wrath –
themes central to Greek asylum – in a scene that to any ancient inhabitant of
western Asia Minor would appear quite familiar.

The seventh chapter of Revelation presents a great multitude of the righteous
who have "come out of the great tribulation" (7:14). They have been through war
and, like the slaughtered souls in Revelation 6, now find themselves under God's
protection. They appear within the heavenly temple standing before the throne
of God with palm branches in their hands. The palm branch, often called the
"supplicant branch," was a common component of the supplication ritual. Although the connections here are less overt than with the fifth seal, this multitude
has the flavor of a crowd of suppliants finding protection and shelter in the temple of God where no longer will they hunger, or thirst, or weep (7:16–17).

Revelation 11 introduces another temple scene, though this one occurs on
earth rather than in heaven (11:1–2). Governing this scene is a contrast between
what is inside the temple and what is outside. While the faithful reside within the
inner courts of the temple, outside the nations trample on the holy city and on
the outer court of the temple. The scene evokes associations of a military siege
with the intended victims gathered within the temple seeking the divine protection of the deity, not unlike the countless examples in Greek sources of individuals fleeing to temples to avoid the violence of war. The violent and threatening
action of the nations outside against God's people is thus balanced here by the
protection afforded God's faithful within the confines of his asylum.

---

[64] For a fuller exploration of this passage in the light of Greek altar asylum, see GREGORY
STEVENSON, *Power and Place: Temple and Identity in the Book of Revelation* (Berlin: Walter de
Gruyter, 2001), 103–13, 286–93.

Finally John's vision of the New Jerusalem in Revelation 21 also incorporates elements that possess cultural resonance with Greek temple asylum. As with the temple scene in chapter eleven, John's vision of the New Jerusalem contrasts insider and outsider. Outside are the impure, the murderers, and those who do harm (21:8, 27; 22:11, 15), while inside are those who are faithful and pure (21:7, 22:14). The righteous find protection and safety within the great high walls of the city and in the presence of God. Most striking is the transformation of the temple that occurs within this city. In Revelation 21:22 John declares, "I did not see a temple in the city, because the Lord God Almighty and the Lamb are its temple." This transformation of the temple from a specific location within the city to wherever God and the Lamb are present has strong implications for the identity of this city. Scholars have long recognized that the New Jerusalem itself functions as a temple.[65] Its square shape recalling the Holy of Holies (21:16), its exclusion of anything impure (21:27), and its description as a place where God dwells and receives worship (21:3; 22:3) support this identification. God and the Lamb dwell directly among the faithful in this city and so the whole city itself functions as the temple and thus a place where the righteous find protection, justice, and safety from those outside. One is reminded of the Hellenistic practice of granting inviolability to cities as well as to temples and the occasional attempts at Ephesos and elsewhere to extend the boundaries of temple asylum to include the city or portions of it within the inviolable area. The goal of these efforts was to gain for the city some measure of the protection and safety enjoyed by the temple. That goal finds fulfillment in John's vision where city and temple essentially merge and become one due to the all-encompassing presence of God and where God's faithful witnesses inherit their reward of permanent asylum in God's city-temple.

E. Conclusion

The area of western Asia Minor had a long and rich history of involvement in Greek asylum, with Ephesos consistently leading the way. Not only did Ephesos trace the origin of its asylum at the Temple of Artemis to mythological times, but the temple became the standard bearer for asylum rights in western Asia Minor through Hellenistic and Roman times. When John, therefore, writes Revelation to Ephesos and other cities in the area, he does so with language and imagery that resonates with them theologically and culturally. One aspect of John's

---

[65] ALFRED LÄPPLE, "Das neue Jerusalem: Die Eschatologie der Offenbarung des Johannes," *BK* 39 (1984): 80; CELIA DEUTSCH, "Transformation of Symbols: The New Jerusalem in Rv 21:1–22:5," *ZNW* 78 (1987): 113, 121; WILFRID J. HARRINGTON, *Revelation* (Minnesota: Liturgical Press, 1993), 215.

message that no doubt resonated with the Christian inhabitants of western Asia Minor was that all those who took up the call to faithful witness would – no matter what opposition or harm the kingdom of the world attacked them with – find ultimate protection, safety, and justice in the presence of their God.

Family and Filial Language in Ephesians

Jerry L. Sumney*

Familial language, and particularly filial language, is far more prominent in Ephesians than in any other Pauline letter. Some comparisons with Colossians, a text the author of Ephesians likely knew, illustrate the point. The term υἱός appears twice in Colossians, four times in Ephesians; τέκνον appears twice in Colossians (both in the household code) and five times in Ephesians; κληρονομία once in Colossians, three times in Ephesians; πατήρ four times in Colossians, eleven times in Ephesians. These examples illustrate what the chart of Appendix 1 demonstrates. This difference is more than incidental. The chart shows that Ephesians uses this language metaphorically far more frequently than the tradition in which the author stands.[1] Yet when commentators discuss themes of Ephesians, familial imagery typically receives no attention.[2] Since its usage is so

---

* I am very pleased to participate in this volume to honor RICHARD E. OSTER. As he did for so many others, he helped me develop the skills needed to read texts well. He did this in no small part by showing us the value of the study of material culture. Working under a very heavy teaching load, he has been able to contribute significantly to the study of Ephesos and the New Testament. Beyond this he has given extensive and quality attention to his students. I am grateful for the ways he expected rigorous study and challenged us to think beyond our familiar constructs as we sought to be faithful as well as scholarly. It seems particularly appropriate to honor Prof. OSTER with a paper on filial imagery because it circles back to my studies with him. He was the director of my Master's thesis that investigated the function of filial language in Galatians. I hope this essay reflects in some measure the skills and sensitivities that Prof. OSTER's life and work exemplify.

[1] It is notable that Ephesians does not use ἀδελφός to express the relatedness of believers generally. It appears only twice in the letter, in 6:21 as a reference to a single individual and in 6:23 as a reference to the church as a whole in the letter's closing. Ἀδελφός is used extensively by Paul, especially in 1 Thessalonians, to talk about the intimate and familial relationships among believers (so PIETER G. R. DE VILLIERS, "Safe in the Family of God: Soteriological Perspectives in 1 Thessalonians," in *Salvation in the New Testament: Perspectives on Soteriology*, ed. by JAN G. VAN DER WATT, NovTSup 121 [Leiden: Brill, 2005], 325–26, who cites ABRAHAM J. MALHERBE, *The Letters to the Thessalonians: A New Translation with Introduction and Commentary*, AYB 32B [New Haven: Yale University Press, 2000], 110). Perhaps part of the reason for this difference is that 1 Thessalonians is not treating the question of the unity of the church, but can presume it. Paul's general use of ἀδελφός seems to reflect the expectation of this relatedness more than being a tool with which he attempts to construct it.

[2] For example, PETRUS J. GRÄBE quotes Eph 1:4–6, which mentions adoption, as an important text for understanding the soteriology of Ephesians. His discussion, however, never mentions filial language as an important lens through which Ephesians understands salvation

extraordinary, this essay will explore the functions this language has in Ephesians. We begin by noting the need in the ancient world for claiming offspring other than one's own biological children and by briefly reviewing adoption practices of the Graeco-Roman era. We will then examine the uses of filial and adoption language in Ephesians.

A. Adoption in the Graeco-Roman World

Adoption was a well-known institution in the Graeco-Roman world. The reasons for its prevalence include concerns about the continuation of family, cultic obligations, and inheritance, including keeping property within the extended family or clan group. Reviewing the evidence about infant mortality in the ancient world will help us set this concern about adoption and inheritance in context.

Adoption was well-known, in part, because of the lack of children in marriages.[3] Children, at least enough of them to pass on one's property, were seen as important throughout the ancient world. Still, many families, including wealthy families, had no heir. Estimates of the infant and child mortality rate range from a low of 20%–30% to over 50%, with most finding it closer to 50%.[4] Archeological evidence from a wide range of sites across the ancient Near East suggests that the higher estimate is more accurate.

Evidence from *necropoli* in Greece and Roman Etruria finds infants and young children almost uniformly absent from cemeteries.[5] Infants and small children

---

("Salvation in Colossians and Ephesians," in *Salvation in the New Testament: Perspectives on Soteriology*, ed. J. G. van der Watt, NovTSup 121 [Leiden: Brill, 2005], 301–3).

[3] Hugh Lindsay, *Adoption in the Roman World* (Cambridge: Cambridge University Press, 2009), 103.

[4] For the earlier estimate see Gershon Galil, *The Lower Stratum Families in the Neo-Assyrian Period*, CHANE 27 (Leiden: Brill, 2007), who bases this estimate on rates in South American countries in the 1970s that were taken from Richard H. Robbins, *Global Problems and the Culture of Capitalism* (Boston, MA: Allyn and Bacon, 1999). The latter estimate: Thomas W. Gallant gives this estimate, basing it on other pre-industrialized societies (*Risk and Survival in Ancient Greece: Reconstructing the Rural Domestic Economy* [Stanford: Stanford University Press, 1991], 21). See also Marshall J. Becker, "Childhood Among the Etruscans: Mortuary Programs at Tarquinia as Indicators of the Transition to Adult Status," in *Constructions of Childhood in Ancient Greece and Italy*, ed. Ada Cohen and Jeremy B. Rutter, Hesperia 41 (Athens: ASCSA, 2008), 282. Carolyn Osiek and Margaret Y. MacDonald, *A Woman's Place: House Churches in Earliest Christianity* (Minneapolis: Fortress, 2006), 78, 272, follow Keith Bradley, "Images of Childhood," in *Plutarch's Advice to the Bride and Groom and A Consolation of His Wife*, ed. Sarah B. Pomeroy (New York: Oxford University Press, 1999), 184, when they estimate that over 50% of children died before the age of ten.

[5] See Becker, "Childhood Among the Etruscans," 288. Becker notes that of the 262 remains discovered in the tombs of Tarquinia, none are of infants. Children of about age 5½ are among the youngest in tombs (285–88). The same absence of infants and small children is found in the Hellenistic tombs of Vitero. See also Anna Lagia, "Notions of Childhood in the Clas-

seem most often to have been interred within residential areas or in places designated for infants. In classical and early Hellenistic Greece, infants and small
children are often found in graves with more than one individual.[6] An extreme
example is the well from the second-century BCE in the Agora of Athens in
which 450 infants were found.[7] Bodies of infants have also been found in other
parts of the living area of cities, including under the floors of empty houses.
Such intramural burials are also present in Etruria.[8] In more recent times, the
cemetery of Tell El-Hesi confirms the high infant mortality rate for pre-indus-
trial cultures. The excavations at this Bedouin cemetery from the seventeenth to
eighteenth centuries explored one plot with 143 graves. Of these, 81 were infants,
18 were children, and 7 were juveniles. A second plot of 310 graves included 147
infants, 39 children and 7 juveniles.[9]

Among the materials collected about Jews from the Greco-Roman period are
inscriptions in family tombs. In one such burial chamber was found the husband,
wife, and three children aged 9¾, 9, and 2¾ (*CIJ* I. 391). Epitaphs found elsewhere included one for two children aged 19 months and 11 months (*CIJ* I. 609),
another for three children aged 3, 4, and 7 (*CIJ* I. 94), and another for three children aged 1, 2, and 4 (*CIJ* II.1527).[10]

In addition to this evidence, the literary evidence for rituals of receiving children into a family point to a reticence to include them in the family before their
survival seemed more probable. Aristotle says that children are not named until
they are seven days old, when the father can have more confidence that the child
will live (*Hist. an.* 588a, 8–10). Similarly, in Etruscan Rome girls are not named
for eight days and boys not until the ninth day.[11] Furthermore, Plutarch asserts
that there is no mourning process for children under the age of three (*Num.*
12.2). This should not lead us to think that parents were unmoved by these losses.
Epitaphs express significant sorrow over these deaths, even those who died before reaching their first birthdays.[12]

---

sical Polis: Evidence from the Bioarchaeological Record," in COHEN and RUTTER, *Constructions
of Childhood*, 299–301.

[6] LAGIA, "Notions of Childhood in the Classical Polis," 302.

[7] LAGIA, "Notions of Childhood in the Classical Polis," 303.

[8] BECKER, "Childhood Among the Etruscans," 288.

[9] J. KENNETH EAKINS, JOHN R. SPENCER, and KEVIN G. O'CONNELL, *Tell El-Hesi: Muslim
Cemetery in Fields V and VI/IX (Stratum II)* (Winona Lake: Eisenbrauns, 1993), 8–14.

[10] All the citations in this paragraph appear in G. H. R. HORSLEY, "A Jewish Family from
Egypt in Rome," *NewDocs* 4 (1987): 221–29.

[11] BECKER, "Childhood Among the Etruscans," 283. The citations of Aristotle and Plutarch
are also found here.

[12] See IGUR 1323 from the imperial period, which is an inscription for an 11 month old
whose mother is taking her ashes back to their homeland ("A Jewish Family from Egypt in
Rome," 182). *IvE* 6.2102 speaks of the guileless young child who died at age 12 ("A Jewish Family
from Egypt in Rome," 186). IGUR 1146, set up by a father for his 7 year old daughter, assures
her that she is in a better place. These are a few of the many epitaphs for children from this era.

The discussion of the exposure of children in many ancient sources seems to counter the view that infant mortality was so high. From at least Hellenistic times forward, the wealthy seem to have intentionally limited the size of families, especially daughters, in order to keep their wealth together.[13] Even so, Sarah Pomeroy estimates that as many as 40 % of families in the classical period might have had no male to inherit the father's household.[14] The result was a shrinking population. Some suggest that it took a significant amount of immigration for an ancient city such as Rome to maintain its population. Given these data, some raise doubts about the frequency of the exposure of infants in Greece and Rome.[15] Still the reticence among the elites to have large families is clear from the Augustan marriage laws that required marriage and the production of children.[16]

In addition to high infant and child mortality rates, another factor also contributed to the concerns about the continuation of family lines, the deaths of fathers. By some estimates, one-third of all Roman children lost their father before they reached puberty and another third before they were twenty-five.[17] Thus, matters of inheritance needed to be settled early in the lives of surviving children.

All of this indicates that issues relating to family membership, adoption, and inheritance were topics well-known to a significant portion of the population.[18] The preserved speeches of Isaeus from Athens in the fourth century BCE give evidence of their importance. All twelve of his extant speeches address disputes about inheritance. The disputes arose either because of questions about the validity of adoptions or because of the deaths of various people in line to receive an inheritance. Such matters attained even higher visibility when emperors began adopting their successors, as was so common in the early empire.[19] Thus, the author of Ephesians can assume that the familial and adoption language he uses

---

[13] D. P. M. WEERAKKODY, "Demography," in *The Encyclopedia of Ancient Greece,* ed. NIGEL G. WILSON (New York: Routledge, 2005), 214, provides significant evidence of wealthy families raising only one daughter.

[14] SARAH B. POMEROY, *Families in Classical and Hellenistic Greece* (Oxford: Clarendon, 1983), 14. Cited by JAMES C. WALTERS, "Paul, Adoption, and Inheritance," in *Paul and the Greco-Roman World: A Handbook* (New York: Trinity, 2003), 46, 70.

[15] GALLANT, *Risk and Survival in Ancient Greece,* 21; BECKER, "Childhood Among the Etruscans," 285.

[16] See BERYL RAWSON, "The Roman Family," in *The Family in Ancient Rome: New Perspectives,* ed. BERYL RAWSON (Ithaca: Cornell University Press, 1986), 9–10. LINDSAY estimates that 2 %–9 % of children in upper-class families were adoptees (*Adoption in the Roman World,* 3).

[17] WALTERS, "Paul, Adoption, and Inheritance," 54, citing RICHARD P. SALLER, *Patriarchy, Property, and Death in the Roman Family* (Cambridge: Cambridge University Press, 1994), 189.

[18] Cf. SABINE R. HÜBNER AND DAVID M. RATZAN, eds., *Growing Up Fatherless in Antiquity* (Cambridge: Cambridge University Press, 2011), and SABINE R. HÜBNER, *The Family in Roman Egypt: A Comparative Approach to Intergenerational Solidarity and Conflict* (Cambridge: Cambridge University Press, 2013), esp. 175–86.

[19] RAWSON notes that through the first two centuries of the empire, only three emperors

will have resonance, even among those who are not of a social class likely to receive an inheritance. While the readers of Ephesians may not have known all the details of particular practices of the institutions of adoption and inheritance, the public nature of civil courts makes it more likely that they would have a rudimentary knowledge of them. Further, as Adolf Deissmann noted, the term υἱοθεσία appears often enough in inscriptions of the period to show that it was a "generally intelligible figure."[20]

Interpreters have given extensive attention to identifying the legal system upon which Paul relied when he used adoption metaphors.[21] The basic options are the Jewish, Greek, or Roman systems. It seems clear that neither Paul nor the author of Ephesians rely on Jewish law about adoption since there are no biblical examples of, or laws about, adoption[22] and very few references to it in any extant Jewish literature of the period.[23] Brendan Byrne, however, notes that the sonship of Israel becomes a topic in some Second Temple period writings. In these works sonship involves the establishment of the prerogatives of Israel in relation to other nations as well as receiving chastisement and an inheritance.[24]

---

were survived by sons: Claudius, Vespasian, and Marcus Aurelius ("The Roman Family," 12). Only Titus succeeded his father as emperor.

[20] G. ADOLF DEISSMANN, *Bible Studies*, trans. ALEXANDER J. GRIEVE (Edinburgh: T&T Clark, 1909), 239.

[21] Even though the author of Ephesians is a disciple of Paul, the same questions arise because he was also a Jewish writer of some social and religious standing, as is evidenced by his ability to compose this letter and his sophisticated treatment of the matters it addresses.

[22] TREVOR J. BURKE notes that some have seen Paul drawing on God making David God's son when he becomes king. But he argues that this elevation of status remains different from adoption (*Adopted into God's Family: Exploring a Pauline Metaphor*, New Studies in Biblical Theology [Downers Grove: IVP, 2006], 56–57). JAMES D. HESTER also argues that Paul's ideas about receiving an inheritance from God stand in substantial continuity with ideas on this matter found in the Hebrew Bible (*Paul's Concept of Inheritance: A Contribution to the Understanding of Heilsgeschichte*, Scottish Journal of Theology Occasional Papers 14 [London: Oliver and Boyd, 1968], vii–viii). But HESTER also recognizes that most of Paul's church members would have known little of Jewish law about inheritance because they were Gentiles. MATTHEW VELLANICKAL is among the few who see understandings of Israel as God's son as the primary lens through which to interpret Paul's metaphor of adoption (*The Divine Sonship of Christians in the Johannine Writings*, AnBib 72 [Rome: Biblical Institute Press, 1977], 69–70).

[23] CAROLINE JOHNSON HODGE notes that Jews recognized adoption in other cultures. This is seen by the references to the adoption of Moses by Pharaoh in Philo and Josephus and by their mentions of the adoptions of emperors (*If Sons, Then Heirs: A Study of Kinship and Ethnicity in the Letters of Paul* [Oxford: Oxford University Press, 2007], 31). Among the most important passages in Philo for our purposes is *Sobr.* 56 where Philo speaks of the one whose lot (κλῆρος) is wisdom being adopted (εἰσποιητός) by God to be God's only son. See also *Conf.* 145–47 where the Logos, as the firstborn, transforms humans into sons of God (cited by FLORENTINO GARCÍA MARTÍNEZ, "Divine Sonship at Qumran and in Philo," *SPhiloA* 19 [2007]: 99). See also the discussion of sonship and adoption in VELLANICKAL, *The Divine Sonship of Christians in the Johannine Writings*, 26–43.

[24] BRENDAN BYRNE, *Sons of God, Seed of Abraham: A Study of the Idea of the Sonship of God of All Christians in Paul against the Jewish Background*, AnBib 83 (Rome: Biblical Institute,

Throughout the rest of the Greco-Roman world, those adopted were usually adults. Adoption was not about caring for children, but preserving family lines to keep estates intact and to perpetuate family cults. In ancient Greece adoptions were public affairs. Some adoptions were carried out through wills, others while the head of the household was still living. While there was no single common set of adoption laws throughout Greece, there were some commonalities. Greek adoptions were concluded in public assemblies. At Gortyn, it was in the market square before a tribunal and had to be approved by the clan group (φρατρία) as well as the assembly of citizens. (δῆμος).[25] The basic purpose of adoption was to perpetuate a family line and keep property within the extended family.[26] Men with legitimate sons were not allowed to adopt another son in Greece. When a son was born to the father after an adoption, the adopted son experienced a lowering of status. In that case, the adopted son received only the size of inheritance given daughters.[27] In fourth-century Athens, only citizens could be adopted; it was even difficult to adopt one's own illegitimate sons.[28] The person adopted was usually a relative, a decision which helped the assets remain within extended families.[29]

We know more about Roman adoption and its detailed rules. It was also primarily about inheritance and the continuation of a family name and cult.[30] The two types of Roman adoptions were distinguished by whether the adoptee was under the *manus* of a *paterfamilias* or was *sui iuris*. If the person about to be adopted was not under the power of a father, he was adopted by adrogation. In this process the adoptee ceded control of all assets to the new father and came under his *manus*. In the *adoptio* process the person still *in potestas* was freed from this power through an ancient law (the Rule of the Twelve Tablets) which said that a son would be free from the power of the father after the father had sold him into slavery three times. With the help of an intermediary, the son was "sold" three times. Then the new father claimed the son who took the new family name and was fully under the power of the new father.[31] Contrary to Greek prac-

---

1979), 23–67. He finds the theme of sonship particularly prominent only in Jubilees, 3 Maccabees, and Wisdom of Solomon.

[25] See WALTERS, "Paul, Adoption, and Inheritance," 47; MARTITZ, "υἱοθεσία," TDNT 8:398; RAPHAEL SEALEY, *The Justice of the Greeks* (Ann Arbor: University of Michigan Press, 1994), 71.

[26] HESTER, *Paul's Conception of Inheritance*, 13. HESTER is commenting on Solon's laws.

[27] See SEALEY, *The Justice of the Greeks*, 71.

[28] An exception to the citizenship requirement could be granted by a vote of 6,000 Athenians according to Demosthenes (*Against Neaera* 59.89).

[29] LINDSAY, *Adoption in the Roman World*, 59–60.

[30] MIREILLE CORBIER, "Divorce and Adoption as Familial Strategies," in RAWSON, *Marriage, Divorce, and Children in Ancient Rome*, 63; LINDSAY, *Adoption in the Roman World*, xii. CORBIER cites Cicero, *Dom.* 35 as evidence for these purposes of adoption.

[31] See the discussion of these procedures in LINDSAY, *Adoption in the Roman World*, 65–82, and GEOFFREY S. NATHAN, *The Family in Late Antiquity: The Rise of Christianity and the Endurance of Tradition* (New York: Routledge, 2000), 25.

tice, a father could adopt multiple sons, and they counted as natural sons in legal matters.[32]

Most Roman adoptions also involved a relative; most often the son of the adopter's brother or sister. This both increased family wealth and strengthened ties within the wider family group.[33] When this was not the case, a person agreed to adoption or adrogation in order to increase their status and wealth.[34] While the adrogated was temporarily made less powerful, that sacrifice came with the promise of more power and status in the future.[35] However, the rise in status had its limits. For example, adoption of a freedman by a freeborn citizen could not confer the rights of a freeborn citizen on the adopted person.[36] Other limits appear in at least some regions. The second-century *Gnomon of the Idios Logos* (*BGU* V 1210; *POxy* XLVII 3014) in Egypt makes it problematic for a person to adopt a son much below his own social class. It penalizes such an adoption by taxing the estate one-fourth of its value.[37] All of this evidence counters the traditional claim among commentators on Ephesians that it was a common practice to adopt slaves.[38] On the other hand, legal discussions and epigraphic evidence indicate that freedmen were, at least on occasion, adopted.[39]

The presence of both this adoption law from Egypt and the discussion of adoption in Aulus Gellius confirm that there was a broad knowledge of Roman adoption practices throughout the empire. It seems likely that the author of Ephesians expects his readers to think of the Roman legal system when he speaks of adoption and other familial matters. As James Walters comments about Paul and the Galatians, however, it is unlikely that this author has or expects his read-

---

[32] LINDSAY, *Adoption in the Roman World*, 109–10; also CORBIER, "Divorce and Adoption as Familial Strategies," 73–74.

[33] LINDSAY, *Adoption in the Roman World*, 103–4. See also CORBIER, "Divorce and Adoption as Familial Strategies," 67–68, who notes that other frequent options include a son-in-law or a grandson.

[34] MICHAEL PEPPARD, "The Eagle and the Dove: Roman Imperial Sonship and the Baptism of Jesus (Mark 1.9–11)," *NTS* 56 (2010): 440.

[35] Still Cicero could be denigrated by someone saying he was a "mere adopted" child of a citizen (Sallust, *Bell. Cat.* 31).

[36] LINDSAY, *Adoption in the Roman World*, 75, citing the second-century provincial writer Aulus Gellius, *Noct. att.* 5.19.

[37] *Gnomon of the Idios Logos*, 41. Cited by KATHLEEN E. CORLEY, "Women's Inheritance Rights in Antiquity and Paul's Metaphor of Adoption," in *A Feminist Companion to Paul*, ed. AMY-JILL LEVINE and MARIANNE BLICKENSTAFF, FCNTECW 6 (New York: T&T Clark, 2004), 115. Logos 41 speaks of a person who adopts a son "from the rubbish heap."

[38] Recent repetitions of this claim include ANDREW T. LINCOLN, *Ephesians*, WBC (Nashville: Thomas Nelson, 1990), 25, and MARGARET MACDONALD, *Colossians and Ephesians*, SP (Collegeville: Liturgical Press, 2000), 199. For discussion of the adoption of relatives see CORBIER, "Divorce and Adoption as Familial Strategies," 67–68.

[39] See JANE F. GARDNER, "The Adoption of Roman Freedmen," *Phoenix* 43 (1989): 236–57. The appendix of this article contains the text of some of the inscriptions that name individuals as freed and adrogated. See also her discussion of whether adopted freedmen were accorded all the rights of an adopted free born citizen.

ers to have extensive knowledge of the intricacies of adoption law. Still they know of the important connections between adoption and inheritance.[40] They would also know of the change in status that an adoption could bring. We should not expect legal expertise, but can rely on the author and readers to have had general knowledge of the practices and meanings of adoption.[41]

B. Fatherhood and Filiation in Ephesians

The familial language of Ephesians, particularly that of parent and children, serves the important functions of establishing the unity of the church, assuring believers of salvation, and identifying the church as the household of God. Thus, it contributes to some of the central themes of Ephesians.

In the undisputed letters, Paul unites the different ethnic groups in his churches by giving them a common ancestor (Abraham). While he does not collapse Jews and Gentiles into a single ethnic group, he does create a fictive kinship through which Gentiles are taken into the people of God.[42] Ephesians, clearly written by a Jewish author (or an author who dons a Jewish mask), often maintains this ethnic difference when it distinguishes the "you" (Gentiles) who were far off (2:13, 17), dead in trespasses and sins (2:1), and strangers and aliens (2:12, 19) from those Jews like himself who were already near and already citizens (2:12, 17). But in places Ephesians mutes this distinction or perhaps even leaves it behind, and does so using familial language.

Chapter 2 begins by identifying Gentiles as those who were dead in sin and who lived in accord with the powers of evil that are at work "in the sons of disobedience" (ἐν τοῖς υἱοῖς τῆς ἀπειθείας; v. 2). This sounds like the usual distinction between Gentile worshippers of many gods and Jews who worship only God.[43] But in v. 3, the author says "we all lived" as people identified with this group.[44] And further that "we" were "by nature children (τέκνα) of wrath, even

---

[40] WALTERS, "Paul, Adoption, and Inheritance," 43–44.

[41] HESTER seems to be on the right track when he acknowledges that Roman law is probably the source of Paul's metaphor, but that he draws on none of its details (*Paul's Concept of Inheritance*, 9). HESTER may go too far when he asserts that all of Paul's illustrations about inheritance can be found in Roman law. VELLANICKAL also identifies specific elements of Paul's use of adoption with specific practices of Roman adoption (*The Divine Sonship of Christians in the Johannine Writings*, 71).

[42] See JOHNSON HODGE and her discussion of the importance of the ideology of patrilinear descent in the construction of this identity for the church (*If Sons, Then Heirs*, 4–23).

[43] BEST, however, argues that the "you" (ὑμᾶς) of 2:1 refers to Jews and Gentiles rather than just Gentiles (*A Critical and Exegetical Commentary on Ephesians*, ICC [Edinburgh: T&T Clark, 1998], 199–200). The regular distinctions drawn between Jews and Gentiles in Ephesians, often signaled by use of second person plural, makes this reading unlikely. Even if BEST is correct, it does no harm to the point I am making.

[44] MARKUS BARTH sees this identification of Jews as one that follows in the tradition of the

as the rest." Here in the space of two verses, Ephesians uses filial language to give Jews and Gentiles a common identity before their admission into the church. Both belong in the same family with respect to their relationship with the powers and because they live by the desires of the flesh. Further, after beginning the paragraph saying *you* were dead because of trespasses (v. 1), the author moves to *we* were dead because of trespasses in v. 5.

There are parallels between the movement in this passage and that in Rom 1–2 where Paul demonstrates that both Gentiles and Jews need the gospel. Romans, however, never identifies Jews with the children of disobedience or says Jews are "by nature" just like "the rest," that is, Gentiles. So, Ephesians has taken a quite different tack or has gone a step further here. It has done more than identify a common need, it has constructed a common identity with filial terminology.[45] Importantly, this common identity is outside the church, and so the author identifies a common familial connection between Jews and Gentiles beyond that found in Christ.[46] At least part of the purpose of this unity of identity is to prepare for proclamation of a common salvation for all: God made *us* alive together in Christ; *we* are saved through grace (2:5).

Following closely behind this construction of common identity, however, Ephesians returns to establishing clear lines between Gentiles outside the church and Jews. In 2:11 the author reminds the readers of when they were formerly Gentiles, estranged from God and outside the people of God. Indeed, all the argument of 2:11–22 rests on an original and deep division between Jews and Gentiles, which is removed for those who become participants in Christ.[47]

The passing reference to the "sons of humans" in 3:5, however, again seems to group together Jews and Gentiles. The mystery of the gospel, the content of which seems to be the inclusion of Gentiles among the people of God,[48] was hidden from all people, Jews and Gentiles alike. The contrast here is eschatological.

---

prophets who spoke about Israel's rebellion (*Ephesians 1–3*, AYB 34 [Garden City, NY: Doubleday, 1974], 217). While this may well be correct, Ephesians is adding a layer of meaning here.

[45] MacDonald comments that it is hard to imagine that Paul or even someone writing in his name could describe Jews as "children of disobedience" or see their prior condition to be the same as Gentiles (*Colossians and Ephesians*, 231).

[46] At the same time, MacDonald notes that "like the rest" is strong sectarian language (*Colossians and Ephesians*, 231). Thus it reinforces the boundary between church and outsiders by creating this common identity for those within.

[47] Nils A. Dahl has noted the tension between "exclusivity and universalism" throughout Ephesians ("Gentiles, Christians, and Israelites in the Epistle to the Ephesians," in *Studies in Ephesians: Introductory Questions, Text- & Edition-Critical Issues, Interpretation of Texts and Themes*, ed. David Hellholm, Vemund Blomkvist, and Tord Fornberg, WUNT 1.131 [Tübingen: Mohr Siebeck, 2000], 442). The succession of these paragraphs is an example of that tension.

[48] Dahl also comments that the mystery in Ephesians is "The Gentiles' incorporation as equal members of Christ" ("Gentiles, Christians, and Israelites in the Epistle to the Ephesians," 431).

All humans belong to one group (those ignorant of the mystery) before the time when the revelation was given to the church's apostles and prophets. While this may be a casual reference with only an eschatological implication, what follows is clearly intentional.

In 3:14–15, the writer praises God as the father of all tribes/clans (πατριά). This assertion certainly claims that God is the creator of all things, particularly all clan groups on earth and in heavenly realms.[49] This identification of God as father and as the one who names all πατριά sets God in a close and authoritative relationship with all peoples.[50] More specifically, Ephesians uses this expression to demonstrate again the unity of Jews and Gentiles.[51] Lincoln rejects the notion that the inclusion of Gentiles is in view here because that is not a theme of the prayer.[52] The repetition of τούτου χάριν in 3:14 signals the resumption of the prayer started but broken off in 3:1. If that is the case, the themes of 3:2–13 indicate that the unity of Jews and Gentiles is in view. Even if 3:14 does not resume 3:1, the immediately preceding discussion of the uniting of Jews and Gentiles strongly suggests that it remains in view as this prayer begins. The change in subject is not so dramatic that the preceding subjects have been completely dropped. The continuity is confirmed by the repetition of identifying God as creator of all things (3:9) and perhaps the mention of heavenly beings (3:10). Further, the mention of Gentiles becoming co-heirs (v. 6) may be yet another thematic connection between the two sections. In addition, the eschatological grouping of all humans as "sons of humans" before the revelation of Christ in 3:5 signals that the theme of God as creator/father has remained a topic within the context.

The explicit way that Ephesians identifies God as Father and namer of all clans, then, creates a common identity for Jews and Gentiles. As we saw in connection with 2:3, this is a unity that exists prior to incorporation into Christ. Here the distinction between those who were "near" and those who were "far away" dissolves into the unity of all having the same father and all being named and so claimed by God. This unity is grounded in the creating (rather than the saving) power of God. This claim about God also authorizes God to give "you" strength that reflects God's glory (3:16). This ὑμῖν may refer to either Gentile believers or all believers. Verse 18 may suggest that this "you" refers to Gen-

---

[49] As noted by Pheme Perkins, "The Letter to the Ephesians: Introduction, Commentary, and Reflections," *NIB*, 11:414, and Harold W. Hoehner, *Ephesians: An Exegetical Commentary* (Grand Rapids: Baker Academic, 2002), 475.

[50] Best, *Ephesians*, 339. See Barth, *Ephesians 1–3*, 382–84, for a review of the ways God's naming of all clans has been interpreted.

[51] So Bonnie Thurston, *Reading Colossians, Ephesians, and 2 Thessalonians: A Literary and Theological Commentary*, Reading the New Testament (New York: Crossroad, 1995), 118. She also asserts that having God give a name follows a Semitic tradition and implies that the named one is included in "the circle of divine concern."

[52] Lincoln, *Ephesians*, 203–4.

tiles because it asserts that the designated group will be enabled to understand "with all the saints." Whether ὑμῖν in 3:16 refers only to Gentile believers or not, vv. 14–15 clearly use familial language to demonstrate the unity of Jews and Gentiles.

Thus, unlike other Pauline writings, Ephesians posits a natural unity of Jews and Gentiles. They have the same father by whom they were named. In addition, both were all "by nature children of wrath." This identity has an eschatological nuance because the change in the state of all comes through God's gracious act in Christ (2:4–6). The eschatological element is explicit in 3:5 as the mystery is withheld from all the "sons of humans." While we expect Pauline literature to posit the unity of all in Christ, it is distinctive – even surprising – to find Ephesians asserting a common nature, status, and circumstance for Jews and Gentiles outside Christ. Ephesians asserts this unity primarily through use of filial and paternal imagery.

Ephesians uses the same familial language to create a fictive kinship for Jews and Gentiles *within* the church. As do all the other Pauline letters, the greeting of Ephesians refers to God as Father, with most referring to "our Father."[53] But Ephesians is unusual in that it takes up the theme of God as father in what immediately follows.[54]

The blessing of 1:3–14, which Dahl speaks of as congratulatory for the Gentile recipients,[55] first identifies God as "Father of our Lord Jesus Christ."[56] This identification of God and Christ prepares readers for the claim that God chose "us for adoption" (ἡμᾶς εἰς υἱοθεσίαν). As is noted by many, the term υἱοθεσία is rare in literary sources until after the first century, though it appears regularly in inscriptions.[57] In the New Testament, it appears only in Pauline letters. Notably,

---

[53] The Pastoral Epistles refer to God as Father, but lack the first person plural possessive pronoun.

[54] Colossians is the only other letter in the Pauline corpus that uses πατήρ in the section immediately following the greeting (1:3). In addition, Galatians uses the term three times in its extensive greeting, but then only once more to refer to God in the entire letter (4:2).

[55] NILS A. DAHL, "Benediction and Congratulation," in *Studies in Ephesians: Introductory Questions, Text- & Edition-Critical Issues, Interpretation of Texts and Themes,* ed. DAVID HELLHOLM, VEMUND BLOMKVIST, and TORD FORNBERG, WUNT 1.131 (Tübingen: Mohr Siebeck, 2000), 303. NILS A. DAHL further sees 1:3–14 as a revision of a preformed baptismal blessing ("Das Proömium des Epheserbriefes," in HELLHOLM, BLOMKVIST, and FORNBERG, *Studies in Ephesians,* 327). But CHARLES TALBERT notes that most interpreters today see it as a composition by the letter's author that does not draw heavily on preformed traditions (*Ephesians and Colossians,* Paideia [Grand Rapids: Baker, 2007], 41). ALLEN MAWHINNEY suggests that this section draws on the baptismal narratives of the Gospels ("Baptism, Servanthood, and Sonship," *WTJ* 49 [1987]: 52). While the author of Ephesians probably did not have the texts of the Gospels, he may have drawn on the traditions found in those narratives.

[56] Ephesians may be drawing on the beginning of Colossians here because the latter begins its thanksgiving with the same identification of God. Following that borrowing, Ephesians goes its own way thematically.

[57] See e. g., BURKE, *Adopted into God's Family,* 22.

one of the five appearances of this term is Rom 9:4 where it is one of the privileges of Israel, even as it is also a gift to the church (Rom 8:15, 23; also Gal 4:5). In
Ephesians, this adoption privilege is a possession of the church and was always
in the plan of God. This first occurrence of the adoption metaphor in Ephesians uses the first person plural ("us"), and thus includes both Jews and Gentiles
in this adoption.[58] Thus it sets them on equal footing within the family of God;
both are adopted. Unlike the fig tree analogy of Romans 11, there are no natural
born sons among believers in Ephesians 1.[59]

Both the foreordination and the adoption show that the initiative for this relationship comes from God.[60] It is the adopter who initiates the process and does
all that is necessary to see it through to its final claiming of an heir for a new
family. Following expectations of both Greek and Roman adoptions, the adopted
child comes under the power of the new father and thus the adoption involves
a shift in allegiances to a new *paterfamilias*.[61] Hoehner comments that with this
adoption, God now "controls their lives and property" as the *paterfamilias* did
following an adoption.[62] Like other Greek and Roman adoptions, this one also
brings new religious/cultic responsibilities. It is unusual, however, to find that
the families are opposed to one another rather than cooperating. That point is
not stressed in 1:3–14, but becomes very evident in chapter 2.

As with most adoptions, this one grants privilege and new status. It confers
on the adoptee the status of the new family. Unlike both Greek and Roman adoptions, the adoptee did not have to possess already a particular status to attain
all the privileges of the new family (in Greece already be a citizen; in Rome not
be a freedman). As is evident in the rest of the letter, the adoption of some of
these sons and the granting of status to them was a surprise to others.[63] Not
only is this conferring of status an expected element of literal adoptions, it is also
found in Philo's discussions of God adopting sons. When God adopts Abraham,
Philo says that it makes him higher than other humans (*Sobr.* 56). Elsewhere,

---

[58] Contra BARTH, *Ephesians*, 81. Best, however, seems to see it referring to both Jews and
Gentiles in the church as he uses "believers" as the recipients of this adoption throughout his
discussion of the verse (*Ephesians*, 123–26). The distinction the author so often draws between
himself as a Jewish believer, and "you" Gentiles, suggests that this "us" refers to all believers,
Jews and Gentiles.

[59] We might, however, bear in mind that Paul uses the fig tree analogy within an extended
argument in Romans. There he says one of the gifts to the Jews is "adoption" (9:4).

[60] So also BURKE, *Adopted into God's Family*, 75. See BYRNE's comparison of 1:3–14 with
Romans 8, particularly v. 29 (*Sons of God, Seed of Abraham*, 126).

[61] HOEHNER, *Ephesians*, 196–97; BURKE, *Adopted into God's Family*, 81–82, here following
WAYNE MEEKS, *The Origins of Christian Morality: The First Two Centuries* (New Haven: Yale,
1993), 170.

[62] HOEHNER, *Ephesians*, 196–97.

[63] The term υἱοθεσία is commonly gender specific. It grants status within the family and
makes the adoptee an heir. See CORLEY, "Women's Inheritance Rights in Antiquity," 108–21.

the Logos as firstborn works as mediator to transform humans into sons of God, which brings them new status (*Conf.* 145–47).[64]

The language of being adopted by a god was also current in imperial propaganda. Octavian used it to assert his status by emphasizing his filial connection through adoption to the divine Julius. Peppard sees imperial usage as so prominent that he asserts that to claim to be a son of god primarily meant you were the son of the emperor.[65] By the time of Ephesians, these imperial adoptions were common and highly visible. Thus, when Ephesians claims that believers are adopted by God we may hear a counter-imperial claim, and we certainly hear the assertion of a privileged position. As in Philo and the imperial family, believers in Ephesians have a higher status than other humans who are "sons of disobedience" (2:2) rather than sons of God.

Best argues that the analogy with Roman adoption breaks down because Christ serves as a mediator in God's adoption of believers and there was no mediator in the Roman process.[66] But perhaps a mediator is not as foreign as it first appears. There were intermediaries in the process of adoption of a son still under a father's *manus*. The symbolic buying and selling of the son required some intermediary. An increasing number of interpreters understand the metaphor of redemption in this context. The most common options for interpreting redemption have been that it is a reference to the slave market, the release of prisoners, or general deliverance.[67] James Hester, however, proposed that the better context in which to see this metaphor when used in Gal 3 is the adoption process in which the new father buys the son who is sold as a slave. Christ then is the means by which the son is bought.[68] Walters builds on this suggestion, noting that the prior obligations and debts of the one adopted became the responsibility of the new father. Thus, Paul sees Christ as the means by which believers are adopted out of their debt.[69] This shift to focus on the prior plight of the adopted makes sense because God does not need to adopt for the usual reason, that is, the preservation of the family line.[70]

If this line of reasoning provides the proper reading for redemption in Ephesians, then filial imagery plays an even larger role in the theology of this letter. Ephesians uses the term ἀπολύτρωσις three times; only Romans among all New Testament books uses it that many times. Two of those occurrences appear in

---

[64] See MARTÍNEZ, "Divine Sonship at Qumran and in Philo," 85–99, for discussion of these passages in Philo and adoption at Qumran.

[65] PEPPARD, "The Eagle and the Dove," 436–37.

[66] *Ephesians*, 125. Burke also cites this as a difference between Paul and Roman practice (*Adopted into God's Family*, 195).

[67] See e. g., LINCOLN, *Ephesians*, 27–28; THURSTON, *Reading Colossians, Ephesians, and 2 Thessalonians*, 96; HOEHNER, *Ephesians*, 205–7; BEST, *Ephesians*, 130.

[68] HESTER, *Paul's Concept of Inheritance*, 18–19.

[69] WALTERS, "Paul, Adoption, and Inheritance," 57–58.

[70] WALTERS, "Paul, Adoption, and Inheritance," 58.

1:3–14 (vv. 7, 14), with the second of those associated with believers receiving their inheritance. If it does not stretch the adoption metaphor too far, this reading shows how God's adoption is transacted "through Christ Jesus." It is the death of Christ that serves as the means by which the adoption of believers is accomplished; it settles their debts and makes the payments required for God to claim them as sons.

As a result of this adoption, Ephesians says believers have access to God as their Father, access that only those in the Spirit have through Christ (2:18).[71] They approach God as members of God's household (2:19). Such access to this father may be another place at which Ephesians sounds a counter-imperial note. The emperor was regularly portrayed as the *paterfamilias* of the empire. Still, only those close to him had immediate access. If the readers of Ephesians understand their adoption to mean that they have been transferred to the control of another and more powerful *paterfamilias*, they may hear this as news that they have an entrance into the presence of this father that they would never have had with the previous one. So not only does the new family line have more power and honor, but the readers have more access to the father who wields the power.

Any discussion of adoption in the first century had a direct connection with inheritance. Inheritance language is also more prominent in Ephesians than in other Pauline writings (see the chart). In 1:14 believers all possess the Spirit as a down payment of their inheritance. That presence of God in their lives is a beginning of the eschatological access to God they will experience in the future. The inheritance that all believers receive is final salvation, life in the full presence of God who is their *paterfamilias*.

A significant shift from the adoption of "us" (1:5) appears in 3:6. Here Gentiles are clearly being brought into the inheritance of Israel; Gentiles are "fellow-heirs." This reflects the understanding that is predominant in 2:11–22, and 3:1–13.[72] In these sections the distinction between Gentiles outside of Christ and Jews is usually clear.[73] The mystery revealed in this eschatological time is that Gentiles are included among those who receive an inheritance from God.[74] In this account of the adoption, Gentiles are at best late-comers. Still, they fully share the inheritance. This description of sharing the inheritance reflects Roman adoption more than Greek adoption in which the adopted son was demoted if

---

[71] PERKINS notes that this claim stands in contrast to the description of Gentiles in 2:12 as "without God in the world" ("The Letter to the Ephesians," 74).

[72] LINCOLN, however, rejects this reading. He contends that Ephesians is not emphasizing relationship with Israel but rather the unity of the church because Ephesians sees those divisions already transcended in the church (*Ephesians*, 180).

[73] See, however, the discussion of 3:5 above.

[74] PAUL L. HAMMER, "A Comparison of *klēronomia* in Paul and Ephesians," *JBL* 79 (1960): 271, correctly notes that συγκληρονόμος refers to the relationship among church members, not that between believers and Christ.

there was a biologically-produced son.[75] In that case, as noted above, the adopted son received a smaller inheritance.[76] In Roman adoptions, the adopted possessed all the legal status that a biological son had. Further, in Roman law a *paterfamilias* could adopt more than one son.

In 3:6, what divides Jews and Gentiles, and makes the latter inferior, remains in place until Gentiles confess Christ and are thus brought into the family of God. This pattern sounds much like that in Romans, where the Gentiles are grafted into Israel, and Israel retains priority in receiving the gospel.[77] Still, both Jewish and Gentile believers enjoy God's promises because they are "in Christ Jesus." Again Ephesians describes final salvation as an inheritance, and thus dependent on being in God's family.

The reference to God's glorious inheritance in 1:18 may refer to either an inheritance that believers receive,[78] or God's possession of believers as God's inheritance.[79] The wording of the text (particularly the pronoun αὐτοῦ) favors the latter reading and thus signals that the inheritance language is being used differently here. This different usage has significant parallels in the Hebrew Bible. Following use of the metaphor in the Hebrew Bible, it is an expression of the claim that God makes on believers and of their value to God. Calling believers, both Jews and Gentiles, God's inheritance expresses their unity and the certainty of their salvation.[80]

---

[75] As MARTÍNEZ notes, talk of Israel as son does not express a genetic relationship, but rather is an expression of the people's relationship with God through election, covenant, and inheritance ("Divine Sonship at Qumran and in Philo," 88). Still in this passage, this sonship grants a privilege that Gentiles do not share. MARTÍNEZ also notes that in Philo there are gradations of sonship, ranging from alien to genuine, with adopted as one of those gradations (95, citing *Mut.* 147). It may be worth noting Philo's Jewish identity since adoption seems to have been rare among Jews. Thus their view of it may have been less favorable than that of others in the first century. Of course, the author of Ephesians is also Jewish and so this way of thinking may have influenced him at this point.

[76] SEALEY, *The Justice of the Greeks*, 71 (citing Demosthenes); LINDSAY, *Adoption in the Roman World*, 38–40 (citing the Gortyn Code). See also the above discussion of adoption in ancient Greece.

[77] This treatment of Gentiles seems close to the way CAROLINE JOHNSON HODGE describes the position of Paul. She sees him identify Gentile believers as somewhere between Gentiles and Jews, they become "an affiliate people" who share with Jews ancestry, Scripture, and God. See "Olive Trees and Ethnicities: Judeans and Gentiles in Rom. 11.17–24," in *Christians as a Religious Minority in a Multicultural City; Modes of Interaction and Identity Formation in Early Imperial Rome*, ed. JÜRGEN ZANGENBERG and MICHAEL LABAHN, JSNTSup 243 (New York: T&T Clark, 2004), 88. Similarly see BYRNE, *Sons of God, Seed of Abraham*, 215, who says that Gentiles come to share the privileges of Israel through aggregation to the people of God through Christ.

[78] So BARTH, *Ephesians*, 151, and BEST, *Ephesians*, 167.

[79] So LINCOLN, *Ephesians*, 59; MACDONALD, *Colossians and Ephesians*, 218; HOEHNER, *Ephesians*, 266–67.

[80] The phrase "redemption of the possession" (1:14) probably has God as the one claiming believers as God's own possession as a part of what it means to receive "our inheritance."

Ephesians calls God 'Father' eight times, twice as often as any other Pauline letter. There are two references to God as Father in the opening lines of the letter and another in the closing lines. The number and placement of this title for God indicates that it constitutes a central way Ephesians presents God. The Hebrew Bible seldom refers to God as Father, and Paul rarely calls God Father outside the greetings of his letters. But Ephesians routinely uses this title for God. It is as father that God gives revelation (1:17), receives praise (5:20), and is related to the church and the whole of humanity (4:6; 3:14). And since it is the father who determines what the inheritance is, God is acting in this role when Ephesians speaks of receiving an inheritance (1:14, 18; 3:6; 5:5).[81] Identifying God as father, then, is a central soteriological theme for Ephesians, even as it establishes the unity of Jews and Gentiles in the church (see above the discussion of 3:14).

A cluster of filial language appears in 5:1–10 (20), especially in vv. 5–8. Most interpreters identify 4:25–5:2 as a section of loosely connected commands that give instructions for how believers should conduct their lives.[82] The exhortations in 5:1–2 are broader instructions with a more detailed sanction, however, and so seem to serve as the introduction of a new section rather than as the conclusion of the previous one.[83] Perkins begins the section at 5:1, noting that vice lists do not typically appear as the first elements in a section, as would be the case if 5:3 is the beginning of a new unit.[84] If the new section begins at 5:1, filial language introduces this hortatory section that contains so much talk about inheritance and familial identity.

Believers are called to imitate God in 5:1. While this is the only instance in the New Testament where believers are told to imitate God, it was a well-known exhortation among moralists and within Hellenistic Judaism. The sanction for this command, and the initial sanction of the section, identifies believers as "beloved children" (τέκνα ἀγαπητά). This sanction follows the common wisdom that children should imitate the virtues of their father.[85] This sanction also reinforces the identity that Ephesians has been asserting for the readers: they are children

---

[81] MARIANNE MEYE THOMPSON notes that when the Hebrew Bible does depict God as Father, God is most often seen as the clan ancestor who bequeaths an inheritance to the people ("'Mercy upon All': God as Father in the Epistle to the Romans," in *Romans and the People of God: Essays in Honor of Gordon D. Fee on the Occasion of his 65th Birthday*, ed. SVEN K. SODERLUND and N. T. WRIGHT [Grand Rapids: Eerdmans, 1999], 205).

[82] So e. g., LINCOLN, *Ephesians*, 292; BEST, *Ephesians*, 442–43.

[83] Perhaps this is the reason the Nestle-Aland 26th–28th and UBS 4th texts begin the new paragraph at 5:1. The Nestle-Aland texts set 5:1–2 apart as an introduction to the following section, while the UBS text makes 5:1–5 a single section.

[84] PERKINS, "The Letter to the Ephesians," 112. Further support comes from her analysis of the way Eph 5:3–8 draws on Col 3:5–8. This seeming connection makes it unlikely that we should see the start of a new section at Eph 5:3.

[85] MACDONALD, *Colossians and Ephesians*, 310, citing Ps.-Isocrates and Demonicus 9–11.

of God. Here the most basic and wide-ranging of ethical injunctions is grounded in that identity. Ephesians asserts that since believers are loved children, they should take on the family likeness.

While most discussions of Roman fathers emphasize their power over other members of the family, that is not a complete picture. A good father was also presented as loving his children and seeking their good. The ideal father was both strict and loving.[86] Calling believers "beloved children" points to the benevolent and affectionate aspect of God's fatherhood.[87]

As important as filial concepts are throughout Ephesians, the writer never uses υἱός to describe believers and uses τέκνον for them only in its exhortations.[88] While the author refers to their adoption and to their status as heirs, 5:1 contains the first reference to believers as children. Since inheritance is not in view, he uses the broader term τέκνον. Had inheritance been in view the writer would have used the gendered term υἱός because being a son rather than a daughter was significant in matters of inheritance.[89] Using τέκνον perhaps makes it yet clearer that these instructions address all members of the church. In any case, this identity for believers serves an anchoring role in the exhortations that follow.

Verse 5 uses language of inheritance to make a threat. Having named vices to which the readers must not succumb, Ephesians reminds them that those who engage in such behavior will have no "inheritance in the kingdom of Christ and God." Hester notes that most places that talk of receiving an inheritance in Paul make a threat.[90] We may recall that within Greek probate law, children had to be explicitly named not to receive a share of the estate.[91] If such rules about required explicit exclusion were known, the places inheritance language is used in this way become more powerful. Then this warning "legally" and unquestionably

---

[86] See EMIEL EYBEN, "Fathers and Sons," in RAWSON, *Marriage, Divorce, and Children in Ancient Rome*, 116–20.

[87] O. LARRY YARBROUGH asserts that intimacy is the "dominant motif in all Paul's metaphorical applications of the parent-child imagery" ("Parents and Children in the Letters of Paul," in *The Social World of the First Christians: Essays in Honor of Wayne A. Meeks*, ed. L. MICHAEL WHITE and O. LARRY YARBROUGH [Minneapolis: Fortress, 1995], 132).

[88] In commenting on 5:1 FRANÇOIS S. MALAN notes that a family theme runs throughout Ephesians ("Unity of Love in the Body of Christ: Identity, Ethics and Ethos in Ephesians," in *Identity, Ethics, and Ethos in the New Testament*, ed. JAN G. VAN DER WATT, BZNW 141 [Berlin: de Gruyter, 2006], 276).

[89] For discussion of this see CORLEY, "Women's Inheritance Rights in Antiquity," 120–21.

[90] HESTER, *Paul's Concept of Inheritance*, 85. Perkins asserts that this inheritance language is "language of Jewish piety" ("The Letter to the Ephesians," 116).

[91] HESTER, *Paul's Concept of Inheritance*, 12–13, cites the WOODHOUSE "Adoption" entry in the Hastings, *Encyclopedia of Religion and Ethics* to make this point. WOODHOUSE cites Demosthenes, [*Leoch.*] 44.63, as evidence. While HESTER's basic point that many Greek wills were written to disinherit those who stood in the line of succession is correct, WOODHOUSE's Demosthenes citation does little to bolster this claim.

excludes those guilty of such behavior. This seems, then, to be a warning to in-siders, those children who might expect to receive an inheritance.[92]

Following this threat of exclusion comes another warning about the "sons of disobedience" (5:6). In 2:2 this expression referred first to Gentiles and then to all people outside of Christ. Perhaps without that explicit extension, it refers primarily to non-believing Gentiles. Still the primary contrast in 5:6 is between those in the church and those outside. Most importantly, this is powerful bound-ary reinforcing language.[93] Those outside are set off starkly from believers.[94] While the expression "sons of ..." is common in Qumran materials and often identified as a Semiticism, its presence here also signals the importance filial imagery has for this letter. It falls between a reference to an inheritance (v. 5) and another expression of the familial identity of believers (v. 8). So a part of the strategy for setting the wicked apart and convincing believers not to act like them is to identify them as people who do not belong among "our" kin.[95]

The "you" who were darkness in 5:8 could refer to Gentiles, but is read better as a reference to all non-believers because it contrasts the state of believers and non-believers. Again, the state of the unbelievers is dramatic; they are not just associated with the darkness, they are the darkness. The description of believers is equally striking; they are not just associated with light, they are light. The con-trast could be no greater. Once this distinction is emphasized, the writer uses filial language to further describe the identity of believers. They are "children (τέκνα) of light." Once again, when inheritance is not in view, the author uses τέκνον. And again it serves as the basis for exhortation. As children they are to act in ways that are appropriate for members of this family, the family into which they have been adopted. Although no specific adoption vocabulary is used, v. 8 makes it clear that once they were not in this family but were the darkness. So now they have been brought into a new family. Thus, their behavior must con-form to their new familial identity.

The general exhortations of Ephesians conclude with another reference to God as father (5:20). Given how unusual it is to call God father in the Pauline corpus, the appearance of this designation again points us to the importance

---

[92] So also BEST, *Ephesians*, 483. Identifying the readers as "children of God" in 5:1 seems to support this reading.

[93] See MACDONALD, *Colossians and Ephesians*, 313. MACDONALD contends that this is one of the passages of Ephesians that calls for withdrawal from the world (321). PERKINS, however, notes that it does not call for withdrawal to the extent seen in Qumran writings ("The Letter to the Ephesians," 118).

[94] Most commentators identify the "sons of disobedience" as non-believing Gentiles. BEST, however, sees them as people within the church (*Ephesians*, 483–84, 486).

[95] This group cohesion function also appears in 4:17, where these non-Jewish readers are told not to live like Gentiles whose minds are futile. Such a statement presumes and reinforces insider identity as it associates the readers' old identity with vice and dishonorable behavior. Be-lievers are no longer members of their originating families; their new identity in Christ makes them members of the household of God.

this understanding of God has in this letter. Its significance may increase if 5:20 serves to close an inclusio that began in 5:1 with the reference to believers as children of God. Whether an intended literary feature or not, a significant section of Ephesians' definition of living as believers is framed by filial language. The concluding mention of God as father reminds the readers that they should behave in the ways set out in these instructions because they are children of God who need to conduct themselves in ways that are appropriate to that identity.

A final reference to God as father appears in the epistolary closing. Ephesians is the only Pauline letter that refers to God as father in the closing. As it was in 5:20, πατήρ appears with no designation that indicates whose father God is. This differs from the epistolary greeting which designated God "our father" (1:2) or the beginning of the blessing that identified God as father of Jesus Christ (1:3). Other usage in Ephesians seems split between referring to God as father of believers (2:18; 5:20) and of all things (that is, as creator; 3:14; 4:6?). Since this instance of πατήρ identifies God and the "Lord Jesus Christ" as the ones through whom the readers receive love, it seems to point to God as father of believers (rather than Christ). If so, the last mention of God as father in the final lines of the letter provides a reminder of the basis on which the unity of the church rests – all believers are in a single family because all have the same father.

C. Conclusions

The pervasive filial language of Ephesians serves a number of important functions. Interpreters agree that a central purpose of the letter is to help the church maintain unity between Jewish and Gentile believers. The writer uses filial language in multiple ways to establish a basis for that unity. He argues for the unity of Jews and Gentiles by asserting that God, as creator and namer, is father of all, and by grouping them together as "sons of disobedience." He also, on the other hand, identifies believers as those taken into the single family of God. At times, some members seem to be adopted while others were born into the family; at other times all believers are adopted. Their unity is reinforced by their receiving of the same inheritance. Finally, filial language serves to reinforce community boundaries with both Jewish and Gentile believers on the inside as children of light and unbelievers on the outside as children of darkness. This identity also serves as a foundation for the letter's ethical exhortations.

Filial language also offers assurance about the salvation of all believers, Jews and Gentiles. Salvation is secure because believers receive it as an inheritance because they are sons of God. Inheritance imagery may also work in multiple ways. If 1:18 (and 1:14) draw on the tradition of God taking Israel as God's possession, it emphasizes the certainty of salvation by accentuating God's love and determination to obtain believers as God's own possession. Elsewhere in Ephesians, believers are the recipients of the inheritance (3:6). Thus, talk of inheritance both makes believers God's possession and promises them a future in which they enjoy God's blessings.

Many have noted how the household code of Ephesians has the married couple serve as the ideal image for the way the church should be structured.[96] This deepens the importance of familial language for the letter, because it appears even more extensively than in the filial and paternal imagery we have examined.

Interpreters often distinguish the Pastorals from other Pauline letters by noting that they conceive of the church as the household of God in ways that the undisputed letters do not. The familial language of Ephesians may represent an intermediate step in that direction. Indeed, one of the expressions of unity among Christ-confessing Jews and Gentiles is that they are not just fellow-citizens, but members of the same household, the household of God (2:19). While the implications of this structure for church organization are not developed in Ephesians, they will be later in the Pastorals.

Whether or not Ephesians represents a stage toward a theological foundation on which the church structures of the Pastorals were built, the filial and paternal language of this letter play major roles in the expression of its theology, including its soteriology and its ecclesiology. These images also serve as an important support for a central purpose of Ephesians. By identifying all believers as (adopted) children of God, Ephesians gives its readers a conceptual means for maintaining the unity of the church.

---

[96] See e. g., OSIEK and MACDONALD, *A Woman's Place*, 121–26.

	Rom	1 Cor	2 Cor	Gal	Phil	Col	Eph	1 Thess	2 Thess	1 Tim	2 Tim	Tit	Phlm
πατήρ (number of references to God)	14 (3 for God)	6 (3 for God)	4	5	4	5 (4 for God)	11 (8 for God)	5 (4 for God)	3	2	1	1	1
πατρίς							1						
υἱός	12	2	4	9		2	4	2					
υἱοθεσία	3			1			1		1				
κληρονομία				1		1	3						
κληρονομέω		4		2									
συγκληρονόμος	1						1						
τέκνον	5	3	3	5	2	2	5	2		5	2	2	1

Table: Filial Language in the Pauline Corpus

Publications and Academic Presentations
of Richard Earl Oster, Jr.

Publications

Books

The Acts of the Apostles Pt. II, chaps. 13:1–28:31. The Living Word Commentary. Austin, Texas: Sweet Publishing Co., 1979.

A Bibliography on Ancient Ephesus: With Introduction and Index. ATLA Bibliography Series, 19. Metuchen, NJ: Scarecrow Press, 1987.

First Corinthians. The College Press NIV Commentary. Joplin, MO: College Press, 1995.

Seven Congregations in a Roman Crucible: A Commentary on Revelation Chapters 1–3. Eugene, OR: Wipf & Stock, 2013.

Articles

"Artemis of Ephesus." Page 60 in *The Oxford Companion to the Bible*. Edited by BRUCE M. METZGER and MICHAEL DAVID COOGAN. Oxford: Oxford University Press, 1993.

"Athens." Page 65 in *The Oxford Companion to the Bible*. Edited by BRUCE M. METZGER and MICHAEL DAVID COOGAN. Oxford: Oxford University Press, 1993.

"Cenchrea." *EDB*, 305.

"Christianity and Emperor Veneration in Ephesus: Iconography of a Conflict." *RQ* 25 (1982): 143–49.

"Christianity in Asia Minor." *ABD* 1:938–54.

"'Congregations of the Gentiles' (Rom. 16:4): A Culture-based Ecclesiology in the Letters of Paul." *RQ* 40 (1998): 39–52.

"Corinth." Pages 134–35 in *The Oxford Companion to the Bible*. Edited by BRUCE M. METZGER and MICHAEL DAVID COOGAN. Oxford: Oxford University Press, 1993.

"Cyrene." Page 227 in *Eerdmans Dictionary of the Bible*. Edited by DAVID NOEL FREEDMAN. Grand Rapids: Eerdmans, 2000.

"Demetrius the Silversmith." *ABD* 1:137.

"The Ephesian Artemis as an Opponent of Early Christianity." *JAC* 19 (1976): 24–44.

"The Ephesian Artemis 'Whom All Asia and the World Worship' (Acts 19:27): Representative Epigraphical testimony to Ἄρτεμις Ἐφεσία outside Ephesos." Pages 212–31 in *Transmission and Reception: New Testament Text-Critical and Exegetical Studies*. Texts and Studies 4. Piscataway, NJ: Gorgias Press, 2006.

"Ephesians, Ephesus." *EEC*, 300–304.

"Ephesus." *ABD* 2:542–49.

"Ephesus." Page 89 in *The Oxford Companion to the Bible*. Edited by BRUCE M. METZGER and MICHAEL DAVID COOGAN. Oxford: Oxford University Press, 1993.

"Ephesus as a Religious Center Under the Principate I. Paganism Before Constantine." *ANRW* 2.18.3 (1990): 1661–728.

"Galatians." Pages 949–56 in *The Transforming Word: A One-Volume Commentary on the Bible.* Edited by MARK W. HAMILTON. Abilene, TX: ACU Press, 2009.

"Going to Worship in Ancient Corinth." *Leaven* 6 (1998): 15–18.

"Greek Inscriptions." *EDB*, 638–39.

"Gymnasiums." *EDB*, 534.

"Holy Days in Honor of Artemis." Pages 74–82 in *NewDocs* 4 (1979).

"Notes on Acts 19:23–41 and an Ephesian Inscription." *HTR* 77 (1984): 233–37.

"Numismatic Windows into the Social World of Early Christianity: A Methodological Inquiry." *JBL* 101 (1982): 195–223.

"Numismatics." *EEC*, 655–56.

"Philadelphia [Lydia]." *EDB*, 1045.

"'Show Me a Denarius': Symbolism of Roman Coinage and Christian Beliefs." *RQ* 28 (1985–1986): 107–15.

"Supposed Anachronism in Luke-Acts's Use of συναγωγή: A Rejoinder to Prof. H. C. Kee." *NTS* 39 (1993): 178–208.

"Use, Misuse and Neglect of Archaeological Evidence in Some Modern Works on 1 Corinthians." *ZNW* 83 (1992): 52–73.

"When Men Wore Veils to Worship: Historical Context of I Cor. 11:4." *NTS* 34 (1988): 481–505.

"Women, Diaspora Synagogues (*proseuche*) and Acts 16:13 (Philippi)." Pages 260–99 in *Faith in Practice: Studies in the Book of Acts: A Festschrift in Honor of Earl and Ottie Stuckenbruck.* Edited by DAVID A. FIENSY and WILLIAM D. HOWDEN. Atlanta: European Evangelistic Society, 1995.

Academic Presentations

"Ancient Ephesus: Christian Conflict with Urban Culture." Paper presented at Southwest Missouri State University. Springfield, MO. April 1986.

"Archaeological and Cultural Background on 1 Corinthians 11:4." Paper presented at the Annual Meeting of the Southeast Region Meeting of the AAR. March 1987.

"Archaeology and Ephesus." Paper presented at the Annual Meeting of the SBL. Baltimore, MD. November 2013.

"Archaeology and the Interpretation of the New Testament." Paper presented at Southwest Missouri State University. Springfield, MO. October 1988.

"Archaeology Assists Exegesis." Paper presented at the Christian Scholars' Conference. Abilene Christian University. Abilene, TX. July 1984.

"Contingent Prophecy and the Openness of God in Interpreting the Book of Revelation." Paper presented at the Central States Meeting of the SBL. April 2003.

"Culture and Counter-Culture: Early Christian Hostilities against the Civil Religion of *Artemis Ephesia*." Paper presented at the Southwest Region Meeting of the AAR. March 1977.

"The Dirt on New Testament Archaeology." Paper presented at the Southeastern Region Meeting of the AAR. March 1986.

"Ephesian Epigraphy and New Testament Studies." Paper presented at the Annual Meeting of the SBL. Atlanta, GA. November 2003.

"Epigraphic Attestation to the Ephesian Artemis and Acts 19." Paper presented at the SNTS. Prague, Czech Republic. August 1995.

"Greek Inscriptions from Roman Oinoanda and the World of Early Christianity." Paper presented at the Annual Meeting of the SBL. Denver, CO. November 2001.

"The Law from a New Testament Perspective." Paper presented at the Christian Scholars' Conference. Abilene Christian University. Abilene, TX. July 1982.

"Men Wearing Veils during Worship (1 Cor. 11:4)." Paper presented at the SNTS. Atlanta, GA. August 1986.

"Numismatic Windows into the Social World of Early Christianity: A Methodological Inquiry." Paper presented at the Annual Meeting of the SBL. New York, NY. November 1979.

"Pagan Religions in Ephesus during the Empire." Paper presented at the Southeast Region Meeting of the SBL. March 1979.

"Recent Attacks on Luke's Depiction of the Second Temple Synagogue in Light of Archaeological Evidence." Paper presented at the Carmichael-Walling Lectures. Abilene Christian University. Abilene, TX. October 1991.

"Reframing the Pentecost Narrative in the Light of the Structure of Acts." Paper presented at the Das Kolloquium für Graduierte (Ausländer und Doktoranden). Tübingen University. Tübingen, Germany. April 1985.

"Research and Reference Tools for New Testament Archaeology." Paper presented at the Annual Meeting of the SBL. December 1987.

"Religion and Philosophy in Ephesian Epigraphy." Paper presented at the Annual Meeting of the SBL. Chicago, IL. November 1994.

"Religion and Philosophy in Ephesian Epigraphy." Paper presented at the SNTS. Edinburgh, Scotland. August 1994

"'Show me a Coin': Numismatic Iconography and New Testament Images." Paper presented at the Southeastern Region Meeting of the SBL. March 1984.

"Thoughts on Archaeological Resources for New Testament Studies in the Classroom." Paper presented at the Annual Meeting of the SBL. New Orleans, LA. November 1996.

"Trust and Obey, for There's No Other Way: Obedience and Works in Paul." Paper presented at the Christian Scholars' Conference. Lipscomb University. Nashville, TN. June 2012.

"Urban Christianity in Imperial Ephesus: A Study in Archaeology, Faith and Life." Paper presented at the 15th Annual University Christian Student Center Lectureship. Oxford, MS. February 1983.

"Use, Misuse and Neglect of Archaeological Information in Recent Works on 1 Corinthians." Paper presented at the Faculty and PhD Student Colloquium. Princeton Theological Seminary. April 1990.

"When Men Wore Veils to Worship: Archaeological and Philological Observations on 1 Corinthians 11:4." Paper presented at the Central States Meeting of the SBL. April 1986.

List of Contributors

ALLEN BLACK, DEAN, Professor of New Testament, Harding School of Theology, Memphis, TN

STEVE J. FRIESEN, Louise Farmer Boyer Chair in Biblical Studies, Department of Religious Studies, University of Texas, Austin, TX

ULRIKE MUSS, Universität Wien, Institut für Klassische Archäologie, Wien, Austria

ELISABETH RATHMAYR, Institut für Kulturgeschichte der Antike, Österreichische Akademie der Wissenschaften, Wien, Austria

GUY MACLEAN ROGERS, Kemper Chair, Department of History, Wellesley College, Wellesley, MA

DANIEL SCHOWALTER, Professor of Religion and Classics, Carthage College, Kenosha, WI

GREGORY STEVENSON, Professor of New Testament, Rochester College, Rochester Hills, MI

JERRY L. SUMNEY, Professor of Biblical Studies, Lexington Theological Seminary, Lexington, KY

CHRISTINE M. THOMAS, Cordano Endowed Chair in Catholic Studies, Department of Religious Studies, University of California, Santa Barbara, CA

TREVOR W. THOMPSON, Instructor at Calvin College, Acquisitions Editor at Eerdmans, Grand Rapids, MI

HILKE THÜR, Institut für Kulturgeschichte der Antike, Österreichische Akademie der Wissenschaften, Wien, Austria

PAUL TREBILCO, Department of Theology and Religion, Te Tari Matauranga Whakapono,University of Otago, Dunedin, New Zealand

Bibliography

ABBOTT, THOMAS K., *A Critical and Exegetical Commentary on The Epistles to the Ephesians and to the Colossians*. ICC. Edinburgh: T&T Clark, 1897.

ALZINGER, WILHELM, *Augusteische Architektur in Ephesos*. Sonderschrift 16. Vienna: ÖAI, 1974.

ALZINGER, WILHELM, and ANTON BAMMER, *Das Monument des C. Memmius*. FiE 7. Vienna: ÖAI, 1971.

AMELUNG, WALTER, *Herodes Atticus*. Hildesheim: Olms, 1983.

ANDREAE, BERNARD, "Vorschlag für eine Rekonstruktion der Polyphemgruppe von Ephesos." Pages 1–11 in *Festschrift für Frank Brommer*. Edited by URSULA HÖCKMANN and ANTJE KRUG, Mainz: von Zabern, 1977.

ARNOLD, CLINTON E., *Ephesians*. Zondervan Exegetical Commentary on the New Testament. Grand Rapids: Zondervan, 2010.

–, *Ephesians: Power and Magic: The Concept of Power in Ephesians in Light of its Historical Setting*. SNTSMS 63. Cambridge: Cambridge University Press, 1989.

AURENHAMMER, MARIA, "Late Hellenistic and Early Roman Imperial Portraits from Ephesos." Pages 101–15 in *Roman Sculpture in Asia Minor: Proceedings of the International Conference to Celebrate the 50th Anniversary of the Italian Excavations at Hierapolis in Phrygia*. Edited by FRANCESCO D'ANDRIA and ILARIA ROMEO, Portsmouth, RI: *JRA*, 2011.

–, "Römische Porträts aus Ephesos: Neue Funde aus dem Hanghaus 2." *JÖAI* 54 (1983): 108–18.

–, "Skulpturen aus Stein und Bronze." Pages 153–208 in *Das Hanghaus 1 in Ephesos: Funde und Ausstattung*. Edited by CLAUDIA LANG-AUINGER, FiE 8.4. Vienna: ÖAW, 2003.

BACHMANN, MARTIN, "Bau Z in Pergamon: Analyse einer Langzeitnutzung." Pages 172–92 in *Städtisches Wohnen im östlichen Mittelmeerraum 4. Jh. v. Chr. – 1. Jh. n. Chr.* Edited by SABINE LADSTÄTTER, DIMITRA ANDRIANOU, and VERONIKA SCHEIBELREITER, AF 18. Vienna: ÖAW, 2010.

BAIR, JENNIFER, "Global Commodity Chains: Genealogy and Review." Pages 1–34 in *Frontiers in Commodity Chain Research*. Edited by JENNIFER BAIR, Stanford: Stanford University Press, 2009.

BAMMER, ANTON, "L'Architecture héllenistique en Asie minuere et ses concepts rétrospectifs et anticipants." Pages 91–101 in *Images et modernité héllenistiques: Appropriation et représentations du monde d'Alexandre à César*. Edited by FRANÇOISE-HÉLÈNE MASSA-PAIRAULT and GILLES SAURON, Collection de l'École française de Rome 390. Rome: École française de Rome, 2007.

–, "Chalcidicum." Pages 88–90 in *Ephesus: The New Guide*. Edited by PETER SCHERRER, Translated by LIONEL BIER and GEORGE M. LUXON, Revised ed. Istanbul: Ege Yayınları, 2000.

–, "Das Denkmal des C. Sextilius Pollio in Ephesos." *JÖAI* 51 (1976–1977): 77–92.

–, "Die politische Symbolik des Memmiusbaues." *JÖAI* 50 (1972–1973): 220–22.

–, "Zu kleinasiatischen Monumentalaltären." Pages 15–27 in *Festschrift für Ramazan Özgan*. Edited by Mustafa Şahin and İ. Hakan Mert, Istanbul: Ege Yayınları, 2005.

–, "Zum Standort des Parthermonuments." *Anatolia/Anadolu* 26 (2004): 11–24.

Barrett, C. K. *The Gospel According to St. John: An Introduction with Commentary and Notes on the Greek Text*. 2nd ed. London: SPCK: 1978.

Barth, Markus, *Ephesians 1–3*. AYB 34. Garden City, NY: Doubleday, 1974.

Bartmann, Elizabeth, *Portraits of Livia*. Cambridge: Cambridge University Press, 1999.

Bauckham, Richard, *The Gospels for All Christians: Rethinking the Gospel Audiences*. Grand Rapids: Eerdmans, 1998.

–, "Papias and Polycrates on the Origin of the Fourth Gospel." *JTS* 44 (1993): 24–69.

Beard, Mary, John North, and Simon Price, *A Sourcebook*. Volume 2 of *Religions of Rome*. Cambridge: Cambridge University Press, 1998.

Beasley-Murray, George R., *Gospel of Life: Theology in the Fourth Gospel*. Peabody: Hendrickson, 1991.

Becker, Jürgen, Hans Conzelmann, and Gerhard Friedrich, *Die Briefe an die Galater, Epheser, Philipper, Kolosser, Thessalonicher und Philemon*. 3rd ed. NTD 8. Göttingen: Vandenhoeck & Ruprecht, 1985.

Becker, Marshall J., "Childhood Among the Etruscans: Mortuary Programs at Tarquinia as Indicators of the Transition to Adult Status." Pages 281–92 in *Constructions of Childhood in Ancient Greece and Italy*. Edited by Ada Cohen and Jeremy B. Rutter, Hesperia 41. Athens: ASCSA, 2008.

Bekker-Nielsen, Tønnes, "Fishing in the Roman World." Pages 187–204 in *Ancient Nets and Fishing Gear: Proceedings of the International Workshop on "Nets and Fishing Gear in Classical Antiquity: A First Approach."* Edited by Tønnes Bekker-Nielsen and Darío Bernal-Casasola, Cádiz (Spain) and Aarhus (Denmark): Servicio de Publicaciones de la Universidad de Cádiz and Aarhus University Press, 2010.

Bendlin, Andreas, "Peripheral Centres – Central Peripheries: Religious Communication in the Roman Empire." Pages 35–68 in *Römische Reichsreligion and Provinzialreligion*. Edited by Hubert Cancik and Jörg Rüpke, Tübingen: Mohr Siebeck, 1997.

Benndorf, Otto and Wilhelm Wilberg, "Studien am Artemision." Pages 205–34 in *Forschungen in Ephesos*. Edited by Otto Benndorf, FiE 1. Vienna: A. Hölder, 1906.

Bennett, Florence M., *Religious Cults Associated with the Amazons*. New York: AMS Press, 1967.

Best, Ernest, *A Critical and Exegetical Commentary on Ephesians*. ICC. Edinburgh: T&T Clark, 1998.

–, *Ephesians*. NTG. Sheffield: JSOT Press, 1993.

–, "Ephesians: Two Types of Existence." *Int* 47 (1993): 39–51.

–, *Essays on Ephesians*. Edinburgh: T & T Clark, 1997.

–, "Recipients and Title of the Letter to the Ephesians: Why and When the Designation 'Ephesians'?" *ANRW* 2.25.4: 3247–79.

–, "Who Used Whom? The Relationship of Ephesians and Colossians." *NTS* 43 (1997): 72–96.

Billington, Clyde E., Jr., "Greek Suppliant Asylum and Its Adoption and Adaptation by the Early Western Christian Church." PhD diss., University of Iowa, 1984.

Black, David A., "The Peculiarities of Ephesians and the Ephesian Address." *Grace Theological Journal* 2 (1981): 59–73.

Boehringer, Erich, and Friedrich Krauss, *Das Temenos für den Herrscherkult*. AvP 9. Berlin: de Gruyter, 1937.

Bohn, Richard, *Die Theater-Terrasse.* AvP 4. Berlin: Spemann, 1896.

Bollmann, Beate, *Römische Vereinshäuser: Untersuchungen zu den Scholae der römischen Berufs-, Kult- und Augustalen-Kollegien in Italien.* Mainz: von Zabern, 1998.

Bosanquet, Robert Carr, "Excavations of the British School at Melos: The Hall of the Mystae." *JHS* 18 (1898): 60–80.

Boschung, Dietrich, *Die Bildnisse des Augustus.* Herrscherbild 1.2. Berlin: Mann, 1993.

Boschung, Dietrich, Hans-Markus von Kaenel, and Hans Jucker, *Die Bildnisse des Caligula.* Das römische Herrscherbild 1.4. Berlin: Mann, 1989.

Bourdieu, Pierre, *The Field of Cultural Production: Essays on Art and Literature.* Edited by Randal Johnson, New York: Columbia University Press, 1993.

–, "The Genesis of the Concepts of Habitus and Field." *Sociocriticism* 1.2 (1985): 19–20.

–, *The Logic of Practice.* Stanford: Stanford University Press, 1990.

–, *Outline of a Theory of Practice.* Cambridge Studies in Social Anthropology 16. Cambridge: Cambridge University Press, 1977.

Bourdieu, Pierre, and Jean-Claude Passeron, *Reproduction in Education, Society, and Culture.* 2nd ed. London: Sage, 1990.

Bourdieu, Pierre, and Loic J. D. Wacquant, *An Invitation to Reflexive Sociology.* Chicago: Chicago University Press, 1992.

Bradley, Keith, "Images of Childhood." Pages 183–96 in *Plutarch's* Advice to the Bride and Groom *and* A Consolation of His Wife. Edited by Sarah B. Pomeroy, New York: Oxford University Press, 1999.

Breresford, James, *The Ancient Sailing Season.* Leiden: Brill, 2013.

Bricault, Laurent, Miguel John Versluys, and Paul G. P. Meyboom, eds. *Nile into Tiber: Egypt in the Roman World: Proceedings of the IIIrd International Congress of Isis Studies.* Leiden: Brill, 2007.

Brodie, Thomas L., *The Birthing of the New Testament: The Intertextual Development of the New Testament Writings.* New Testament Monographs 1. Sheffield: Sheffield Phoenix Press, 2004.

Brodie, Thomas L., Dennis R. MacDonald, and Stanley E. Porter, "Conclusion: Problems of Method-Suggested Guidelines." Pages 284–96 in *The Intertextuality of the Epistles: Explorations of Theory and Practice.* Edited by Thomas L. Brodie, Dennis R. MacDonald, and Stanley E. Porter, New Testament Monographs 16. Sheffield: Sheffield Phoenix Press, 2006.

Brown, Raymond E., *The Churches the Apostles Left Behind.* New York: Paulist, 1984.

–, *The Gospel According to John: Introduction, Translation, and Notes.* 2 vols. AYB 29. New Haven: Yale University Press, 1966.

–, *An Introduction to the Gospel of John: Edited, Updated, Introduced, and Concluded by* Francis J. Moloney, AYBRL. New Haven: Yale University Press, 2003.

Bruneau, Philippe, *Recherches sur les cultes de Délos à l'époque hellénistique et à l'époque impériale.* BEFAR 217. Paris: de Boccard, 1970.

Bultmann, Rudolf, *Theology of the New Testament.* 2 vols. London: SCM, 1955.

Burrell, Barbara, *Neokoroi: Greek Cities and Roman Emperors.* Leiden: Brill, 2004.

Burke, Trevor J., *Adopted into God's Family: Exploring a Pauline Metaphor.* New Studies in Biblical Theology. Downers Grove: IVP, 2006.

Burkert, Walter, *Antike Mysterien.* Munich: Beck'sche Verlagsbuchhandlung, 1994.

–, *Greek Religion.* Cambridge: Harvard University Press, 1985.

Butcher, Kevin, *Roman Provincial Coins: An Introduction to the 'Greek Imperials.'* London: Seaby, 1988.

BYRNE, BRENDAN, *Sons of God, Seed of Abraham: A Study of the Idea of the Sonship of God of All Christians in Paul against the Jewish Background*. AnBib 83. Rome: Biblical Institute, 1979.

CAMPBELL, WILLIAM S., "Unity and Diversity in the Church: Transformed Identities and the Peace of Christ in Ephesians." *Transformation: An International Journal of Holistic Mission Studies* 25 (2008): 15–31.

CHANIOTIS, ANGELOS, "Conflicting Authorities: Asylia between Secular and Divine Law in the Classical and Hellenistic Poleis." *Kernos* 9 (1996): 65–86.

–, "The Conversion of the Temple of Aphrodite at Aphrodisias in Context." Pages 243–74 in *From Temple to Church: Deconstruction and Renewal of Local Topography in Late Antiquity*. Edited by JOHANNES HAHN, STEPHEN EMMEL, and ULRICH GOTTER, Leiden: Brill, 2008.

CHRISTOF, EVA, "Skulpturen." Pages 656–67 in *Das Hanghaus 2 in Ephesos: Die Wohneinheiten 1 und 2: Baubefund, Ausstattung, Funde*. Edited by FRIEDRICH KRINZINGER and INGRID ADENSTEDT, FiE 8.8. Vienna: ÖAW, 2010.

CLAUSS, MANFRED, *Kaiser und Gott: Herrscherkult im römischen Reich*. Munich: Sauer, 2001.

COLE, SUSAN GUETTEL, *Landscapes, Gender and Ritual Space: The Ancient Greek Experience*. Berkeley: University of California Press, 2004.

–, *Theoi Megaloi: The Cult of the Great Gods at Samothrace*. Leiden: Brill, 1984.

COOK, JAMES I., *Edgar Johnson Goodspeed: Articulate Scholar*. BSNA 4. Chico, CA: Scholars Press, 1981.

CORBIER, MIREILLE, "Divorce and Adoption as Familial Strategies." Pages 47–78 in *Marriage, Divorce, and Children in Ancient Rome*. Edited by BERYL RAWSON, Oxford: Oxford University Press, 1991.

–, "The *Lex Portorii Asiae* and Financial Administration." Pages 202–35 in *The Customs Law of Asia*. Edited by MICHEL COTTIER, MICHAEL H. CRAWFORD, C. V. CROWTHER, JEAN-LOUIS FERRARY, BARBARA LEVICK, and MICHAEL WÖRRLE, Oxford: Oxford University Press, 2008.

CORLEY, KATHLEEN E., "Women's Inheritance Rights in Antiquity and Paul's Metaphor of Adoption." Pages 98–121 in *A Feminist Companion to Paul*. Edited by AMY-JILL LEVINE and MARIANNE BLICKENSTAFF, FCNTECW 6. New York: T&T Clark, 2004.

CRAMME, STEFAN, "Die Bedeutung des Euergetismus für die Finanzierung städtischer Aufgaben in der Provinz Asia." PhD diss., Cologne, 2001.

COTTIER, MICHEL, MICHAEL H. CRAWFORD, C. V. CROWTHER, JEAN-LOUIS FERRARY, BARBARA LEVICK, and MICHAEL WÖRRLE, eds. *The Customs Law of Asia*. Oxford: Oxford University Press, 2008.

CULPEPPER, R. A. "The Quest for the Church in the Gospel of John." *Int* 63 (2009): 341–54.

CURTIUS, ERNST, *Beiträge zur Geschichte Kleinasiens: Abhandlung der königlich preußischen Akademie der Wissenschaften*. Berlin: G. Vogt, 1872.

DAHL, NILS A., "Benediction and Congratulation." Pages 279–314 in *Studies in Ephesians: Introductory Questions, Text- & Edition-Critical Issues, Interpretation of Texts and Themes*. Edited by DAVID HELLHOLM, VEMUND BLOMKVIST, and TORD FORNBERG, WUNT 1.131. Tübingen: Mohr Siebeck, 2000.

–, "Das Proömium des Epheserbriefes." Pages 315–34 in *Studies in Ephesians: Introductory Questions, Text- & Edition-Critical Issues, Interpretation of Texts and Themes*. Edited by DAVID HELLHOLM, VEMUND BLOMKVIST, and TORD FORNBERG, WUNT 1.131. Tübingen: Mohr Siebeck, 2000.

–, "Gentiles, Christians, and Israelites in the Epistle to the Ephesians." Pages 442–32 in *Studies in Ephesians: Introductory Questions, Text- & Edition-Critical Issues, Interpretation of Texts and Themes.* Edited by DAVID HELLHOLM, VEMUND BLOMKVIST, and TORD FORNBERG, WUNT 1.131. Tübingen: Mohr Siebeck, 2000.

–, *Studies in Ephesians: Introductory Questions, Text- & Edition-Critical Issues, Interpretation of Texts and Themes.* WUNT 1.131. Tübingen: Mohr Siebeck, 2000.

DAHMEN, KARSTEN, *Untersuchungen zu Form und Funktion kleinformatiger Porträts der römischen Kaiserzeit.* Münster: Scriptorium, 2001.

DALLY, ORTWIN, "Pflege und Umnutzung heidnischer Tempel in der Spätantike." Pages 98–114 in *Die spätantike Stadt und ihre Christianisierung: Symposion vom 14. bis 16. Februar 2000 in Halle-Saale.* Edited by GUNNAR BRANDS and HANS-GEORG SEVERIN, Wiesbaden: Reichert, 2003.

DECKERS, JOHANNES, "Die Wandmalereien im Kaiserkultraum von Luxor." *JDAI* 94 (1979): 600–52.

DEISSMANN, G. ADOLF, *Bible Studies.* Translated by ALEXANDER J. GRIEVE, Edinburgh: T&T Clark, 1909.

DEONNA, WALDEMAR, *Le mobilier délien.* Exploration archéologique de Délos 18. Paris: de Boccard, 1938.

DEUTSCH, CELIA, "Transformation of Symbols: The New Jerusalem in Rv 21:1–22:5." *ZNW* 78 (1987): 106–26.

DICKMANN, JENS-ARNE, *Domus frequentata: Anspruchsvolles Wohnen im pompejanischen Stadthaus.* Studien zur antiken Stadt 4. Munich: Pfeil, 1999.

DMITRIEV, SVIATOSLAV, *City Government in Hellenistic and Roman Asia Minor.* Oxford: Oxford University Press, 2005.

DRÄGER, MICHAEL, *Die Städte der Provinz Asia in der Flavierzeit: Studien zur kleinasiatischen Stadt- und Religionsgeschichte.* Europäische Hochschulschriften 3. Geschichte und ihre Hilfswissenschaften 576. Frankfurt a. Main: Lang, 1993.

DRÄGER, OLAF, *Religionem significare: Studien zu reich verzierten römischen Altären und Basen aus Marmor.* MDAI (R) Supp. 33. Mainz: von Zabern, 1994.

EAKINS, J. KENNETH, JOHN R. SPENCER, and KEVIN G. O'CONNELL, *Tell El-Hesi: Muslim Cemetery in Fields V and VI/IX (Stratum II).* Winona Lake: Eisenbrauns, 1993.

ECK, WERNER, *Monument und Inschrift.* Berlin: de Gruyter, 2010.

EGELHAAF-GAISER, ULRIKE, "Religionsästhetik und Raumordnung am Beispiel der Vereinsgebäude von Ostia." Pages 155–57 in *Religiöse Vereine in der römischen Antike.* Edited by ULRIKE EGELHAAF-GAISER and ALFRED SCHÄFER, STAC 13. Tübingen: Mohr Siebeck, 2002.

ELSNER, JAŚ, "The Origins of the Icon: Pilgrimage, Religion, and Visual Culture in the Roman East as 'Resistance' to the Centre." Pages 178–99 in *The Early Roman Empire in the East.* Edited by SUSAN E. ALCOCK, Oxbow Monographs 95. Oxford: Oxbow Books, 1997.

ENGELMANN, HELMUT, "Ephesos und die Johannesakten." *ZPE* 103 (1994): 297–302.

–, "Inschriften aus Metropolis," *ZPE* 125 (1999): 143–46.

–, "Inschriften und Heiligtum." Pages 33–44 in *Der Kosmos der Artemis von Ephesos 2001.* Edited by ULRIKE MUSS, Sonderschriften des ÖAI 37. Vienna: Phoibos, 2001.

–, "Zum Kaiserkult in Ephesos." *ZPE* 97 (1993): 279–83.

ENGELMANN, HELMUT, and DIETER KNIBBE, eds. *Das Zollgesetz der Provinz Asia: Eine neue Inschrift aus Ephesos.* EA 14. Bonn: Habelt, 1989.

EYBEN, EMIEL, "Fathers and Sons." Pages 114–43 in *Marriage, Divorce, and Children in Ancient Rome*. Edited by BERYL RAWSON, Oxford: Oxford University Press, 1991.

FLEISCHER, ROBERT, "Die Amazonen und das Asyl des Artemisions von Ephesos." *JDAI* 117 (2002): 185–216.

–, "Der Fries des Hadrianstempels in Ephesos." Pages 23–71 in *Festschrift für Fritz Eichler*. Edited by EGON BRAUN, Vienna: ÖAI, 1967.

FOWL, STEPHEN E., *Ephesians: A Commentary*. NTL. Louisville: Westminster John Knox Press, 2012.

FRASER, PETER M., *Rhodian Funerary Monuments*. Oxford: Clarendon Press, 1977.

FRIESEN, STEVEN J., *Twice Neokoros: Ephesus, Asia, and the Cult of the Flavian Imperial Family*. Leiden: Brill, 1993.

FRIESINGER, HERWIG, and FRITZ KRINZINGER, eds. *100 Jahre österreichische Forschungen in Ephesos: Akten des Symposions Wien 1995*. Vienna: ÖAW, 1999.

FRÖHLICH, THEODOR, *Lararien- und Fassadenbilder in den Vesuvstädten: Untersuchungen zur 'volkstümlichen' pompeianischen Malerei*, MDAI (R) Supp. 32. Mainz: von Zabern, 1991.

GALIL, GERSHON, *The Lower Stratum Families in the Neo-Assyrian Period*. CHANE 27. Leiden: Brill, 2007.

GALLANT, THOMAS W, *Risk and Survival in Ancient Greece: Reconstructing the Rural Domestic Economy*. Stanford: Stanford University Press, 1991.

GARDNER, JANE F., "The Adoption of Roman Freedmen." *Phoenix* 43 (1989): 236–57.

GIEBEL, MARION, *Das Geheimnis der Mysterien: Antike Kulte in Griechenland, Rom und Ägypten*. 3rd ed. Düsseldorf: Patmos, 2003.

GNILKA, JOACHIM, *Der Epheserbrief*. 3rd ed. HTKNT 10.2. Freiburg: Herder, 1982.

GOLDA, THOMAS MATTHIAS, *Puteale und verwandte Monumente: eine Studie zum römischen Ausstattungsluxus*. Mainz: von Zabern, 1997.

GOODSPEED, E. J. *The Meaning of Ephesians*. Chicago: University of Chicago Press, 1933.

GOULD, JOHN, "Hiketeia." *JHS* 93 (1973): 73–104.

GRÄBE, PETRUS J., "'And He Made Known to Us the Mystery of His Will …': Reflections on the Eschatology of the Letter to the Ephesians." Pages 256–68 in *Eschatology of the New Testament and Some Related Documents*. Edited by JAN G. VAN DER WATT, WUNT 2.315. Tübingen: Mohr Siebeck, 2011.

–, "Salvation in Colossians and Ephesians." Pages 294–303 in *Salvation in the New Testament: Perspectives on Soteriology*. Edited by JAN G. VAN DER WATT, NovTSup 121. Leiden: Brill, 2005.

GRAINDOR, PAUL, *Un milliardaire antique: Hérode Atticus et sa famille*. Cairo: Misr, 1930.

GRANT, ROBERT M., "American New Testament Study, 1926–1956." *JBL* 87 (1968): 42–50.

GUARDUCCI, MARGHERITA, *Epigrafia Greca*. Rome: Istituto poligrafico dello Stato, 1978.

GÜNTHER, MATTHIAS, *Die Frühgeschichte des Christentums in Ephesus*. Arbeiten zur Religion und Geschichte des Urchristentums 1. Frankfurt am Main: Peter Lang, 1995.

HAMDORF, FRIEDRICH WILHELM, *Dionysos-Bacchus: Kult und Wandlungen des Weingottes*. Munich: Callwey, 1986.

HAMMER, PAUL L., "A Comparison of *klēronomia* in Paul and Ephesians." *JBL* 79 (1960): 267–72.

HARLAND, PHILIP, *Associations, Synagogues, and Congregations: Claiming a Place in Ancient Mediterranean Society*. Minneapolis: Fortress, 2003.

–, *Dynamics of Identity in the World of the Early Christians*. New York: T&T Clark, 2009.

HARRINGTON, WILFRID J., *Revelation*. Minnesota: Liturgical Press, 1993.

HARTER-UIBOPUU, KAJA, "Kaiserkult und Kaiserverehrung in den Koina des griechisch-en Mutterlandes." Pages 218–21 in *Die Praxis der Herrscherverehrung in Rom und seinen Provinzen*. Edited by HUBERT CANCIK and KONRAD HITZL, Tübingen: Mohr Siebeck, 2003.

HAYS, RICHARD B., *The Conversion of the Imagination: Paul as Interpreter of Israel's Scripture*. Grand Rapids: Eerdmans, 2005.

–, *Echoes of Scripture in the Letters of Paul*. New Haven: Yale University Press, 1989.

HEAD, BARCLAY V., *Catalogue of the Greek Coins of Ionia*. Bologna: Arnaldo Forni, 1964.

–, *On the Chronological Sequence of the Coins of Ephesus*. Chicago: Obol International, 1880.

HECKEL, ULRICH, "Die Einheit der Kirche im Johannesevangelium und im Epheserbrief. Ein Vergleich der ekklesiologischen Strukturen." Pages 613–40 in *Kontexte des Johannesevangeliums: das vierte Evangelium in religions- und traditionsgeschichtlicher Perspektive*. Edited by JÖRG FREY and UDO SCHNELLE, WUNT 1.175. Tübingen: Mohr Siebeck, 2004.

HEIL, JOHN PAUL, *Ephesians: Empowerment to Walk in Love for the Unity of All in Christ*. SBLStBL 13. Atlanta: SBL, 2007.

HERRMANN, PETER, "Rom und die Asylie griechischer Heiligtümer: Eine Urkunde des Dictators Caesar aus Sardeis." *Chiron* 19 (1989): 127–58.

HERMANN, WERNER, *Römische Götteraltäre*. Kallmünz: Lassleben, 1961.

HESTER, JAMES D., *Paul's Concept of Inheritance: A Contribution to the Understanding of Heilsgeschichte*. Scottish Journal of Theology Occasional Papers 14. London: Oliver and Boyd, 1968.

HICKS, E. L., *The Collection of Ancient Greek Inscriptions in the British Museum*. Oxford: Clarendon Press, 1890.

HILL, CHARLES E., *The Johannine Corpus in the Early Church*. Oxford: Oxford University Press, 2004.

HODGE, CAROLINE JOHNSON, *If Sons, Then Heirs: A Study of Kinship and Ethnicity in the Letters of Paul*. Oxford: Oxford University Press, 2007.

–, "Olive Trees and Ethnicities: Judeans and Gentiles in Rom. 11.17–24." Pages 77–89 in *Christians as a Religious Minority in a Multicultural City: Modes of Interaction and Identity Formation in Early Imperial Rome*. Edited by JÜRGEN ZANGENBERG and MICHAEL LABAHN, JSNTSup 243. New York: T&T Clark, 2004.

HOEHNER, HAROLD W., *Ephesians: An Exegetical Commentary*. Grand Rapids: Baker Academic, 2002.

HOEPFNER, WOLFRAM, "Zum Typus der Basileia und der königlichen Androne." Pages 29–31 in *Basileia: Die Paläste der hellenistischen Könige: Internationales Symposium in Berlin vom 16.12.1992 – 20.12.1992*. Edited by WOLFRAM HOEPFNER and GUNNAR BRANDS, Mainz: von Zabern, 1996.

HOEPFNER, WOLFRAM, and GUNNAR BRANDS, eds. *Basileia: Die Paläste der hellenistischen Könige: Internationales Symposium in Berlin vom 16.12.1992 – 20.12.1992*. Mainz: von Zabern, 1996

HÖLSCHER, TONIO, *Victoria Romana: Archäologische Untersuchungen zur Geschichte und Wesensart der römischen Siegesgöttin von den Anfängen bis zum Ende des 3. Jhs. n. Chr.* Mainz: von Zabern, 1967.

HOOKER, MORNA, *Jesus and the Servant: The Influence of the Servant Concept of Deutero-Isaiah in the New Testament*. London: SPCK, 1959.

HOPKINS, TERENCE K., and IMMANUEL WALLERSTEIN, "Commodity Chains in the World-Economy prior to 1800." *Review* 10.1 (1986): 159.

HORSLEY, G. H. R., "A Fishing Cartel in First-Century Ephesus." *NewDocs* 5 (1989): 95–114.

–, "The Inscriptions of Ephesos and the New Testament." *NovT* 34 (1992): 105–68.

–, "A Jewish Family from Egypt in Rome." *NewDocs* 4 (1987): 221–29.

HORSTER, MARIETTA, *Landbesitz griechischer Heiligtümer in archaischer und klassischer Zeit*. Berlin: de Gruyter, 2004.

HÜBNER, SABINE R., *The Family in Roman Egypt: A Comparative Approach to Intergenerational Solidarity and Conflict*. Cambridge: Cambridge University Press, 2013.

HÜBNER, SABINE R., and DAVID M. RATZAN, eds. *Growing Up Fatherless in Antiquity*. Cambridge: Cambridge University Press, 2011.

ILIEVA, PETYA, "Samothrace: Samo- or Thrace?" Pages 138–70 in *Material Culture and Social Identities in the Ancient World*. Edited by SHELLEY HALES and TAMAR HODOS, Cambridge: Cambridge University Press, 2010.

İNAN, JALE, and ELISABETH ALFÖLDI-ROSENBAUM, *Römische und frühbyzantinische Porträtplastik aus der Türkei: Neue Funde*. Mainz: von Zabern, 1979.

JACOB-FELSCH, MARGRIT, *Die Entwicklung griechischer Statuenbasen und die Aufstellung der Statuen*. Waldsassen: Stiftland, 1969.

JOBST, WERNER, *Römische Mosaiken aus Ephesos 1: Die Hanghäuser am Embolos*. Vienna: ÖAW, 1977.

KARWIESE, STEFAN, "Ephesos 1980: Liste der Fundmünzen." *AAWW* 118 (1981): 154–68.

KAUFMANN-HEINIMANN, ANNEMARIE, *Götter und Lararien aus Augusta Raurica: Herstellung, Fundzusammenhänge und sakrale Funktion figürlicher Bronzen in einer römischen Stadt*. Forschungen in Augst 26. Augst: Römermuseum, 1998.

KEIL, JOSEF, *Ephesos: Ein Führer durch die Ruinenstätte und ihre Geschichte*. Vienna: Alfred Hölder, 1915.

–, "XV. Vorläufiger Bericht über die Ausgrabungen von Ephesos." *JÖAI* 26 (1930): 48–49.

–, "Zum Martyrium des heiligen Timotheus in Ephesos." *JÖAI* 29 (1935): 82–92.

KIRBIHLER, FRANÇOIS, and LILLI ZABRANA, "Archäologische, epigraphische und numismatische Zeugnisse für den Kaiserkult im Artemision." *JÖAI* 83 (2014): 101–31.

KIRBY, JOHN C., *Ephesians: Baptism and Pentecost: An Inquiry into the Structure and Purpose of the Epistle to the Ephesians*. London: SPCK, 1968.

KLOPPENBORG, JOHN S,, and RICHARD S. ASCOUGH, *Attica, Central Greece, Macedonia, Thrace*. Vol. 1 of *Greco-Roman Associations: Texts, Translations, and Commentary*. Berlin: de Gruyter, 2011.

KNIBBE, DIETER, "Private Euergetism in the Service of the City-Goddess: The Most Wealthy Ephesian Family of the 2nd Century CE Supports Artemis in Her Struggle Against the Decline of Her Cult after the Meteorological Catastrophe of 186 CE." *Mediterraneo Antico* 5.1 (2002): 49–62.

–, "Via Sacra Ephesiaca: New Aspects of the Cult of Artemis Ephesia." Pages 144–55 in *Ephesos: Metropolis of Asia*. Edited by HELMUT KOESTER, HTS 41. Valley Forge, PA: Trinity Press International, 1995.

KNIBBE, DIETER, and BÜLENT İPLİKCİOĞLU, "Neue Inschriften aus Ephesos 8." *JÖAI* 53 (1981–1982): 87–150.

KNIBBE, DIETER, HELMUT ENGELMANN, and BÜLENT İPLİKÇİOĞLU, "Neue Inschriften aus Ephesos XI." *JÖAI* 59 (1989): 162–238.

–, "Neue Inschriften aus Ephesos XII." *JÖAI* 62 (1993): 113–50.

KNIBBE, DIETER, and GERHARD LANGMANN, *Via Sacra Ephesiaca I.* BerMat 3. Vienna: Schindler, 1993.

KNIBBE, DIETER, and HILKE THÜR, *Via Sacra Ephesiaca II.* BerMat 6. Vienna: Schindler, 1995.

KOESTER, HELMUT, "Ephesos in Early Christian Literature." Pages 119–41 in *Ephesos, Metropolis of Asia: An Interdisciplinary Approach to its Archaeology, Religion, and Culture.* Edited by HELMUT KOESTER, HTS 41. Valley Forge: Trinity Press International, 1995.

KOLLER, KARIN, "Marmor." Pages 259–71 in *Das Hanghaus 2 in Ephesos: Die Wohneinheit 7: Baubefund, Ausstattung, Funde.* Edited by ELISABETH RATHMAYR, FiE 8.10. Vienna: ÖAW, 2016.

–, "Marmor." Pages 227–54 in in *Das Hanghaus 2 in Ephesos: Die Wohneinheit 6: Baubefund, Ausstattung, Funde.* Edited by HILKE THÜR and ELISABETH RATHMAYR, FiE 8.9. Vienna: ÖAW, 2014.

–, "Die Pilasterkapitelle aus dem 'Marmorsaal' der Wohneinheit 6: Bemerkungen zu Dekoration und Zeitstellung." Pages 119–36 in *Das Hanghaus 2 von Ephesos: Studien zu Baugeschichte und Chronologie.* Edited by FRIEDRICH KRINZINGER, Vienna: ÖAW, 2002.

KREIKENBOM, DETLEV, *Griechische und römische Kolossalporträts bis zum späten ersten Jahrhundert nach Christus.* Berlin: de Gruyter, 1992.

KRINZINGER, FRIEDRICH, ed. *Hanghaus 2 in Ephesos: Die Wohneinheiten 1 und 2: Baubefund, Ausstattung und Funde.* FiE 8.8. Vienna: ÖAW, 2010.

KRINZINGER, FRIEDRICH and INGRID ADENSTEDT, *Das Hanghaus 2 in Ephesos: Die Wohneinheiten 1 und 2: Baubefund, Ausstattung, Funde.* FiE 8.8. Vienna: ÖAW, 2010.

KUKULA, RICHARD C., "Literarische Zeugnisse über den Artemistempel von Ephesos und inschriftliche Zeugnisse über das Artemision." Pages 237–82 in *Forschungen in Ephesos.* Edited by OTTO BENNDORF, FiE 1. Vienna: A. Hölder, 1906.

LADSTÄTTER, SABINE, "Die Chronologie des Hanghauses 2." Pages 9–39 in *Das Hanghaus 2 von Ephesos: Studien zu Baugeschichte und Chronologie.* Edited by FRIEDRICH KRINZINGER, AF 7. Vienna: ÖAW, 2002.

LADSTÄTTER, SABINE, and ELISABETH RATHMAYR, "Rekonstruktion der Bauphasen." Pages 81–104 and 426–42 in *Hanghaus 2 in Ephesos: Die Wohneinheiten 1 und 2: Baubefund, Ausstattung und Funde.* Edited by FRIEDRICH KRINZINGER, FiE 8.8. Vienna: ÖAW, 2010.

LAGIA, ANNA, "Notions of Childhood in the Classical Polis: Evidence from the Bioarchaeological Record." Pages 293–308 in *Constructions of Childhood in Ancient Greece and Italy.* Edited by ADA COHEN and JEREMY B. RUTTER, Hesperia 41. Athens: ASCSA, 2008.

LANG-AUINGER, CLAUDIA, "Skulpturen aus Stein und Bronze." Pages 153–208 in *Das Hanghaus 1 in Ephesos: Funde und Ausstattung.* Edited by MARIA AURENHAMMER, FiE 8.4. Vienna: ÖAW, 2003.

LÄPPLE, ALFRED, "Das neue Jerusalem: Die Eschatologie der Offenbarung des Johannes." *BK* 39 (1984): 75–81.

LEHNER, MICHAEL F., "Die Agonistik in Ephesos der römischen Kaiserzeit." PhD diss., Munich, 2004.

LEWIS, NAPHTALI, ed. *Greek Historical Documents on The Roman Principate 27 BC–285 AD.* Hakkert: Toronto, 1974.

LINCOLN, ANDREW T., *Ephesians.* WBC. Dallas: Word Books, 1990.

–, *The Gospel According to John.* BNTC. London: Continuum, 2005.

Lincoln, Andrew T., and Alexander J. M. Wedderburn, *The Theology of the Later Pauline Letters*. Cambridge: Cambridge University Press, 1993.

Lindsay, Hugh, *Adoption in the Roman World*. Cambridge: Cambridge University Press, 2009.

Longfellow, Brenda, *Roman Imperialism and Civic Patronage: Form, Meaning, and Ideology in Monumental Fountain Complexes*. Cambridge: Cambridge University Press, 2011.

Lytle, Ephraim, "A Customs House of Our Own: Infrastructure, Duties and a Joint Association of Fishermen and Fishmongers [*IK*, 11.1a-Ephesos, 2]." Pages 213–24 in *Tout vendre, tout acheter: Structures et équipements des marchés antiques: Actes du colloque d'Athènes, 16–19 juin 2009*. Edited by Véronique Chankowski and Pavlos Karvonis, Bourdeaux-Athènes: Diffusion de Boccard, 2012.

MacDonald, Margaret, *Colossians and Ephesians*. SP. Collegeville: Liturgical Press, 2000.

MacMullen, Ramsay, *Christianizing the Roman Empire A. D. 100–400*. New Haven: Yale University Press, 1984.

Magie, David, *Roman Rule in Asia Minor: To the End of the Third Century after Christ*. Princeton: Princeton University Press, 1950.

Malan, François S., "Unity of Love in the Body of Christ: Identity, Ethics and Ethos in Ephesians." Pages 257–88 in *Identity, Ethics, and Ethos in the New Testament*. Edited by Jan G. van der Watt, BZNW 141. Berlin: de Gruyter, 2006.

Malherbe, Abraham J., *The Letters to the Thessalonians: A New Translation with Introduction and Commentary*. AYB 32B. New Haven: Yale University Press, 2000.

Mangartz, Fritz, *Die byzantinische Steinsäge von Ephesos: Baubefund, Rekonstruktion, Architekturteile*. Monographien RGZ 86. Mainz: RGZ, 2010.

Martin, Ralph P., "An Epistle in Search of a Life-Setting." *ExpTim* 79 (1968): 296–302.

Martínez, Florentino García, "Divine Sonship at Qumran and in Philo." *SPhiloA* 19 (2007): 85–100.

Marzano, Annalisa, *Harvesting the Sea: The Exploitation of Marine Resources in the Roman Mediterranean*. Oxford: Oxford University Press, 2013.

Maschek, Dominik, "Domitian und Polyphem: Kritische Anmerkungen zur hermeneutischen Methode in der antiken Kunstgeschichte am Beispiel Ephesos." *JÖAI* 76 (2008): 279–99.

Mawhinney, Allen, "Baptism, Servanthood, and Sonship." *WTJ* 49 (1987): 35–64.

Megow, Wolf-R., "Tiberius in Ephesos." *JÖAI* 69 (2000): 249–95

Meeks, Wayne, *The Origins of Christian Morality: The First Two Centuries*. New Haven: Yale, 1993.

Mendel, Gustave, *Catalogue des sculptures grècques, romains et byzantines 1*. Constantinople: Musée imperial, 1912.

Merkelbach, Reinhold, "Ephesische Parerga (13): Der Prytanis und Hierokeryx Fabius Faustinianus." *ZPE* 28 (1978): 82–83.

–, "Ephesische Parerga (18): Der Bäckerstreik." *ZPE* 30 (1978): 164–65.

–, *Die Hirten des Dionysos: Die Dionysos-Mysterien der römischen Kaiserzeit und der bukolische Roman des Longus*. Stuttgart: Teubner, 1988.

Michaels, J. Ramsey, *The Gospel of John*. NICNT. Grand Rapids: Eerdmans, 2010.

Mitchell, Stephen, "Geography, Politics, and Imperialism in the Asian Customs Law." Pages 165–201 in *The Customs Law of Asia*, eds. Michel Cottier,, Michael

H. Crawford, C. V. Crowther, Jean-Louis Ferrary, Barbara Levick, and Michael Wörrle, Oxford: Oxford University Press, 2008.

Mitton, C. L. *The Epistle to the Ephesians: Its Authorship, Origin and Purpose*. Oxford: Clarendon Press, 1951.

Moffatt, J. *An Introduction to the Literature of the New Testament*. Edinburgh: T&T Clark, 1911.

Moormann, Eric M., *Divine Interiors: Mural Paintings in Greek and Roman Sanctuaries*. Amsterdam Archaeological Studies 16. Amsterdam: Amsterdam University, 2011.

Moss, Christopher F., "Roman Marble Tables." PhD Diss., Princeton, 1988.

Muddiman, John, *The Epistle to the Ephesians*. BNTC. London: Continuum, 2001.

Murphy-O'Connor, Jerome, *St. Paul's Ephesus: Texts and Archaeology*. Collegeville: Liturgical Press, 2008.

Murray, J. O. F. *The Epistle of Paul the Apostle to the Ephesians*. CGTSC. Cambridge: Cambridge University Press, 1914.

Muss, Ulrike, "Arsinoe IV, eine Schwester Kleopatras VII, Grabinhaberin des Oktogons von Ephesos? Ein Vorschlag." *JÖAI* 60 (1990): 43–56.

–, "The Artemision at Ephesos: Paul, John and Mary." Pages 495–511 in *Contested Spaces: Houses and Temples in Roman Antiquity and the New Testament*. Edited by David L. Balch and Annette Weissenrieder, WUNT 1.285. Tübingen: Mohr Siebeck, 2012.

–, "The Artemision in Early Christian Times." *EC* 7.3 (2016): 293–312.

–, "Das Artemision von Ephesos in römischer Zeit." Pages 249–63 in *Festschrift für Ramazan Özgan*. Edited by Mustafa Şahin and İ. Hakan Mert, Istanbul: Ege Yayınları, 2005.

–, "Republik und Kaiser im Artemision von Ephesos." Pages 243–50 in *Neue Zeiten, Neue Sitten: Zu Rezeption und Integration römischen und italischen Kulturguts in Kleinasien*. Edited by Marion Meyer, Vienna: Phoibos, 2007.

Nathan, Geoffrey S., *The Family in Late Antiquity: The Rise of Christianity and the Endurance of Tradition*. New York: Routledge, 2000.

Nielsen, Inge, *Hellenistic Palaces: Tradition and Renewal*. Studies of Hellenistic Civilization 5. Aarhus: Aarhus University, 1994.

Nilsson, Martin P., *Cults, Myths, Oracles, and Politics in Ancient Greece*. Göteberg: Paul Aströms, 1986.

Nohlen, Klaus, and Wolfgang Radt, *Kapıkaya: Ein Felsheiligtum bei Pergamon*. AvP 12. Berlin: de Gruyter, 1978.

Nongbri, Brent, *Before Religion: A History of a Modern Concept*. New Haven: Yale University Press, 2013.

Oberleitner, Wolfgang, *Das Parthermonument von Ephesos*. Vienna: Phoibos, 2009.

Oliver, James Henry, *Greek Constitutions of Early Roman Emperors from Inscriptions and Papyri*. Philadelphia: American Philosophical Society, 1989.

–, *The Sacred Gerusia*. Athens: ASCSA, 1941.

Omanson, Roger L., *A Textual Guide to the Greek New Testament: An Adaptation of Bruce M. Metzger's Textual Commentary for the Needs of Translators*. Stuttgart: Deutsche Bibelgesellschaft, 2006.

Osiek, Carolyn, and Margaret Y. MacDonald, *A Woman's Place: House Churches in Earliest Christianity*. Minneapolis: Fortress, 2006.

OUTSCHAR, ULRIKE, "The Memmius Monument." Page 96 in *Ephesus: The New Guide*, ed. PETER SCHERRER, Translated by LIONEL BIER and GEORGE M. LUXON, Rev. ed. Istanbul: Ege Yayınları, 2000.

–, "Zum Monument des C. Memmius." *JÖAI* 60 (1990): 57–85.

PADILLA MONGE, AURELIO, "Notas sobre la explotación de las cantoas imperiales hasta al reinado des Hadriano: El caso de Dokimeion." *Habis: Filología clasíca, historia antiqua, arquelogía clasíca* 33 (2002): 433–46.

PICARD, CHRISTIAN, "Percées Tympanales ou Niches de Fronton?" *RAr* (1949): 31–39.

PEKÁRY, THOMAS, *Das römische Kaiserbildnis in Staat, Kult und Gesellschaft, dargestellt anhand der Schriftquellen*. Herrscherbild 3.5. Berlin: Mann, 1985.

PEPPARD, MICHAEL, "The Eagle and the Dove: Roman Imperial Sonship and the Baptism of Jesus (Mark 1.9–11)." *NTS* 56 (2010): 431–51.

PERKINS, PHEME, "The Letter to the Ephesians: Introduction, Commentary, and Reflections." *NIB* 11:414.

PLATTNER, GEORG A., "Architekturausstattung." Pages 147–69 in *Das Hanghaus 2 in Ephesos: Die Wohneinheit 7: Baubefund, Ausstattung, Funde*. Edited by ELISABETH RATHMAYR, FiE 8.10. Vienna: ÖAW, 2016.

POLAND, FRANZ, *Geschichte des griechischen Vereinswesens*. Leipzig: Teubner, 1909.

POMEROY, SARAH B., *Families in Classical and Hellenistic Greece*. Oxford: Clarendon Press, 1983.

PRIGENT, PIERRE, *Commentary on the Apocalypse of St John*. Tübingen: Mohr Siebeck, 2001.

QUATEMBER, URSULA, "Funde aus Marmor und anderem Gestein." Pages 707–18 in *Das Hanghaus 2 in Ephesos: Die Wohneinheit 6: Baubefund, Ausstattung, Funde*. Edited by HILKE THÜR and ELISABETH RATHMAYR, FiE 8.9. Vienna: ÖAW, 2014.

–, "Das Hanghaus 2 in Ephesos im Spiegel seiner Hausheiligtümer." Masters Thesis, University of Vienna, 2000.

RADT, WOLFGANG, *Pergamon: Geschichten und Bauten einer antiken Metropole*. Darmstadt: Primus, 1999.

–, "Pergamon: Vorbericht über die Kampagne 1985." *AA* (1986): 422–25.

–, "Pergamon: Vorbericht über die Kampagne 1986." *AA* (1987): 400–22.

RATHMAYR, ELISABETH, "Auswertung." Pages 688–97 in *Das Hanghaus 2 in Ephesos: Die Wohneinheiten 1 und 2: Baubefund, Ausstattung, Funde*. Edited by FRIEDRICH KRINZINGER and INGRID ADENSTEDT, FiE 8.8. Vienna: ÖAW, 2010.

–, "Auswertung: Eingangssituation und Peristylhof." Pages 837–38 in *Das Hanghaus 2 in Ephesos: Die Wohneinheit 6: Baubefund, Ausstattung, Funde*. Edited by HILKE THÜR and ELISABETH RATHMAYR, FiE 8.9. Vienna: ÖAW, 2014.

–, "Die Besitzerfamilie." Pages 846–49 in *Das Hanghaus 2 in Ephesos: Die Wohneinheit 6: Baubefund, Ausstattung, Funde*. Edited by HILKE THÜR and ELISABETH RATHMAYR, FiE 8.9. Vienna: ÖAW, 2014.

–, *Das Hanghaus 2 in Ephesos: Die Wohneinheit 7: Baubefund, Ausstattung, Funde*. FiE 8.10. Vienna: ÖAW, 2016.

–, "Das Haus des Ritters C. Flavius Furius Aptus. Beobachtungen zur Einflussnahme von Hausbesitzern an Architektur und Ausstattung in der Wohneinheit 6 des Hanghauses 2 in Ephesos." *MDAI (I)* 59 (2009): 307–36.

–, "Götter- und Kaiserkult im häuslichen Bereich anhand von Skulpturen aus dem Hanghaus 2 in Ephesos." *RHM* 48 (2006): 119–49.

–, "Rekonstruktion der Bauphasen." Pages 103–46 in *Das Hanghaus 2 in Ephesos: Die Wohneinheit 7: Baubefund, Ausstattung, Funde*. Edited by ELISABETH RATHMAYR, FiE 8.10. Vienna: ÖAW, 2016.

–, "Skulpturenfunde." Pages 367–434 in *Das Hanghaus 2 in Ephesos: Die Wohneinheit 6: Baubefund, Ausstattung, Funde*. Edited by HILKE THÜR and ELISABETH RATHMAYR, FiE 8.9. Vienna: ÖAW, 2014.

–, "Stuckdekorationen der Räume 8a und 36c." Pages 324–29 in *Das Hanghaus 2 in Ephesos: Die Wohneinheit 6: Baubefund, Ausstattung, Funde*. Edited by HILKE THÜR and ELISABETH RATHMAYR, FiE 8.9. Vienna: ÖAW, 2014.

–, "Skulpturen." Pages 207–29 in *Das Hanghaus 2 in Ephesos: Die Wohneinheit 4: Befund, Ausstattung, Funde*. Edited by HILKE THÜR, FiE 8.6. Vienna: ÖAW, 2005.

–, "Skulpturen." Pages 333–42 in *Das Hanghaus 2 in Ephesos: Die Wohneinheiten 1 und 2: Baubefund, Ausstattung, Funde*. Edited by FRIEDRICH KRINZINGER and INGRID ADENSTEDT, FiE 8.8. Vienna: ÖAW, 2010.

–, "Skulpturen." Pages 543–84 in *Das Hanghaus 2 in Ephesos: Die Wohneinheit 7: Baubefund, Ausstattung, Funde*. Edited by ELISABETH RATHMAYR, FiE 8.10. Vienna: ÖAW, 2016.

–, "Skulpturenfunde." Pages 370–72 and 412–13 in *Das Hanghaus 2 in Ephesos: Die Wohneinheit 6: Baubefund, Ausstattung, Funde*. Edited by HILKE THÜR and ELISABETH RATHMAYR, FiE 8.9. Vienna: ÖAW, 2014.

–, "Wasserwirtschaftliche Einrichtungen." Pages 144–46 in *Das Hanghaus 2 in Ephesos: Die Wohneinheit 7: Baubefund, Ausstattung, Funde*. Edited by ELISABETH RATHMAYR, FiE 8.10. Vienna: ÖAW, 2016.

RATHMAYR, ELISABETH, ALFRED GALIK, MARTINA SCHÄTZSCHOCK, HILKE THÜR, BARBARA TOBER, and ALICE WALDNER, "Hellenistische Strukturen und Funde: Ergebnisse und Interpretationen." Pages 833–36 in *Das Hanghaus 2 in Ephesos: Die Wohneinheit 6: Baubefund, Ausstattung, Funde*. Edited by HILKE THÜR and ELISABETH RATHMAYR, FiE 8.9. Vienna: ÖAW, 2014.

RAWSON, BERYL, "The Roman Family." Pages 1–57 in *The Family in Ancient Rome: New Perspectives*. Edited by BERYL RAWSON, Ithaca: Cornell University Press, 1986.

REBER, KARL, "Die Architekturelemente." Pages 55–74 in *La Quartier de la Maison aux mosaïques, Eretria: Fouilles et recherches VIII*. Edited by PIERRE DUCREY, INGRID R. METZGER, and KARL REBER, Lausanne: Payot, 1993.

REMIJSEN, SOFIE, "The *alytarches*, an Olympic *agonothetes*." *Nikephoros* 22 (2009): 129–43.

REYNOLDS, JOYCE, *Aphrodisias and Rome*. JRS Monographs 1. London: Society for the Promotion of Roman Studies, 1982.

RICHTER, GISELA M. A., *The Furniture of the Greeks, Etruscans and Romans*. London: Phaidon, 1966.

RIEGER, ANNA-KATHRINA, *Heiligtümer in Ostia: Architektur, Ausstattung und Stellung öffentlicher Heiligtümer in einer römischen Stadt*. Studien zur antiken Stadt 8. Munich: Pfeil, 2004.

RIGSBY, KENT J., *Asylia: Territorial Inviolability in the Hellenistic World*. Berkeley: University of California Press, 1996.

ROBBINS, RICHARD H., *Global Problems and the Culture of Capitalism*. Boston, MA: Allyn and Bacon, 1999.

ROBERT, LOUIS, "Dans une maison d'Éphèse un serpent et une chiffre." *CRAI* (1982): 126–32.

ROBERTS, J. H., "The Enigma of Ephesians: Rethinking Some Positions on the Basis of Schnackenburg and Arnold." *Neot* 27 (1993): 97–103.

ROBINSON, BETSEY ANN, *Histories of Peirene: A Corinthian Fountain in Three Millennia.* Princeton: ASCSA, 2011.

ROBINSON, THOMAS A., *The Bauer Thesis Examined: The Geography of Heresy in the Early Christian Church.* Lewiston/Queenston: Edwin Mellen Press, 1988.

RÖDER, JOSEF, "Bericht über Arbeiten in den antiken Steinbrüchen von Isçehisar (Dokimeion)." *TAD* 18.1 (1969): 109–16.

ROGERS, GUY M., "From the Greek Polis to the Greco-Roman Polis: Augustus and the Artemision of Ephesos." Pages 137–45 in *Regionalism in Hellenistic and Roman Asia Minor: Acts of the Conference Hartford, Connecticut (USA), August 22–24 August 1997.* Edited by HUGH ELTON and GARY REGER, Paris: Ausonius, 2007.

–, *The Mysteries of Artemis of Ephesos: Cult, Polis, and Change in the Graeco-Roman World.* New Haven: Yale University Press, 2012.

–, *The Sacred Identity of Ephesos: Foundation Myths of a Roman City.* London: Routledge, 1991.

ROSE, CHARLES B., *Dynastic Commemoration and Imperial Portraiture in the Julio-Claudian Period.* Cambridge: Cambridge University, 1997.

ROSSNER, MARGARETE, "Asiarchen und Archiereis Asias." *Studii Clasice* 16 (1974): 101–42.

RÜPKE, JÖRG, "Collegia sacerdotum: Religiöse Vereine in der Oberschicht." Pages 41–67 in *Religiöse Vereine in der römischen Antike.* Edited by ULRIKE EGELHAAF-GAISER and ALFRED SCHÄFER, STAC 13. Tübingen: Mohr Siebeck, 2002.

SALLER, RICHARD P., *Patriarchy, Property, and Death in the Roman Family.* Cambridge: Cambridge University Press, 1994.

SAPORITI, NADA, "A Frieze From the Temple of Hadrian at Ephesus." Pages 269–78 in *Essays in Memory of Karl Lehman.* Edited by L. F. SANDLER, New York: Institute of Fine Arts, 1964.

SCHÄFER, ALFRED, "Dionysische Gruppen als Phänomen der römischen Kaiserzeit." Pages 161–80 in *Gruppenreligionen im römischen Reich: Sozialformen, Grenzziehungen und Leistungen.* Edited by JÖRG RÜPKE, STAC 43. Tübingen: Mohr Siebeck, 2006.

–, "Raumnutzung und Raumwahrnehmung im Vereinslokal der Iobakchen von Athen." Pages 173–220 in *Religiöse Vereine in der römischen Antike.* Edited by ULRIKE EGELHAAF-GAISER and ALFRED SCHÄFER, STAC 13. Tübingen: Mohr Siebeck, 2002.

SCHÄTZSCHOCK, MARTINA, "Glas." Pages 429–65 in *Das Hanghaus 2 in Ephesos: Die Wohneinheit 7: Baubefund, Ausstattung, Funde.* Edited by ELISABETH RATHMAYR, FiE 8.10. Vienna: ÖAW, 2016.

SCHEIDEL, WALTER, "Progress and Problems in Roman Demography." Pages 1–81 in *Debating Roman Demography.* Edited by WALTER SCHEIDEL, Leiden: Brill, 2001.

SCHEIBELREITER-GAIL, VERONIKA, "Mosaiken." Pages 255–71 in *Das Hanghaus 2 in Ephesos: Die Wohneinheit 6: Baubefund, Ausstattung, Funde.* Edited by HILKE THÜR and ELISABETH RATHMAYR, FiE 8.9. Vienna: ÖAW, 2014.

–, "Mosaiken." Pages 273–83 in *Das Hanghaus 2 in Ephesos: Die Wohneinheit 7: Baubefund, Ausstattung, Funde.* Edited by ELISABETH RATHMAYR, FiE 8.10. Vienna: ÖAW, 2016.

SCHERRER, PETER, "Anmerkungen zum städtischen und provinzialen Kaiserkult: Paradigma Ephesos: Entwicklungen von Augustus bis Hadrian." Pages 93–112 in *"… und verschönerte die Stadt …": Ein ephesischer Priester des Kaiserkultes in seinem Umfeld.* Edited by HILKE THÜR, ÖAI Sonderschriften 27. Vienna: ÖAI, 1997.

–, "Augustus, die Mission des Vedius Pollio und die Artemis Ephesia." *JÖAI* 60 (1990): 87–101.

–, ed. *Ephesus: The New Guide*. Istanbul: Ege Yayınları, 2000.

–, "Kathodos with Embasis." Page 86 in *Ephesus: The New Guide*. Edited by PETER SCHERRER, Translated by LIONEL BIER and GEORGE M. LUXON, Revised ed. Istanbul: Ege Yayınları, 2000.

–, *Der neue Führer*. Vienna: ÖAI, 1995.

–, "Die Stadt als Festplatz: Das Beispiel der ephesischen Bauprogramme rund um die Kaiserneokorien Domitians und Hadrians." Pages 35–65 in *Festrituale in der römischen Kaiserzeit*. Edited by JÖRG RÜPKE, STAC 48. Tübingen: Mohr Siebeck, 2008.

SCHINDEL, NIKOLAUS, "Fundmünzen." Pages 425–28 in *Das Hanghaus 2 in Ephesos: Die Wohneinheit 7: Baubefund, Ausstattung, Funde*. Edited by ELISABETH RATHMAYR, FiE 8.10. Vienna: ÖAW, 2016.

SCHNACKENBURG, RUDOLF, *Ephesians: A Commentary*. Edinburgh: T&T Clark, 1991.

SCHÖRNER, GÜNTHER, *Votive im römischen Griechenland*. Stuttgart: Steiner, 2003.

SCHUMACHER, ROB W. M., "Three Related Sanctuaries of Poseidon: Geraistos, Kalaureia and Tainaron." Pages 62–87 in *Greek Sanctuaries: New Approaches*. Edited by NANNO MARINATOS and ROBIN HÄGG, London: Routledge, 1993.

SCHWARZER, HOLGER, "Die Bukoloi in Pergamon: Ein dionysischer Kultverein im Spiegel der archäologischen und epigraphischen Zeugnisse." Pages 153–67 in *Zwischen Kult und Gesellschaft*. Edited by INGE NIELSEN, Hephaistos Themenband 24. Augsburg: Camelion, 2006.

–, "Der Herrscherkult der Attaliden." Pages 110–17 in *Pergamon: Panorama der antiken Metropole: Begleitbuch zur Ausstellung*. Edited by RALF GRÜSSINGER, VOLKER KÄSTNER, and ANDREAS SCHOLL, Petersberg: Imhof, 2011.

–, *Die Stadtgrabung: Teil 4: Das Gebäude mit dem Podiensaal in der Stadtgrabung von Pergamon*. AvP 15.4. Berlin: de Gruyter, 2008.

–, "Untersuchungen zum hellenistischen Herrscherkult in Pergamon." *MDAI (I)* 49 (1999): 249–300.

–, "Vereinslokale im hellenistischen und römischen Pergamon." Pages 221–60 in *Religiöse Vereine in der römischen Antike*. Edited by ULRIKE EGELHAAF-GAISER and ALFRED SCHÄFER, STAC 13. Tübingen: Mohr Siebeck, 2002.

SCHWEIZER, EDUARD, *Church Order in the New Testament*. London: SCM, 1961.

SCHWINDT, RAINER, *Das Weltbild des Epheserbriefes: Eine religionsgeschichtlich-exegetische Studie*. WUNT 1.148. Tübingen: Mohr Siebeck, 2002.

SEALEY, RAPHAEL, *The Justice of the Greeks*. Ann Arbor: University of Michigan Press, 1994.

SIEBERT, ANNE VIOLA, *Instrumenta sacra: Untersuchungen zu römischen Opfer-, Kult- und Priestergeräten*. Berlin: de Gruyter, 1999.

SIM, DAVID C., "Matthew and the Pauline Corpus: A Preliminary Intertextual Study." *JSNT* 31 (2009): 401–22.

SINN, ULRICH, "Greek Sanctuaries as Places of Refuge." Pages 88–109 in *Greek Sanctuaries: New Approaches*. Edited by NANNO MARINATOS and ROBIN HÄGG, London: Routledge, 1993.

SMITH, R. R. R., "The Imperial Reliefs from the Sebasteion at Aphrodisias." *JRS* 77 (1987): 88–138.

SMITH, WILFRED CANTWELL, *The Meaning and End of Religion*. New York: Harper & Row, 1978.

STANTON, GRAHAM N., *The Gospels and Jesus*. 2nd ed. Oxford: Oxford University Press, 2002.

STEUERNAGEL, DIRK, "Synnaos Theos: Images of Roman Emperors in Greek Temples." Pages 241–53 in *Divine Images and Human Imaginations in Ancient Greece and Rome*. Edited by JOANNIS MYLONOPOULOS, Religions in the Graeco-Roman World 170. Leiden: Brill, 2010.

STEVENSON, GREGORY, *Power and Place: Temple and Identity in the Book of Revelation*. Berlin: de Gruyter, 2001.

STRELAN, RICK, *Paul, Artemis, and the Jews in Ephesus*. BZNW 80. Berlin: de Gruyter, 1996.

STROCKA, VOLKER MICHAEL, "Zeus, Marnas und Klaseas: Ephesische Brunnenfiguren von 93 n. Chr." Pages 77–92 in *Festschrift für Jale İnan*. Edited by NEZIH BAŞGELEN and MİHİN LUGAL, Istanbul: Arkeoloji ve Sanat Yayınları, 1989.

TAEUBER, HANS, "Graffiti und Steininschriften." Pages 331–44 in *Das Hanghaus 2 in Ephesos: Die Wohneinheit 6: Baubefund, Ausstattung, Funde*. Edited by HILKE THÜR and ELISABETH RATHMAYR, FiE 8.9. Vienna: ÖAW, 2014.

TALBERT, CHARLES, *Ephesians and Colossians*. Paideia. Grand Rapids: Baker, 2007.

TALLOEN, PETER, "One Question, Several Answers: The Introduction of the Imperial Cult in Pisidia." Pages 233–42 in *Neue Zeiten, Neue Sitten: Zu Rezeption und Integration römischen und italischen Kulturguts in Kleinasien*. Edited by MARION MEYER, Vienna: Phoibos, 2007.

TANG, BIRGIT, *Delos, Carthage, Ampurias: The Housing of Three Mediterranean Trading Centres*. Analecta Romana Instituti Danici Suppl. 36. Rome: "L'Erma" di Bretschneider, 2005.

TELLBE, MIKAEL, *Christ-believers in Ephesus: A Textual Analysis of Early Christian Identity Formation in a Local Perspective*. WUNT 1.242. Tübingen: Mohr Siebeck, 2009.

THIESSEN, WERNER, *Christen in Ephesus: Die historische und theologische Situation in vorpaulinischer und paulinischer Zeit und zur Zeit der Apostelgeschichte und der Pastoralbriefe*. Texte und Arbeiten zum neutestamentlichen Zeitalter 12. Tübingen: Francke Verlag, 1995.

THIELMAN, FRANK, *Ephesians*. BECNT. Grand Rapids: Baker Academic, 2010.

–, *Theology of the New Testament: A Canonical and Synthetic Approach*. Grand Rapids: Zondervan, 2005.

THOMAS, CHRISTINE M, "At Home in the City of Artemis: Religion in Ephesos in the Literary Imagination of the Roman Period." Pages 81–118 in *Ephesos: Metropolis of Asia*. Edited by HELMUT KOESTER, Valley Forge, PA: Trinity Press International, 1995.

THOMPSON, MARIANNE MEYE, "'Mercy upon All': God as Father in the Epistle to the Romans." Pages 203–16 in *Romans and the People of God: Essays in Honor of Gordon D. Fee on the Occasion of his 65th Birthday*. Edited by SVEN K. SODERLUND and N. T. WRIGHT, Grand Rapids: Eerdmans, 1999.

THOMPSON, TREVOR W., "Claiming Ephesus: Pauline Legacy in The Acts of John." Pages 379–400 in *The Rise and Expansion of Christianity in the First Three Centuries of the Common Era*. Edited by CLARE K. ROTHSCHILD and JENS SCHRÖTER, WUNT 301. Tübingen: Mohr Siebeck, 2013.

THÜR, HILKE, "Architekturausstattung." Pages 141–74 in *Das Hanghaus 2 in Ephesos: Die Wohneinheit 6: Baubefund, Ausstattung, Funde*. Edited by HILKE THÜR and ELISABETH RATHMAYR, FiE 8.9. Vienna: ÖAW, 2014.

–, "Arsinoe IV, eine Schwester Kleopatras VII, Grabinhaberin des Oktogons von Ephesos? Ein Vorschlag." *JÖAI* 60 (1990): 43–56.

–, "Art and Architecture in Terrace House 2 in Ephesus: An Example of Domestic Archi-
tecture in the Roman Imperial Period." Pages 237–59 in *Contested Spaces: Houses and
Temples in Roman Antiquity and the New Testament*. Edited by DAVID L. BALCH and
ANNETTE WEISSENRIEDER, WUNT 285. Tübingen: Mohr Siebeck, 2012.

–, "Auswertung: Badeanlage." Pages 842–45 in *Das Hanghaus 2 in Ephesos: Die Wohneinheit 6: Baubefund, Ausstattung, Funde*. Edited by HILKE THÜR and ELISABETH RATH-
MAYR, FiE 8.9. Vienna: ÖAW, 2014.

–, "Auswertung: Repräsentationsräume." Pages 838–42 in *Das Hanghaus 2 in Ephesos:
Die Wohneinheit 6: Baubefund, Ausstattung, Funde*. Edited by HILKE THÜR and ELIS-
ABETH RATHMAYR, FiE 8.9. Vienna: ÖAW, 2014.

–, "Baubeschreibung." Pages 29–120 in *Das Hanghaus 2 in Ephesos: Die Wohneinheit 6:
Baubefund, Ausstattung, Funde*. Edited by HILKE THÜR and ELISABETH RATHMAYR,
FiE 8.9. Vienna: ÖAW, 2014.

–, "Die Bauphasen der Wohneinheit 4 (und 6)." Pages 41–66 in *Das Hanghaus 2 von Ephesos: Studien zu Baugeschichte und Chronologie*. Edited by FRIEDRICH KRINZINGER, AF
7. Vienna: ÖAW, 2002.

–, "Domitian's Terrace with Imperial Temple and Altar." Page 92 in *Ephesus: The
New Guide*. Edited by PETER SCHERRER, Translated by LIONEL BIER and GEORGE
M. LUXON, Revised ed. Istanbul: Ege Yayınları, 2000.

–, "Einleitung." Pages 3–17 in *Das Hanghaus 2 in Ephesos: Die Wohneinheit 6: Baubefund, Ausstattung, Funde*. Edited by HILKE THÜR and ELISABETH RATHMAYR, FiE 8.9.
Vienna: ÖAW, 2014.

–, *Das Hanghaus 2 in Ephesos: Die Wohneinheit 4: Befund, Ausstattung, Funde*. FiE 8.6.
Vienna: ÖAW, 2005.

–, "Heizungsanlagen." Pages 219–25 in *Das Hanghaus 2 in Ephesos: Die Wohneinheit 6:
Baubefund, Ausstattung, Funde*. Edited by HILKE THÜR and ELISABETH RATHMAYR,
FiE 8.9. Vienna: ÖAW, 2014.

–, "Hydreion." Pages 96–97 in *Ephesus: The New Guide*. Edited by PETER SCHERRER,
Translated by LIONEL BIER and GEORGE M. LUXON, Revised ed. Istanbul: Ege Yayınları,
2000.

–, "Rekonstruktion der Bauphasen." Pages 121–40 in *Das Hanghaus 2 in Ephesos: Die
Wohneinheit 6: Baubefund, Ausstattung, Funde*. Edited by HILKE THÜR and ELISA-
BETH RATHMAYR, FiE 8.9. Vienna: ÖAW, 2014.

–, "Sonstige Ausstattung." Pages 175–95 in *Das Hanghaus 2 in Ephesos: Die Wohneinheit 6: Baubefund, Ausstattung, Funde*. Edited by HILKE THÜR and ELISABETH RATH-
MAYR, FiE 8.9. Vienna: ÖAW, 2014.

–, "Wasserwirtschaftliche Einrichtungen." Pages 197–218 in *Das Hanghaus 2 in Ephesos:
Die Wohneinheit 6: Baubefund, Ausstattung, Funde*. Edited by HILKE THÜR and ELIS-
ABETH RATHMAYR, FiE 8.9. Vienna: ÖAW, 2014.

–, "Die Wohneinheit 4: Zusammenfassung und Ergebnisse." Pages 427–38 in *Das Hanghaus 2 in Ephesos: Die Wohneinheit 4. Baubefund, Ausstattung, Funde*. Edited by HILKE
THÜR, FiE 8.6 Vienna: ÖAW, 2005.

–, "Die Wohneinheit 6: Vereinshaus eines dionysischen Kultvereins?" Pages 849–53 in
Das Hanghaus 2 in Ephesos: Die Wohneinheit 6: Baubefund, Ausstattung, Funde. Edited
by HILKE THÜR and ELISABETH RATHMAYR, FiE 8.9. Vienna: ÖAW, 2014.

–, "Zum Stadtpalast des Dionysospriesters C. Flavius Furius Aptus im Hanghaus 2 in Ephesos: Ein Zwischenbericht." Pages 1057–72 in *Thiasos: Festschrift für Erwin Pochmarski zum 65. Geburtstag.* Edited by CHRISTIANE FRANEK, Vienna: Phoibos, 2008.

–, "Zur Dach- und Deckenkonstruktion des Marmorsaales der Wohneinheit 6 im Hanghaus 2 in Ephesos." Pages 235–45 in *Holztragwerke der Antike.* Edited by ALEXANDER VON KIENLIN, Byzas 11. Istanbul: Ege, 2011.

–, "Zur Datierung der Bauphasen: Anmerkungen zur Methodik." Pages 13–18 in *Das Hanghaus 2 in Ephesos: Die Wohneinheit 6: Baubefund, Ausstattung, Funde.* Edited by HILKE THÜR and ELISABETH RATHMAYR, FiE 8.9. Vienna: ÖAW, 2014.

THÜR, HILKE, and ELISABETH RATHMAYR, ed. *Das Hanghaus 2 in Ephesos: Die Wohneinheit 6: Baubefund, Ausstattung, Funde.* FiE 8.9. Vienna: ÖAW, 2014.

THURSTON, BONNIE, *Reading Colossians, Ephesians, and 2 Thessalonians: A Literary and Theological Commentary.* Reading the New Testament. New York: Crossroad, 1995.

TREBILCO, PAUL R., *The Early Christians in Ephesus from Paul to Ignatius.* WUNT 1.166. Tübingen: Mohr Siebeck, 2004.

–, *Self-Designations and Group Identity in the New Testament.* Cambridge: Cambridge University Press, 2012.

TRELL, BLUMA L., "The Temple of Artemis at Ephesos." Pages 78–99 in *The Seven Wonders of the Ancient World.* Edited by PETER CLAYTON and MARTIN PRICE, London: Routledge, 1988.

TRÜMPER, MONIKA, *Wohnen in Delos: Eine baugeschichtliche Untersuchung zum Wandel der Wohnkultur in hellenistischer Zeit.* Internationale Archäologie 46. Rahden: Marie Leidorf, 1998.

USENER, HERMANN, *Acta Sancti Timothei.* Bonn: Georgi, 1877.

VAN BREMEN, RIET, *The Limits of Participation: Women and Civic Life in the Greek East in the Hellenistic and Roman Periods.* Amsterdam: J. C. Gieben, 1996.

VAN DER WATT, JAN G., "Eschatology in John: A Continuous Process of Realizing Events." Pages 109–40 in *Eschatology of the New Testament and Some Related Documents.* Edited by JAN G. VAN DER WATT, WUNT 2.315. Tübingen: Mohr Siebeck, 2011.

VAN NIJF, ONNO, "The Social World of Tax Farmers and their Personnel." Pages 279–311 in *The Customs Law of Asia.* Edited by MICHEL COTTIER, MICHAEL H. CRAWFORD, C. V. CROWTHER, JEAN-LOUIS FERRARY, BARBARA LEVICK, and MICHAEL WÖRRLE, Oxford: Oxford University Press, 2008.

VÁSQUEZ, MANUEL A., *More than Belief: A Materialist Theory of Religion.* Oxford: Oxford University Press, 2011.

–, "Studying Religion in Motion: A Networks Approach." *MTSR* 20 (2008): 151–84.

VELLANICKAL, MATTHEW, *The Divine Sonship of Christians in the Johannine Writings.* AnBib 72. Rome: Biblical Institute Press, 1977.

VETTERS, HERMANN, "Basilica privata." Pages 211–15 in *Classica et provincialia: Festschrift Erna Diez.* Edited by GERDA SCHWARZ and ERWIN POCHMARSKI, Graz: Akademische Druck- und Verlagsanstalt, 1978.

–, "Ephesos: Vorläufiger Grabungsbericht 1973." *AAWW* 111 (1974): 211–24.

–, "Ephesos: Vorläufiger Grabungsbericht 1979." *AAWW* 117 (1980): 249–66.

–, "Ephesos: Vorläufiger Grabungsbericht 1980." *AAWW* 118 (1981): 137–68.

–, "Ephesos: Vorläufiger Grabungsbericht 1981." *AAWW* 119 (1982): 62–102.

–, "Ephesos: Vorläufiger Grabungsbericht 1982." *AAWW* 120 (1983): 111–69.

–, "Ephesos: Vorläufiger Grabungsbericht für die Jahre 1984 und 1985." *AAWW* 123 (1986): 75–161.

–, "Nochmals zur Basilica privata." *RHM* 23 (1981): 209–12.

–, "Der Schlangengott." Pages 967–79 in *Studien zu Religion und Kultur Kleinasiens: Festschrift für Friedrich Karl Dörner zum 65. Geburtstag.* Edited by FRIEDRICH KARL DÖRNER, SENCER ŞAHİN, ELMAR SCHWERTHEIM, and JÖRG WAGNER, EPRO 66.2. Leiden: Brill, 1978.

–, "Ein weiterer Schlangengott in Ephesos." Pages 315–20 in *Echo: Beiträge zur Archäologie des mediterranen und alpinen Raumes: Johannes Trentini zum 80. Geburtstag.* Edited by BRINNA OTTO and FRIEDRICH EHRL, Innsbruck: University of Innsbruck, 1990.

VILLIERS, PIETER G. R. DE, "Safe in the Family of God: Soteriological Perspectives in 1 Thessalonians." Pages 305–30 in *Salvation in the New Testament: Perspectives on Soteriology.* Edited by J. G. VAN DER WATT, NovTSup 121. Leiden: Brill, 2005.

VOGLIANO, ACHILLE, and FRANZ CUMONT, "La Grande Iscrizione Bacchica del Metropolitan Museum." *AJA* 37 (1933): 215–63.

VON WAHLDE, URBAN C., *The Gospel and Letters of John.* 3 vols. ECC. Grand Rapids: Eerdmans, 2010.

WALDNER, ALICE, and SABINE LADSTÄTTER, "Keramik." Pages 435–588 in *Das Hanghaus 2 in Ephesos: Die Wohneinheit 6: Baubefund, Ausstattung, Funde.* Edited by HILKE THÜR and ELISABETH RATHMAYR, FiE 8.9. Vienna: ÖAW, 2014

WALTERS, JAMES C., "Paul, Adoption, and Inheritance." Pages 42–76 in *Paul and the Greco-Roman World: A Handbook.* New York: Trinity, 2003.

WEERAKKODY, D. P. M., "Demography." Pages 213–14 in *The Encyclopedia of Ancient Greece.* Edited by NIGEL G. WILSON, New York: Routledge, 2005.

WEINSTOCK, STEFAN, *Divus Julius.* Oxford: Clarendon Press, 1971.

WIEGAND, THEODOR and HANS SCHRADER, *Priene: Ergebnisse der Ausgrabungen und Untersuchungen in den Jahren 1895–1898.* Berlin: Reimer, 1904.

WINKES, ROLF, *Livia, Octavia, Iulia: Porträts und Darstellungen.* Archaeologia Transatlantica 13. Providence, RI: Brown University, 1995.

WITETSCHEK, STEPHAN, *Ephesische Enthüllungen 1: Frühe Christen in einer antiken Grossstadt: zugleich ein Beitrag zur Frage nach den Kontexten der Johannesapokalypse.* BTS 6. Leuven: Peeters, 2008.

WITT, R. E. *Isis in the Graeco-Roman World.* Ithaca, NY: Cornell University Press, 1971. Reprint *Isis in the Ancient World.* Baltimore: Johns Hopkins, 1997.

WOOD, J. T. *Discoveries at Ephesus: Including the Site and Remains of the Great Temple of Diana.* Boston: James R. Osgood and Co., 1877.

WULF-RHEIDT, ULRIKE, *Die Stadtgrabung: Die hellenistischen und römischen Wohnhäuser von Pergamon.* AvP 15.3. Berlin: de Gruyter, 1999.

YARBROUGH, O. LARRY, "Parents and Children in the Letters of Paul." Pages 126–41 in *The Social World of the First Christians: Essays in Honor of Wayne A. Meeks.* Minneapolis: Fortress, 1995.

YAVIS, CONSTANTINE GEORGE, *Greek Altars: Origins and Typology: Including the Minoan-Mycenaean Offertory Apparatus: An Archaeological Study in the History of Religion.* St. Louis: St. Louis University Press, 1949.

YEGÜL, FIKRET K., "The Street Experience of Ancient Ephesus." Pages 103–4 in *Streets: Critical Perspectives on Public Space.* Ed. ZEYNEP ÇELIK, DIANE FAVRO, and RICHARD INGERSOLL, Berkeley: University of California, 1994.

ZABRANA, LILLI, "Vorbericht zur sogenannten Tribüne im Artemision von Ephesos: Ein neues Odeion im Heiligtum der Artemision." *JÖAI* 80 (2011): 341–63.

ZIMMERMANN, NORBERT, "Wandmalerei." Pages 175–231 in *Das Hanghaus 2 in Ephesos: Die Wohneinheit 7: Baubefund, Ausstattung, Funde*. Edited by ELISABETH RATHMAYR, FiE 8.10. Vienna: ÖAW, 2016.

–, "Wandmalerei und Stuckdekoration." Pages 273–330 in *Das Hanghaus 2 in Ephesos: Die Wohneinheit 6: Baubefund, Ausstattung, Funde*. Edited by HILKE THÜR and ELISABETH RATHMAYR, FiE 8.9. Vienna: ÖAW, 2014.

–, "Wandmalerei." Pages 105–31 in *Das Hanghaus 2 in Ephesos: Die Wohneinheit 4: Baubefund, Ausstattung, Funde*. Edited by HILKE THÜR, FiE 8.6 Vienna: ÖAW, 2005.

ZIMMERMANN, NORBERT, and SABINE LADSTÄTTER, *Wandmalerei in Ephesos*. Vienna: Phoibos, 2010.

ZUIDERHOEK, ARJAN, *The Politics of Munificence in the Roman Empire Citizens: Elites and Benefactors in Asia Minor*. Cambridge: Cambridge University Press, 2009.

Index of Passages

Dead Sea Scrolls

Ancient Jewish Writers

New Testament

Early Christian Writings

Graeco-Roman Literature

Index of Modern Authors

Index of Subjects

Wissenschaftliche Untersuchungen
zum Neuen Testament

Edited by Jörg Frey (Zürich)

Associate Editors:

Markus Bockmuehl (Oxford) · James A. Kelhoffer (Uppsala)
Tobias Nicklas (Regensburg) · Janet Spittler (Charlottesville, VA)
J. Ross Wagner (Durham, NC)

WUNT I is an international series dealing with the entire field of early Christianity and its Jewish and Graeco-Roman environment. Its historical-philological profile and interdisciplinary outlook, which its long-term editor Martin Hengel was instrumental in establishing, is maintained by an international team of editors representing a wide range of the traditions and themes of New Testament scholarship. The sole criteria for acceptance to the series are the scholarly quality and lasting merit of the work being submitted. Apart from the specialist monographs of experienced researchers, some of which may be habilitations, *WUNT I* features collections of essays by renowned scholars, source material collections and editions as well as conference proceedings in the form of a handbook on themes central to the discipline.

WUNT II complements the first series by offering a publishing platform in paperback for outstanding writing by up-and-coming young researchers. Dissertations and monographs are presented alongside innovative conference volumes on fundamental themes of New Testament research. Like Series I, it is marked by a historical-philological character and an international orientation that transcends exegetical schools and subject boundaries. The academic quality of Series II is overseen by the same team of editors.

WUNT I:
ISSN: 0512-1604
Suggested citation: WUNT I
All available volumes can be found at
www.mohrsiebeck.com/wunt1

WUNT II:
ISSN: 0340-9570
Suggested citation: WUNT II
All available volumes can be found
at *www.mohrsiebeck.com/wunt2*

Mohr Siebeck
www.mohrsiebeck.com